# The Two-Headed Household

# Pitt Latin American Series

Billie R. DeWalt, General Editor

Reid Andrews, Associate Editor

Carmen Diana Deere, Associate Editor

Jorge I. Domínguez, Associate Editor

*Susana Lastarria C.*
*Madison, September 2000*

# The Two-Headed Household

Gender and Rural Development in the Ecuadorean Andes

Sarah Hamilton

University of Pittsburgh Press

Published by the University of Pittsburgh Press, Pittsburgh, Pa. 15261

Copyright © 1998, University of Pittsburgh Press

Manufactured in the United States of America

Printed on acid-free paper

10 9 8 7 6 5 4 3 2 1


*Library of Congress Cataloging-in-Publication Data*

Hamilton, Sarah, 1946–
   The two-headed household : gender and rural development in
the Ecuadorean Andes / Sarah Hamilton.
   p.   cm. — (Pitt Latin American series)
   Includes bibliographical references and index.
   ISBN 0-8229-4072-8 (acid-free paper)
   ISBN 0-8229-5677-2 (pbk. : acid-free paper)
   1. Indian women—Ecuador—Hacienda Chanchalo—Economic
conditions.   2. Indian women—Ecuador—Hacienda Chanchalo—
Social conditions.   3. Indians of South America—Agriculture—
Ecuador—Hacienda Chanchalo.   4. Rural development—
Ecuador—Hacienda Chanchalo.   5. Sex role—Economic
aspects—Ecuador—Hacienda Chanchalo.   6. Sex discrimination
against women—Ecuador—Hacienda Chanchalo.   7. Hacienda
Chanchalo (Ecuador)—Economic conditions.   I. Title.   II. Series.
   F3721.1.H33 H35   1998
   305.3'09866—ddc21                    98-9029


A CIP catalog record for this book is available from the British Library.

# Contents

# Tables

# Acknowledgments

Many individuals and several institutions contributed to the production of this book. Fieldwork in Cantón Salcedo, Ecuador, was supported by a Fulbright Dissertation Research Fellowship; Gonzalo Cartagenova, director, Comisión Fulbright, Quito, and Helena Saona were especially kind and helpful. Fieldwork was carried out in conjunction with National Science Foundation Project "Farming Systems and Socio-cultural Determinants of Child Growth in Two Ecological Zones of Ecuador," Kathleen DeWalt, principal investigator, and in collaboration with Fundación para el Desarrollo Agropecuario (FUNDAGRO), Quito. I am especially grateful to Jorge Uquillas, director of evaluation at FUNDAGRO during 1992–1993; NSF Project Household Survey coordinator Jim Stansbury; and FUNDAGRO field research team members Oscar Silva, Alex Portillo, Favian Tapia, Gloria Cordoba, Susana Chávez, Lilián Leyedra, and Patricia Gutiérrez. Jorge's guidance and the hard work of the survey coordinator and team produced highly reliable data that form the quantitative basis for this book. I am also grateful on many counts to Bill Leonard, NSF project co-principal investigator.

Colleagues in the field of Gender and Development have contributed knowledge, institutional support, and good-humored collegiality both in the field and at home. Susan Poats, Virginia Lambert, Deborah Caro, and Rae Blumberg provided guidance and encouragement during my fieldwork. When I was planning field research, Andrea Allen generously shared her firsthand knowledge of Ecuadorean indigenous communities. The ideas and experience of these colleagues enriched this work, and I continue to be grateful for their friendship.

This book originated as a Ph.D. thesis in the University of Kentucky Department of Anthropology. My thesis work was directed and inspired by Billie R. DeWalt and Kathleen M. DeWalt. Kathleen designed the NSF project with which my research was affiliated, creating space for the investigation of women's work and intrahousehold resource dynamics. Throughout my graduate preparation, she enabled intellectual and professional growth as only a great teacher can. Bill directed my graduate research and study, serving as academic advisor and repeatedly providing encouragement and opportunities for professional development. He provided careful training in research design, invaluable experience in collaborative research, and an exemplum of discerning, uncompromising policy analysis and vision. I am grateful, also, to Tom Dillehay for his acute thesis comments and for the pleasure of learning from a distinguished scholar who cherishes Andean people and places. Peter Little, John van Willigen, William Y. Adams, and Mike Webb also contributed helpful comments and concepts that improved this work. A dissertation fellowship awarded by the University of Kentucky Graduate School provided support for writing the thesis.

My colleagues in Virginia Tech's Office of International Research and Development deserve my thanks for enabling me to devote time to the revision of this book, and for being unfailingly kind and supportive. I am grateful to OIRD's director, S. K. De Datta, and to Mike Bertelsen, Keith Moore, Peggy Lawson, and Martha Bower for their help in moving this book forward.

I am grateful to the University of Pittsburgh Press for selecting reviewers whose scholarly and editorial judgment have greatly improved this book. I also appreciate the fine editorial work of Eileen Kiley and Kathy Meyer and the painstaking copy editing performed by Pippa Letsky.

Ultimately, the greatest debt I owe is to the Andean people who incorporated me into their families and community, and to my own family. This book would not have been possible without the love and support of these compañeros. Chanchaleños shared their daily lives with me, giving the book its essence; their kindness and courage taught me a great deal about the potential of humanity for collaborative survival. They also introduced me to sociocultural institutions that enable gender equality, refreshing my appreciation for the gender-egalitarian practice of my parents, Helen and John Hamilton, and my marriage partner, Alan Moorer. This book is dedicated to them, and to Carmelina Chicaiza Cha Cha.

# The Two-Headed Household

ONE ✦ **Gender and Rural Development**

---

THE PEOPLE OF CHANCHALÓ, an indigenous farming community in the Ecuadorean Andes, say that their households have two heads.[1] Chanchaleños find themselves repeatedly explaining this to officials and others who expect households to be headed by an individual, and generally by a male individual. I began to understand why local people were so intent on making plain to me that their households have *dos cabezas* (two heads) soon after beginning fieldwork in 1992, when I accompanied my landlord to the public utility agency and courthouse in the county seat. After waiting in long lines, we were further delayed as he engaged in lengthy conversations with officials. While remarking that it takes a long time to transact official business, my landlord showed me the form he was working on:

They say they want the name of the household head; I say this is the name of the household head. They say there are two names here, which one is the head? I don't know why they can't understand. *We* are the head, my wife and I.[2]

This was my first inkling that, in Chanchaló, gender relations are constituted from both ideological and material bases that differ radically from those in urban Ecuador and in my own country.

Chanchaló is located in a region once characterized by an agricultural abundance created by both women and men. In highland communities where people maintain traditional indigenous forms of social organization,

1

women and men control the means and fruits of agricultural production in an egalitarian manner. Sustaining a balance of power between wife and husband is considered essential if a household is to flourish. Tradition alone does not define a woman's place in Chanchaló, however, as local women and men earn their livelihoods, rear their children, and build their community within a national socioeconomic context that has long promoted male control of economic resources and patriarchal social forms. This book will document gender relations in Chanchaló and examine the dynamic interactions of tradition and change that engender processes of rural development in the central Ecuadorean sierra.

In the nearly five hundred years since the Spanish Conquest, agricultural production in the Ecuadorean highlands has been restructured repeatedly by colonial and modern state interventions, reflecting the distribution of political power among landholders, and by processes associated with the expansion of world capitalism. The feudalistic hacienda system of land tenure, through which mestizo overlords came to control vast tracts of formerly indigenous lands and to indenture an indigenous labor force, persisted through the late twentieth century in highland Ecuador.[3] From the earliest memory of the oldest community member until the 1970s, Chanchaleños labored under a system of debt peonage in which men contracted the labor of their entire households to the hacienda owner in exchange for access to subsistence plots of hacienda-controlled land and advances of grain or cash. Women were obligated to work for the hacienda until the debts assumed by their husbands were repaid; for many tasks women's labor was credited at half the rate of men's labor.

Planned agricultural development initiatives and market structures that contributed to the belated demise of the hacienda system did not alleviate gender bias in the allocation of productive assets to indigenous households. Land-reform statutes—under which Chanchaleños sought title to the small plots they had accessed on hacienda lands—favor male household heads. Planned development projects that focus on increasing the market competitiveness of small-scale agriculture, such as those channeling financial and technical assistance through production credit associations, generally have been targeted only to men. Regional labor market structures ensure that most off-farm cash income will be earned by men. Relatively well-paying jobs open to rural people with little education, such as those in the urban construction sector, are not open to women. Many men from Chanchaló migrate seasonally to take advantage of this market, where they can earn at least four times the local agricultural wage available to their wives.

Supporting the gender bias of past and present economic institutions, nationally dominant cultural models sanction patriarchal organization of economic and social entities ranging from the household to the national level. For generations countless to Chanchaleños, the national legal system, Roman Catholicism, and hacienda culture have brought to the community ideological models of female subordination influential within institutions exerting coercive power over the lives of indigenous people. The men who migrate temporarily to highland cities live and work in a national, mestizo cultural context. They may return with more patriarchal values as well as with the lion's share of household income.

Within social science research devoted to gender and development in the Andes and elsewhere in Latin America, a dominant and compelling paradigm posits the inevitable erosion of indigenous women's economic and social status under conditions of unequal access to macroeconomic institutions and hegemonic cultural change. The present study is a natural experiment designed to test the comparative usefulness of this paradigm in predicting the likely costs and benefits of certain forms of economic development for indigenous women, and in theorizing how the fabric of gender relations is constructed.[4] This book is also an ethnography. I shall attempt to give human form to "the gender variable" in economic-development analysis through narrative presentation of images and voices from the lived realities of women and men in Chanchaló.[5] My introduction to the policy issues and theoretical perspectives that inform the book will begin, therefore, with a glimpse of the people who will exemplify those issues.

## An Introduction to the Women of Chanchaló

The settings for these narrative snapshots include an indigenous agricultural community on the eastern Andean slopes of the Valley of Salcedo in Ecuador's Cotopaxi Province, and the large mestizo market town in the heart of the valley. The women of Chanchaló and their families derive a more or less precarious living from small-scale agriculture practiced in a fragile environment. As smallholders with little political-economic power, they are marginal participants in their national market economy, operating largely without access to agricultural infrastructure that enables larger producers to become more economically competitive. For many families, agricultural production must be supplemented or supported by off-farm wage labor.

Two of the women introduced here are affluent, by community standards. They and their husbands have accumulated landholdings of sufficient size to practice modernized commercial agriculture on a scale that has enabled them to secure private education for their children, private health care, comfortable

homes, and nest eggs. Two women are members of very poor, semiproletarianized households with none of these assets. The others struggle to compete
in commodities markets with varying levels of success. The year is 1993.

## Negotiating the Household Budget

Beatriz (aged thirty-three) and her husband Luis (aged thirty-four) have
come to town for the baptism of their infant daughter. Before returning home
for the party in her honor, there is shopping to do. The family needs food, alcohol, fuel, and fertilizer. Decisions must be made concerning how much of
each of these goods should be purchased; which deals to accept from merchants; and how all purchases relate to the family's major production-invest-
ment goal, saving for a tractor.

As the family drives around town in a borrowed truck, Beatriz remains in
the cab with the baby while Luis and their two teenaged daughters make purchases. Marketing is a social occasion, an opportunity to visit with friends
from home, other communities, and town. Many friends greet Luis and come
over to the truck to say hello to Beatriz. Luis is well known and well liked; he
has a reputation as an honest and economically successful man. He holds a
regionally important political office. Luis is also famous for the gusto with
which he occasionally consumes alcohol, as his friends are doing today.

Beatriz dispatches her daughters to the food market with instructions
concerning food and drink selections, quantities, and acceptable prices. They
return with some purchases completed and questions about others. Beatriz
tells them which deals to accept and hands out more money. Luis is socializ-
ing in the street. He stops his elder daughter, Nancy; they laugh together as
he adopts a number of exaggerated facial expressions—hopeful, pleading,
disappointed—while she shakes her head, "No way." The girls return with all
purchases completed and the right amount of change. Nancy says Luis wanted some money "for 'lunch'—you know what that means," but she didn't
give him any. Their mother laughs and tells them they have done well. Although this is a day for celebrating with family and friends and Beatriz expects they will be drinking and dancing soon, she says they must finish the
shopping first and she wants Luis to be in good shape for bargaining with
merchants.

Luis drives away from the food market, rolling up onto the sidewalk outside a number of agricultural supply stores and gasoline suppliers'. At each of
these establishments he obtains a baseline price per quantity and information
about current and future pricing trends. He also enters into negotiation with
vendors.

Luis brings his best deal from each store out to the truck. He states his case
for purchase of a large quantity of fertilizer on sale and for a fairly large pur-

chase of gas at a good price. Beatriz is not sure the fertilizer purchase is such a good idea. They do not need such a large quantity for the coming applications and, although she agrees the price is good, she's not convinced the deal is the best they can hope for. Luis cajoles. Beatriz remains firm; the larger purchase is not a bargain. She agrees that the gas purchase makes sense and they plan to complete negotiations the following day. She hands him money and he buys the fertilizer—half as much as he wanted.

On the way home they discuss their saving for the tractor. Beatriz has recently been to the lending institutions; she reviews the terms available to them, how much they now have, and how long it will probably take them to repay the loan if they can get it. She does not like any of the deals. She explains to Luis why not, and he agrees with her evaluation. She concludes that she'll have to find another source of credit.

## Deciding What to Plant

Susana (twenty-three) is feeding her animals after returning from market. She discusses crop choice for her small parcel, located at the relatively low altitude of 3,000 meters. She produces potato, two varieties of maize, and barley and pasture grasses to feed her cow, pigs, and chickens. She also tried to raise garlic, but the crop failed owing to a soil disease she was unable to treat. Failure of the garlic crop was a severe blow to household finance, as a relatively large investment was required to plant the crop. Susana remarks that the wage her husband earns managing the local small-scale cheese factory will not cover the lost production investment. Susana was also disappointed because garlic is a high-value (though also a high-risk) crop, and garlic production would represent a good investment of her small land base. She has not been able to remedy the problem that afflicted her garlic crop, so she is "resting" the land by growing pasture. Her husband returns from visiting a new cheese factory in a neighboring community and joins the conversation. He says crop choice is up to Susana because she knows more about farming than he does, although he generally works on the farm after mornings spent at the cheese factory.

## Marketing a Cash Crop

Valentina (forty-eight) heads to the wholesale market in town to sell five *quintales* (hundred-pound sacks) of potatoes. She rides to town with her uncle, Rosalino, who is selling ten times as much as she. Her husband is not with them. Rosalino says that bargaining is a waste of time, as all wholesalers offer the same price. He parks his truck and strikes a deal immediately. Valentina jokes with several wholesalers and farmers. She has quiet personal conversations with a few, patting one man on the back. She tells me that the wholesalers have colluded to cap the price per variety and quality grade, but that quality grade is negotiated between buyer and seller. Valentina turns down some offers; her eventual deal is 30 percent better than Rosalino's for the same variety.

## Managing Labor

Alegría (thirty-five) and Rubén (thirty-six) have one remaining day in which to complete their fava bean harvest. Weather conditions threaten the harvesting. By local standards Alegría and Rubén are affluent; they own about sixty hectares of land in the Amazon basin, on which they raise cattle, and they cultivate smaller holdings locally, some sharecropped with Rubén's father. They have invested in hiring ten workers for the bean harvest. The workers—including Rubén's father, who owns the fava field—pick beans while Alegría and Rubén sort and bag them. Alegría directs workers to parts of the field, exhorts them to hurry, and chastises them if they do not work well. Most of them work energetically; the largest amounts are picked by two tiny, fragile-looking indigenous women from another province. When storm clouds lower, Alegría tells Rubén to stop sorting; everyone must pick, including the two of them. Later she organizes the packing of burros with *quintales* of favas to be hauled up a steep slope to the top of the rise where their truck waits. Rubén directs the loading of these onto the truck and drives the load to town to be sold.

Alegría does not go into town because she wants to check a distant field of potatoes she sprayed with pesticide a few days earlier. Perhaps she will have to apply more the next day. She tells me they've been spraying once a week during the wet season when *lancha* (late blight) threatens their crop. On our way to town, I follow up an earlier conversation by asking Rubén if most farmers pay women and men the same daily wage, as he does. He tells me there is a single local wage for all workers per task; he volunteers the information that his *peones* are worth it because Alegría recruits good workers.

Rubén then launches into an expansive speech concerning his wife's expertise in agricultural management. He says Alegría works harder than he does because they both perform the same agricultural labor, and in addition she has to "organize" the work. She decides who will perform each task and then sees to it that all tasks are performed efficiently. Having just observed her direct the labor of several employees, her husband, and her father-in-law, I am not surprised that Rubén sums up his wife's administrative efforts by saying that she is *bien organizada,* the local phrase for a person or organization that consistently manages to achieve positive results. He feels sorry for his father, who no longer has a marriage partner: "It is no good alone."

*Putting In a Day's Work*

At seven o'clock in the morning, Rosa has been up for two hours cooking, cleaning, and tending animals. With her husband, she makes the trip from their home (at around 3,000 meters) to their potato fields some four kilometers away (at nearly 4,000 meters). Rosa digs potatoes for eight hours, stopping only briefly for lunch. The work is hard; her husband says they were old at twenty, worn out by hard labor. On the trip back down the mountainside, Rosa strikes out on her own to collect cattle and drive them home for the night. She runs down a steep slope on bowed legs that make her appear to be listing from side to side as she runs. When she returns home she will have food to prepare, animals to tend, and housework to do before she rests a bit and goes to bed. Rosa's working day is typical of women in Chanchaló. What is not typical is that she is nearly sixty, and wealthy by local standards. Her household hires labor, yet she keeps working.

*Banking on Land*

Mariana (thirty-eight) has important banking to do on market day. Her husband has been working in Quito, the capital city located about two hours by bus from Salcedo. He has returned for one of his regular visits, and they must deposit his earnings, deducting the amount he will need for living expenses in the city. Enrique explains that he stays with relatives in the city and takes them produce from the farm to help cover his board; Mariana must approve the amount he will have to spend before his next payday. She says that he does not ask for much, as the family will need most of the money for subsistence and for savings. Mariana and her husband have an important accumulation goal: they own only a very small amount of land and want to buy more. Their ultimate goal is to have enough land to support their family of four children without his having to work in the city for several months every year.

*Talking About Women in the United States*

Marina (twenty-one) and I are chatting about her visit to the United States. Marina has inherited a small parcel from her parents and also is an agricultural wage worker in Chanchaló. She is locally famous because she and her sister-in-law won scholarships financed by USAID to study horticulture in Jackson, Mississippi, during the summer of 1992. Many Ecuadoreans dream of working in the United States and becoming dollar rich. Because my husband is from Jackson, I know the city fairly well and anticipate a pleasant talk comparing our impressions. Marina thinks Jackson is a very beautiful place. She particularly admired the profusion of large trees (nonexistent in her community) and flowers. But she would not want to live there; I ask why not, and Marina answers, "Women do not earn as much as men for the same work. Not nearly as much. And women have to be afraid in the street. Here we earn the same as men and we are not afraid. No one wants to hurt us."

*First Impressions*

These momentary impressions suggest that women in Chanchaló have considerably more control over household economic resources than we might expect given the gender bias of national agricultural-development and labor-market structures. Chanchaleñas appear to have control of their own and others' agricultural labor; a strong voice in household decisions concerning land use, agricultural technology, product marketing, and finance; equal pay for equal work within the local community; and relative freedom from gender-based physical violence. Given the body of research to be reviewed in the remainder of this chapter, however, it is also plausible that these introductory snapshots mask inequalities within the household arising from gender bias in wage structures, access to the means of agricultural production, and social and political institutions.[6] In the chapters that follow, I will argue that vignettes such as these do not mask asymmetries but instead reflect an extraordinary degree of economic, social, and political gender-egalitarianism. I will argue, also, that the abundant contradictions between the gender bias that characterizes national-level institutions and the egalitarian behavior and values of Chanchaleños who participate in these same institutions offer important lessons for analysts of gender and development.

These snapshots have introduced women and men in whose lives are realized interactions of structure and culture, of exogenous and indigenous impetus, and of institutional imperative and individual human agency that are central to the discourse of gender and development. In the remainder of this chapter, I will present an overview of this discourse, and of development practice during the twenty-five years since "Women in Development" emerged as an item on international development menus. The discussion will then "get down to cases" of gender and development in sierran Ecuador and throughout the Andes, and the chapter will conclude with an overview of research questions that emerge from gender-and-development theory and from patterns of contrast, similarity, and prediction among the Andean cases.

## Gender, Households, and Rural Development

Policy-oriented studies of rural women's roles in developing-country economies have revealed the central impact of three processes on women's work and access to economic resources: (1) the evolution of peasant systems into capitalist modes of production; (2) the imposition of political authority by colonial and modernizing nation states over local-level traditional patterns of resource control; and (3) the persistence of patriarchal sociocultural systems. The emergence of a unified trend resulting from these forces, often in concert, has been widely documented: in many parts of the developing world, women farmers have decreasing access to the means of production and to productive decision-making.[7]

Although women may be incorporated into the rural capitalist workforce, they are concentrated in nonmanagerial, low-wage, temporary jobs (Faulkner and Lawson 1991; Birdsall and McGreevey 1983; Deere and León 1982). Even on family farms, women are increasingly marginalized from control of productive resources (Nash 1986; Jaquette 1985; Bossen 1981, 1989; Katz 1995). Both market-based and centrally planned economies have created or perpetuated gender bias in both off-farm employment and household-based production (IDB 1995; Padilla, Murguialday, and Criquillon 1987; Stubbs and Alvarez 1987; but see Babb 1996).

Analysts find that planned agricultural development initiatives often exacerbate the marginalization of female producers. Women have been excluded from agricultural development programs aimed at restructuring smallholder access to the means of production and at improved productivity and sustainability, even in circumstances in which they are responsible for much of smallholder production.[8] Men have received assistance in gaining restructured landholdings, technology, marketing infrastructure, and other means of making an agricultural living; their wives, in many circumstances, have become field laborers with no decision authority over resources accessed through development projects.

Women's productive resource bases have been reduced by both planned and unplanned development of commercialized crop, livestock, fishing, and forest-resource production among small-scale, former subsistence producers in Africa, Asia, and Latin America.[9] Men may have greater access to commodities markets through production contracts (Carney and Watts 1991), control of transportation (Bourque and Warren 1981), or wider experience of national or global economies and cultures (Bourque and Warren 1981). Although women may resist unreciprocated demands on their labor or lands by household patriarchs engaged in commercialized production, most analysts conclude that in developing countries men control cash cropping on small farms (Warren and Bourque 1991). One of the central questions to be explored in this study is whether this generalization can be applied to Andean farming systems.

It is not only women who suffer from gender bias in planned and unplanned economic development. In farming systems where women are responsible for food crops and men for nonfood cash crops that command increasing amounts of household lands and labor, losses both in food production and in women's income adversely affect children (Buvinić and Mehra 1990; Blumberg 1988; Guyer 1988a). In many societies women bear the greater responsibility for meeting nutritional and other subsistence needs of children and other household dependents (Mencher 1988; Roldán 1988; Kennedy 1989; Jaquette 1993). These responsibilities increase with some forms of economic change, notably structural adjustment packages that cut public support for social programs, even as women's income and agricultural output may decrease (Benería 1995). Analysts working within diverse theoretical perspectives have documented the disproportionate costs borne by women and children of many forms of planned and unplanned economic development.

## Planned Development and the "Black Box"

Women have been marginalized from productive processes in part because governments and donor agencies have perceived the small-farm production unit as a male-headed household in which property rights and management decisions are vested in the head (Poats, Feldstein, and Rocheleau 1989; Blumberg 1988). When questions of distribution within the household have been considered at all, it has been generally assumed that the head determines how development benefits will be allocated and that he will consider the needs of his family. Within many of the largest or "mainstream" bilateral and multilateral donor agencies, the household itself long remained a "black box," its internal social and economic dynamics of little interest to development planners.[10] Practitioners desired a simple and practical way to use a single production function per production unit in the delivery and monitoring of development programs (Blumberg 1988, 52) and in comparing results across programs (Bossen 1989).

The "black-box" approach not only obscures relations of production and consumption within the "box"; it also puts artificially impermeable sides on the box itself. Small-farm production "units" may incorporate extrahousehold members of kinship and other reciprocity networks, a fact that has implications for their access to productive resources and investment patterns. Moreover, households are never totally isolated or self-sufficient (Laslett 1984) but are always "penetrated by other affiliations through age, kinship, gender and class" (Wilk 1990, 326). Consequences of the "black-box" approach for rural women have been summarized effectively by Laurel Bossen:

The use of this "head" concept implicitly diminishes the economic roles of women . . . ignoring any independent productive, managerial, or commercial activities they carry out in other cultures. As a result, development programs intending to work with what is erroneously and ethnocentrically believed to be the status quo tend to deliver training, technology, and resources to men. In the process, these programs can revolutionize systems of gender relations by putting men in charge of all major material resources. At the same time, benefits to the assumed household head are often falsely perceived as equally benefitting the household members. (Bossen 1989, 341)

## Emergence of "The Gender Variable" in International Development Discourse and Practice

During the last twenty-five years, analyses of women's productive and re-productive roles in developing societies have contributed to the breaking open of the black box. Scholars working within competing development paradigms and diverse feminist perspectives, practitioners working within mainstream and alternative development institutions, and political activists concerned with the economic and social well-being of women have contributed to a maturing gender-and-development discourse. Central to this discourse are questions relating to both (1) the impact of planned and unplanned economic change in women's lives and (2) the impact of gendered patterns in household production and reproduction on the results of macroeconomic policy. From the modernization schemes of the 1950s and 1960s through structural adjustment programs of the 1980s and 1990s, disappointing performance in the areas of economic growth, poverty reduction, and social justice have been linked to inadequate knowledge of gendered economic and social processes within households, and to gender bias within both macro-level and micro-level economic, social, and political structures.

Ester Boserup's pioneering analysis of women's productive roles in traditional agricultural and trade systems (1970) convinced early proponents of gender equity in development that colonial and postwar modernization schemes had channeled access to land, credit, technology, and training to men, using inappropriate Western models of household agricultural production, in which men are the primary agricultural producers. This process marginalized women—who in fact had heavy production responsibilities within their households—from access to the means of production. As modernization advanced, the exclusion of women from developing labor and commodities markets deepened the income gap between women and men, rendering household gender hierarchies more patriarchal. Boserup's solution, embraced within some international development institutions, was to promote the integration of women into modernization programs.

Boserup argued that opening modernization processes to women would both redress gender inequities caused by these processes and improve the efficiency of development projects and developing markets (Jaquette 1990). Boserup presented a case for considering women to be the "missing links" in development programs that had produced disappointing results through the 1960s (Mair 1986, cited in Tinker 1990b, 31). If half of the producers were excluded from development efforts, it followed that enormous productive potential was being wasted. Furthermore, women might seek to undermine projects that threatened their livelihoods.

This efficiency-based argument in favor of including women in development projects and developing markets had more appeal to many international development institutions than an equity-based argument alone. Including women in development could be legitimized as a strategy conducive to economic growth and market development. Since women, despite their productive potential, made up a disproportionately large percentage of "the poorest of the poor" in developing countries, some donors also found it appealing to include women in integrated rural development programs of the 1970s that focused on self-help poverty reduction and the more equitable distribution of development benefits.

Many development analysts argued, however, that the cure for modernization programs' disappointing results after more than two decades was not to be found in making them more inclusive. Dependency theorists argued that policies promoting improved economic and social well-being for rural populations through modernization and poverty reduction had created, instead, structures of dependent capitalist development that extended the power of "First World" institutions controlling money and technology flows while deepening class inequalities within "Third World" societies. From this perspective, true rural development would not result from continued public investment in capitalist agriculture, which contributed to increasing land concentration. Along with their decreasing access to land, smallholders faced increasing dependence on off-farm wages kept artificially low by the continuation of family subsistence production. Economic growth resulted in increased domestic demand and investment primarily for a small and predominantly urban elite. In the absence of hard political choices supporting a more socially equitable distribution of productive resources, continued modernization would only exacerbate the production of neocolonial underdevelopment.[11]

Many gender-and-development analysts found the broad implications of dependency theory compelling. Latin American researchers argued that the solution to women's marginalization by development schemes that target productive resources to men, and to commodities and labor markets segmented by gender, was not to incorporate women into these structures. Alternative forms of development that would address both class and gender inequities—exacerbated under dependent capitalism—were called for.[12]

Within both modernization- and dependency-influenced models, redressing gender inequities associated with economic development was largely approached as an economic problem during the 1970s. As the decade drew to a close, however, many scholars and activists concluded that the focus on employment and resource-access opportunities had failed to improve women's economic and social status in many settings, because patriarchal social structures in workplace, home, and state had not been challenged by development processes (Benería 1979; Benería and Sen 1986). Social norms could prevent women from working outside their homes. For women who did seek outside employment, opportunities were concentrated in low-wage, insecure positions. In many societies, women had little recourse to defend themselves against physical violence or to control their own fertility. Moreover, policies designed to reduce poverty did not address social determinants of women's subordination that cut across class lines.

During the 1980s gender-and-development discourse increasingly focused on the social construction of gender hierarchies. With respect to household structures, a number of studies investigated whether earning her own income would improve a woman's well-being and that of her children. In many sociocultural settings, earning income proved the single most important factor in improving women's access to both household economic resources and decision-making processes; women's income and improved bargaining positions tend to improve children's welfare (Blumberg 1988). In some settings, having access to secure employment proved the most important determinant in allowing women to limit the size of their families (Handwerker 1992; see Blumberg 1988).

However, positive outcomes were far from universal. In patriarchal households, women's income can be appropriated by men and allocated for their own pleasures or for household expenditures that do not benefit women and children (Jacobs 1991). Women's greater responsibility for providing food and other subsistence needs for dependents can offset gains in access to income and decision-making within the household (see A. Sen 1990; Benería and Roldán 1987). Aside from earned income, other resources brought into the household by women, such as land, often are not under their control and do not provide access to resulting incomes (Bourque and Warren 1981).

Moreover, cultural ideals and social norms play important roles in determining the valuation of women, women's perceived obligations to their families, and resulting patterns in resource entitlement within households (Papanek 1990; A. Sen 1990; see discussion below). Perceptions of women's in-come-earning performance or potential may be as important as the income they actually produce in terms of entitlements within the household. The per-ception that there is a viable labor market for women may raise the status of women who do not earn income. Conversely, the perception that income-earning women are housewives rather than breadwinners can both keep wages low and lower women's bargaining position concerning the amount of reproductive labor they must perform for their households.

By the mid–1980s, most analysts were in agreement that women's primary responsibility for the social and biological reproduction of their households had not diminished with their incorporation into markets or into centrally planned economies. Across theoretical and political perspectives, it was pro-posed that development policy focus on linkages between women's produc-tive and reproductive roles within households, and on linkages among women's roles within the household, macrolevel political and economic structures, and women's well-being. To the equity and efficiency arguments of the 1970s were added both an approach demanding women's social and political empowerment through social transformations (Mosse 1993; Sen and Grown 1987) and a more nuanced economic and social efficiency approach contextualized by the economic crises and public-spending austerity pro-grams of the 1980s (G. Sen 1996; Blumberg 1995a, 1995b; Tinker 1990a, 1990b). To the voices of Western proponents of gender equity were increas-ingly added the voices of non-Western women with their own diverse ideas regarding women's well-being and institutional pathways to sustainable social and economic development (DAWN 1987).

Macroeconomic policy featuring Structural Adjustment Packages (SAPs), which emphasized both austerity with respect to social programs and national economic competitiveness arising from the comparative advantage of cheap labor within a global economy, placed increasing economic stress on poor and, in many Latin American countries, middle-income women and families (Benería 1995; Acosta-Belén and Bose 1995; Babb 1996; but see Gladwin and Thompson 1995). During the 1980s and into the 1990s, Latin American women had greater access than men to many forms of wage labor, but they earned less than men and primarily worked in jobs lacking benefits and secu-rity; women participated in the informal sector as the smallest operators, gen-erally earning less than men and less than the minimum wage (IDB 1995, 58–59, 67). Throughout the developing world, women's unpaid reproductive labor was "taxed" to compensate for reduced social services (Palmer 1992; Moser 1989).

Structural adjustment policies also encouraged production of nontradition-

al cash crops for export; agricultural development programs channeled resources for such production to men while increasing demands were placed on
women's unpaid agricultural labor and on women's earnings from seasonal,
low-paying field and processing work (DAWN 1987; Buvinić and Mehra
1990). While some researchers stressed variability in women's employment
and social contexts within the new international division of labor—pointing
to both absolute gains and to improvements in women's positions relative to
those of men in some settings (see Gladwin and Thompson 1995)—most concluded that SAPs resulted in increased work for women without commensu-
rate gains in economic and social well-being (Rakowski 1995b; Moser 1989;
Benería 1995; G. Sen 1996).

A number of researchers have argued that the gender-segmented commodities and labor markets of the 1980s and 1990s, together with the "reproduction tax," allocate resources inefficiently as well as inequitably (Palmer
1992; G. Sen 1996). Social constraints to women's participation in labor markets and the increasing concentration of women in the least remunerative
niches of the informal sector bias allocative efficiency. One Latin American
study showed that, for women to earn as much as men, they must have four
more years of formal education (Krawczyk 1993, cited in IDB 1995, 60). In
addition, reliance on unpaid (zero-valued) women's labor to subsidize family
social welfare overtaxes women in a context of unsustainably low capital-
labor ratios (Palmer 1992; Moser 1989).

In the 1990s proponents of efficiency, equity, and empowerment approaches to gender and development address an institutional climate in
which market allocation of resources is generally viewed as the unquestioned
linchpin of economic development (G. Sen 1996; IDB 1995). Economic efficiency arguments for removing gender bias from labor and commodities markets (Elson and McGee 1995) are joined by social efficiency arguments for
forging creative alliances between public and private entities to improve social
welfare and reduce nonsustainable demands on women's labor (see Çağatay,
Elson, and Grown 1995; Palmer 1992). As did Boserup, these proponents of
gender equity and empowerment in the 1990s seek to show that more equitable markets will also be more efficient. During the years of structural adjustment, the critical importance of interactions among economic and social variables contributing to women's well-being has been made evident in work
from diverse perspectives.

## The Cultural Dimension

An issue that frequently has been raised within gender-and-development
discourse (but less frequently investigated) is the interaction of structural and

cultural factors in producing gendered patterns in economic development. Reference to "the culture variable" often encompasses undifferentiated non-structural factors that contribute to cross-cultural differences in women's economic and social roles. The cultural construction of gender ideologies—ideas concerning, for example, women's and men's physical and mental attributes, their appropriate economic and social roles, and the maintaining of these roles for the perpetuation of families and societies—has seldom been analyzed together with the structural determinants of women's economic and social status (see discussion in Wolf 1992, 7–29; Papanek 1990; Hart 1992). More than ten years ago June Nash called for

a dialectical analysis of cultural and structural interrelations. . . . Such a perspective embraces values, beliefs, and expectations conditioning behavior and attitudes about society at the same time that it relates to the structural constraints of a given mode of production and level of capital accumulation. We are not limiting the culture concept to that which is transmitted from one generation to another, but rather we shall assert that culture is the generative base for adapting to and redefining basic relations in production and reproduction. (Nash 1986, 15)

During the past decade, studies engaging this dialectic have demonstrated that ideologies of gender (and of ethnicity, kinship, class, and capital) can interact with structural factors in ways that profoundly affect the impact of economic change in women's lives (Guyer 1988a, 1988b; Carney and Watts 1991; Lockwood 1993; Rakowski 1995a; Safa 1995a; and see Bourque and Warren 1981 for an earlier example).[13]

Among the questions most frequently asked regarding the interaction of structure and culture is whether women's integration into capitalist agriculture, industry, or trade translates into a reconceptualization of "housewives" as "producers," "breadwinners," or "providers," and the more gender-equitable division of household reproductive labor that might be expected to accompany such a reconceptualization. In theoretically diverse recent studies of Latin American populations, the answer to this question is a qualified no. Among rural Mexican populations in which women engage in wage labor, industrial piecework or craft production in their homes, and/or agricultural production and marketing, Patricia Arias finds "a common thread":

women's difficulty in transforming economic activities into social and cultural resources that can modify their position within their families and societies. According to the possibilities of their culture, women have traveled, traded, brought money and goods home, and earned a regular income, but this did not lead to a modification in their domestic roles or their traditional community roles, where obligations and rights are defined by land possession and agricultural work and status hierarchies are ordered according to age and sex. (Arias 1994, 172)

Other analysts studying similar populations find "incipient" but important cultural and social change partly attributable to women's cash-earning activities (González Montes 1994; Mummert 1994). Liberalized courtship rules and marriage residence patterns within families who have come to value the earning ability of young female industrial workers; inheritance patterns that are becoming more gender-egalitarian; and an increase in women's ability to resist spouse abuse and found independent households have been observed for at least a small percentage of research samples.

In all of these studies, however, married women are found to be constrained by cultural rules requiring their cash-earning work to be performed within their homes. Although this is the least-remunerative labor in most cases, women bow to cultural constructs of appropriate behavior for married mothers, whose leaving home to work would shame both their husbands and themselves. Women must also perform most reproductive labor, as their husbands consider it an "insult" to be asked to perform housework or child care. The essentially patriarchal nature of household social organization has not been renegotiated along more gender-egalitarian lines between breadwinning marriage partners.

In three Caribbean countries, Helen Safa (1995a) finds that women who earn most of their households' cash income through industrial wage labor, and whose income gives them more leverage within their households, are still perceived both at home and at work as housewives or supplemental wage earners rather than breadwinners. Safa delineates the traditional, Spanish colonial *casa/calle* (home/street) cultural divide, which has not been breached by women's leaving home to earn their families' livelihoods. At home, working women retain primary responsibility for reproductive labor, a process many have not attempted to alter, as traditional social status for women is based on motherhood and unilateral responsibility for the domestic component of household survival. At work, women are perceived as supplemental wage earners who can be counted on to work for low wages within patriarchal management hierarchies. Women are viewed by themselves, as well as by men, as "wives and mothers with economic responsibilities," rather than as breadwinners (Safa 1995a, 48). Safa concludes that so long as these cultural values do not change, women will continue to be doubly burdened with productive and reproductive labor, and employers will continue to profit from the subordination of women.[14]

Both Safa and Cathy Rakowski (1995a) demonstrate that state institutions can also maintain, or help create, household patriarchal hierarchies through development and other policies based in the perception that women are, or should be, housewives. In a study of planned industrial communities in Venezuela, Rakowski finds that programs promoting women's self-identification as housewives contributed to ideological constructions of gender that outlasted the economic structure on which they were originally based. When economic hardship threatened their families, many women were ill-prepared and hesitant to seek work, as they believed income generation and effective execution of their reproductive responsibilities to be incompatible. Women who had not been targeted by planned "housewifization" did not face such barriers.

These studies demonstrate that ideological factors cannot be discounted in explanations of women's continued subordination within their households and workplaces. Earlier reluctance to focus on cultural constructions of gender stemmed partly from a well-founded desire to emphasize structural issues rather than to blame cultural institutions for economic inequality. However, both delineation of cultural norms and analysis of the constitution of those norms in practice is essential for an understanding of women's "places" in developing economies (Guyer and Peters 1987; Hart 1992).

### Engendered Human Agency: Interactions Among Macro- and Microlevel Factors

Studies of gender and development have succeeded in identifying patterned gender inequalities resulting from linkages among factors at varying levels of analysis: household, kin group, community, ethnic group, economic sector, nation, region, world capitalist system. Much of this research has concentrated on the influence of macrolevel factors on more microlevel configurations. This is a component of critical importance in analysis of the negative effects of planned and unplanned development—which often originate within international or national-level institutions—on women's labor, control of household economic resources, and social roles. Both macrostructural economic change and hegemonic cultural change associated with Western colonialism, capitalism, and planned modernization have been shown to contribute to the subordination of women (Lockwood 1993; Weismantel 1988; Collins 1986).

However, observed variation in the results of these linkages indicates that local-level institutions can mediate the effects of macrolevel directed economic change and capitalist institutions. Research conducted in Africa and Asia has demonstrated the formative role of locally distinctive intrahousehold social relations in mediating and even shaping broader processes.[15] Moreover, neither women nor local-level institutions should be viewed as the inevitably more or less passive victims of exogenous development processes. In many contexts, women should be viewed as economic agents who have successfully resisted or adapted development processes to their own ends (see de Groot 1991). Local-level institutions may provide vehicles for their success.

Studies of gender and development in Latin America have been strongly influenced by a global-economy perspective that emphasizes both the unequal articulation of peasant agricultural systems with national and international political-economic institutions (Nash 1986; Arizpe and Botey 1987) and the exploitation of class and gender inequities by multinational corporations (see essays in Nash and Fernández-Kelly 1983; discussion in Warren and Bourque 1991). Although increasingly focused on intraregional differences in these articulations and on the incorporation of sociocultural variables and household-based processes in their analyses of women's subordination (Deere and León 1987; Babb 1989; Rakowski 1995a, 1995b; IDB 1995), macrostructural loci of causation are emphasized.

Studies of the interaction of structure and culture in Latin America generally emphasize the hegemonic influence of cultural change originating at the macro level in colonial political, economic, and religious institutions; modern state and planned development institutions; or capitalism (Weismantel 1988; see Papanek 1990). With respect to capitalism, for example, this perspective is succinctly summarized by Rakowski: "under capitalism, definitional power [the ability to impose values and norms] accrues to those who have economic power" (1995a, 53). Poor or socially subjugated peoples—including most indigenous populations and women—are expected to be oppressed ideologically as well as economically, politically, and physically (Rakowski 1995a; see Chafetz 1991). Although historical and ethnographic studies reveal the indigenous agency of Latin American institutions that elsewhere are assumed to be the result of colonial capitalist hegemony (Smith 1985; Bourque and Warren 1981), most researchers expect that macrolevel institutions will dominate economic and sociocultural change at the local level.

## *Gender-and-Development Institutional Ideology: Postmodern Feminist Critique*

The universal victimization of Third World women by economic and social processes associated with modernization, structural adjustment, and traditional patriarchy is a form of conceptual and political essentialism strongly contested by postmodern feminist critics, both Western and non-Western.[16] Critics of Western models of development and gender equity argue that deconstruction of gender-and-development discourse reveals a neocolonial agenda typifying Third World women as poor, vulnerable, oppressed, exploited, and by implication in need of salvation by Western (or Western-trained) development specialists. Mitu Hirschman characterizes this agenda and some of its "progressive" proponents:

Like the good Samaritans (reminiscent of the missionary zeal of the eighteenth- and nineteenth-century colonial administrators), many of these development specialists have sought to represent and rescue at the same time the "silent and mute victims" (i.e. poor Third World women) from their own men (symbolizing patriarchal oppression and domination), who are in league with capitalism (symbolizing the hierarchical, oppressive and the exploitative international division of labor), the "bad guys" in other words. Through their analysis of the development process, conjoined with their understanding of feminism, they (the Subject) have sought to empower the oppressed and poor women (the subject/object) in various Third World countries and to engage them in grass roots struggles to recuperate the subjecthood (agency) which they presumably lost, in some cases, during the capitalist penetration of their societies. (1995, 50)

Critics challenge researchers and development practitioners to allow their "subject/objects" to speak for themselves, to seek "previously silenced women's voices, particularly their interpretation of the world they inhabit, their successes and failures and their desires for change" (Parpart 1993, 454), and thus to cease "coloniz[ing] the material and historical heterogeneities of the lives of women in the third world" (Mohanty 1988, 62).

Moreover, concepts of gender equality associated with Western development agendas are also questioned, together with component constructs such as the gendered division of labor, wage rates, access to the means of production, and women's sexual or political autonomy. Analysts are challenged to overcome ethnocentric bias in their work by deconstructing their own ideologies concerning what is good for women (see Mukhopadhyay and Higgins 1988). Further, critics argue that any agenda reflecting "the binary thought structures and patriarchal character of most Western knowledge" (Parpart 1995, 239) relies on conceptual frameworks that misrepresent experience. A life cannot be encoded meaningfully into (binary) categories such as "the sexual division of labor," or women's "practical gender needs" and "strategic gender interests," which are then used to target components of lived experience for development agendas (Hirschman 1995; Marchand 1995).

Many of these points are well taken. Although there is ample evidence of a growing effort to avoid the victimization perspective (Blumberg 1995a, 1995b; Kabeer 1994) and to stress the diversity of experience of women in developing countries (IDB 1995; Rakowski 1995b), examples of continuing essentialism abound in gender-and-development discourse. Even critics who reject uniform, Western-based development menus continue to make statements such as: "What unites all women in developing nations is the remaining hope that organization, education and resistance would in the long run provide many with a means of escaping from, or at the very least loosening the tight grip of, poverty and subordination" (Afshar 1991, 2). In a survey of gender and development in Latin America that expresses commitment to exploring diversity, analysis of negative agricultural development outcomes for women arrives at the conclusion: "The traditional division of labor and allocation of resources have been reinforced rather than challenged by existing agricultural and rural development policies" (IDB 1995, 64). Allowing for the necessity to generalize, this statement illustrates a subtle essentialism and victimization subtext; I would argue that among the wide variety of gendered divisions of agricultural labor and resources in Latin America, some traditional forms are gender-egalitarian. Most analysts (including this author) continue to utilize binary constructs such as gendered divisions of labor or practical versus strategic needs, although there is a growing awareness that such oppositions are often artificial and should be placed in a holistic context, both for understanding gendered processes and for targeting development investment (Rakowski 1995b). Although some progress has been made in the push for *locally defined*, socially transformative empowerment, this effort has been more successful in alternative development institutions than in mainstream contexts.

## Gender-and-Development Studies: Conclusion

During twenty-five years of research and practice concerning gender and development, competing theoretical perspectives have matured and their advocates have advanced the field by challenging and enriching one another's work. Whether the focus has been on efficiency or equity goals in development; on economic or sociocultural linkages through which development processes have marginalized women; on macro- or microlevel processes; on ideologies of gender alone, or of gender and development, we have seen that women make a difference in development processes and are affected differentially by development processes. The black box has been cracked open. Gender has emerged as a critical variable in analysis of development outcomes and of the sustainability of succeeding development agendas. Analysis of development processes has informed the comparative study of gender status, as well. Scholars and practitioners have successfully pursued a rigorous search for patterned gender inequalities related to planned and unplanned economic development processes.

To the degree that knowledge is power, the interests of women in developing countries are now better represented within international and national development institutions. Some of the largest international donors consider gender reciprocities within the household and the marginalization of women by past development processes in project design (Jaquette 1993). A few are beginning to consider the "strategic" needs of women for long-term, socially transformative empowerment as well as "practical" (specific or daily) needs (Moser 1989; Parpart 1993; IDB 1995). Within agencies reluctant to tackle problems of social transformation, individual practitioners continue to push for more inclusive development agendas (Rathgeber 1995).

However, the work of making development beneficial for women in developing countries has not yet achieved widespread results. Although most Latin American countries now have women's bureaus and development plans calling for the incorporation of women into economic and social institutions, few have delineated concrete policies and even fewer have developed mechanisms or channeled resources sufficiently for these policies to be executed (Deere and León 1987). More heartening are the results of bottom-up development approaches, many organized through NGOs in partnership with local entities, although these may be underfunded or difficult to replicate (Mosse 1993). Although some bilateral donors have incorporated lessons learned from bottom-up successes into their gender-and-development programs, putting their financial and political muscle behind programming of local origination, this approach does not characterize the majority of development initiatives exported from the First World (Mosse 1993).

It is beyond the scope of this discussion to analyze the institutional and other problems not related to research that have limited the incorporation of gender analysis into economic development policy and the effectiveness of gender-and-development policy implementation throughout Latin America and the developing world. As the research base becomes more inclusive, in terms of population and process coverage and in terms of attention to subjective voices and local realities, let us hope that development agendas informed by it will yield more inclusive results.

## Gender and Development in the Andes: Five Hundred Years of Political, Economic, and Cultural Hegemony

Studies of women's agricultural roles in the Andes attest to the potentially negative influence of planned and unplanned development on indigenous women's access to economic, social, and political resources. In many Andean countries, indigenous populations constitute a majority of rural highland populations. In Ecuador, 43 percent of the total population of 10 million is indigenous; most of these people live in the rural highlands (IDB 1992, 9). In Peru and Bolivia, both total populations and indigenous percentages are larger. Thus, indigenous populations constitute a significant proportion of humanity in a large geographical area. In the following discussion I will focus on threats posed to indigenous women's productive and social bases by the legacy of Spanish colonial regimes, modernizing nation states, and capitalism as these have interacted with indigenous Andean patterns of landholding and production.

## Colonial and Republican Regimes, 1533–1964

In pre-Incaic Ecuador, Peru, and Bolivia, women held independent usufruct rights to communal lands and controlled their own production on these lands (Stark 1984; Silverblatt 1980, 1987). Elite women in my own study region in Cotopaxi Province also inherited and held land independently (Oberem 1988, 160). During the Inca empire, bilateral and parallel inheritance of land continued to be recognized. In addition, both women and men filled agricultural production quotas for the state while also producing for household consumption (Silverblatt 1980; LeVine 1987; Salomon 1986). It is likely that women served indigenous chieftains as long-distance traders, positions that could carry a great deal of wealth and prestige (Salomon 1986, 106).

With the coming of colonialism, indigenous women and men became economic wards of the state. Most indigenous people in Ecuador lost their rights to land and to control their own labor (Hurtado 1980). Although men were more likely to be subject to colonial labor drafts, leaving women to fend for their families (Stark 1979), both women and men were forced to work for the conquerors without regard for their own families' agricultural consumption needs.

In accordance with Spanish patriarchal cultural norms, colonial governments considered women to be the social and economic wards of male "household heads"; under colonial law, women lost the right to inherit (Stark 1979) or otherwise own land officially (Silverblatt 1980). In Ecuador, women were not allowed to inherit usufruct rights to the small marginal plots provided by hacienda owners to the indigenous families who worked their lands (Stark 1979). Women could, however, inherit the debts of their husbands in the onerous debt-peonage system prevalent on the haciendas.

## Contemporary Planned Development

The economic contributions of rural women have become increasingly "invisible" to national-level institutions, as colonial exploitation has been replaced by modernization policies based upon perceived male responsibility for agricultural production. Andean land-reform and other development efforts have largely excluded women by law (Phillips 1987; Deere 1986; Deere and

León 1987). As agricultural modernization reformed Peru's highland hacienda system in the 1960s, peasant women lost access to hacienda productive resources. Only official household heads, however, were permitted to apply for land grants (Deere 1986). Most women lived in households including adult males who were considered by the state to be the heads of their households.

In Ecuador during the 1960s and 1970s only household heads were permitted to participate legally in land reform. Women were required by law to secure their husbands' permission to apply for membership in agricultural cooperatives and were prohibited from joining the same cooperatives as their husbands (Agricultural Cooperatives Law, 1973, Titulo III, Art. 17b; Art. 19; referenced in Phillips 1987, 113). Recent efforts to redress these inequalities through legislation have yet to affect women's direct access to national-level agricultural development benefits. Thus national development policy has perpetuated the internationally observed pattern of institutional exclusion of women from access to productive resources. (Indigenous responses to national law and policy will be delineated throughout this study.)

Development projects aimed at increased crop productivity and agricultural sustainability have also excluded Ecuadorean women. With very few exceptions, the limited technical-assistance and other programs that do reach small-scale producers are targeted to men.[17] The rationale for excluding women is the widespread perception among national-level policy makers that male household heads make most production decisions, including those related to land use and input selection. Training materials for extensionists emphasize the desirability of dealing with productive decision-makers, specifically men who work away from home and will be available only on weekends or seasonally. To the degree that perceived male control of agricultural production does not reflect local realities, excluding women from technical assistance and other programs may result in considerable productivity, income, and sustainability losses for women and their families.

A number of state and private organizations have offered development benefits to women. However, these organizations have concentrated on women's reproductive roles and productive activities perceived to be extensions of these roles.[18] The Ministry of Health, the Roman Catholic Church, and other institutions have organized community-based "mothers' groups" to receive information and aid in the areas of nutrition and family health. Both public and private agencies have limited production-oriented or income-generating projects to sewing and crafts production (Belote and Belote 1988) or kitchen gardens and small-animal production (Garrett and Espinosa 1988). Many analysts conclude that such programs do not generate much income, although they may be of benefit in organizational terms (see Chaney 1987;

Flora 1987; Bourque and Warren 1981). There is no evidence that programs aimed at mothers or "housewives" have redefined the economic roles or self-concepts of indigenous women farmers, but neither have they addressed women's potential production needs.

*Unplanned Development: Capitalist Labor and Commodity Markets
and Women's Loss of Access to Resources and Decision-Making*

Several studies find that the effects of unplanned development have disadvantaged indigenous women agriculturalists, as male participation in capitalist labor markets has served to reduce women's agricultural productivity, access to income, and social status within their households. In traditional communities where indigenous social forms have survived, husband and wife may mobilize labor independently through kinship and other reciprocity networks. Men's participation in wage labor has left their wives with less household labor to exchange (Collins 1986; Radcliffe 1986). In some communities, certain agricultural tasks can be performed only by men (Bourque and Warren 1981). Women must pay for labor, depending on access to their husbands' cash or on their own small cash earnings (Collins 1986). Female children, whose work is considered nonproductive by male heads, may have to migrate to work for wages, which they remit to the household to cover these costs (Radcliffe 1986).

Women's subsistence production, reproductive labor, and even cash incomes have become devalued within households dependent on male wages (Collins 1986; Radcliffe 1986; Weismantel 1988; Phillips 1987; Balarezo 1984). Balarezo (1984) finds that women's earnings are devalued even if they earn more cash than their husbands, who characterize their wives' wage labor as low-paying "women's work." Mary Weismantel (1988) and Jane Collins attribute the devaluation of women's income to male migrants' contact with "a dominant cultural tradition that defines men as household heads and women's work as domestic in nature and thus less important" (Collins 1986, 667). Collins also emphasizes the state's role in transforming male householders within a gender-egalitarian society into household heads responsible for paying taxes and for the actions of their dependents.

An important result of this devaluation of women's production is that women have decreasing entitlements to men's income (Weismantel 1988) and to economic decision-making (Balarezo 1984). Family structure can collapse under this strain. When men migrate to work for wages and women cannot mobilize extrahousehold labor but must perform all agricultural work themselves, their production is likely to decrease and they will no longer be able to supply the level of subsistence they once did. Their husbands will either have to provide more or abandon the family. Some migrant husbands have chosen to leave their wives and children rather than bear an increased proportion of the burden of family support (Weismantel 1988; Gisbert, Painter, and Quitón 1994).

Thus, much of the evidence concerning indigenous women's economic roles in Ecuador and the Andes indicates that women have been disadvantaged by both planned and unplanned capitalist development. Women producers have become, at least in the perception of many policy makers and social scientists, unpaid domestic agricultural labor. They have lost access to both productive resources and household economic decision-making.

The view that traditional Andean institutions are more gender-egalitarian than national capitalist institutions has been challenged by Bourque and Warren (1981), who find that even the poorest women in a more market-oriented Peruvian community have access to more economic opportunities than women in a more traditional, less commercially oriented community within the same microregion. In their analysis, women in the more traditional community are found to be disadvantaged by gender complementarity in the division of agricultural labor, which prohibits women from participating in important activities. Patriarchal gender ideology views women as physically and emotionally weaker than men; thus, their labor is materially devalued relative to that of men.

Bourque and Warren also find that participation in capitalist commodity markets by traditional households threatens women's control of economic resources. In wealthier cash-cropping households, men control the marketing of agricultural commodities and cash income. Bourque and Warren conclude that the *interaction* of capitalist institutions and traditional gender cultural norms is more damaging to women than either capitalist institutions or traditional gender ideology alone. Both the poorest women described above whose husbands migrate to wage labor and the wealthier women whose husbands control the fruits of commercial agriculture have become marginalized from control of their households' most valuable economic resources.

## Can Indigenous Ecuadorean Women Hold Their Own?

In contrast to the evidence reported above, three Ecuadorean studies (Poeschel 1988; Belote and Belote 1988; Alberti 1986) attest to the survival of what the researchers consider to be traditional Andean gender-egalitarian intrahousehold resource control in communities and households integrated into capitalist labor and/or commodity markets. (These formations will be elaborated in later chapters.) The general pattern emerging from these three studies is that in surviving traditional Andean production systems women

continue, however precariously, to hold land and control productive processes equally with men, and to enjoy an equal measure of power and prestige
within their communities.

Some analysts have attributed the survival of gender-egalitarian power-
sharing and control of household economic resources to a traditional system
of sexual parallelism or complementarity in household economic production
and in public institutions, based upon both gender-egalitarian inheritance of
material wealth and upon traditional gender ideology (Belote and Belote
1977, 1988). Traditional forms of land tenure have been shown to exist in areas where colonial governments chose to exploit resources other than land
(Belote and Belote 1988), or where traditional forms of equal male and female inheritance have begun to equalize ownership of land-reform properties
that are now being passed on to a second generation (Stark 1984). Vestiges of
parallel male and female ritual systems survive, whereas male-dominated political organizations chartered in accord with land-reform legislation often
lack power and influence (Belote and Belote 1977, 1981, 1988).

Gender complementarity in household economic production essentially
means that women and men control differing—but equally valued—productive domains (such as crops versus livestock production), activities, products,
and resource bases. Although both men and women may participate in the
domains of the opposite gender and sometimes even have prescribed subordinate roles within their partners' domains, particular domains and their attendant required skills are perceived to belong exclusively to men or women
(Allen 1988; Belote and Belote 1988). Additionally, many productive activities (such as land preparation) may involve prescribed male and female complementary tasks. Ideally, both male and female participation is required for
the successful completion of these activities. Thus women's labor, expertise,
products, and individually owned or controlled resources are critical to
household survival. Owing to their material productive value to their households and to egalitarian gender ideology, women also enjoy equal participation with their husbands in joint decisions affecting important household resources, such as land, labor, and income.

Where this form of complementarity is strictly observed, women may be
disadvantaged if they cannot mobilize additional labor to compensate for the
absence of their migrant husbands, or if they cannot perform tasks themselves. However, in the research area studied by Linda and Jim Belote in the
southern Ecuadorean sierra, women were able to manage in their husbands'
absence (Belote and Belote 1981, 1988). Saraguro families own an average of
fifteen hectares of land and are thus wealthier than most indigenous families
studied in Ecuador. Most Saraguro women can afford to hire extrahousehold

labor. In addition, the amount of labor required by a Saraguro household for plowing (the one agricultural task that must be performed by men) is relatively small. The Saraguros farm relatively small amounts of their total land-holdings, allotting most land to livestock production on which they rely for their farm-produced cash income. Thus, in their husbands' absence, women can manage nearly all agricultural production alone or with hired labor.

The Saraguro form of sexual complementarity has benefited women by enabling them to participate in job-training and other development programs. Women are able to remain away from home for longer periods than their husbands, who have greater responsibility for livestock management (Belote and Belote 1988). During the 1960s women participated in vocational training courses offered by development organizations in urban centers; they were able to obtain work as medical assistants and to earn other types of off-farm income in greater numbers than were men.

The high valuation placed on women's productive capacity also enabled women to take advantage of formal educational opportunities. Once laws were passed freeing indigenous young people to attend secondary school with mestizos in the late 1960s, Saraguro families invested in education for both female and male children. The first Saraguro graduate from a four-year university was a woman. Many young women obtained posts as teachers, nurses, and in government service (Belote and Belote 1988). Thus integration into planned development programs and national culture increased income-earning opportunities for Saraguro women during the 1960s and 1970s, rather than decreasing or devaluing their productive capacity relative to that of men.

In Chimborazo Province in the central Ecuadorean sierra, Amalia Alberti (1986) reports that women are involved in most agricultural and livestock-production activities. Alberti finds that *inclusiveness* of women's labor participation, rather than complementarity and exclusively female economic contributions, helps to account for gender-egalitarian control of productive resources. Involvement in productive domains is associated with the development of expertise, an important basis for inclusion in decision-making. The more labor domains open to a woman, the wider her decision authority.

In Alberti's analysis, however, the ultimate basis for women's authority is cultural. Although women do not earn much of their households' cash income, they have equal or greater control of this income than men. Alberti concludes that cultural norms indicating shared male and female economic responsibility remain unaffected by increased household reliance on men's wages. Alberti does not postulate why these norms—which appear to have been reconstituted elsewhere (Weismantel 1988)—have been maintained in the indigenous region she studied.

Ursula Poeschel (1988) also attributes the survival of women's control of economic resources in households heavily reliant on male wages to the survival of cultural norms. Women's subsistence economic contributions, produced on small land bases in Tungurahua Province, are small compared to those of their husbands (who are beginning to exhibit the devaluation of those material contributions described above). However, women continue to control household income, including their husbands' earnings. Poeschel concludes that men place a high value on ethnic identity and thus value their wives' roles as guardians of traditional culture. Women work hard to maintain cultural principles, including the importance of extrahousehold reciprocity and community solidarity, and to reinforce cultural identification in their children's upbringing. This role accords them high status within the household, in the face of their eroding share of household economic production.

Poeschel, Linda Belote, and Jim Belote fear that indigenous women may yet lose their precarious hold on household economic processes through continuing incorporation into the capitalist national economy and patriarchal national culture. Poeschel expresses concern that incipient negative valuation of women's subsistence production may herald a trend that will come to outweigh men's positive valuation of women as cultural conservators. Belote and Belote report that Saraguro men increasingly work in occupations that are closed to women, such as building and road construction, which alters the earlier pattern of greater female participation in wage labor. In the 1980s many more men than women earned off-farm income. Although "this shift does not appear to have gone far enough to have had a serious impact on male-female relationships" (Belote and Belote 1988, 112), the authors conclude that it may be only a matter of time before greater integration into capitalist labor markets exerts the probable negative effect.

Thus even those researchers who find that planned and unplanned development have not disadvantaged indigenous Ecuadorean women relative to men in terms of household economic authority expect that continued participation by men in labor markets and national culture may soon overwhelm currently surviving patterns of gender equality. And household reliance on off-farm income earned by migrating men is likely to continue. Although men move in and out of labor markets as agricultural and labor-market conditions vary, high levels of population growth together with a highly unequal distribution of land mean that household land bases will become even smaller. Opportunities for earning off-farm income in rural areas are not being developed. Reliance on off-farm income, earned largely by migrating men, is likely to increase for smallholding families (see Blumberg and Colyer 1990).

*Theoretical Consensus: Andean Forms of Gender Equality*
*Will Not Survive State Modernization Programs and*
*Household Integration into Market Economies*

All of these Andean studies—those focusing on the unequal articulation of indigenous agricultural households with national and international political and economic institutions; those with a more positive view of women's past incorporation into planned development programs; and those with a more negative interpretation of women's position in traditional production systems—view the incorporation of indigenous householders into national and international market economies and national society as demonstrably or potentially damaging to women. These cases reveal the following patterned inequalities: Women have been excluded from land reform, cooperative agricultural income-earning projects, and production-oriented agricultural assistance. Unplanned or capitalistic development has also disadvantaged women whose households participate in labor or commodity markets. Small-farm households are increasingly dependent on wages earned by migrating males, who are exposed to the patriarchal value system dominant in national mestizo Ecuadorean society. This value system, as it is perpetuated by the owners and bosses who control the working lives of migrant men, will exert a hegemonic influence on them. Women also do not have equal productive roles in cash cropping and thus have decreasing entitlements to the income it produces. Even those women who currently maintain equal control of household economic assets are in danger of losing this control to the combined effects of their increasingly unequal earning power and of changing attitudes on the part of their more cash-rich partners. Women are generally viewed as the more or less successful defenders of a traditional production and ideological system that accords them equal responsibility for household economic survival and equal access to the means and fruits of economic production. The eventual capitulation of this system seems inevitable.

## Research Questions and Methods

This chapter began with an introduction to the women and men of Chanchaló. In this indigenous Andean farming community, households and their individual members exhibit a wide range of variation in wealth, involvement in agricultural development projects and commercialization, dependence on off-farm income, current and past outmigration, and integration into national society and culture. Chanchaló is thus an appropriate setting in which to examine interactions among processes of economic change and traditional forms of productive resource control, social organization, and gender identity—interactions identified in comparative and Andean studies as significant determinants of women's economic and social well-being.

The literature is largely devoted to observed or anticipated gender inequalities resulting from household participation in gender-biased commodities and labor markets. An evolutionary process has been more or less explicitly postulated. In comparing findings and methodologies across studies I concluded, however, that a unidirectional effect for these variables is not supported in the literature. Neither can we dismiss the political-economic pull felt, if not observed, across these studies (Hamilton 1995, 323–36). I will examine associations between increased household reliance on cash cropping or on men's off-farm income and gendered access to productive resources and incomes. If resource control patterns have become more patriarchal in cash-cropping or wage-dependent households, then the trend identified in the literature will be confirmed for an additional population studied more recently. If resource control patterns have not become more patriarchal, then an alternative interpretation will be proposed.

Results of this analysis will contribute to an understanding of the managerial roles of indigenous women on commercial farms—a subject that has been little investigated. Under conditions of national-level structural adjustment and increasingly stringent criteria for development investment by international donors, relatively successful small-scale commercial producers may appear particularly attractive to institutions practicing development triage (see de Janvry and Sadoulet 1990). Knowledge of relations of production within the household can help planners ensure that access to projects aiming to improve agricultural productivity and sustainability is offered to all agricultural decision-makers, regardless of gender. The inclusion of all decision-makers is a first step toward ensuring that public investment will yield positive results, both for farm families and in terms of sectoral output, by expanding household production options. Further, an understanding of the gendered effects of household participation in current development projects and in developing markets will help planners design projects that will not marginalize women from access to economic resources.

Currently most analysts and policy makers expect that women will control productive resources on only the poorest and smallest subsistence-oriented farms, where men have abandoned agriculture for wage labor (de Janvry and Sadoulet 1990). Examining interactions among household wealth, male outmigration, agricultural commercialization, and women's control of productive resources will indicate whether use of this stereotype is justifiable. I will present both quantitative and qualitative information in this analysis; both quantitative and qualitative methods are described in appendix A and throughout the text.

One of the problems in evaluating the usefulness of the evolutionary/marginalization perspective for purposes of generalization to Andean populations is that much of the research on which it rests does not analyze variation among units of analysis smaller than the community. Normative statements regarding women's work and control of economic resources often are not supported by evidence of the representativeness of samples. Most of the studies that do examine variation in processes within the household either rely on very small samples or do not analyze social or cultural contexts for economic processes (Hamilton 1995, 323–36). For these reasons it is important to examine variation within a demonstrably representative and relatively large sample and to provide detailed ethnographic description of both intrahousehold processes and their structural and cultural contexts.

Gender-and-development research and practice have pointed to the need for analysis of interactions among structural and cultural factors and among macro- and microlevel institutions that influence women's socioeconomic status. Economic processes are embedded in social, cultural, and political contexts; and economic behavior reflects values basic to understanding these contexts. As Gillian Hart has said: "we have to engage directly with questions of ideology and the construction of meaning, and recognize how struggles over resources and labor are simultaneously struggles over meaning" (1992, 121).

In my attempt to identify relevant behavior and discover its meanings during nine months in Chanchaló, I found that the most reliable information often emerged from sustained observation and from thematic conversational currents that reappear throughout the course of personal relationships. Rather than abstract this information, I have attempted to place readers literally on the scene to experience concretely, as I did, the interplay of cooperation and conflict within marital partnerships; the balance of power between women and men in household, kin group, and community; the valuation of women in these groups; and the perpetual constructing of valuation from material and ideational bases. In framing narrative passages that are relevant to gender-and-development policy issues, I have allowed a great deal of space for my informants to express themselves and for the unfolding of daily life.

Nonetheless, some readers will be disappointed that the resulting ethnography is neither truly multivocalic—composed of a multitude of voices, each shaping her own tale—nor explicitly reflexive. This disappointment is well founded. Each of the women and men who shared their lives with me has a life history to impart, which deserves more space than the present treatment provides and which should be told, in its entirety, by the person who lived it. Further, the truths and realities on which I must rely take shape in the spaces between observer and observed, between subject and object, between writer and reader. The ethnographic information I collected is a social construct; as an actor, as well as an observer, I participated in the creation of that information. I have placed myself in this book's narrative action and have described relationships with informants and institutional affiliations that limit the field of action I was able to encompass.

Beyond providing the personal context in which data were collected and interpreted, however, I did not think it useful to focus on myself as an actor in this book, a policy-oriented ethnography. In a gender-and-development policy context, consumers of quantitative and qualitative information search for reliable and valid indicators of social and economic well-being, and of the development processes expected to affect well-being. The myriad limitations inherent in conceptualizing, operationalizing, and measuring these indicators come to bear on both field experience and analytical methods. Not only the interpretation and presentation of observed data but also the lenses through which observations are made are products of professional training, research agenda, and habits of mind. I did not think that telling more of my own story would address these limitations, which will be more obvious to readers than to me.

Because this book is about indigenous people whose Andean traditions influence contemporary gender relations, the term *ethnicity* may be used to capture many of the patterned differences observed between gender relations in Chanchaló and in nonindigenous (mestizo) Ecuador. In gender-and-development discourse, ethnicity has emerged as a critical factor influencing both positive and negative outcomes for women under conditions of economic change. However, I will often use the term *local*, rather than an ethnic identifier, to demarcate Chanchaló's place in the universe of gender relations. In my usage, *local* refers to the local particularities of political-economic history. That history and the gender relations that are part of it continue to be generated by interactions of exogenous and indigenous factors, of class and ethnicity. I will also use the term *local knowledge* interchangeably with *indigenous knowledge* to refer to the views of Chanchaleños regarding gender relations (such as the evaluation of gendered wage rates and violence victimization offered by Marina early in this chapter) and regarding the probable outcomes of competing development agendas.

Local knowledge should be an important component in a rigorous search for patterned inequalities related to development processes. I set out for Chanchaló with the intention of balancing indigenous measures of women's well-being against my own. However, I perceived relatively little dissonance between my own analysis of gender relations in Chanchaló and local knowledge. I will employ constructs such as abstract equality, and I will evaluate component measures such as the egalitarian division of household labor; access to the means of production and to social and political institutions; and control of sexual reproduction. In my interpretation of their words and actions, the women of Chanchaló also value these goods, as they are locally constituted. Their successes in attaining them reveal patterns I believe to be informative for the study of gender and development.

TWO ✺ An Introduction to Chanchaló

ACCORDING TO a regional historian, the name Chanchaló means "well hidden" (Navas 1986, 40). And, in many ways, the community is well hidden. San José de Chanchaló took its name from the hacienda that had encompassed all local land until the 1970s, when hacienda workers pressed their rights to obtain hacienda land under the Ecuadorean land-reform initiative. In the 1990s, despite its political status as an independent community with juridically well-defined rights to access state institutions and public environmental resources, Chanchaló remains so well hidden from national political, social, and economic institutions that its people are virtually on their own as they struggle to improve their lot in life.

Chanchaló is certainly well hidden from those who designate the recipients of state infrastructural resources. There is no paved road, no telephone, no clean drinking water. Government plans to privatize rural health services will have the effect of eliminating even the poor basic service currently supplied to the community. Only the few families who can afford to send their children to the county seat for schooling have access to secondary education. Irrigation works and other agricultural development benefits have been directed primarily to large landowners; smallholders must compete without benefit of subsidies targeted to less needy producers.

Chanchaló, being an indigenous community, is also well hidden from Ecuadorean national culture. Many urban mestizos hold the stereotypical

35

view that *indios* (Indians, an often-derogatory term for indigenous persons) are lazy, drunken, dirty, and dangerous (*El Comercio*, January 8, 1993). Well-meaning mestizos, including development professionals, who extolled the hard work and managerial expertise of indigenous women explained this phenomenon by saying that indigenous women must manage their households' resources or their husbands would drink up any profits. Other mestizos, who want to appreciate the indigenous heritage of their country, also hold stereotypical (albeit more positive) views. These aficionados of folk art and mythology believe that indigenous communities remain untouched by external events both past and present. I was repeatedly told that "Indians" speak their own language, have their own religion, wear colorfully distinctive clothing, and survive economically outside the market economy. Although some of these characteristics describe some Ecuadorean indigenous groups, none is accurate for Chanchaló; thus the sociocultural patterns of life in Chanchaló remain well hidden.

It is obvious that stereotypical views rob indigenous people of individuality, and that negative perceptions rob them of dignity. Indigenous people suffer materially, and perhaps emotionally, under such bigotry. It is also obvious that the people of Chanchaló suffer from their lack of access to many social and economic institutions.

What may not be so obvious is that the obscurity of Chanchaló, behind a veil of social indifference and cultural misunderstanding, robs Ecuador and the world community of valuable resources: the economic potential and social exemplum of the people of Chanchaló and the rural Ecuadorean sierra. The people of Chanchaló are industrious members of national and international market economies. Though often effectively disenfranchised from institutions that would make them more economically competitive, they are shareholders in the economic and environmental future of their country and the world beyond her national borders. They want to become more productive shareholders. They are also the conservators of sociocultural patterns that contribute to the enfranchisement of all community members—women as well as men, poorer families as well as richer. These patterns have helped to maintain the people of Chanchaló under difficult political-economic conditions and merit our attempts at understanding.

So let us explore this well-hidden community. First we shall locate Chanchaló geographically and uncover its place in history. An introduction to the community's ecology, demography, economy, social-welfare infrastructure, social organization, political institutions, ethnicity, and religious life will serve as a general orientation. Much of the information will not be disaggregated by gender; the following chapters will be devoted to analysis of gender relations in Chanchaló and Cantón Salcedo. This chapter places Chanchaleños in their physical, political-economic, social, and cultural contexts.

## Regional Geography: The "Ladder of Fire"

Chanchaló is an agricultural community of some 135 households located on the eastern slopes of the inter-Andean valley of central Ecuador. As it is used here, the term *community* refers both to the people who live or own land in a particular geographical area and to the contiguous agricultural and grazing lands accessed by community members. An Andean community's boundaries encompass a great deal more space than simply the central area, where institutions such as school, church, and community meeting place are located. Chanchaló covers approximately six square kilometers, ranging in altitude from 2,900 meters to nearly 4,000 meters.

The Ecuadorean Andes comprise two volcanic mountain chains, or *cordilleras,* running north–south the length of the country, and the inter-Andean valley flanked by them (see map). The Eastern Cordillera, where Chanchaló is located, peaks at 6,003 meters (the height of the active volcano Cotopaxi) and declines in altitude eastward into the Amazon Basin. The Western Cordillera peaks at 6,310 meters (the height of the volcano Chimborazo) and declines more precipitously to the coastal plains and the Pacific.

The inter-Andean valley is not an unbroken expanse. A series of transverse ranges running east–west connect the Eastern and Western Cordilleras, forming a string of bounded interior valleys. This formation popularly has been called the "ladder of fire" (Sarmiento 1988, 191): the volcanic cordilleras form the sides of the imagined ladder, and each transverse range forms a rung. In terms of relief, climate, and rainfall each inter-Andean valley is both distinct from its neighbors and internally heterogeneous.

In these valleys *(hoyas)* are situated all the large towns and cities of the Ecuadorean sierra; each interior valley constitutes an administrative unit of the Ecuadorean state as well as a geographical zone. Together with its protective mountains, each valley also comprises a drainage system. These basins, the basic units of regional hydraulic dynamics, include a number of smaller valleys. Locating Chanchaló in the county, or *cantón,* of Salcedo within the province of Cotopaxi also refers to the Valley of Salcedo within the east-central basin of Patate (also called the Ambato-Latacunga Basin [Basile 1974, 10]). Cantón Salcedo comprises 50.4 square kilometers; Chanchaló is located on the valley's eastern slopes.

As I approached Chanchaló for the first time, climbing the ten kilometers from the county seat of Salcedo in the valley floor, I was impressed by two

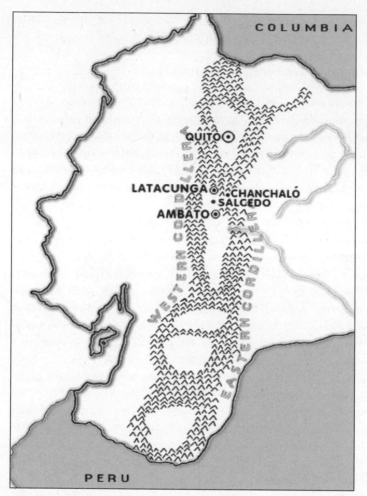

*The Equadorean Andes. Source: MAS Media*

things: the beauty of the landscape and the contrasts within it. Green fields with large healthy plants alternate with severely eroded dry areas where only sparse scrub survives. The promise and the fragility of this environment were immediately apparent.

Although any ecological formation must be conceived of as dynamic rather than static, the volatility of the central Ecuadorean sierra's physical environment is one of its defining features. The region is subject to frequent earthquakes and severe climatic fluctuations. Volcanic eruptions occur periodically throughout the ladder of fire. The crystalline beauty of the perfectly conical volcano Cotopaxi, from which Chanchaló's province takes its name, masks fire below. The highest active volcano in the world, Cotopaxi is expected by geologists to erupt again in the near future.

Climatic variation is most strikingly demonstrated in the range of annual precipitation. During the ninety years preceding 1983, annual rainfall for the city of Quito varied from 692 to 1,905 millimeters. Rainfall fluctuations are influenced by both the Pacific El Niño torrential downpour phenomenon and by winter weather patterns in the northern hemisphere (Knapp 1991, 28). The early months of 1993 were disastrously wet for all of sierran Ecuador, with severe flooding to the south of Chanchaló. The community itself was visited by both drought and excessive rainfall from mid-1992 to mid-1993. Thus, even a measure of cumulative rainfall for one year can mask severe and potentially destructive fluctuations.

During any year there are marked wet and dry seasons. The wet season generally extends from November through May, with peak precipitation usually around the spring equinox. A dry spell typically occurs in December. In Ecuador the terms *winter* and *summer* refer to precipitation, not to temperature. Winter *(invierno)* means wet; summer *(verano)* means dry. Thus the short dry season associated with the winter solstice is called the "little summer." The longer and more intense dry season of the summer months extends through October but often includes a very wet spell during September. Seasonal rainfall tends to peak at the equinoxes and the driest times occur around the solstices (Knapp 1991, 21).

The importance of fluctuation notwithstanding, some measures of average precipitation and other characteristics of Chanchaló's ecological formations will serve to contextualize the community in terms of its physical environment. The following discussion is based on a study by the Integrated Rural Development Secretariat (SEDRI 1981) and employs the classification system developed by Leslie R. Holdridge (1967). This system is based upon the interplay between values of precipitation, biotemperature, potential evaporation and transpiration of water, and plant formations. Holdridge and others take as their point of departure the fact that the physical environment has been radically altered by humans. Original vegetation, which included extensive forests, no longer covers the landscape. Deep rich soils have become eroded to varying degrees (Holdridge 1947, 26, cited in Salomon 1986, 35).

Chanchaló encompasses two ecological formations. This is not surprising, as precipitation, temperature, and soils vary dramatically across even short vertical distances. In the inter-Andean valleys, precipitation tends to increase with both altitude and distance from the valley center (Knapp 1991, 21). This is the case in the Valley of Salcedo.

At altitudes between 3,000 and 3,500 meters, Chanchaló exhibits Holdridge's Humid Mountain Forest formation. Precipitation is expected to vary between 1,000 and 1,500 millimeters annually. The topographic configuration is strikingly uneven. Mean temperatures are eight–ten degrees centigrade, with little seasonal or annual variation but considerable diurnal fluctuation. At the upper elevations frosts occur, usually at night. Soils are black, volcanic, and deep to moderately deep. Soils have a high clay content and thus retain water well. In place of the aboriginal forests, the landscape is punctuated by small stands of non-native eucalyptus and pine. Predominant crops include potato and other Andean tubers (*melloco,* oca), maize, barley, quinoa, a goosefoot *(Chenopodium quinoa)* native to the Andes and cultivated for its high-protein grain, fava beans, and other legumes.

At altitudes of 3,400–4,000 meters, Chanchaló exhibits the Subalpine Floor formation. Known as the *páramos* (high plains), this land slopes gently. Precipitation tends to be higher and can range up to 2,000 millimeters per year, in rare instances. The temperature is colder, averaging around six degrees centigrade annually. Soils are very black, volcanic, deep, and muddy. In the past this land surface was completely covered by grasses and was used for grazing. Today the subalpine floor is largely devoted to high-altitude crops, chiefly potato and other tubers. The more gentle slopes help discourage erosion, and these fertile lands are highly prized.

Water supply is the result of the interaction between precipitation, transpiration, evaporation, and irrigation. In Chanchaló the latter introduces a political dimension into any discussion of the environment. Precipitation and soil content vary dramatically within Cantón Salcedo. Farmers in the central valley must deal with both low rainfall and the low water-retention capability of the soil. One area of the valley floor receives an average of only 450 millimeters per year (SEDRI 1981, 22), and this area is not the cantón's driest region.

Salcedo's irrigation networks and potable water supplies depend heavily upon high mountain sources, yet political power is concentrated among the urban residents and large landowners of the central valley. Although the state officially controls irrigation and potable water networks, and Chanchaló is supposed to have access to a small-scale irrigation system, powerful landowners divert irrigation waters with impunity (SEDRI 1981; Jiménez 1990). Therefore, it is difficult to determine the actual volume of water available from local irrigation canals. Chanchaló farmers agree with the SEDRI assessment: the irrigation infrastructure of Cantón Salcedo is not adequate to supply most farmers during the dry season (SEDRI 1981, 29). Farmers consistently cite lack of water as their primary production constraint.

## The Community's Place in History

The diverse physical landscape of Chanchaló, both rich and challenging, has been the setting of an equally dramatic historical passage. Indigenous communities in the Valley of Salcedo developed thriving economies based on high-technology agriculture before A.D. 500. They had become integrated into wealthy and politically aggressive chiefdoms before the Inca invasion of the fifteenth century; they treated with Inca invaders and absorbed ethnic colonies transplanted by the conquerors. After suffering nearly five hundred years of economic indenture and political subservience to autocratic Spanish and mestizo landholders, they became reconstituted in the late twentieth century as independent agricultural communities. Chanchaló's heritage includes resilient indigenous institutions that strengthen the community in its current struggle to survive economic, social, and political marginalization.

An examination of political, economic, and social institutions of the period A.D. 500–1500 reveals indigenous lifeways that are reflected in contemporary Chanchaló. The basic unit of indigenous political, economic, and social organization before the Conquest was the local chiefdom community, a "group of persons sharing hereditary rights over certain factors of production (particular lands, the labor of certain people, and specific tools and infrastructure), and recognizing as a political authority a privileged member of their own number" (Salomon 1986, 45). These communities ranged in size from several dozen to several thousand people (Alchon 1992, 7); many belonged to larger federations or were controlled by militarily powerful overlords. The territory of contemporary Chanchaló was federated within the chiefdom of Mullihambatu, centered in the Valley of Salcedo (see Zuñiga 1936, 23). The Mullihambatus were controlled by the overlord of the large and powerful chiefdom of Latacunga (Moreno Yánez 1988, 77).

Communities exploited a variety of vertically arrayed ecological niches—some within and some contiguous to their boundaries—and thus produced a wide variety of tubers, grains, legumes, fruits, and vegetables. The term *microverticality* has been used to describe the exploitation of locally contiguous ecological floors of varying altitude (Oberem 1976, cited in Salomon 1986, 70). Contemporary Chanchaleños also prefer to maintain holdings at varying altitudes.

To obtain products not locally produced, chiefdoms participated in a sophisticated system of interregional trade, employing community trade representatives who exchanged local products for commodities produced in the lowlands and for luxury goods. Exchange took place through a system of permanent regional marketplaces, located throughout the sierra, and was dependent upon political trading alliances among chiefdoms (Salomon 1986, 97–102). One of the largest of these trading centers was located at Latacunga, around twelve kilometers west of Chanchaló.

Some communities deployed groups of colonists to lower elevations for additional production (Salomon 1986, 111–15, 169; Knapp 1991, 107). This "archipelago" pattern of long-distance verticality—the exploitation of ecological niches located at higher or lower elevations than the community had access to in its home territory—is still practiced by many families in Chanchaló. (See Weismantel 1988 for a description of similar practice elsewhere in Cotopaxi Province.)

Communities were highly stratified socially, and politically centralized under the rule of their chief.[1] Political and legal powers were vested in the chief, who had the authority to deploy troops and colonists, regulate communal labor requirements, sanction marriages, settle disputes, negotiate trade agreements and military alliances, distribute agricultural surpluses and imported trade goods, and officiate in important ceremonial events. The chief enjoyed a number of prerogatives not accorded commoners, among them the right to marry more than one wife. His household was consequently the largest in any community, at times comprised of extended-family members, attached retainer families, and dependent servants, as well as wives and children. In some communities, the chief's household included as much as 20 percent of the population (Knapp 1991, 105).

In exchange for his privileged position the chief was responsible for military and internal security, the management of communal economic production, and the equitable portioning out of surpluses to the community. Succession was not hereditary; the chief's power was contingent upon his ability to provide access to sufficient agricultural surplus as well as security. Although possessed of coercive power, chiefs were required to request formally the cooperation of the community in public maintenance and productive activities. Several students of Ecuadorean indigenous society have pointed out that a form of asymmetrical reciprocity existed between chief and commoner that mirrored the more symmetrical form characterizing alliances among commoners: each party executed obligations that legitimized claims to the labor and largesse of the other (Salomon 1986; Hurtado 1980; Alchon 1992).

The chief held large tracts of lands that were worked by communal labor for the sustenance of his household and to produce surpluses for trade and communal distribution. Beneath the noble house but exempt from the communal obligations of other commoners were the *mindalaes*, an elite and often wealthy caste of long-distance traders, which may have included women.

These privileged persons managed the exchange of locally produced surpluses for lowland products and luxury goods (Salomon 1986, 102–6).

Commoners held rights to work and retain the usufruct of lands specified for each household. These lands were heritable although unalienable. In addition, commoners were responsible for communally maintaining infrastructure. The participation of most adult women and men in agricultural production and public works continues in Chanchaló today.

Among commoners, a complex system of rights and obligations bound extended kinship groups, which included blood relatives, affinal relatives, and perhaps people related by residence or even occupation (Alchon 1992, 7). Members of reciprocity networks aided one another in private agricultural production, house construction, and fulfilling ritual obligations. Extrahousehold reciprocity networks remain essential to economic survival in contemporary Chanchaló.

Although status differences were great, status exogamy was practiced, as well as group exogamy (see Feldman and Moseley 1983). Marriage among social strata continues today in Chanchaló, as well as group exogamy. The distribution of wealth is similar, as well, although the economic elite no longer hold coercive political power or practice polygyny.

It is perhaps ironic that this structure, which maintained political stability and economic prosperity before the invasions, also facilitated the conquest of indigenous chiefdoms by the Incas and the Spanish, who imposed new overlords atop the existing structure and ruled through it. Central features of the indigenous social contract would also help conquered peoples survive hardship and subjugation, however. The Inca invasion of Ecuador was a protracted process; numerous and costly campaigns were required to subjugate the indigenous population. In the Valley of Salcedo, repeated revolts caused the rulers from Cuzco to move some of the local population elsewhere and resettle their territories with colonists from Peru, Bolivia, and other regions of the Ecuadorean sierra, who would be easier to govern and would help dilute the spirit of native rebellion (Salomon 1986, 159; Moreno Yánez 1988, 62; Oberem 1988; Zuñiga 1936, 1968).

Indigenous political organization was retained, subject to the conquerors' authority; however, tribute payments were extracted from both chiefs and commoners. The Latacunga chief treatied with the conquerors that he and his wife each retain their large landholdings (Moreno Yánez 1988, 79). The Inca state required that all adults be married; Inca officials married the Latacunga to his sister, according to indigenous tradition, although under Inca law only the royal house of Cuzco was permitted this form of marriage (Moreno Yánez 1988, 78; Oberem 1988, 160). The Incas' accommodation of local tradition and authority did not earn the support of the Latacunga during the Spanish invasion (Oberem 1988).

From the early sixteenth through the mid–twentieth centuries, the history of the indigenous communities of sierran Ecuador is one of radical and increasing economic, political, social, and cultural disenfranchisement. The state, the established state religion, and the landholding economic elite mutually reinforced the development and maintenance of a feudal society in which indigenous people became serfs on their own lands. Lacking the mineral wealth found in many other colonial territories, Spanish colonists in the land that is now Ecuador extracted, instead, the labor and wealth of the indigenous population.

As the source of both labor and tribute, native Americans were the single greatest resource on which the colonial economy was based. *Conquistadores* were rewarded not by payment from the Spanish crown but by the assignment of a number of indigenous people to be protected, converted to Christianity, and taxed to pay for their own subjugation. These *encomienda* grants did not include title to indigenous lands nor the right to extract labor from the population. However, both land and labor were claimed by *encomenderos*, who were legally possessed of private armies with which to enforce their control (Hurtado 1980, 22).

Independence from Spain in the early nineteenth century did not improve the lot of indigenous peoples. One-third of the state treasury was provided by a head tax levied only against indigenous persons, who were not permitted to share benefits subsidized by their labor. The church was legally permitted to collect a tithe of 10 percent of an indigenous household's harvest, and it was not unusual for the church to receive as much as one-third of the household's production (Hurtado 1980).

Under the largely private, hacienda-dominated system that evolved from colonial land tenure patterns, landholdings became increasingly concentrated as hacendados bought out their less successful neighbors and bequeathed their estates to a single heir. This landholding elite held overwhelming political influence, in a "nation" in which only 5 percent of the population held voting rights (Hurtado 1980, 62). Hacendados became governors and mayors; counties were created in order for them to hold political office. Through patronage, they controlled the rural police force and those offices they did not hold directly. Estate owners also held legislative and executive office at the national level and exerted tremendous influence through political factions dependent on their patronage. During the late nineteenth century, political leverage enabled large landholders to declare the size and location of their previously untitled holdings and to claim vast tracts of public domain land

(Seligson 1984, 12). This system was sanctioned by the Roman Catholic Church, which held large haciendas and also depended upon the patronage of hacendados.

## *Concertaje* and *Huasipungaje:* "The Hacendado Was the Law"

During the nineteenth century, the state enforced a system of debt peonage *(concertaje)* that bound indigenous families for life to the service of a landowner. Begun in the seventeenth century, this system of indenture allowed for indigenous men to contract their labor and that of their families to a landowner in return for an advance in nominal wages, grains, or animals, and for a plot of land *(huasipungo)*, on which the family would produce their subsistence. Because indebted workers were often unable to compensate the landlord to his satisfaction for the advances they had received, this contract developed into life indenture for the indigenous family (Cosse 1984, 24). An individual's debt could be inherited by his wife and children (Hurtado 1980, 48). *Conciertos* could be imprisoned for debt; as indigenous people did not have the right to defend themselves in court, they remained in prison at the will of the hacendado while their families tried to pay off the debt. When haciendas changed hands, the right to enforce the debt peonage of bound workers was transferred with the land.

Although concertaje was legally abolished at the beginning of the twentieth century, in Chanchaló the conjunction of landholding and political power continued into the 1970s. Hacendados mediated disputes, assigned fines, meted out criminal justice, and attempted to control the religious life and private morality of their peons. The patrón retained absolute authority to punish his workers, even to execute them (Hurtado 1980, 51). Local informants report having been beaten and whipped and having observed the punishment of others who were shackled in stocks and left to die for failing to report to work (Waters 1985). Imprisonment on the estates was a common practice (Waters 1985; see Deere 1990).

A series of reforms enacted during the first half of the twentieth century required landlords to pay their de facto permanent labor force a nominal wage, and gave *huasipunguero* families legal recourse to claim they had settled their debts. In practice, however, landlords were free to enforce contracts at will and to their own advantage (Barsky et al. 1984; Martínez 1984; Waters 1985). Many local landowners simply ignored wage laws, paying huasipungueros and other obligated workers a nominal fraction of the legal wage (Waters 1985). As long as it remained advantageous to retain a large labor pool obligated to agricultural and domestic labor in exchange for usufruct rights, powerful hacendados could simply refuse to settle their workers' accounts, thus forcing them and their families to continue servile labor relations.

From the 1930s through the early 1970s, the people of Hacienda Chanchaló labored under servile relations *(huasipungaje)* with two families, related by marriage, who owned large tracts of land in Cantón Salcedo. Their labor was occasionally loaned by their landlord to a hacendado in the Latacunga Valley (see A. Allen 1993, 53). For their labor they received "humiliation, bad treatment, and low wages" (Pumasunta Chacha 1992, 1), together with usufruct rights to marginal subsistence plots.

The owners of Chanchaló resorted to both political and economic pressure to retain their permanent labor force following national land-reform legislation mandating the sale or granting of huasipungos to workers who had labored for a specified number of years. Although legally freed during the 1960s, workers were threatened when they began their struggle to form a juridically independent *comuna* (community) in accordance with laws designed to integrate free indigenous communities into national political and economic institutions. Less intimidated than many of their neighbors (Waters 1985), Chanchaleños resorted to a labor strike rather than abandon their quest for political and economic freedom. While some hacendados sponsored community religious fiestas during which workers enjoyed a measure of social license, large quantities of food and drink, and perhaps a reaffirmation of collective identity (see Thurner 1993), the local patrón did not support this tradition. He objected to the construction of a workers' community chapel, which Chanchaleños eventually built and which now stands as a symbol of independence from political and economic coercion. One informant summed up the landlord's political authority saying, "The hacendado was the law."

## Household and Hacienda Labor Relations

Within huasipunguero families, the male household head contracted with the hacendado to provide five–six days per week of adult labor for productive activities.[2] This obligation could be met by the male or female household head and, in some cases, by adult children. The labor of the female household head was contracted seasonally for agricultural and domestic work; these arrangements were made between the male head and the hacendado or his overseer. Depending on the amount of labor contracted, which could vary according to the amount of land provided by the hacendado, many entire families were tied to the hacienda. Contracts often specified that members of huasipunguero families under labor obligation were not permitted to leave the hacienda without permission.

Another form of labor relations included the extended family of the huasipunguero, or even landless nonrelatives, who contracted with those estate families whose huasipungos were large enough to absorb extrahousehold labor. These workers raised subsistence crops in a share arrangement with the huasipunguero family on their usufruct parcel; in exchange sharecroppers supplied labor to both the huasipunguero family and to the hacienda. Since many labor contracts required the huasipunguero family to supply labor to the landlord six days a week, arrangements that would increase the amount of labor available for household production could provide a great advantage.

Thus hacienda dependents comprised distinct social strata, and a variety of land-access levels and contractual obligations evolved, some of them depending on the individual household's ability to gain favor with the landlord (see Waters 1985 and Deere 1990). Limited upward mobility was possible. A very few indigenous families were able to accumulate capital through wages and sales of huasipungo produce from relatively large usufruct parcels. They bought land bordering Hacienda Chanchaló and eventually became owners of relatively large holdings and choice parcels in contemporary Chanchaló. Earnings by family members who were not contracted for daily labor, some of whom migrated to wage labor on coastal plantations, also enabled some families to buy land near Chanchaló and to bid on land following the dissolution of the hacienda.

Women and men performed similar agricultural work when executing the household's daily labor obligation *(tarea)* or during times of peak agricultural activity, when all huasipunguero household labor was mobilized for hacienda production. As the *tarea* could be fulfilled by wife or husband, women substituted for their husbands or joined them when it would be advantageous for the men to have more time for family production.[3] Women also labored on the family parcel throughout the agricultural cycle. Women worked for the hacendado independently of the household *tarea* during times of peak agricultural activity, such as planting and harvesting. Women were paid less than men for seasonal labor, in some cases receiving only half a man's cash wage or as little as a quintal (one hundred pounds) of grain for an entire season's labor (see Waters 1985; Barsky et al. 1984; Salamea and Likes n.d.).

Informants emphasize that there were no differences in agricultural labor assignments for women and men. Much like the system described by Osvaldo Barsky and others for the northern sierra (1984, 71), the gendered division of labor was fluid, and women performed all tasks except those requiring exceptional physical strength. Local people remember that even the one task not performed by women in most indigenous communities—plowing with oxen—was assigned to women on the hacienda (contemporary divisions of labor are discussed in chapters 3 and 4). The words of one woman summarize a pattern reported by several elders: "I worked in the hacendado's fields. We women worked in the fields. We did the heavy work. We even plowed with the *yunta* [yoke of oxen]. We worked on the family plot, too, as we do now. The children pastured animals. Women and men did the milking. The work was the same for women and men."

Women also supplied the hacendado with domestic labor. In a pattern reported throughout the sierra, women from huasipunguero households could be required to serve an annual one-month's rotation performing domestic labor *(huasicamia)* in the hacendado's houses in the country and in the city, or in the households of the clergy or others, by arrangement with the hacendado (Rosero 1984, 35). Some men also reported for huasicamia, which included care of domestic animals. Only selected girls, those aged eight to fifteen who were specially trained and expected to exhibit "superior personal presentation" (Barsky et al. 1984, 75–77), were assigned exclusively to domestic labor throughout the year. These young women performed all domestic chores *(servicia)* but were primarily responsible for child care.

Many, but not all, local women reported for a month's huasicamia on Hacienda Chanchaló or, by arrangement with the local landlord, on a larger hacienda near Latacunga. A few girls performed the servicia. One handsome and well-spoken woman who was in her teens during the last decade of hacienda rule reported performing both forms of domestic service. It is not difficult to imagine that, as a girl, her personal presentation was superior. This woman also reported that she was pleased to have the opportunity to work for the Latacunga hacendado because "we were paid more for that." In a pattern reported in both Peru and Ecuador, women could be drafted for huasicamia service without remuneration; it was considered a part of the huasipunguero family's obligation (Deere 1977; Barsky et al. 1984).[4] By the late 1950s, a token wage was paid for huasicamia in Chanchaló.

## Indigenous Resistance and Socioeconomic Organization

Although a majority of indigenous Ecuadoreans were legally and economically forced to serve the landed elite, they did not submit meekly. Processes of land concentration and legal disenfranchisement were punctuated by a series of military uprisings, labor strikes, and social and legal protests.[5] Less dramatic daily forms of resistance included crop theft, foot dragging, and "organized, gradualistic invasion of the demesne" (Thurner 1993, 61). In addition to their attempts to undermine asymmetrical/vertical state and class structures, indigenous communities also activated symmetrical/horizontal exchange networks—both within and beyond hacienda borders—which enabled individual households to share resources during the leanest times, lessen their hacienda debt burden, and accumulate surplus.

Formed along lines of traditional economic reciprocity, these networks were based on the exchange of hacienda products or resources that huasipunguero households could access (such as pasture, forest, and water resources) for needed goods and agricultural products (Chiriboga 1983; Casagrande 1974; Thurner 1993). Chanchaleños formed trading partnerships with outside farmers and urban mestizos in Salcedo, as well as within the hacienda workforce community. The value of maintaining collaborative social and economic networks is stressed by Chanchaleños, who conclude that collaboration enabled them to survive hardship and has been instrumental in organizing to secure freedom and to gain a measure of economic and social viability as an independent community (see Chiriboga 1983, 74). The importance of traditional socioeconomic reciprocity to community and household survival is a theme that recurred during Chanchaleños' descriptions of their community's past and present struggles (and will recur during this study).[6]

Although the agrarian-reform movement in Ecuador legally liberated indigenous people from the political control of local oligarchs, in many regions of the sierra including Salcedo the process did not redistribute land more equitably, nor did the state's efforts facilitate the ability of small-scale agricultural producers to survive on their newly acquired land base. Both political liberation and land transfers were accomplished largely because huasipungo labor was no longer advantageous to the landlords (Barsky 1978; Handelman 1981, 5–6; Redclift and Preston 1980; Zevallos 1989) or because hacienda laborers staged land invasions or work strikes (Guerrero 1984, 118; Andrade and Rivera 1988, 263–65), not because powerful hacendados were forced to obey a series of laws. Before land-reform laws were passed, increasing campesino mobilization (together with political fallout from the Cuban Revolution and encouragement by the U.S. Alliance for Progress) and a modernizing agricultural economy created political and economic conditions under which many hacendados were willing to abandon claims to huasipungo labor (Redclift and Preston 1980; Seligson 1984, 18; Zevallos 1989; this chapter, note 4). Nonetheless, many landlords held on to the old patterns.

For the huasipungueros of Chanchaló, both market forces and campesino mobilization contributed more to the transfer of land than did national laws. Although the Agrarian Reform Law of 1964 outlawed the huasipungo labor agreement and specified that huasipungueros were to receive title to their plots and fair payment for past labor if they had worked on the hacienda for

over ten years, the local owner did not release Chanchaló huasipungos until
1968–1972, following a protracted labor strike. In order to obtain land, Chanchaleños had to agree to continue working for the hacendado for a few years
under much the same relations of production as before the law was passed.
The landlord and his heirs were able to set the terms for land transfers. Although some Salcedo landlords did compensate workers for past labor, this
appears not to have been the case in Chanchaló. In effect, nonpayment of
past wages subsidized any land transfers that were "granted" (see Waters
1985).

The hacendado turned over the estate to his children in the early 1970s;
his heirs decided to sell out rather than remain and modernize production.
Many landlords did this, investing in urban sectors of the economy, which
yielded higher returns during the oil boom of the 1970s (Zevallos 1989, 47;
Cosse 1984; Redclift and Preston 1980). Most of the land in Chanchaló was
bought by former huasipungueros and other campesinos, rather than ceded
to them.

## The Legacy of Agrarian Reform

For small-scale farmers in sierran Ecuador, limited attempts by the state to
transform the hacienda system into one of modernized capitalist production
produced limited results. During the 1970s oil revenues furnished the state
with funds to encourage agricultural modernization, but these were disseminated to large- and medium-scale landowners (Zevallos 1989; Seligson 1984).
Cheap credit, input subsidies, tax breaks, and irrigation projects were directed
to large landholders who retained influence within the Ministry of Agriculture (Seligson 1984; Zevallos 1989).

The distribution of landholdings did not change greatly in many parts of
the sierra. Preferring to open coastal and Amazonian lands to colonization
rather than enforce private land expropriations in the sierra, during the 1970s
and 1980s the government titled little former hacienda land to campesinos
(Zevallos 1989, 51; Seligson 1984). In Cantón Salcedo in 1984, 63 percent of
the land surface was controlled by holdings of one hundred hectares or more,
a reduction of only 1.5 percent since 1974 (Chiriboga 1988b, 54). Only 2.4
percent of properties of this size had been affected by twenty years of land reform. Holders of fewer than twenty hectares averaged only 1.8 hectares per
family. Including all of the sierra, 92 percent of all holdings fell into this category, while less than 1 percent of farmers held properties of more than one
hundred hectares (Chiriboga 1986, 51). The agrarian reform laws of 1964,
1970, 1973, and 1979 did little to restructure agricultural landholding and

small-scale production in the Ecuadorean sierra (Chiriboga 1988b; Zevallos 1989, 54; Hurtado 1980, 232; Farrell 1983, table 9).

The legacy of agrarian reform for the community of Chanchaló is contradictory: political independence and stability coexist with economic dependence on unequal market access. Under terms established in the 1930s and 1960s, the people of Hacienda Chanchaló formed a pre-comuna in 1968. The independent comuna of San José de Chanchaló was chartered in 1972. Chanchaleños gained both independent juridical status and the right to work for themselves and to enter labor markets. When comparing the days of the hacienda to the present, members of the community emphasize the critical importance of having attained freedom. Although still poor, they now have the freedom to apply their labor to their own accumulation. The people of Chanchaló are free, that is, to attempt survival on a small land base, without formal credit, subsidized inputs, or infrastructure; for most families, levels of accumulation have remained low in spite of the hard work of all family members.

## The Economic Base

The realities of economic survival under these circumstances will be described quantitatively for households and qualitatively with respect to communitywide institutions. All quantitative measures of individual and household well-being reported in the remainder of this chapter are based on a series of household surveys fielded by National Science Foundation (NSF) project, "Farming Systems and Socio-cultural Determinants of Child Growth in Two Ecological Zones of Ecuador," together with the Fundación para el Desarrollo Agropecuario (FUNDAGRO), a private Ecuadorean development agency (see appendix A for a full description of this project). Chanchaló is one of three communities included in the surveys. Information was collected in three seasonal rounds from late summer 1992 through midsummer 1993. The sample from Chanchaló includes forty-two households.

### The Importance of Agriculture to Household Livelihood

Although the average household has only a small land base of around three hectares, the economy of Chanchaló is primarily agricultural. For most families, both cash incomes and food consumption depend heavily on farm production. The high prevalence of male outmigration to temporary wage labor that has been observed among smallholders throughout the sierra—including the Western Cordillera of Cantón Salcedo (Chiriboga 1985)—is not characteristic of Chanchaló. This is partly because, on average, families in

Chanchaló have larger and more productive landholdings than people living in the more severely eroded Western Cordillera across the inter-Andean valley.

Temporary outmigration in the Eastern Cordillera also appears to have decreased since the late 1980s (B. DeWalt et al. 1990). This pattern reflects increased urban underemployment during the early 1990s (ILDIS 1993, 150–52). Among the more attractive jobs for Chanchaleños are those in the construction industry in sierran cities, especially in Quito, the capital city. Although the industry was rebounding from declines suffered during the late 1980s, high rates of unemployment in other sectors resulted in increased competition for construction work (ILDIS 1993, 182–87). The effects of national economic crisis and restructuring of the public sector also meant that employment opportunities in provincial cities were becoming more difficult to find (CEPLAES-ILDIS 1993, 53–64). Although harvests did not live up to early expectations, bumper crops had been expected in 1992 (see ILDIS 1993). Most families invested most of their labor in agriculture.

On average, families earn 90 percent of their cash income from the sale of agricultural products, animal products, and livestock (table 1). Although nearly half of all households recorded some form of off-farm income during the year, and although the individual household's reliance on particular crop and livestock income sources varies by season depending on farm output and markets, the average percentage of total household income derived from farm production does not vary seasonally. On average, household reliance on crop versus livestock income also does not vary seasonally. Nearly all households (93 percent) sold crops; over two-thirds sold dairy products and nearly two-thirds sold animals during the year.

*Table 1. Composition of Household Income, Chanchaló, 1992*

| Income Source | Percentage of Cash Income | | Percentage of Total Income | |
|---|---|---|---|---|
| | Mean | SD | Mean | SD |
| Crops | 65% | 33 | 43% | 22 |
| Livestock production | 4 | 11 | 2 | 4 |
| Dairy products | 19 | 28 | 11 | 15 |
| Off-farm income | 10 | 22 | 7 | 19 |
| Subsistence production | 0 | | 35 | 21 |
| TOTAL | 100% | | 100% | |

*Source:* NSF/FUNDAGRO Household Surveys, round 1, August–October 1992 (42 households).

    *Note:* N = 40 male household heads who provided information on all income sources.

According to the amount of land planted, as well as cash income and sub-sistence production derived, crops include (in order of importance) potato, maize, melloco, barley, fava beans, and pasture (Hamilton 1995, table 3-2). The predominant crop is potato, accounting for nearly 60 percent of all land devoted to cropping, agricultural cash income, and subsistence production during mid-1992. Potato is produced and marketed year-round. Most house-holds also produce common beans, intercropped with maize, and many also grow peas, lupine beans, onions, and carrots.

The level of technology varies from mechanized, relatively high-input pro-duction and processing by several families to total reliance on human labor and simple tools in a very few households. Agrochemicals are widely avail-able for sale in Salcedo. Agrochemical companies advertise heavily, visiting the community to demonstrate the efficacy of their goods. Farmers generally apply as much fertilizer and pesticide as they can afford. Improved varieties are grown by many farmers. Access to credit and irrigation is limited; crop in-surance is not available.

Marketing infrastructure is also limited. All families sell their produce to intermediaries at the weekly wholesale market in Salcedo. Richer families can afford to hold products for sale when short supply has improved prices, and better bargainers can obtain better prices, but the intermediaries collude to cap their top price and will not go far beyond that. A few people have sold small quantities of products not purchased by intermediaries in Salcedo—such as garlic—in Ambato or Latacunga, cities within an hour's drive from Chanchaló. One farmer told me he was thinking of selling melloco in Quito, where the price was twice as high as in Salcedo, but that he would have to pay dearly to rent a truck and might not be able to manage it. It is fair to say that the community does not have access to competitive markets for their produce.

Dairy production is also an important source of daily income for most households, although on average dairy production accounts for only one-fifth of all household cash income. Salcedo is famous for its dairy ranches and fine dairy products, consumed throughout the country. In Chanchaló, dairying is a developing small-scale industry. Most families sell milk daily, averaging about five liters. This milk is purchased by agents of cheese factories else-where in Cotopaxi Province and by the local quesería (cheese factory). Farm-gate milk prices do not vary greatly.

Those families who derive cash income from off-farm sources depend on wage and salaried labor (33 percent of the sample), commerce (7 percent), work as marketing intermediaries (5 percent), and transportation (12 per-cent). Some households report more than one off-farm source of income. With the exception of commerce, most of this income is earned by male household heads. The sale of crafts produced by women also brings income to several families, although most men and women did not quantify amounts.

The families of Chanchaló consume a significant proportion of their agricultural production. During mid-1992 more than one-third of total household income was destined for household consumption. Most of this measure was provided by potato production and consumption, but households consumed portions of all crops. Households provided most of their food and nearly all dairy products from home production. On average, 56 percent of calories consumed during our first-round survey were supplied by household production.

## Small-Scale Industries

Local industries are based on dairy and livestock production and are cooperatively managed. The recently constructed cheese factory is located in the community. The cattle and fish production cooperative is located several hours' distance from the community in the *monte* of the Eastern Cordillera. Although both organizations require a large membership deposit and considerable labor from members, half of the households in the community participate in one of these endeavors.

The members of the quesería production association work on a rotational basis in the processing of cheese and other milk products and in maintenance of the factory building, as they did in the building's construction. One permanent half-time employee supervises production and coordinates marketing in Salcedo and elsewhere. The association does not produce milk cooperatively; milk is purchased locally. Income provides a credit fund for members. This association was chartered with help from FUNDAGRO in obtaining credit and technical assistance. A number of other public and private institutions were also instrumental in the provision of funds and the development of the factory.

According to informants, the primary function of the quesería is to earn money that will then provide credit for members. Campesinos do not have access to cheap agricultural credit from development banks; other banks and institutions charge up to 58 percent interest and require short-term repayment. Chanchaleños have instead organized to supply their own credit.

Members of the cooperative also provide the labor on which their production depends. Each member must travel to the cooperative to work one week out of each month. The heavier work and financial investment requirements of the cooperative provide greater benefits, in terms of both the income-earning potential of livestock production and in terms of provision of land for pasture, which is in short supply in the community.

These two industries are providing income and credit to local families on the bases of local knowledge of dairy and livestock production, and a local tradition of cooperative labor. The number of families that have invested considerable money and labor in these ventures is indicative of the confidence Chanchaleños have in the industriousness of their neighbors and the future of agricultural productivity in their community.

The Women's Production Association has functions other than the cooperative production of crops and animals, but productive efforts are central to their goal of providing increased social welfare for members and their families. Members grow potatoes and pasture and are beginning to raise guinea pigs, all for sale. Each member contributes labor, and many also recruit family members to help in weekly work parties. Land for crop production and for the guinea-pig house has been contributed by members on a share arrangement or gratis. Membership dues are nominal. Profits form a credit fund that loans money to members at 5 percent interest. One-fifth of all households participate in the women's association.

## Levels of Wealth, Health, and Education

On average, households have access to 2.9 hectares of land, a small base but one that is higher than in many other small-farming communities in the sierra (Chiriboga 1985; Hamilton 1992). During summer 1992 households reported a gross median per capita income of US $23 per month (table 2). This figure includes subsistence value of agricultural production but may underestimate all incomes (see Rozelle 1991). The daily wage for agricultural labor in the community varied between $1 and $1.25 per day. During the three seasonal rounds of the NSF/FUNDAGRO Survey, average household income did not vary greatly.

At the median, reported per capita daily income is sufficient to purchase one of the following items: twelve pounds of potatoes, two pounds of fresh beans, one-third of a chicken including bones, or four pounds of barley. The average daily wage would purchase a one-way bus ticket from Salcedo to the capital city, two hours distant, or a round-trip ticket to the nearest city. Consultation with a private doctor in Salcedo costs four days' wages; treatment costs would be added. Although reported incomes are often underestimated, gross income exceeds the actual buying power of the household and includes subsistence value of production. The community must be considered poor in terms of income.

Measures of well-being other than income and material wealth indicate that many people in the community lack important goods. Weekly food consumption recalls indicate that more than one-third of all households did not have enough food on hand to provide sufficient calories during the autumn of 1992 (Hamilton 1995, table 3-4).[7] Two-thirds of children under the age of five

Table 2. Basic Measures of Material Well-Being, Chanchaló, 1992

| | Percentage Owning/ Accessing | Mean | SD | Median |
|---|---|---|---|---|
| Land | 95% | 2.85 ha. | 2.56 | 2.06 |
| Income per cap./mo. (N = 40)[a] | 100% | $42 | $60 | $23 |
| Cattle | 97% | 2.6 | 2.0 | 2.0 |
| Pigs | 85% | 2.1 | 1.8 | 2.0 |
| Chickens | 87% | 4.9 | 3.9 | 5.0 |
| Electricity | 91% | | | |
| Piped Water[b] | 93% | | | |
| Housing: | | 2.4 | .8 | 2.0 |
| number of rooms | | | | |
| 1 | 8% | | | |
| 2–3 | 80% | | | |
| 4 | 12% | | | |
| Indoor bath | 12% | | | |
| Truck | 10% | | | |
| Refrigerator | 2% | | | |
| Gas range | 5% | | | |
| Sewing machine | 32% | | | |
| Television | 42% | | | |

Source: NSF/FUNDAGRO Household Surveys, round 1, August–October 1992 (42 households).
 Notes: a. Income includes subsistence value of agricultural production and was measured for the previous six months during summer–fall 1992. Income amounts are 1992 U.S. dollar equivalents. N = 40 male household heads who provided information on all income sources.
 b. Piped water is chemically treated but contaminated.

had experienced chronic undernutrition, as measured by current height for age; nearly one-third exhibited low weight for age (Hamilton 1995, table 3-4).[8] Levels of nutritional health for children do not differ by sex (Leonard, K. DeWalt, and Uquillas 1993). Although many households have access to piped water, the supply is contaminated. Chronic respiratory diseases and parasitosis endanger the health of the community, especially that of the children.

Most adults in Chanchaló have completed only primary education (see table 3). Women have had significantly less education than men. Among the school-age population, girls are now receiving as much education as boys, but

*Table 3. Levels of Education by Age and Sex, Chanchaló, 1992*

| Years of Education | Adults | | |
| | Total (N = 88) | Female (N = 45) | Male (N = 43) |
| --- | --- | --- | --- |
| 0 | 40% | 53% | 26% |
| 1–6 | 57% | 46% | 70% |
| More than 6 | 3% | 1% | 4% |
| Means | 3.10 yrs. | 2.24 yrs[a] | 3.93 yrs[a] |
| SD | 3.00 | 2.71 | 3.10 |

| Years of Education | Children Aged 6 to 12 | | |
| | Total (N = 47) | Female (N = 25) | Male (N = 22) |
| --- | --- | --- | --- |
| 0 | 0% | 0% | 0% |
| 1–6 according to age | 100% | 100% | 100% |

| Years of Education | Young People Aged 13 to 18 | | |
| | Total (N = 28) | Female (N = 19) | Male (N = 9) |
| --- | --- | --- | --- |
| 0 | 0% | 0% | 0% |
| 1–6 | 96% | 95% | 100% |
| More than 6 | 4% | 5% | 0%[b] |

Source: NSF/FUNDAGRO Household Surveys, round 1, August–October 1992 (42 households).
 Notes: a. Difference in means is significant at .008 using t-test.
 b. Owing to the small number of males in this category currently living in the community, this number is difficult to interpret. Of those young people living in the community, females and males are being educated equally.

most young people complete only the primary grades. The quality of primary education is very poor. Many adults who read do so with some difficulty, although they enjoy reading newspapers and are proud of their few books. Those who are proficient in mathematics seem to be primarily self-taught; their calculations of production costs and benefits are often labored but correct.

## Distribution of Economic and Social Goods

Both reported income and land, the primary resource necessary for producing income, are unequally distributed among households in Chanchaló. Income is not always reliably recalled by informants whereas ownership of land is both a matter of public record and more reliably described by informants; thus, ownership of land will serve as the primary indicator of wealth in this study.[9] The distributions of household income and land are similar. Although nearly all households own land, the wealthiest one-fifth of the sample hold 50 percent of the land; the poorest one-fifth hold only 3 percent (see table 4). As will be discussed in later chapters, land is owned by equal numbers of women and men, in holdings of similar size. In terms of household income, the wealthiest one-fifth hold 47 percent of the wealth, and the poorest only 4 percent (see table 5).

Local key informants analyzing the community's distribution of wealth report a picture that is consistent with survey results. Approximately one-fifth of the community is considered wealthy by local standards; three-fifths are considered middle-income; one-fifth is considered poor. This information comes from both informal interviews and from a card-sorting technique in which informants are given cards representing each surveyed household and asked to group the cards according to socioeconomic position (B. DeWalt 1979, 106–8). Informants are free to use as many or as few categories as they wish. I asked three informants to rank households independently. Their rankings are consistent, and all identify the same wealthy, middle income, and poor households.[10] Families from each of the income groups will be profiled.

Several families who bought hacienda land on relatively advantageous terms have increased their holdings during the twenty-five years since land became available. The richest family in the community, headed by a woman

*Table 4. Percentage Shares of Household Landownership by Population Quintiles, Chanchaló, 1992*

|  | Lowest Quintile | Second Quintile | Third Quintile | Fourth Quintile | Highest Quintile |
|---|---|---|---|---|---|
| Hectares, mean | .6 | 1.2 | 2.0 | 3.3 | 6.8 |
| Land share | 3% | 10% | 13% | 24% | 50% |

*Source:* NSF/FUNDAGRO Household Surveys, round 1, August–October 1992 (42 households).

*Table 5. Percentage Shares of Monthly Household Income by Population Quintiles, Chanchaló, 1992*

|  | Lowest Quintile | Second Quintile | Third Quintile | Fourth Quintile | Highest Quintile |
|---|---|---|---|---|---|
| Income, mean | $43 | $73 | $159 | $267 | $474 |
| Income share | 4% | 7% | 16% | 26% | 47% |

*Source:* NSF/FUNDAGRO Household Surveys, round 1, August–October 1992 (42 households).
    *Notes:* Income includes subsistence value of agricultural production. Income amounts are 1992 U.S. dollar equivalents. N = 40 households in which male head gave complete income information.

and a man in their late fifties, holds around twenty hectares. This couple lives in a relatively large concrete and tile house equipped with refrigerator and gas range, rare luxuries in Chanchaló. They also own a truck and a tractor. Although the vehicles are old, they are in perfect condition; renting the tractor is a lucrative source of income for the family. The family practices high-technology agriculture. In addition to their own machinery, they rent a combine for threshing wheat and barley. They apply agrochemicals as often as once every week or two during seasons of peak infestation. In addition, this family has sent a younger son and daughter to high school in Salcedo and to a technical college in Latacunga, paying for housing and living expenses away from home, as have a few other families. They eat well, including a variety of fruits and vegetables in their diet, and sufficient meat and dairy products to satisfy their preference for moderate consumption. They are able to seek medical attention in Salcedo or a nearby city.

This wealthy family is credited with attaining their unique level of economic success through hard work. Indeed, both husband and wife still put in a hard day's field labor every day. A few other families have either as much land, as much machinery, as large a house, as many material items, or the educational commitment of this family. None has all of these goods, although all are considered wealthy.

A typical middle-income family has between one and four hectares of land and lives in a two- or three-room concrete and tile house with piped water but no indoor plumbing. They own a small gas stove for cooking but also cook over a eucalyptus or straw fire, which provides warmth as well as energy. A television set and a tape player will be found in many homes. Middle-income people own two or three head of cattle, a couple of pigs, and some chickens and guinea pigs. They hold the larger animals for dairy production or for sale in times of economic necessity and eat the smaller ones on special occasions. They also have burros, horses, or llamas to use for local transportation and hauling. They may be able to rent a tractor for land preparation, but are also likely to use their own or borrowed oxen. They will apply agrochemicals if they can afford to do so but will need to borrow the money to purchase them and will apply only as much as they can afford.

Some middle-income families sacrifice to send their children to high school or to the better elementary schools in Salcedo; most do not or cannot. Most have enough potatoes and grains to supply sufficient calories and consume dairy products; they eat little meat and few fruits or vegetables. These families can muster the cost of a visit to the doctor in Salcedo if it is a medical emergency, but have great difficulty paying for extended or surgical treatment.

The poorest families of Chanchaló own very little land; 5 percent of all

*Women and men work together in high-technology barley production.*

families have none. Poorer people live in one-room dwellings made of adobe
with thatch roofs, usually without piped water. They do not have much furniture of any kind, nor do they have televisions. They may have a radio or small
tape player. These families cook over a wood fire. Most have a cow but no
pigs; they also have guinea pigs. Although some families may perform all agricultural labor without the aid of machinery or draft animals, most manage to
rent draft animals. Some very poor families invest scarce resources in agrochemicals and other inputs but apply lower levels. Most have a burro for
transportation and hauling. Their children attend the local elementary school
and will begin full-time farming as soon as they complete the sixth grade. The
poor families consume mostly potato and home-produced barley, supplemented by other grains; at times they do not have enough to eat. They must
rely on home remedies or the local free health service for medical treatment.

In this poor community, then, most people have enough to eat, a smallish house without indoor plumbing and with few amenities, some animals for savings and local transportation, a small income from their land and agricultural labor, and no access to secondary education or private health facilities. A few families have accumulated enough assets to improve their housing, enjoy more amenities, and educate their children. A few families are nearly landless and hungry.

## Community Services

Rural electrification, piped water, and the services of a medical dispensary of the rural national health insurance scheme, Seguro Campesino, are accessible to most families. These services have been provided by the national government at nominal fees. However, the quality of the water and health services is poor, and campesinos must wait months to qualify for electrical service. The community is served by a winding, deeply rutted dirt road that connects to a secondary paved road a few kilometers' distance from the community center.

The medical dispensary is staffed by a nurse's assistant with minimal medical training. She is qualified to dispense medications for body aches, digestive problems, and other mundane illnesses. The dispensary is supposed to be served periodically by a physician and a dentist, but during the nine months I lived in the community the doctor visited only once and the dentist never appeared. Employees of the social security administration were on strike during part of this time, in response to the national government's plan to privatize most services. However, informants state that under normal conditions physicians appear only rarely. Fewer than half the families in Chanchaló use the dispensary. They say that the health worker is a good soul who understands them and their illnesses but she is not trained to treat serious problems, nor is the facility equipped with the medicines and other services they need. They are unimpressed with the occasional physicians' services, citing the doctors' lack of understanding of the constraints of their lives and of their preferences.

Contamination of the local piped water supply is a serious health problem in a region that experienced a cholera epidemic during 1992. The community's water supply originates in the upper *páramos*, and water must travel many kilometers before it reaches storage tanks. During the rainy season, heavy accumulations of silt are deposited in the tanks. The water is literally black; often the filters are clogged and the community is without water. During all seasons, untreated water contributes to high rates of parasitosis and diarrheal disease.

## Demography and Social Organization

Chanchaló is a densely populated and very young community (table 6). Families are large; parents in their fifties and forties generally have between five and eight living children. Parents in their thirties and twenties express the desire to limit their families to two or three children but are likely to have four. Access to family planning is limited (see chapter 6). Considering the small land base of most families and the size of families, it is not surprising that population density is high. Although the research sample is younger than the population, the population is also very young; 43 percent of the population is under the age of fifteen. Considering the current low level of education and income, as well as the lack of family planning, the population of Chanchaló is likely to continue to grow rapidly, controlled only by infant mortality and the outmigration that will probably result as families subdivide their small farms into minifundia that will not support a household.

The primary distinguishing feature of Chanchaló, according to both Chanchaleños and people from bordering communities, is its social solidarity. Chanchaló is considered *mas colaborador* (more collaborative) than many other communities. Chanchaleños are neither richer nor poorer than their less collaborative neighbors; they do not have better land or climate or roads or schools. Wealth is not more equitably distributed. The legacy of hacienda repression and past necessity for socioeconomic collaboration is not unique to Chanchaló. Extended families and friends practice economic and social reciprocity in all neighboring communities. Yet Chanchaleños have developed local industries their neighbors lack. They have successfully collaborated in a number of community-based development projects and activities, whereas their neighbors have refused to contribute time and material resources to cooperative endeavors. The traditional Andean social contract of reciprocal public obligation and benefit has survived here and has been translated into communal social and economic institutions.[11]

It is not that Chanchaleños cheerfully sacrifice for the good of all. Rather, the perception is strong that everyone will benefit more from participation in cooperative endeavors than from going it alone. If an individual objects to required contributions of labor or material resources, a neighbor is likely to reply that cooperative endeavor is the only way to provide genuine social security for the community, and that this is the right thing to do. A combination of individual cost-benefit analysis and social conscience is at work.

Economic and social reciprocity continues to bind extended families, as well. Although most households are comprised of nuclear families, household structure is fairly fluid, with families often taking in relatives whose nuclear

*Table 6. Demographic Measures, Chanchaló, 1992*

| Population size: | 135 households | 6 persons per household, average |
|---|---|---|
| Population density: | 137 persons/km$^2$ | 219 persons/km$^2$ of land under production[a] |
| Temporary outmigration: | 10% of male household heads worked outside community, 1992 | Average time away: 12.5 wks. (SD = 7.6) |
| Family structure: | 83% nuclear-family households | 0% woman-headed households |

| | Population[b] | | Sample[c] | |
|---|---|---|---|---|
| Age structure: | Females (N=421) | Males (N=389) | Females (N=126) | Males (N=112) |
| 0–4 years | 12.7% | 14.2% | 22.2% | 29.5% |
| 5–9 years | 13.5% | 15.2% | 20.7% | 14.3% |
| 10–19 years | 24.6% | 25.6% | 21.4% | 19.6% |
| 20–39 years | 26.5% | 21.6% | 30.1% | 30.4% |
| 40–59 years | 13.8% | 14.4% | 4.0% | 4.4% |
| 60+ years | 8.9% | 9.1% | 1.6% | 1.8% |
| | 100% | 100% | 100% | 100% |

*Notes:* a. Population/km$^2$ arable land is considered the nutritional density of a population, that is, the density of population that must be fed per km$^2$ of land that can be used to provide food (Peters and Larkin 1989). This is a more accurate measure of population density for geographical comparison, as large tracts of nonarable land are not included. Most arable land in Chanchaló is under production.

b. Population figures are taken from INEC 1991, 1990a, checked against local comuna lists and against projections from a census of 115 households performed by staff of NSF project "Farming Systems and Socio-Cultural Determinants of Child Nutrition in Two Ecological Zones of Ecuador," July 1992.

c. Probabilistic sample selected for NSF project household survey.

families are undergoing some sort of hardship, or simply for convenience. Extended families also work together, although land and houses are individually owned by individuals or couples.

Traditionally, reciprocal labor was exchanged without cash payment. Today, it is more likely that cash will change hands. What has not changed is family members' perceived obligation to provide labor even if its opportunity cost is relatively high. Extended family members also engage in sharecropping of one another's land and in managing one another's animals, as well as borrowing and lending money. These arrangements are perpetuated even though the terms may not be more advantageous than similar deals with nonrelatives. Families at all economic levels cooperate in this manner—not only those who cannot afford to pay for labor or those who have so little land they must seek out sharecrop opportunities.

Kinship is reckoned bilaterally, and marital residence is ambilocal. Marriage in Chanchaló is monogamous and universal. Although there have been cases of divorce or desertion, adults do not remain unmarried for long. While endogamy is not a rule, and many families include a spouse from nearby communities, most Chanchaleños are lifetime residents.

The institutions of bilateral kinship and inheritance, and of the reciprocal social contract, have contributed to a system in which all community members are socially enfranchised. Gender equality is a central feature of social organization in Chanchaló. Women are visibly important contributors to community projects, communal work, and public office. Women hold property individually and jointly with their husbands. The nature of women's substantial economic contributions to their households and the egalitarian control of household economic and social resources will be the central focus of the remaining chapters in this study.

## Political Organization

The community's juridical constitution is vested in the body of the comuna (community), its local governing agency. The 1937 Law of Comunas established the basis for juridical legitimacy of local-level chartered communities in rural Ecuador (Hurtado 1980). A body of fifty or more persons was entitled to establish a local government and, under certain conditions during the years of land reform, to claim hacienda land (Redclift 1978). Currently, a group must also be registered with the Ministry of Agriculture to be legally recognized, following the Constitution of 1979 (Blumberg and Colyer 1990, 254).

The organization of the comuna includes the general assembly and the council *(cabildo)*. All adult residents are qualified to be voting members of the general assembly, which elects the council and determines policy. The council is composed of the president and other officers; its duty is to carry out the policies of the assembly (Blumberg and Colyer 1990, 256). The council also represents the community to the executive committee of the regional or "second-level" association of campesinos in Salcedo, the Casa Campesina. All comuna members are required to participate in public works projects, such as road and irrigation canal maintenance.

The comuna functions primarily to manage construction and maintenance of community infrastructure, and to promote education, health, other services, and community development. Whereas many other comunas administer communal lands, the formerly communal lands of Chanchaló have been sub-divided and are now the property of individuals. Control of water rights is in the hands of a parish-level committee and is locally administered by a board composed of representatives from the four communities that share the same water resources. The comuna does not manage a peacekeeping force nor does it include a judicial body.[12]

The political life of the community is not restricted to the comuna. Political interests are largely represented by the Casa Campesina, made up of repre-sentatives from sixteen comunas in the cantón. Among other activities, this organization presses for the rights of indigenous communities to access na-tional institutions and negotiates on their behalf with international develop-ment agencies. The Casa Campesina president strongly influences the direc-tion of the regional organization and serves for two years. The president of the comuna has considerable political leverage; he is an important representa-tive to the Casa Campesina and currently is the only community member who has a vote in elections for the presidency of the Casa Campesina. Howev-er, officers from all of the community's organizations are represented on the Casa Campesina executive committee, which establishes electoral policy and oversees voting for the office of president. It is likely that all of these will vote in future elections.

Official status in the community's production associations is an important measure of community political leadership, as these institutions manage eco-nomic resources while the comuna does not. Membership on the parish and local water boards is also a measure of community political influence, as wa-ter rights are critical for agricultural production. The comuna, then, is not the community's most important interest group, nor does it determine economic development policy. Rather, it is perceived as a means to organize the com-munity for development and maintenance of infrastructure and to promote local development. (Women's roles in the comuna, Casa Campesina, and eco-nomic organizations will be delineated in chapters 3 and 6.)

## Ethnicity

The people of Chanchaló are, by self-definition and by observable qualities, *indígena* (indigenous). This is an ethnic distinction. Unlike the Otavaleños of the northern sierra or the Salasacas of neighboring Tungurahua Province, the indígena status of Chanchaleños is no longer evidenced by locally distinctive clothing or other markers.

The term *indígena* has social, political, and economic implications. Al-though many urban Ecuadoreans use the term to indicate a racial or genetic-endowment classification, indígena status is in fact fluid, both within indigenous communities and outside them (see Crandon 1984, 1986). An indígena individual who moves to the city, or simply adopts city ways, may then be considered *blanco* (white), a term used by Chanchaleños and other Ecuadorean indigenous people to describe mestizos (Poeschel 1988). The term *cholo* is also used by city people to label an urbanized indigenous person. Moreover, the physical features of persons of indigenous ancestry are visible in the faces of "blancos" who do not have mixed ancestry but who have become blanco/mestizo by virtue of their behavior.[13]

Local informants define the term *indígena* historically and socially. They say that indigenous people are the descendants of the inhabitants of the sierra before the Spanish came. They also say that indigenous people are those descendants who continue to live in the country or participate in community affairs, and who preserve at least some of the traditional lifeways, as these are currently perceived.

Chanchaleños do not consider dress or language to be definitive markers of ethnicity, although they are proud of Quichua, the language they have inherited from the Inca occupation and which belongs to them but not to city people. Quichua is spoken by elders in Chanchaló. Some of the young people are asking their grandparents to teach it to them in hopes that it will not be lost. Dress identifies Chanchaleños as indigenous people to outsiders. Men wear ponchos, although they sometimes also wear jackets, with Western-style pants. Women wear shawls over sweaters and knee-length skirts. All wear narrow-brimmed dark brown or black felt hats and rubber boots. A few of the younger women dress more blanco in jeans and T-shirts or dresses for social occasions, but they work in country clothes. One couple who lived near Quito for three years always wear blanco clothing but are not considered to be ethnically differentiated by the rest of the community.

The term *indígena* is used interchangeably with *campesino* by people in Chanchaló, referring to peasants or small-scale farmers of indigenous descent. The term does not differentiate socioeconomic class within the community. The richest family, who own city clothes and physically transform themselves when they travel to the city for an important occasion, are considered as indigenous as the rest of the community. They participate in all community functions and consider themselves indigenous campesinos. They have not adopted city ways.

The political implications of the term *indígena* are important and are interpreted variously by indigenous and nonindigenous people. I was told by well-meaning Ecuadorean development workers familiar with the community that *indígena* is no more than a political category, chosen by campesinos because it enables them to qualify for grants and other benefits. Less well-meaning mestizos or blancos told me that *indígena* has no meaning at all because, in the words of a physician from Quito: "Indians are being manipulated by communist insurgents who have fabricated this indigenous identity; their only community identity was created by the state during land reform." I hope the previous discussion has shown that this is not the case.

On the other hand, ethnicity is consciously manipulated by the Casa Campesina and other indigenous political interest groups. For example, the Salcedo Casa Campesina president encourages the use of Quichua phrases as a mechanism of reinforcing solidarity and ethnic pride; he has had little success, however, as members consider these expressions merely quaint. They would prefer that he concentrate on political-economic issues. This president has a laissez-faire attitude about political protest on behalf of indigenous rights. Some *comuneros* have expressed dissatisfaction with his failure to organize local participation in countrywide protests by indigenous organizations against (1) the government's restructuring of communal landholdings and rural social services, (2) the celebration of the five-hundredth anniversary of the arrival of the Spanish in the New World, and (3) human rights abuses.

During 1993 people from Chanchaló participated in peaceful protests concerning these issues. They privately expressed sympathy for other indigenous groups who are in danger of losing their communal lands, and for Amazonian indigenous people whose territories and lifeways are threatened by oil production and exploration. And they are acutely aware that their strength lies potentially in numbers and coordinated political activity. Yet, Chanchaleños are much more concerned with making a living and protecting the community's welfare through their own social work than they are with political action. And they express concern for poor or disenfranchised people who are not indigenous, but who are also victims of the policies they protest.

It is fair to say that indigenous identity has a political component. It is not fair to say that indigenous identity has been created by a political environment. Chanchaleños refer to themselves as indígena primarily because they are descended from pre-Hispanic inhabitants, have preserved indigenous social forms, and make their living as smallholding agriculturalists. Ethnicity is a self-conscious component of community and individual identity. Although ethnic identity can be altered by behavior, it is not a politically situational construct.

## Religion

The people of Chanchaló practice a syncretic form of folk Roman Catholicism. Although Protestant missionaries are active in Cantón Salcedo, their presence has not been felt in Chanchaló. There is one small church, more a symbol of community autonomy than of Christianity. The community is served by a priest who is scheduled to visit three communities every Thursday, which is market day in Salcedo. Consequently, the community is fairly empty when he holds services. The current priest is often absent for months at a time, as he was during my time in Chanchaló.

There are no shamans or magico-religious healers practicing in Chanchaló. One man told me he had seen a television show about shamanistic healing in the Oriente (Amazonian Ecuador). Several people mentioned religious healers they had heard about who practice among coastal indigenous groups. The general idea concerning shamans and other religious healers is that they are both exotic and very expensive. I did not talk to anyone who reported consulting a religious healer.

Before the Conquest, indigenous mythology centered on belief in the power and sentient character of mountains or of features within the mountain landscape. In the region of Chanchaló, a creation myth held that the world was created through marriage between the snow-capped volcanos that dominate the landscape (Murra 1946). Sky dwellers such as the rainbow were conceived of as powerful forces, capable of causing great mischief, especially in the form of ill health, for humans. Places of worship were outdoors; there is no archaeological evidence of buildings having been used for religious purposes (Salomon 1986, 126). Aside from ceremonial activities that took place in the chief's compound, ritual life was expressed in the vicinity of the spirits.

Although beliefs have changed over the centuries, the people of Chanchaló continue to perform Roman Catholic rituals of great importance outdoors, to express awe for their powerful landscape, and to conceive of supernatural power in terms of that landscape. Objects of ritual significance are likely to be removed from the church to the outdoor area where spiritual blessing is desired. On Easter Sunday, the statue of the Virgin was removed from the church and displayed under a small tent during the afternoon so that all could pay their respects individually. On the day the local cheese factory was to be opened and blessed by the priest, statues of the Virgin and Saint Joseph, the community's patron, were removed from the church and placed outdoors next to the factory, where the ceremony of blessing took place.

People continue to express awe in the presence of endless Andean vistas, taking great pride in the vastness of mountains and skies as well as their beauty. It is not unusual for a person engaged in field labor to look out across the inter-Andean valley at the massive waves of the Western Cordillera and ask the visitor if this view is not the grandest on earth. Pride, anger, and fear are all mingled in human responses to the devastating power of an environment featuring frequent earthquakes, landslides, and torrents, as well as the present threat of volcanic eruption. In the midst of natural calamity, the forces of nature are addressed by daredevil laughter as well as by prayers. The people of Chanchaló both love and curse their powerful landscape; they do not find it quotidian.

It has often been remarked that religion is not a separate component in the lives of people in traditional communities, but a way of looking at things that permeates all of life. This is a fairly accurate description of religious life in Chanchaló. When the going gets tough, people try to help themselves but they also invoke the power and succor of the Virgin and, through her, the power of God. When my landlord's sister was planning a trip to the shrine of the Virgin of Laja in Columbia, he sent along a candle to be lighted on behalf of the family's endangered potato crop. He also sent a candle with which he had touched the four corners of my living room where wall and ceiling meet, and a spot in the center of the floor. He assured me that the house would be safe from intruders because he had done this.

These practical appeals are made sincerely but without great affect—part of covering all of one's bases in a practical sense and also an expression of a generalized respect for forces greater than humanity. But religious life also has an affective component, and it seems to be directly related to the power manifest in the physical environment. Some Chanchaleños express the affective component of their faith through devotion to the Virgin of Baños, who in visions appeared to emerge from within a mountainside or from the source of a waterfall. Powerful spirits of their ancestors, also, were imaged as dwelling within mountainsides and were associated with water sources.

Baños is a small resort town featuring pools that capture mineral spring water heated by geological activity in the volcano Tungurahua. The region is prone to earthquakes. The Virgin of Baños, Our Lady of the Holy Water, is credited with so many miracles—often involving interdiction of the more dangerous forces of nature loosed by geological activity—that the walls of her large shrine are completely covered with small plaques in her honor given by grateful devotees. This shrine is always crowded with visitors from throughout the sierra who pay their respects to the Virgin and also enjoy the tourist attractions of the town.

People from Chanchaló who can afford to do so like to take day trips to Baños, some two hours from Salcedo by bus. I asked why they visit the Virgin—expecting answers such as "to ask for good health" or "to ask for help with the crops." I was told that, while they do often ask the Virgin in her many incarnations for help, they like to visit this particular shrine because, as one man put it, "it makes my heart big." He said that the Virgin of Baños has the power to inspire him; in other shrines he has not felt the same. The Virgin of mountainsides and waterfalls has the power to disarm the forces of nature—those earthquakes, floods, and fires that in U.S. legal contracts are termed "acts of God." She has the power to call forth an emotive response. In her, natural and supernatural are one.

Awe is reserved for the landscape and for the abstract power of God and the more immediately perceived power of the Virgin. Yet people do not walk in fear of God. Nor are they afraid of the disapproval of his human representatives in the church. The concept of eternal damnation does not appear to be present in Chanchaló, although it exists in Ecuadorean national culture, together with the fear of God and desire for the approbation of the clergy. When moral lessons are delivered to them by the clergy, Chanchaleños voice appropriate responses. Sometimes the name of God is invoked when an individual is making a moral point. Yet the concept of sin—supernaturally punishable sin—is lacking.

It seems to me that Christianity has been layered over traditional Andean ethics, and that the Christian God serves primarily as an abstract and distant overseer of human activity, one whose authority backs the traditional system. The moral basis of social reciprocity is now at times expressed in Christian terms. There is little evidence of direct survival of pre-Hispanic mythology. I was indulgently teased for asking if rainbows harm people. Yet this concept survives in indigenous communities in the northern sierra. Several other indigenous religious/medical beliefs that are widespread throughout the highlands do not exist in Chanchaló to my knowledge.

Ritual life is rich. Ritual marks the progress of individual lives, inaugurates economic projects, refreshes community spirit—and involves consumption of much refreshment in the form of alcoholic spirits at all of these occasions. Traditional Andean fiestas have been well described in the ethnographic literature (Isbell 1978; Allen 1988), as have the celebrations of baptism, first haircutting, coming of age, and marriage, together with the rites of death and devotion to the ancestors during the Day of the Dead (Poeschel 1988). Chanchaleños exuberantly celebrate all of these occasions. Because the blessing of an individual, a project, or of the community is an important component in all of these ceremonies, they cannot be considered apart from religion.

Roman Catholic priests perform the duties of ritual specialists with varying degrees of involvement in community spirit; some also provide support for the economic and social struggle of their parishioners. Chanchaleños say that, at times, they have been assigned circuit-riding padres who were derelict in their duties and held only contempt for local people, hypocrites who lay about with women while away from their post. But they also say that many other priests are good men. Occasionally they attend mass in Salcedo on Sunday, also a market day, if the service is said by Padre Antonito, a priest known for his social work with campesinos and for his strength of spirit and compassion. Another good priest was invited to say the inaugural service and blessing for the quesería. People express affection for the nuns who live next to the Casa Campesina compound in Salcedo and who work with Father Tony and others to improve the quality of rural life.

Chanchaleños take advantage of many services offered by the Ecuadorean and international Roman Catholic Church. Among these the most prominently mentioned is the financial lending service of the Fondo Ecuatoriano Populorum Progressio (FEPP), headquartered in Latacunga. As sources of credit are so limited for campesinos, this service is especially appreciated.

In sum, Chanchaleños are a religious people. For them natural and supernatural are not always conceptually separate. They are mindful of a religious basis for moral living. Their lives are enriched by individual and communal ritual, and also by spiritual devotion. They view the Roman Catholic religious community not as the awesome representatives of supernatural power, but as men and women who either respect and help them or do not. They cannot imagine life without religion.

## Conclusion

The people of Chanchaló are survivors. They are making a living in a volatile and fragile environment on a hard-won yet barely adequate land base. They are fighting, against long odds, for access to national economic and social infrastructure, for full citizenship, for an even chance at a better future. In this struggle they are mindful of the weapons that helped them to survive nearly five hundred years of oppression and to win land and freedom: community solidarity; a desire to continue their agricultural way of life; hard work; respect for their environment, whether as enemy or friend; and an uncompromising view of their place in that environment as rightful heirs. The people of Chanchaló take great pride and delight in these things. Only delight has come easily.

# THREE ❋ Managers, Mothers, Maiden, and Matriarch

*Five Women and Their Families*

IN A FINE ETHNOGRAPHY of Andean life, Catherine Allen states that her best "informants" were not people chosen because they possessed desired information, but people with whom she became friends because she and they enjoyed one another's company. These good friends considered themselves her teachers (1988, 38). The same is true of my own field study. After a very short time in Chanchaló I stopped thinking of the three women I came to know best as potential informants.

The women I shall call Clemencia, Marina, and Beatriz took me into their homes and family life with such generosity of spirit that we quickly became close friends. We laughed and gossiped together in the evenings after work. We helped each other deal with sadness. We loaned each other money and exchanged gifts. We became fictive kin. We shared the stories of our lives: our aspirations, trials, loves, disappointments, enthusiasms, the pleasures and problems encountered in making a living and rearing a family, the things we are proud of and the things we wish we could change in our societies. These experiences were not confined to one gender or generation but often included husbands, children, parents, other family, and community members.

These women and others volunteered to be my teachers. As a person who had never lived far from the comforts and ease of modern Western life, I needed a great deal of teaching. In addition to agricultural tasks I learned how to build a fire, cook locally grown foods, treat illness with herbs, bargain in the market, dance, take the best shortcuts through the fields, and innumerable other lessons in daily living. My friends and neighbors appeared to enjoy teaching the gringa, especially on those many occasions when my ineptitude or confusion provided a good laugh.

In addition to my close friends, many women and men volunteered to teach me about local history, kinship, economic reciprocity networks, agriculture, marriage, the sexual division of labor, resource ownership, and experience with development organizations, among other subjects. I was often invited to join them as they engaged in activities they thought would interest me. These teachers were not surprised that a person from the United States would want to learn about agricultural production and the economic roles of men and women in their community. Their curiosity about life in the United States often centered on these topics.

From this group of voluntary teachers, and from the sample of female household heads identified by the NSF Child Growth Project, I chose seven additional women to complement my close friends in forming an ethnographic sample of ten women that would be representative of variation within the community on the following variables: household wealth, male outmigration and experience of national culture, life cycle of the household, and participation in traditional forms of extrahousehold kinship-based and communal economic cooperation. All of these women regularly welcomed me to their homes and fields for observational visits and rarely let me leave empty-handed. Most of them became friends and some of them raised intimate topics for conversation. I observed their activities for periods of two–four hours approximately once every two weeks, and I visited with them more often. All of these women also invited or allowed me to participate in a variety of economic and social activities. In the following case studies, I shall profile two of these women as well as my three most intimate friends.

## Some Limitations of the Ethnographic Data

During my first months in Chanchaló I began interviewing informants by asking fairly technical questions about agricultural production, labor, and decision-making in order to map the domains of agricultural work and decision-making and to get a general idea of how people view men's and women's participation in these. For example, to gain a preliminary understanding of the gendered division of labor, whether women are excluded from any phases of production or particular tasks, and the ideological basis for any such exclusion, I asked which members of households would perform particular tasks:

the male head, the female head, or other members of the household. After repeatedly eliciting the information that both male and female heads perform all tasks, I began to ask if there are any tasks that are generally performed by men or by women, and if there are any tasks that only men or women perform well. I did not use terms I thought would be socially loaded, such as *permit, exclude,* or *equality.* I used the same technique when asking who decides what to plant, how much and what kind of fertilizer or pesticide to use, how much of a crop or animal product to sell, the lowest acceptable price for produce, how to invest savings, and other areas of economic decision-making. I interviewed both women and men: individually, as couples together, and in small groups of people working together or congregated together for social reasons.

I did not want to be perceived by Chanchaleños as a person who has a sexual-equality agenda against which she is measuring the lives of her informants. I felt that questions from an outsider regarding what I considered sensitive aspects of gender relations within the household—such as domestic violence and women's control over their own sexual fertility—might be regarded as invasive or perceived as negatively critical. I am aware (as will be discussed below) that these particular sensitive subjects are important to an understanding of engendered social relations and relate in no small way to women's economic status.

My research was conducted in association with FUNDAGRO, a development agency that operates a field project concentrating on dairy commodity production and nutrition in Chanchaló. The NSF research project of which my own study is a part was designed to provide an evaluation instrument for the dairy commodity project as well as to study the farming-systems and sociocultural determinants of child nutrition (see appendix A for a full description of the NSF Child Growth Project). I was asked by the NSF project survey coordinator to avoid entirely the topic of sexual reproduction; he felt that raising this issue would compromise the work of our FUNDAGRO colleagues by angering religious workers who are socially active in campesino communities.

For all of these reasons, I limited my samplewide questioning to matters of intrahousehold economic relations and women's access to social, economic, and political community institutions. In retrospect, I think this was a mistake. Although I did talk about issues such as domestic violence and women's control of their own bodies with my close friends, I now believe that I could have asked many informants about virtually any aspect of gender relations, with reference to both their own families and their community. Many people volunteered extremely personal information or raised what I consider sensitive issues. It was not unusual, for example, for a woman I had just met to ask me if I knew how she could obtain reliable contraception. Many people felt quite free to ask me personal questions.

Among the questions put to me included the state of my own marriage. Men and women who expressed surprise that I would want to work so far away from my family for such a long period sometimes also asked me if things were going well with my husband and if he was good to me. One especially solicitous gentleman, whose family were not close friends but had been very kind to me, quizzed me on this subject for a full half-hour during a trip to town with his family. He remarked that in some places, like the Ecuadorean coast, men beat their wives; he wondered if I had run away from a cruel husband. When I assured him that my husband and I get along very well and that I have never been harmed, he persisted, "Yes, but does he love you? Does he treat you well?" I refrained, however, from asking such questions myself because I did not want to risk offending anyone or eroding the rapport that had developed with several friends and teachers.

There are other areas of marital relations I did not pursue, including marital infidelity. All my informants except one are married. None of them raised the subject of infidelity within their own marriages, and, although gossip often included remarks about how other couples were getting along, I never heard talk of ongoing sexual affairs. I also did not hear of any cases of desertion of families by husbands within the community. One recently remarried forty-year-old widow had left her new husband, who received much commiseration from friends who assured him that it was sometimes hard for older persons who had developed their own ways of doing things to adjust to a new partner, but she'd surely be back to give it another try. When I asked about desertion and divorce I was told that marriages dissolve occasionally, but no one could think of anyone who was currently or had been divorced. In retrospect, I think I should have asked questions about infidelity and about the circumstances under which people might change partners. As my friends always seemed willing to talk about anything that interested me, I expect they would have discussed this subject candidly, at least concerning the frequency of extramarital affairs in the community.

Information concerning frequency of domestic violence, control of biological fertility, frequency of extramarital affairs, and the conditions under which marriages might dissolve may be relevant in several ways to the investigation of women's economic status within the household. If a woman lives in fear of her husband's physical attacks, it is not unreasonable to say that her economic decision input would be at the pleasure of her husband, who ultimately holds coercive power over her. Her ownership of resources may be in name only. And her physical labor may not be her own to control. A woman who has no say in the number of children she will bear does not control her own health, may find her agricultural labor constrained by pregnancy and the necessity of caring for small children, and may find that being distanced from agricultural work and income earning lessens her economic decision input. A woman who must share her husband with other women may suffer resource deprivation for herself and her children. If marriages are brittle, that is, perceived in the community as being dissolvable, the partner who would face greater difficulty surviving outside a marriage may be disadvantaged in intrahousehold bargaining, as this partner would have more to lose from dissolution and would perhaps put up with greater inequality within the household. In most societies this partner would be female.

Thus these intimate "noneconomic" aspects of marriage may be integrally related to women's economic status and roles in household agricultural production. I am satisfied that the quality of observation and conversation I enjoyed with my closest women and men friends, together with observation of other couples and conversation with them concerning intimate topics, accords an understanding of their marriages sufficient to discuss with confidence levels of women's control over their own bodies, labor, and individual and household economic resources. I have not, however, produced a precise map of all potential threats to women.

The marital landscape to be presented in the following case descriptions is peopled by wives and husbands who consider themselves partnered for life, and who have learned (or are learning) to capitalize on one another's strengths and to compensate for one another's weaknesses in matters of economic survival. Although the need to resolve conflict is a part of these marriages, there is also evidence in most of them of mutual tolerance, tenderness, and respect. Although they joked or complained about their spouses' foibles, not one of my informants expressed dissatisfaction with her or his marriage. I must ask if my informants are atypical, if they did not feel free or inclined to discuss deep dissatisfactions with me, if perhaps they are better able to resolve differences, or face greater necessity to resolve differences, than my own compatriots. I do not know the answer to this question. I do know that all of the female household heads in the probabilistic sample drawn from Chanchaló by the NSF project currently live in marital unions.

Another potential limitation of my ethnographic data is the possible perception by some informants that I worked for (rather than with) FUNDAGRO. I tried in several ways to counter this impression, as I did not want to be perceived as a development worker promoting a particular agenda. Only three of the women in my ethnographic sample were affiliated with FUNDAGRO activities. This is roughly the same percentage as the proportion of community members who participate in FUNDAGRO-affiliated groups. I did not make it a habit to attend meetings of groups affiliated with FUNDAGRO, which included the quesería and women's associations, but I did accept invitations by friends to participate in women's association work projects and other activities. I was careful to tell all my informants and anyone else who asked that I did not come to Chanchaló to promote or evaluate FUNDAGRO activities but to study the economic and social life of the entire community.

It is quite possible that my efforts did not erase the initial impression many people had of me as an employee of FUNDAGRO, however. This impression helped me make friends, as FUNDAGRO field staff treat campesinos with respect and are, in turn, respected by most Chanchaleños who participate in their projects. It may also have limited the information I received from some informants.

Although people often remarked that, as a matter of general knowledge, "it is good to know" about the ways of life of people in countries other than one's own, they also pointedly asked me what I intended to do with the information I collected from them. I replied that I would write a thesis describing their ways of life because some people in my country also think "it is good to know" about other peoples, especially about those who have survived for so many centuries under difficult political and economic circumstances and must therefore possess a great deal of valuable knowledge. I also stated that I would share some of this information with development agencies, so that assistance could be offered that would meet local needs and would not exclude previously unidentified groups of farmers—such as, perhaps, women.

These explanations were apparently accepted at face value. Several people remarked that well-meaning development workers sometimes do not seem to understand how they live. Many people stated that they are proud of their community and want me to use its name in my writing. My friends told me that they "have confidence in" me to make good use of information about them.

While I believe that such community pride and confidence in the ethnographer's good intentions are conducive to the providing of reliable information, I must also wonder if there were times when people did not reveal what they considered shameful behavior in their own families or in their community. For example (as will be discussed later), violence against women is considered shameful behavior, the kind of behavior that goes on elsewhere but is not tolerated in Chanchaló. Not one of my teachers mentioned violent or otherwise coercive behavior as an aspect of his or her own or generalized relations between husbands and wives. Perhaps if I had not emphasized the public uses I intended to make of the information they gave me, or if I had developed a line of questioning designed to reveal the existence of coercive behavior, I would have discovered its presence.

In sum, I focused on economic matters within the household and women's access to social and political institutions in their community, including conflictive aspects of intrahousehold economic decision-making and gendered access to economic and social resources. I did not focus on marriage or community institutions as arenas of conflict. It is possible that this focus—together with my stated aim to provide information to development institutions—may have circumscribed the information I received and was permitted to observe. It is certain that both my focus and aims limited my fields of observation and interpretation.

## Case Study Approach

The five women presented in this chapter range in age from twenty-one to forty-seven; in socioeconomic circumstance from poor to affluent, by local standard; in household social status from unmarried daughter to matriarch; in experience of the world outside Chanchaló from scholarship recipients who spent six weeks in the United States, to a returned urban migrant who lived near the capital city for three years, to a woman who has lived every day of her life in Cantón Salcedo. Some of their husbands have spent considerable time outside the community, working or serving in the military; others have never left Chanchaló. Reflecting the composition of the community census and probabilistic sample, no households headed by unmarried women are available for study.

I will introduce each woman, together with her husband or parents, by orienting the reader to their individual socioeconomic circumstances, the composition of their households, and their public roles in the community. I will describe working days, resource ownership, mothering, affective relations with husbands, economic and social goals, division of labor and economic decision-making within the household, and interaction with development agencies and projects. Some case descriptions (notably the first) will include interpretive analysis; others will include very little analytical discussion. Interpretive discussion is intended primarily to clarify subsequent use of concepts such as egalitarianism, which are illustrated by a particular case. As each woman's experience and perspective contributes a unique strand to the texture of economic survival and gender relations in Chanchaló, I will focus on those areas about which I learned the most from each individual woman.

My aim in this chapter is to describe each woman's circumstances in sufficient detail so that these cases may be used to contextualize subsequent discussions of cross-sectional variation in economic and social relations within the household. I have limited the number of case descriptions to five in order to provide considerable detail for each case, rather than describing less completely each woman in my ethnographic sample. The remaining five women will be profiled briefly in subsequent chapters. The five women I have chosen to introduce here are neither older nor younger, richer nor poorer, better nor worse endowed with social networks or prestige than the five women who will receive less descriptive attention. Rather, they are the three friends and teachers I know best, and two additional women chosen to increase the range of household and intrahousehold social and economic circumstances described.

## Clemencia and Alejandro

Clemencia is thirty-three, a daughter of the richest family in Chanchaló. Although her parents have become wealthy by local standards and now educate their younger sons and daughter at least through high school, Clemencia has only four years of education. She has been married for twelve years to Alejandro, the son of her parents' less affluent next-door neighbors. Alejandro's father is one of Chanchaló's legal founders; his mother is Clemencia's first cousin. They have four children: Diego, aged ten; Mauro, aged eight; Estella, aged four; and Milton, aged two. Clemencia also delivered three babies who died.

Clemencia and Alejandro are doing well economically and are considered middle-income by informants. They are full-time farmers who planted five hectares during 1992, growing potato, maize, beans, barley, pasture, and other crops. They own about half this land; the remainder is sharecropped with Clemencia's parents. They also sell milk from two cows and occasionally sell an animal.

They live in a relatively large and well-built cement-block and tile house that Alejandro and hired laborers constructed at the time of their marriage. The house is well furnished by local standards; Clemencia has a kitchen sink, unlike most everyone else in Chanchaló. They had to work a long time for that sink, she says. They also have a kitchen range (another rarity), a television set, and a stereo. Like most other families they do not have upholstered furniture or dining tables and chairs. They do have a bathroom. The house is situated on land that Clemencia will inherit, equidistant from her parents' and Alejandro's parents' homes in the central sector of Chanchaló.

Although they are not formally educated beyond their local grammar school, both Clemencia and Alejandro read and write fluently and are good at mathematics. Both are effective public speakers. Clemencia and Alejandro send their children to Salcedo to school and plan to educate them at least through high school.

## The Working Day

During the spring and summer of 1993 Chanchaló suffered an unusually long and unremittingly wet rainy season. Crops became waterlogged and infested with fungus. Humans slogged through mud well over the ankles and worked soddenly in the fields, where they huddled frozenly under plastic sheets during the heaviest deluges. Everyone cursed the weather. Many people became ill.

Toward the end of February, Clemencia developed an illness, diagnosed as respiratory, whose symptoms included chest pain, fatigue, fever, and loss of appetite. The debilitating effects of this illness could be read in her lovely oval face. Her smooth caramel-colored complexion paled to a mottled greenish yellow, and the light that often played behind her smiling eyes disappeared. She took antibiotics prescribed by a physician from Salcedo, but the illness persisted for two months. Although Alejandro implored her to rest, and she did rest more than usual, she continued to work in the fields, doing the most difficult tasks in the worst weather. The illness showed in her face and pace but did not seriously interrupt her agricultural work or community obligations.

Clemencia and Alejandro balance household productive and reproductive labor with public duties. I will describe two working days during Clemencia's illness. I choose these two days because they illustrate the variation in household responsibilities during the potato-cropping cycle, the activity that produces most of the household's income, and trade-offs between household and extrahousehold reciprocity-network duties. In mid-March Clemencia had been ill for about three weeks and everyone was becoming seriously concerned for her health. In spite of Alejandro's protestations that he could manage field labor without her, Clemencia put in a full working day, which included working in the field as well as community service.

She arose around 5:30, as usual, to prepare breakfast for her family. She prepared the usual hearty meal of cereal (oats, milk, and sugar today) and potato-and-grain-based soup (rice today) seasoned with vegetables (carrots and onion today). While she worked in the kitchen, Alejandro dressed the small children and straightened the bedrooms. He fed the animals and did the milking. After breakfast Clemencia cleaned the kitchen and sent her small daughter and toddler son next door to stay the morning with Alejandro's mother. Her older sons were in Salcedo, where they board with Clemencia's younger sister while attending school during the week. With the morning's reproductive and animal-care chores attended to, Clemencia and Alejandro left the house.

Clemencia is vice president of the women's association; she crossed the road to attend an association work party that would last all morning. Alejandro was to travel a kilometer or so up the slope to spray one of their potato fields with chemical pesticide; he would then climb further up to spray their highest potato field, at nearly 4,000 meters. He would not be home for the midday meal.

The women's association has been encouraged by FUNDAGRO field staff to produce guinea pigs for sale. The morning's work party *(minga)* was devoted to working on the building that will house the guinea pigs. Clemencia and a crew composed of young women together with a few of their male relatives dug damp earth, mixed it with water, and formed adobe bricks. They also raised part of the walls of the building with bricks made earlier. This was a slow process because the wet weather inhibited the drying of the bricks and some of them had to be reformed. Despite her illness and the arduousness of the task, Clemencia felt that all hands were necessary to catch up on the project. Clemencia worked from 8:00 to 12:00 noon, leaving with the others who also had chores to attend to during the afternoon.

She collected her small children, fed them breakfast leftovers for lunch, and spent the afternoon weeding and applying fertilizer in their lower potato field near the house. At around 4:00 she began to cut alfalfa to be fed to the cattle, a chore performed by her older boys when they are home. She fed the animals as Alejandro was returning from the upper fields.

When I ask how she is able to work so hard when she isn't feeling well, she replies that Alejandro usually makes sure she has some time to rest, by increasing his own workload, but she's had no time to rest today because she was in Latacunga and Salcedo the entire day yesterday, as well as working at the *minga* today, and now there is simply too much work for Alejandro to do alone. Her day away from the farm was well spent, she says. In the morning she met with officials of the Abrigada Patria, a social welfare organization that is considering a loan to the women's association to pay for industrial materials needed to finish the guinea-pig house. In the afternoon, she was elected president of the five women's associations affiliated with the Casa Campesina of Cantón Salcedo. She is pleased that she's been elected, although the job will require a lot of work, planning and coordinating courses and other activities to be held at the Casa Campesina, and the thought of this extra work seems to add to her tiredness.

Alejandro brought home eucalyptus branches for the evening's cooking

*Members of the Women's Production Association build a guinea-pig house with the help of male volunteers.*

fire. While Clemencia heated water for the evening's cauldron of potato-and-vegetable soup and began preparing the vegetables, Alejandro washed clothes in the outdoor laundry sink equipped with running water. He then joined her in the kitchen and finished the vegetables while she ground *achiote*, a pungent spice. When they had eaten, he washed the dishes while Clemencia bathed the children. Alejandro put the children to bed while Clemencia and I visited. By 8:30 they were ready to retire. This was a relatively light day for Clemencia.

A month later, not yet recovered, Clemencia was putting in even more demanding days. Potato harvesting was underway and it was imperative to finish as quickly as possible because potatoes were absorbing too much water in the saturated fields. A rare sunny day found Clemencia, Alejandro, his eighteen-year-old sister, Maria Elena, and the four children in the field by

8:00 A.M. The adults were digging up potatoes and the remains of peas, turnips, and radishes that had been intercropped with them, using short-handled hoes. The ten-year-old helped a bit but was easily distracted by the antics of his younger siblings. It would take the three workers one week to harvest the *cuadra*, about three-quarters of a hectare.

Although I had told Clemencia I would be observing only and would try to avoid interrupting their work with questions, Alejandro stopped working when I arrived and seemed to expect me to begin interviewing. I asked a few questions about the production of the potatoes in this field, concentrating on amounts and costs of seed, fertilizer, pesticides, machinery rental, and labor required. Alejandro answered but paused often and looked at Clemencia, who continued to work and did not say anything. He computed his answers concerning the amount of chemicals they had bought, but when I asked about labor, Clemencia interrupted her work and began to answer. She supplied the information about the amount of labor needed to weed and harvest the crop, plus the time required for land preparation, planting, fertilization, and fumigation. I thanked them for the information and wandered off to another part of the field where I could watch the work without their feeling they had to talk to me.

An hour or so later I returned and asked about the quality of the harvest. Alejandro replied that the field is not irrigated and the harvest is poor, owing to the earlier drought as well as the recent superfluity of water. I then asked about the relative strengths of the potato variety they were harvesting compared to other varieties, and Clemencia began to answer. She said they had chosen to plant the Garrisco variety for several reasons. It produces a higher yield in less time than other varieties, and at the altitude of this particular field (about 3,000 meters) they can harvest two crops per year. Although it brings a lower price than some other varieties, the total yield is so much higher it is a good choice. Alejandro agreed. Once again, I removed myself from the adults and took up my observation post.

Clemencia worked hard, digging as much as the healthy Maria Elena and nearly as much as Alejandro. I was not surprised when she told me that, in Chanchaló, female and male workers are paid the same amount for a day's work. Workers receive between 2,000 and 2,500 sucres per day, about US $1.25, depending on the activity. Although Maria Elena is expected to exchange labor with her brother, who will help with her own harvest on the *cuadra* she owns, they paid her 2,000 sucres and a hearty lunch for her eight hours of work.

While the adults labored, the children provided comic relief, playing with plants, animals, and equipment as well as one another. They busily harvested the landscape, piling on to tree branches to weight them down so they could pick *capulis,* a cherry-like fruit, and pulling up ocas in a nearby field to eat the sweet stalks. They played hide-and-seek among the tall maize plants in the field next to the potatoes. They made swings of potato sacks and rope and performed amazing aerial feats upside down. Eight-year-old Mauro sneaked up behind one of the cows grazing on the upturned turnips and squirted his older brother with milk from her teat, a stunt that convulsed everyone except Diego. This brought on a wrestling match, with much giggling and rolling down the hillside. Clemencia enjoyed the antics of her children, while Alejandro exhorted Diego to pitch in and help them work and sternly warned Maurito that he was asking for trouble. But Alejandro could not keep from laughing at the cow stunt and none of the youngsters seemed to worry about adult interference.

One of Alejandro's sisters once remarked, "Clemencia's children run wild," and I observed them running all over the community, usually encrusted with grime and often involved in daredevil escapades. When I heard Diego and Maurito calling "Watch me, Sarita!" I was afraid to look up because I knew they would be dangling from the highest branches of the biggest tree or otherwise working without a net. Four-year-old Estella favored activities closer to the ground, sliding and somersaulting down muddy banks and playing stealthy tricks on everyone. Two-year-old Milton was fearless, charging ahead like a miniature human tank, clambering over any obstacle in his path (including me) on sturdy legs. All four of them roamed the neighborhood together on a daily basis unless the older boys were in Salcedo. I did not think them wild but, rather, lively and curious.

Once when I was trying to find the right word to comment on the brightness of her children's eyes, Clemencia smiled, widened her eyes, and suggested *abierto* (literally "open" or "clear"). I think this exchange captures both the children's energetic curiosity and Clemencia's encouragement of it. She was never too busy to help with homework, including praise for the usually well-done work, and told me several times that above all she wanted her children to develop their intelligence and to become well educated. Her indulgence of their creative pranks reflects her own playfulness, more in evidence when she is well than during her months of illness.

After four hours of digging potatoes, it was time for the large midday meal, which Alejandro missed because he had to rush off to a meeting in Latacunga. As president of the quesería, it was his responsibility to meet with a representative of the national rural development bank who was coming to Latacunga that afternoon. The quesería production association had requested a loan from this organization. It was the worst time for one of them to miss agricultural work, but Clemencia said Alejandro had no choice. She said the community needs the quesería because no one can afford to borrow from the banks at 58 percent interest, and organizations such as the women's association and the quesería use their profits to provide loans to members for as little as 5 percent interest. "We don't work with the banks," she emphasized.

By the time we had finished discussing the lack of affordable credit for smallholders, we had prepared the potato-rice-and-vegetable soup and ground-corn-and-milk dish the children like. Clemencia ladled out bowls of soup and bowls of hot cereal for the children, accompanied by wheat and corn bread. Milton ate little, although he was served as much as his older sister. Clemencia said the two-year-old has a poor appetite and doesn't sleep well; he is often fretful. He also suffers from recurrent diarrhea. I am not surprised, as I have observed him eating grass as well as handfuls of *capulis*. Clemencia also boiled an egg and made sweetened herbal tea for me, saying I don't eat enough. We all enjoyed lunchtime, sitting cross-legged on the dirt floor in the kitchen as we ate and talked.

After lunch I left, taking the children with me to an interview with their Aunt Marina, another of Alejandro's sisters, who was at home caring for their ailing mother. From Marina's front porch I saw Alejandro return to the harvest and later attend to the animals. Diego and Mauro cut pasture grasses for the animals. Clemencia dug potatoes until nearly dusk.

On my way home I stopped in to ask about the loan negotiations. Alejandro was peeling potatoes and oca for soup while Clemencia pulled carrots and scallions from a small plot near the house. The development bank official had promised to come to Chanchaló to evaluate the potential of the cheese factory. Alejandro seemed to think his time had been well spent but worried that the loan was far from certain.

Clemencia was chilled in spite of the heat generated by the eucalyptus cooking fire she keeps burning (even though she has a gas range). She went into the bedroom to wrap additional layers of crocheted woolen scarves around her chest and waist, making her look decidedly plump although she had lost weight during her illness. Tired and ill, worried about the potato harvest and the fretting two-year-old, she could still express concern for her guest who should have some of these scarves to protect against the cold. "It's so cold now. I'll crochet a wrap for you if you will wear one. They really help to keep you warm. I'm going to do some needlework after supper. Would you rather have a wrap or a tote bag?"

Like many women in Chanchaló, Clemencia has learned new styles of needlecraft from development and religious workers who also help find buyers for traditional and modern crafts. Selling the traditional *shigra* (individually patterned bags of sisal fiber thread, woven by needle) to intermediaries who supply tourist markets earns income in many households. Past efforts to organize small-scale clothing production in Chanchaló left a legacy of expertise in several forms of knitting and crochet, for which Clemencia and others have been seeking new markets. She also makes many garments for her family.

Clemencia's working day would not be over until she had devoted an hour or two to clothing or craft production. Professing that she likes to crochet and knit, especially since she can do these things while resting or watching TV, Clemencia insisted that making a wrap or bag for me would be no trouble at all. She sent me home with a half-dozen eggs and an admonition to eat enough and dress warmly so I wouldn't become ill.

Clemencia regained her health and with it the glowing beauty and playfulness she had been too exhausted to enjoy during the worst of the wet season. I have chosen to describe working days during her illness to illustrate the depth of her determination to manage household production and community service despite her fatigue. These scenes also illustrate the joint commitment of this couple to support community organizations even when the opportunity cost for doing so is high.

## Public Life and Community Leadership

I first met Clemencia in Salcedo outside the post office, where she had gone to mail letters. Clemencia had heard I was looking for a place to live in Chanchaló and asked me to come and live with her. She said she had plenty of room and didn't want me to have to live alone. However, I did not want to live with a family because I wanted a house where I could work undisturbed and control my own diet; I declined Clemencia's kind invitation and soon located a house. In Chanchaló where stray humans often are sheltered, Clemencia's generous offer of hospitality to a stranger is not unique. Her concept of sheltering is, however, remarkably expansive. Clemencia nurtures the entire community.

I was drawn to Clemencia immediately by qualities that have helped make her a respected community leader: her intense vitality is both seriously goal-directed and ebulliently open to the enjoyment she finds in most aspects of her life. Both these qualities and her hard work on behalf of others have led to her election as past president and current vice president of the Women's Production Association and as president of the federated women's associations belonging to the Casa Campesina of Cantón Salcedo.

Clemencia is an effective organizer of social and economic projects. With good humor and her own example of hardworking purpose, she encourages women to contribute labor and other resources to cooperative economic en-

*Members of the Women's Production Association sort potatoes for sale.*

deavors. In order to raise money for their credit fund, the women's association decided to produce and market potatoes. Clemencia provided the land and in exchange received a share of the harvest. According to other association members, this arrangement was not as advantageous to her as if she had sharecropped privately, but she wanted the income-producing project to succeed. Clemencia not only contributed her own labor to this project, she also mobilized Alejandro to work as well.

Clemencia worked hard on the association's guinea-pig project, mixing and carrying adobe bricks on cold wet days when she was ill. She also facilitates activities introduced to the association by the FUNDAGRO nutrition extensionist and other promoters. With an impish twinkle in her eye, she volunteered to help the extensionist demonstrate the use of suspension scales for weighing babies. She teased the group into trying it with her and soon had everyone laughing and enjoying the exercise.

Clemencia will also challenge a promoter if she feels the individual is offering inappropriate technical assistance or otherwise operating from a flawed conception of circumstances in Chanchaló. When a male visitor to the women's association made casual but erroneous statements about the degree of campesino political activism in Cantón Salcedo, during a time when national structural adjustment policies threatening indigenous landholding and rural services had caused unrest, she briskly set him straight. She then posed a series of rapid-fire questions about what was going on in the national capital and offered her opinion of what campesinos should be doing.

While eager to learn from development agencies, Clemencia is also aware of the tremendous gulf between a variety of national and international development agendas and the realities of economic struggle in Chanchaló. When the nutrition extensionist exhorted women to increase vegetable production using free seeds from FUNDAGRO and to use the vegetables in cooking, Clemencia replied that the group needs help with obtaining inputs and information on intercropping and other production techniques as well as seed. She further remarked that growing vegetables and preparing them for cooking takes a great deal of time and some labor-saving hints would be welcome. The nutritionist had been concentrating on the health and beauty benefits of eating vegetables, ideas to which the women were mildly receptive, but had said nothing about production or time constraints. She had been operating under the assumption that women already manage kitchen gardens and that all they would have to do is to add more vegetable crops. In fact, as Clemencia pointed out, many families do grow small amounts of onions, carrots, and herbs near their homes for household consumption, but with limited land, the idea of a kitchen garden is foreign to Chanchaló.

Clemencia has successfully mobilized traditional work and social-welfare motivation while also applying organizational skills and technical information learned from several external sources. In 1992 she was one of three women from Cotopaxi Province who received USAID scholarships to study horticulture and organizational skills for six weeks in the United States.[1] As president of the federated women's associations, she regularly attends organizational and informational meetings in Latacunga, the provincial capital. She also frequents the FUNDAGRO office in Salcedo, seeking information about pesticide use and other production-related information. With some of this information, she has presented talks to the women's association in Chanchaló. She applies some of it to her own agricultural and dairy production.

Although Clemencia dresses in traditional plain woolen skirt, sweater, shawl, and narrow-brimmed dark brown felt hat for everyday life in the country, she also has a small wardrobe of town clothes, many of which she has made. One day Clemencia and I had a date to meet at the FUNDAGRO office in Salcedo before setting off for a doctor's appointment she had asked me to arrange for her. It was the first time I had seen her in town clothes, and it is not an exaggeration to say that I hardly recognized her. Indigenous women braid their longer-than-waist-length hair, but on this occasion she wore her hair cascading over her shoulders. Her working clothes had been replaced with an immaculate white silken blouse, navy polyester trousers, a lacy pale green shawl, and high-heeled loafers worn with sheer stockings. Pictures from her visit to the United States reveal an even greater transformation, as she responded to the Mississippi climate by donning tank tops and cotton slacks and winding her hair on top of her head. She also has a navy suit for formal occasions.

Clemencia's wardrobe choices provide a superficial illustration of her ability to move among contrasting social worlds. Ecuador is a dual society: rural indigenous people and urban mestizos inhabit distinct social and cultural landscapes as well as economic niches. Clemencia meets the urban world dressed in protective coloration, but she has not adopted what she perceives as urban attitudes nor does she aspire to adopt urban lifeways:

When I was in the United States I saw many beautiful things. The hotel we stayed in was beautiful. The farms and flower gardens, too, and many of the houses. People have things we don't have in the country: nice furniture, matching sets of tableware. Like in the cities here. I would like to have those things, but I don't think I could live in the United States. There is so much *egoismo* [self-centeredness, selfishness].

I think that people in your country want those things too much, they are greedy for things. This is very bad for them. They can love things but things cannot love them back. I think many people in the United States are lonely and fearful. Like my sister-in-law who lives in Salcedo and wants only money, more money. She isn't like me.

To me the most important thing is not money but family and community. I don't think families are as strong in the United States as they are here. And collaboration in the community is important, too. We help one another here. If someone needs something, family members will help. The community, the same. If someone is in trouble, people will help. That is why we are brave, not afraid like some people in your country and in the cities of this country.

When I asked members of the women's association why they had elected Clemencia to office, I was told that she is admired because, although a daughter of the wealthiest family in the community, she "likes to work with poor people." Several women described her as *muy seria,* a characterization implying seriousness of purpose, earnestness, and reliability. This description of Clemencia was also offered by her husband.

## Marriage

Alejandro, also an energetic and well-respected community leader, is proud of his wife's strength of character and achievements. He was eager to tell me that she had been elected to the regional post and that she will do a good job although the responsibilities are heavy. His letters continue to re-count the accomplishments of "my Clemencia."

Clemencia and Alejandro's marriage is built upon mutual respect. Alejandro says that he fell in love with Clemencia because she was the sweetest and the most beautiful girl in Chanchaló. He has come to admire her even more as her sweetness has matured into concern for the welfare of others. Among the qualities Alejandro admires are Clemencia's intelligence and determination:

Clemencia is smarter than most people. You know, Sarita, that she's got a lot between her ears. And she works hard. She works too hard—that's the way she was raised. They work all the time in that family, even if they're sick. I can't make her leave work when she feels bad. My Clemencia is *muy decidida* [decided, determined], *muy fuerte* [strong, forceful; *fuerte* is a term that can refer to physical healthiness or hardiness as well as to forceful character].

Theirs is a love story. One morning when she, Marina, and I were listening to rock and roll and enjoying some girl talk, as they sorted potatoes for market, Clemencia told me how they came to be married. Clemencia's wealthy parents did not want her to marry the boy next-door, who had left home for a tour with the Ecuadorean army and who would inherit little land. Alejandro was not considered a stable prospect. Clemencia is very beautiful, in addition to her other fine qualities and economic prospects, and she was highly sought after by the local eligibles. Her parents forbade the marriage, even resorting to physical abuse in an attempt to dissuade her. She would not be dissuaded. In Clemencia's words:

A marriage is no good if it is not based on love. Alejo and I have always loved one an-other, and we were determined to marry. It was terrible. My parents had always treat-ed me well, but they were so desperate to prevent my marriage that they became cruel. They hit me. They boxed my ears. It only made me want to get married sooner. So I did. In the end, they gave the land for our house. Alejo and I have been very happy. He is a good man. Now my parents love him.

I asked Clemencia what she meant by "a good man." She thought a moment before replying:

Alejo loves me and the children very much. He takes care of the children, worries about their education, takes them to the doctor, does anything for the children. He worries when I'm ill. He wants me to be happy. He works hard for us and for the com-munity. He doesn't drink much at all. [Pause . . . Clemencia has been speaking intent-ly, her brows drawn down. Now her face opens into a wide smile, light playing behind her eyes. She lengthens her frame and preens a bit.] And, you know, he is very, very handsome. Women always think their own husbands are handsome, but my husband really is.

On another evening of potato-sorting after a hard day's work, when Alejandro was feeling rested and talkative, both spoke of their wedding day. Alejandro was quizzing me about the strange North American Protestants who, he had heard, perform marriages as well as baptisms in the river. I asked about their marriage, which took place in the large Roman Catholic church in Salcedo, where their favorite priest performed the ceremony. Clemencia said that both her mother and Alejandro's mother served as marriage sponsors. When I asked what marriage sponsors do, she replied with a raised eyebrow and sly look at her husband, "When we fight, they give us advice." Alejandro burst out laughing, caressed his wife's shoulder, and added, "They never stop, the mamas."

## Household Agricultural Production and Division of Labor

Clemencia and Alejandro cooperate economically with her parents to their mutual benefit. Alejandro and Clemencia have been able to buy only about one hectare of land. Alejandro has inherited one hectare from his parents, who gave the same amount to each of their six children. Clemencia's parents own around twenty hectares, and none of their children lives at home to provide labor. Thus the sharecropping arrangement brings land into Clemencia's household and provides income to her parents.[2] Clemencia's parents also own a tractor, which they lucratively rent out. Alejandro drives the tractor for them and receives in exchange an occasional small monetary wage and use of the tractor for household production and for women's group production activities.

Clemencia and Alejandro practice high-technology commercial agriculture. For this they use not only the tractor but also rented threshing equipment and chemical fertilizers and pesticides. Approximately 90 percent of their total income, including the retail value of foods consumed in the household, is derived from the sale of potato, other crops, livestock, and milk. Potato provides the bulk of this income. All income is pooled.

Clemencia is both a full-time farmer and a full decision-making partner in household agricultural production. When I first interviewed Clemencia and Alejandro concerning the division of labor in their household agricultural production, both used the term *igual* ("equal" or "the same") to describe their participation in agricultural labor and management. I did not ask if she participated equally; I asked only (in separate interviews with Clemencia and Alejandro) if each would tell me what men and women do on the farm. I followed general categorical information with questions about male and female participation within particular labor and decision domains. I then asked about their own household production. Clemencia and Alejandro independently provided the following generalizations concerning the gendered division of agricultural labor: (1) they put in equal time; (2) although there are jobs generally performed by one or the other there are no jobs performed exclusively by either; (3) the person most immediately available will do any job that needs doing; (4) there are no crops, animals, or animal products that are the exclusive domains of wife or husband. Clemencia and Alejandro both emphasized that she participates in all phases of agricultural production, from seed selection and soil preparation to the harvesting and processing of products.

There are, however, specific tasks that Clemencia avoids when possible. Milking is one of these. In several Andean farming systems, women and children are primarily responsible for milking cattle (Fernández 1988), and this specialization is evidenced to some degree in Chanchaló. However, Clemencia says that she doesn't like to milk, and therefore Alejandro does it. When Alejandro isn't available, she does the milking. She also doesn't like to spray chemical pesticides and usually doesn't do so, although she applies chemical fertilizers that do not require spraying and participates in decisions concerning the type and amount of pesticide or fertilizer to be applied. She says that pesticide spray makes her respiratory problems worse but that she will pitch in and do a little "fumigating" when she isn't ill and her help is needed. The one task Clemencia never does is market the family's cash crops:

> I don't like to haggle in the marketplace. My mother doesn't do it either. Many women do sell in the marketplace. Some tell their husbands the price they want, and their husbands do the selling. I don't mark the *quintales* [hundred-pound sacks]. Alejo and I decide on the price we think we should get and then he deals with the intermediaries. I never sell potatoes in the market.

Alejandro agreed with Clemencia's assertion that she avoids the tasks she dislikes when he is available to perform them. He says that selling in the marketplace "bothers" her, so he does it. He also says that they generally try to accommodate one another's preferences in terms of agricultural labor domains. When I ask if there are any tasks he hates that she will do for him, he replies that he hates to keep accounts whereas she is adept at it, and that this is one area in which she usually does most of the work.

### Decision-Making: Consultative, Consensual, Egalitarian

Clemencia and Alejandro both maintain that all decisions concerning agricultural production, use of the family's productive resources, and disposition of income are taken jointly. They refine this generalization by delineating certain areas of decision-making for which wife or husband bears greater responsibility but emphasize that the process is consensual. No action will be taken until they have considered the weight of one another's arguments. (I did not participate in economic decision processes with Clemencia and Alejandro. The following discussion is drawn from several individual interviews with them and delineates their perceptions of the way economic decisions are reached and enacted in their household.)

Concerning the general process, Clemencia sets me straight regarding how one should speak of economic decision-making in Chanchaló. In an early interview I ask if women make decisions concerning land use. She replies heatedly: "You ask me if women here in Chanchaló 'make decisions.' The answer is no. Women do not make decisions. Men do not make decisions. Women and men make decisions together. Both participate or there is no decision, there is no action. You should say that women participate, men participate, in making decisions."

At this point in the interview Clemencia's mother, Rosa, a dignified woman of fifty-eight, arrived and seconded Clemencia's evaluation of the decision-making process. In Rosa's words: "*Dos cabezas* [two heads]. In each family there are two heads. You have seen the two names on our deeds. Well. We buy the land together; we work the land together; we manage the land together. It is always both, the wife and the husband, who make decisions."

During several other interviews, Clemencia reported that she and Alejandro both analyze the costs and benefits of agricultural options and express their recommendations regarding varietal choice, type and amount of agrochemical to be used, how much labor they will employ, when to market products and prices they will accept:

Maybe I think we should grow *uvilla* [a potato variety] up high and *garrisco* down lower. We discuss the altitude, the soil, how much labor we will need, the yield, how much fertilizer we will have to use, the price we can get, everything. . . . Or maybe I think we need more fertilizer or that we should buy a different fertilizer that will be better for the crop. Maybe he thinks we don't need to change. Well, we will talk about it. Sometimes we decide to do what I said. Sometimes we do what he said. We always talk about it.

I ask if there are any areas of agricultural decision-making that tend to be the responsibility of one household head, such that one person usually makes the recommendation and the other either ratifies or challenges it: "Well, I don't know. I don't think so. We do the same work, you know. He knows more about some things than I do, but if I want to learn he teaches me and he teaches the boys, too. I learned things he doesn't know about from my parents and in the United States and I taught him. It is good to learn." I ask if Alejandro occasionally relies on her for information he doesn't have, or if she relies on him in this way:

Oh, yes. I have to tell him if we can afford things. He knows how much things cost and he isn't greedy, but I know how much we have and how much we will have to spend on everything. You know he wants a Betamax. I want him to have it if it will make him happy, but we cannot afford it this year. Maybe next year. I want him to have it because he wants me to have things I like. But I have to say no.

I ask if they have arguments about how they will spend their money and if either of them keeps money aside for something he or she wants. She laughs:

No. We worry about how to make it, not how to spend it. Seriously, if I say we can't afford it, he accepts. If he says we can't afford it, I accept. We try to manage it if it's something one of us really wants. Then we will save for it together. We don't keep money aside. I know exactly how much we make, and that's what we have to spend. I probably say "no" more than he does, but we don't fight about it. What do you and your husband fight about?

Alejandro's description of their joint decision process is similar. He reports that they both contribute information and recommendations regarding specific agricultural decisions, and that Clemencia ultimately bears greater responsibility for household financial decisions.

Concerning the decision areas about which Clemencia spoke, Alejandro agrees that she participates equally in decisions concerning land use, and she computes cost-benefit analysis regarding all agricultural inputs. Concerning agrochemicals (a major expenditure in potato production), for example, she will evaluate the efficacy and cost-effectiveness of various chemical fertilizers per crop and environmental conditions. Both prefer to minimize use of expensive chemical pesticides, and to rely on a mix of natural pesticides, pest-resistant varieties, and interplanting and rotation patterns to minimize the need for agrochemicals. Alejandro is particularly knowledgeable concerning biological pesticides, while Clemencia has learned a great deal about chemical pesticides during her course in the United States. They will discuss the advantages and disadvantages of any chemical input purchase, and only when they have agreed is the decision final. Alejandro will then make the purchases.

Clemencia is the keeper of the family budget and is thus prepared to assess the expenditure required to supply sufficient labor and additional inputs. Concerning land use, they decide together how much, when, and what to plant. No action will be taken until they have reached consensus. Alejandro sums up the process:

She tells me what she thinks we should do about what to plant and all the rest of it. She has her ideas about everything, and she knows a lot about the soil and the crops and what to do about problems like this terrible fungus and the worms that are in the potatoes now. She is a good farmer. No, I do not make decisions without her. Never.

I ask if she ever makes decisions without him. He replies: "No. Always to-gether." I ask if either of them is more responsible for any particular decision domains. He replies: "Sure. She decides about the food and she knows what she needs for the kitchen. And she knows more about savings. She is always thinking about what we will need then, in the future. And what we will have. We both think about the children, of course, but she can see them in the future." I ask him if they ever disagree about agricultural matters or how to spend their money. "We start out disagreeing sometimes. But we end up agreeing. I don't know how to explain it. About the money, I have to listen to her because she keeps it. No, I don't mean that she keeps it in the house, I mean that she keeps it in her head. Do you understand?" I reply that I think I understand, but will he correct me if I do not? I then summarize his statements by saying that they both participate in all economic decisions, and that she has more responsibility for decisions about food consumption and financial planning and budgeting. Alejandro agrees with this summary. When I ask him if he has more responsibility for any particular decisions, he replies:

About the crops, no. About the money, no. About the children, yes. Clemencia won't punish them sometimes when they need it, so I have to do it. Her parents punished her and she doesn't want to do the same with our children. She doesn't try to prevent me from punishing them, she just doesn't do it herself. Or maybe she does it if I'm not home, but if I'm here I have to do it. It's all right. I don't mind doing it so much, but she hates to.

Several recurring motifs in these and other statements indicate that economic decision-making is gender-egalitarian in this household. First, both female and male household heads assert that both partners participate fully in the decision process and that neither partner always holds sway. In their views, a balance of authority is maintained.

Second, neither household head controls more valuable resources than the other. Both have their say regarding use of the land—their most valuable ma-terial resource—and both direct the ultimate use of income. Although Clemencia has more direct responsibility for managing the household budget and must be more vigilant concerning expenditure, Alejandro has equal input in deciding the ultimate disposition of funds. The division of labor, which I observed, bears out their generalizations that there are no labor domains from which either is excluded and Clemencia's statement that she is able to avoid disliked tasks when Alejandro is at home to perform them. Both household heads control their own labor to the same degree.

Third, both Clemencia and Alejandro acknowledge respect for the other's expertise, which forms the informational base on which decisions partly depend. Within this consensual and egalitarian pattern there is a moderate amount of short-term conflict. Two household heads, both with decision authority and assertive personalities, are involved in virtually every economic decision. Both Clemencia and Alejandro emphasize the consensual result of the resolution process and appear to be satisfied with their amount of input into the process.

Moreover, Clemencia and Alejandro both maintain that they have worked out a mutual accommodation of one another's major productive and reproductive goals. They have agreed to sacrifice in order to educate their children, a priority of Clemencia's. They also have agreed to contribute considerable time and material resources to the activities of the women's association and the quesería, of which Alejandro is president. Community service was an early priority of Alejandro's that he has successfully encouraged Clemencia to share during their years of marriage. They have agreed they do not want more children and have invested in family planning services. This was a priority of Clemencia's. She described her pregnancies as becoming increasingly difficult and debilitating. At my suggestion, Alejandro accompanied her to the medical consultation she had asked me to arrange for her concerning contraceptive options. He agreed to abide by her decision concerning choice of method.

The bases for admission to the economic decision-making process in this household include shared and mutually valued expertise and labor, as well as complementary fields of vision or personality traits. Clemencia is future-oriented in a practical way, which serves the household well in financial management; Alejandro manages to discipline the children and deal with market intermediaries, possessing a temperamental edge that Clemencia lacks but values. I find no indication in their statements that intrahousehold power or authority is conceived of as a limited good, so that the strength of one partner implies weakness in the other, or that acquiescence within any single decision process implies subordination.

In many Andean farming systems, particular labor domains and related expertise are perceived by both women and men as belonging to one gender, such as animal husbandry (Fernández 1988; Harris 1978). Consequently, egalitarian decision processes are believed by analysts to rest on the need of the household to benefit from both female and male expertise. However, in this household no one owns special knowledge. Clemencia has greater fluency with financial matters, while Alejandro is more knowledgeable regarding integrated pest management; neither of them owns all expertise in the relevant decision domain. Rather than individually held, complementary domains of expertise and labor, these are shared. Neither partner buys in to the decision process via exclusive control of labor or knowledge domains.

Although neither partner mentioned ownership of resources as a factor in securing access to decision processes, a connection between ownership and management was suggested by the parallel structure and content of Rosa's statement "we buy the land together, we work the land together, we manage the land together." Perhaps the consciousness that both partners have provided land—as well as the equally valued labor that has enabled them to buy additional land—forms a base for the economic decision process. Perhaps, as Rosa is a more acquisitive and materially motivated woman than Clemencia, the conscious association between ownership and management is entirely the mother's. Certainly I saw no indication that either Clemencia or Alejandro considers that one has to buy one's way into intrahousehold economic decision processes via ownership of the means of production. I do consider it important that egalitarian decision processes take place in a household where both wife and husband access or own land independently and also have bought land together.

The decisions taken by Clemencia and Alejandro reflect concern for one another's well-being and tolerance for one another's desires. The obvious mutual affection revealed in glances, caresses, and tone of voice may also be a factor in the mutuality of decision processes in this household. Certainly mutual respect is a factor. Emotional factors need not enter into every analysis of intrahousehold decision processes—it is entirely possible for two people who are bored with or who even dislike each other to maintain equitable or otherwise mutually satisfying economic relations. In the case of Clemencia and Alejandro, I think the affective quality of the union contributes to the overall balance they have achieved.

The description of decision processes provided by Clemencia and Alejandro may be ideologically flavored. During interviewing, the more general implication that all decisions are the result of equal participation becomes refined to show that one partner may hold greater sway in a particular decision domain such as household expenditure or child discipline. It may be that the more general statements simply reflect overall equality in access to the decision process and mutual satisfaction with the results of the process. But it is also true that both partners chose to emphasize the inclusiveness of economic processes rather than the differences in individual participation that emerged in subsequent questioning. The amount of conflict or asymmetry in decision processes may have been underrepresented by Clemencia and Alejandro. Certainly the process described lies within the ideal pattern defined by Clemencia and Rosa: it is fitting that both partners make decisions together; it is not fitting that either partner make decisions alone. Observed egalitarian patterns in labor and access to resources lead me to conclude that, within this household, decision processes are symmetrical in practice as well as in perception or ideology.

## Goals for the Future: Sustainable Agriculture

Both Clemencia and Alejandro are forward-thinking, progressive farmers who independently seek technical information and consider, but do not necessarily adopt, all innovations presented to them. They are worried because the only information available in the community concerning soil conservation and the health and environmental costs of agrochemical use comes from the FUNDAGRO dairy commodity project, the Peace Corps, and chemical companies. In their opinion, this outreach is not sufficient to help farmers adopt sustainable practices.[3] The problem is serious because nonsustainable practices have contributed to severe soil erosion. Agrochemicals are used intensively by many farmers.

Clemencia reports that, in contrast to the dearth of information provided by development workers, agrochemical companies regularly visit Chanchaló. They use the local media—radio spots and loudspeakers blaring from atop jeeps—to inundate the countryside with information and invitations to attend their promotional meetings. At these meetings, company agronomists inform their audiences about the efficacy of various products against late blight, a fungus that threatens the potato crop and that was particularly virulent during the rainy season of 1993. They recommend weekly treatments (a very high level of usage). Although they do sometimes discuss safety measures for those applying chemicals, they never mention health problems caused by pesticide contamination of water supplies and food crops. They do not discuss making their products part of an integrated-pest-management approach.

Clemencia and Alejandro are concerned about what they consider to be the misuse of chemical pesticides in Chanchaló. Clemencia learned about the dangers of some of the pesticides used in Chanchaló during her USAID-sponsored course in the United States. These pesticides have been restricted in the United States, and so they were not used by her horticulture teachers.[4] She says the products used in the course aren't for sale in Salcedo. Alejandro says that most Chanchaló farmers buy as much pesticide as they can afford, and many use more than they need because they lack reliable information concerning optimal usage and integrating chemical pesticides into a pest-management strategy that includes intercropping, crop rotation, and biological pesticides. Many of the farmers who have come to rely on chemical pesticides can no longer name biological pesticides traditionally considered reliable.

Clemencia and Alejandro have availed themselves of literature concerning integrated pest management in the FUNDAGRO field office in Salcedo. Clemencia also presented a lecture on soil conservation to the women's association. She was not able to address fully the issue of agrochemical selection, however, as the products she would prefer are not available in Salcedo.

In Clemencia's opinion, women might be more receptive to alternative pest-management strategies than men, because chemical pesticides are expensive and it is women who must manage the production budget. However, she says that women, like men, have been convinced by the chemical companies that they need to apply heavy dosages of agrochemicals, and FUNDAGRO has not offered alternative information to the women's association:

You say that FUNDAGRO says they will talk to us about chemicals if we ask them to. I believe that. But it is a problem. The women have not given any thought to asking about pesticides because they don't know about the problems. How could they know? I tell them, but I am only one person. I ask FUNDAGRO, but I am only one person. Maybe it will happen, but it will take a long time.

Besides, they talk to us about many other things we didn't ask for. You have visited the women's association. What did you see? [I answer that I saw presentations concerning child-growth monitoring and kitchen vegetable gardens, among others.] Well, we didn't ask for that: not for weighing babies or planting vegetables. We were pleased to learn, but we didn't have to ask to learn about those things.

### Summary: Equal Partnership Between Community Leaders

Clemencia is a strong community leader whose commitment to sustainable agriculture and community development can serve Chanchaló well. By nature a serious and determined woman, she was influenced by her husband to devote much of her energy to community affairs. Alejandro supports her community work by increasing his own workload in household productive and reproductive labor while she performs public responsibilities. She supports his community activities in the same manner. Clemencia and Alejandro share agricultural labor and decision-making in an egalitarian manner. They depend on one another's expertise, goodwill, and sense of responsibility. Their consensual management has been materially successful, and both seem satisfied with an interdependent style. We shall now turn to a very different kind of household, in which mutuality in labor and decision processes is neither expressed as an ideal nor observed in practice, the household of Clemencia's elder first cousin and political rival, Valentina.

## Valentina and Esteban

Valentina is forty-seven and has been married for thirty years to Esteban. They have five children, ranging in age from twenty-eight to nine. The eldest,

José, lives next door to Valentina with his wife Leonor and two daughters. Valentina's house is not as large, as well built, or as well equipped as Clemencia's; it contains an original homestead of adobe and thatch as well as a small cement-block and tile addition. Valentina, however, is considered wealthier than Clemencia by most informants because she has more land. Valentina has received her inheritance from her parents: nearly three hectares, the same as each of her siblings. She has also bought land together with her husband: five hectares, some in the high *páramo* and some surrounding the house at around 2,950 meters. Her husband has not inherited any land.

Valentina has never attended school and does not read or write. She is not a great believer in the value of investing in secondary education. Her eldest son is doing well enough to buy a truck without benefit of education beyond the sixth grade. Her children become full-time farmers at the age of twelve.

## Public Leadership

When I met Valentina on my first visit to Chanchaló, I had no idea of her importance in the community. Crossing the small earthen plaza I found a woman sitting on the stoop outside the community center, bent over some needlework. She lifted her face, revealing large strong features and a compelling gaze. She offered her hand in a firm handshake and, in a forthright, businesslike, and friendly manner welcomed the unexpected gringa to her community: "¡Compañera! ¿Cómo estás?"

Valentina then quizzed me politely regarding my intentions in Chanchaló, expressed satisfaction with my answers, and invited me to attend the meeting of the women's association due to begin shortly. She rose slowly and drew herself up to her full height of about five feet three inches, several inches taller than other adult women in Chanchaló. A quietly imposing figure, she led the way into the community center. I did not need a formal introduction to know that Valentina is a powerful woman.

Like Clemencia, Valentina has an important public role in the community. She is the current president of the women's association, and a gifted group leader and politician. Like Clemencia, Valentina uses a combination of humor and serious purpose to foster an atmosphere of goodwill for public projects. Unlike Clemencia, Valentina wields considerable public authority and enjoys it. Whereas Clemencia is likely to lead by example, Valentina is more likely to lead by instruction and exhortation. Although Valentina does pitch in and join the work in women's association *minga*s, she will also boss an activity full-time while everyone else works. She has threatened to use her considerable influence in the community to block development efforts or individuals she considers to be harmful. Valentina wanted very badly to be reelected president of the women's association and was demonstrably relieved when the election had the desired effect.

Several informants agreed that Valentina is an effective leader. The phrase most often used to describe her, *Valentina tiene mucho carácter*, means that she is a woman of strong character. Several members of the women's association expressed admiration for Valentina's ability to influence others, stating, "Valentina has a lot of influence," and "she can make people do what she wants." When I asked for an explanation of these phrases, I was given a catalogue of people who, following meetings with Valentina, had agreed to provide or help secure resources for the association. This list included the director of dairy projects for FUNDAGRO, representatives from Roman Catholic lending institutions, the president of the Casa Campesina, a church worker serving as market intermediary for local handcrafts, and two priests—and these were only the most recent conquests. The FUNDAGRO program director and one of the lending-institution representatives agreed with the women's assessment of Valentina's persuasiveness. I was not able to ascertain from the other individuals their impressions of the extent of Valentina's influence over their favorable decisions. The members of the women's association, however, were convinced that she had brought about their cooperation.

I have some personal experience of Valentina's ability to "get what she wants" in striking deals advantageous to the women's association. When I went to interview or observe Valentina at her farm, I always ended up promising to contribute labor, material resources, or networking assistance to the women's association. Valentina never asked for anything for herself; but she always asked for something, and she has an uncanny ability to gauge just how much she might be able to raise. For example, when I did not flinch at the idea of providing part of the money needed to purchase cement for the building to house the women's association's guinea pigs, she told me that $40 would provide one-fourth of the cement. I gave the association $50 for this purchase, only to learn later that my contribution provided a good deal more than one-fourth of the flooring. She had correctly figured me for a collaborator who prefers to contribute to, rather than provide sole support for, any project. If I had known the flooring could be completed for, say, $100, I would have donated only $25–$30.

Valentina's strong character and political acumen have been recognized by campesino leaders throughout Cantón Salcedo. She invited me to attend the biannual election of the president of the regional Casa Campesina by the organization's executive council. During debate about the legitimacy of current practice, which limits voting rights in presidential elections to the sixteen comuna presidents, several members of the executive council recommended that women's groups be given voting rights because "women like Valentina C—— should be allowed to vote." I do not know how much Valentina's reputation for effective leadership influenced the council's decision, but it was decided that future elections should be opened to women's group officers, following an interval of two years to allow women in all sixteen affiliated communities to organize associations if they choose to do so.

Valentina interacts with the world beyond Chanchaló and Cantón Salcedo, but on a more limited basis than Clemencia. Like Clemencia, she displays no hesitation in dealing with professional people in urban settings. The forthright manner she used with me on my first day in her community serves also for her dealings with officials from Ecuadorean national-level institutions. Valentina does not change her dress when she goes to town or to the provincial capital for meetings. She dresses her best for local fiestas and frets that she is not prepared to have her picture taken when I arrive with camera for an interview, but she does not adjust her clothing to interact with city people.

Although Valentina and I did not become close friends, she was very kind to me, invited me for visits frequently, and always gave me presents of food to take home. We laughed a lot together, and she usually seemed glad to see me. But I think she was always aware of what she considered my affiliation with FUNDAGRO, and of her position as president of a production association that cooperated with FUNDAGRO in many activities. She often invited me to visit when a women's association activity would be underway at her house, where the guinea-pig project was located. She was intent that I record correctly the extent of collaboration evidenced by women working on this and other projects. On one occasion, she checked my notes to make sure I had recorded her statement regarding the number of women working on a project, including women no longer in the field, as well as my own observation of the number in the field. During my months of research, she continued to ask about the uses I would make of my research.

## Historical Context

Valentina remembers life on the hacienda before the people of Chanchaló gained the freedom to choose their work. The following interview took place one Sunday afternoon when she had returned from market day in Salcedo and was weaving a *shigra*, sitting in the sunshine in front of her house. Although Valentina is ordinarily full of earthy humor and loves to tease, during this interview she seemed self-consciously aware of her position as a public leader and spokesperson. And the topic is not one that lends itself to humor. She spoke gravely and with passion concerning the past servitude of her family and community.

As a child, Valentina cared for animals and helped with agricultural work on Hacienda Chanchaló. She tells, also, of working in the house of a larger estate near Latacunga called Tiobamba during the month-long labor rotation that Chanchaleños performed according to an agreement between Chanchaló's owner and the owner of Tiobamba.

We had to work from the time we were children. Everyone had to perform service to the hacienda. My mother milked and sometimes worked in the fields, the same as the men. Sometimes we worked in the house. At Tiobamba I washed dishes, washed clothes, mopped the floors. I did some cooking, mostly I prepared hens for cooking. . . . At Chanchaló I pastured animals: lambs, pigs, cows, horses. And I played. I also worked in the fields, in agriculture.

I asked if the people of Chanchaló were free to refuse to work on the haciendas:

We had to work for Sr. R.C. You know there was no land here except his land. He paid us a little and allowed us to cultivate small plots of land for ourselves. We were free to refuse the work at Tiobamba. But we always did it because we were paid more for that. And you must understand that we were not free to refuse to work for R.C.

Then we went on strike, and after that [there was] no more huasipungo. Before the strike, my mother and father had saved some money. Before I married, my parents were able to buy a piece of land across the *quebrada* [small ravine] in Chanchalito. But there wasn't any land for us in Chanchaló.

I asked how it is that they went on strike if they were not free to refuse to work. Valentina became more emphatic as she discussed the hacendado's refusal to grant land and political freedom to the people whose labor had made him rich.

It was *because* we were not free that we went on strike. The government said the hacendados must hand over the huasipungos to the campesinos. R.C. would not do this. We told him we wanted to have an independent community with a charter. He said no. We knew he couldn't operate the hacienda without us, so we went on strike. Then he agreed to let us have a little land, but only if we would continue to work for him. In truth we were not yet free. And that was very little land. We were not free until he left and then the families bought the land from his children.

I asked how R.C. was able to deny campesinos the right to establish an independent community.

Well, there was no community before then [1968]. The community began when the hacendado left. Before, we had no independent charter, no human rights. There were no *minga*s [communal work parties that build and maintain public facilities and infrastructure]. All of the work was for the hacienda. The hacendado had everything—all of the land and all of the authority. The government made a law that said we could have a community, but in Chanchaló, the hacendado was the law.

## The Value of Independence

As the interview continued, we watched Valentina's son plow a field adjoining her house. I asked if women's work had changed much since the days of the hacienda.

Work isn't as hard now. We work with animals and in the fields, the same as on the hacienda. And we work all the time, the same as on the hacienda. But it is different, too. Now we decide what to do. We work with our own families in our own fields. If I want my son to plow a field, I can decide when to do it. If I want to do easy work or work for the community I can do it: I can work in the house, wash clothes, or cook for a fiesta if I want to. I can say. We still have to work all the time, you know that. You know the work I do.

But no one can tell us what to do or how to do it. Maybe you cannot understand that. You work with FUNDAGRO. You know they are always telling us how to cure the animals or some other thing. Good. It is good to learn. But here we do not all do livestock production or agriculture in the same way. Each person has his or her own way. It was different on the hacienda.

Clearly independence is highly valued by Valentina. She remembers the burden of dependence on an owner who not only controlled her surplus and her political freedom, but also the manner and rhythms of her work. She is not alone in placing a high value on the freedom to pursue idiosyncratic agricultural practices. In my efforts to learn how people think about soil conservation, for example, I often asked why some people practice contour plowing and others don't. I hoped to elicit an explanation of the benefits perceived for both techniques. I expected that I might be told, as well, that noncontour plowing is "just the way we do it." However, the most frequent response I received was that individuals practice varying methods of soil preparation because "No one tells us how we have to do it. We can decide."

Valentina is alone in my sample, however, in the degree of independence she claims for herself in matters of economic decision-making within the household. Both privately and publicly Valentina asserts her leadership. If Clemencia is her own boss in cooperation with her husband, Valentina wants to be top boss. It is a tribute to her political skill that she has been able to align friends, colleagues, and husband in this effort.

## The Affectionate Matriarch

Within her household, as well as in the community, Valentina is more authoritarian than Clemencia. Whereas Clemencia will stop work to convulse in laughter at the antics of her children, Valentina may smile indulgently at her adored granddaughter's misbehavior but will also issue orders to her adult male children in a manner that brooks no insubordination. Clemencia's children are young, the oldest near the age of Valentina's granddaughter, but different management styles are also indicated. Clemencia consults with her husband on all economic decisions, and she serves as a sort of background consultant for her children. Clemencia's brood know where they can find their mother if she is needed, but she allows them considerable freedom to roam the neighborhood. Valentina is a more authoritarian, if affectionate, presence for even her younger children.

Valentina does not order her husband around (not in my presence, at least). However, her economic consultations often seem pro forma. In their thirty years together, Valentina and Esteban have developed a pattern in which she suggests a course of action, rather than proposing one and expecting his input in return. She will then proceed to enact her suggestion, often with his participation. Not all decisions are taken in this way, but those involving household labor, marketing of agricultural products and animals, and control of household income are the outcome of Valentina's direction or greater influence.

The vignette in chapter 1 featuring Valentina in the potato market is a case in point. Given that much of the literature concerning women's roles in Andean farming systems focuses on semiproletarianized households in which women control marginally productive subsistence agriculture while their husbands earn the bulk of household income working off-farm, it would be reasonable to expect that Valentina's solo marketing reflects this general division of labor and resources. In fact, Valentina went to the market alone, not because her husband was unavailable or because she was selling marginal or individually owned produce. According to both Valentina and her husband, she went alone because she is the better bargainer in the family.

On that particular market day, I arrived at Valentina's house after lunch, just as she was preparing to hitch a ride to town with her potatoes. She told Esteban that he should be able to finish spraying the lower potato field before she returned from town and that she would be back in time to supervise the children working in another field. She suggested that after spraying he move on to collect the cattle and send the oldest boy along to help her in the field next to the house.

Tagging along with Valentina in the marketplace, I asked why she was selling potatoes alone without Esteban and if the crop belongs to her. She replied patiently:

The crop belongs to the family. I say these are my potatoes because I am the one selling them. But the money is for the family. It doesn't matter who sells the potatoes or

*Buying and selling potatoes: the buyer (right) presses cash, but the hard-bargaining Chanchaleña (center) holds out for a better deal.*

whose field they come from. All of the money from all of the crops is for the family. It's the same with everybody.

Now, why do you ask about Esteban? I sell the potatoes because I get a better price. And why should two people do together what one can do alone? Esteban is spraying today.

Now I am going to talk to some people about buying my potatoes. You can watch, but don't say anything.

Valentina and Esteban often work separately. Whereas Clemencia and Alejandro prefer to work together in the same field when possible, Valentina and Esteban are more independent. During most of my observational visits that took place during agricultural working hours, Valentina worked in one field with some of the children while Esteban worked in another field with other children. This pattern may reflect Valentina's larger child labor pool. The family may simply be able to cover a larger territory than Clemencia and Alejandro can manage, even with hired help. But Valentina also remarked once that she didn't think much of all that togetherness over at Clemencia's:

I don't have to work all the time with my husband like Clemencia. Señora Clemencia does everything together with her husband. I like to be independent of my husband. Well, not like you. It must be terrible to be alone for so long, like you. During the day, I like to be independent. At night I want to sleep with my husband and be warm.

Valentina's marriage appears to be a love match. I did not discuss the affective quality of their marriage with Valentina or Esteban. However, on more than one occasion I observed Valentina flirting with her husband while firmly holding the floor during family discussions. She makes labor assignments to the entire family, without pausing for his input, then turns to glance coquettishly over her shoulder at him as she walks out the door. She interrupts him and even answers questions directly addressed to him, while at the same time gazing warmly into his eyes. Perhaps flirting simply helps Valentina get her own way; whether for political or romantic reasons, she seems to enjoy it. During a visit in her kitchen, she told me she was cooking a *menestra* (a mixture of beans and peas flavored with garlic and spices) because it is his favorite dish and that is why she grows so many types of beans. Laughingly, she added, "Not only because they bring a good price."

Esteban does not exhibit visible signs of anger or exasperation while Valentina is "organizing" household labor or holding other discussions without his equal input. He appears to be satisfied with the mixture of flirtation and bossiness Valentina deals out, smiling broadly in response to her coquettishness and going about the business she has organized for the day. He expressed considerable satisfaction with the *menestra*.

Moreover, Esteban struck me as an extraordinarily contented and gentle man. Most of the conversations I had with him apart from Valentina were held walking along the road at the end of the day's work, as he drove cattle home from pasturage, a forty-five-minute walk. When I would ask him what he intended to do the next day, the invariable lighthearted reply was "I don't know. Whatever Valentina says. I don't worry about that."

The household's long-range social and financial goals also reflect Valentina's priorities. During one of our conversations on the road home, Esteban talked about his younger children's schooling. I had asked his opinion of the local elementary school. He said his children had learned to read and write well, and that all but one of them had enjoyed school. He explained that the decision to put the children to work after they had completed elementary school was taken jointly, but that his personal view was overridden by Valentina, whose plan was also accepted by the children.

I thought maybe we should send Edgar and Pati to high school in Salcedo. We couldn't afford to send José [now twenty-eight], but we could have managed with Edgar [now sixteen] and Pati [fourteen]. They are very intelligent. When I was younger I worked on the coast to make money so we could buy land. I know how it is in the cities, too. People with education make much more money than people like us who have little. I thought: the children will not inherit much land and maybe they will need to work in the city.

But my wife, no. She said, "Look how well José is doing. He is a good farmer and makes money with his truck. He didn't need to go to high school. The others don't need to go to high school. And we need them to work on the land." Well, the children were content to stay here and work on the land.

You see, it was more important to Valentina than it was to me. It was so important to Valentina.

I asked Esteban if there were anything that is "so important" to him. He replied, with twinkling eyes and a broad grin, "Well, what makes her happy also makes me happy." The gently ironic tone mixed with the smile in Esteban's voice reminded me of a sweatshirt slogan I had seen in the United States: "If Mama ain't happy ain't nobody happy." Perhaps Esteban pays a price for peace in his household. Perhaps he simply wants to please Valentina, as she seems to want to please him in some matters. Certainly there was not a trace of bitterness in his voice.

Esteban is very popular among the men and women of Chanchaló. Known for his bonhomie rather than for his public leadership, he is always welcomed by everyone. Although several of my friends remarked that Valentina is likely to call the shots in her household, no one ever commented or even implied that her exercise of power renders Esteban weak or unmanly. Indeed, authority within the household, together with the respect it implies, does not appear to be conceived of as a limited good in Chanchaló. Just as Clemencia's household has room for two strong-willed decision-makers, Valentina's greater authority does not diminish her husband's stature in the community.[5]

## Management of Household Income Streams

Valentina's family practice commercial agriculture on their eight hectares. They use animal traction and hand tools rather than renting agricultural machinery. They do apply agrochemical inputs liberally. Potatoes are harvested throughout the year; Valentina sells potatoes regularly in fairly small increments, as well as maize, beans, and melloco. Maize can be sold incrementally, as well. Although maize requires nearly a year to ripen fully, it can be sold at six months' maturation. Maize can also be kept in fully ripened, dried form until supplies are low and prices rise. Valentina's family produces a surplus of maize and can thus market small quantities advantageously throughout the year. They do not sell barley, at least during the current cropping cycle. Barley provides a highly valued source of calories in Valentina's household, both for humans and for animals. Current yields are low, and in Valentina's opinion the price for barley is not conducive to production for sale.

Like many Andean female household heads, Valentina decides how much of the harvests the family should keep and how much they should sell (Bourque and Warren 1981; Allen 1988). She decides when to sell crops such as maize that can be kept until supply is low and the price becomes most advantageous. Perhaps because of her famous ability to negotiate in a variety of markets, Esteban says this aspect of economic decision-making is entirely up to Valentina as well as decisions about household consumption of crops.

Valentina taught me a good deal about the confluence of income streams in her household. As crops are sold throughout the year, income from each crop blends into a single continuous stream. Valentina states that in her household—and generally in the community—the income from all household production is pooled in a household fund used for meeting daily expenses and for investment in savings accounts. Valentina does not bank the household subsistence fund but disburses it from a closely guarded kitty.

Valentina maintains that she does not divert any of this stream into a separate stash aside from the household's earnings, nor does Esteban. She says that by the time they pay for daily living expenses, production expenses, and put a bit aside for the future, there is no money left over for her to keep for herself. When I ask if she keeps any separate, not to spend on herself but rather to hold for emergencies, she says no. Esteban is not so sure: "My wife manages the money. I don't. She tells me how much we have and what we should spend. Sometimes she comes up with some more. I don't know where she gets it."

I did not pursue this line of questioning. The salient fact for me is that in both Clemencia's and Valentina's households, the female household head has an equal say in decisions concerning major expenditures and savings goals, as well as daily living expenses. Valentina and Clemencia do not merely administer household finances but have an equal voice in determining the use of funds.

### Women's Work: Egalitarian Ideology

Despite her apparently more dominant role in economic decision-making and the complementarity of independent task assignments she devises for her own household, Valentina used the term *igual* to describe the roles of women and men in household agriculture. Concerning the division of labor, she explained that there are absolutely no tasks that women are incapable of performing, even plowing with draft animals, a task reserved for men in many Andean communities (Bourque and Warren 1981; Stolen 1985). This conversation took place during a women's association *minga*. Several women and a few men were preparing land donated by Valentina and planting alfalfa, which would feed the population of the association's planned guinea-pig project. I joined the women, who turned the soil using the *azadón*, a fairly short-handled hoe. In another part of the field, three men drove oxen and guided a plow. When the field had been prepared, Valentina sowed the seed. The men then covered the furrows by dragging a thatch of small tree branches over them. I turned down their invitation to provide ballast by riding on this prickly thatch.

I asked Valentina why only men plowed this field. She replied that Marianita B—— had "volunteered" the labor of her husband, son, and brother for the purpose of plowing the field. "Why should we take on that job when we have three men to do it for us?" she demanded. Valentina insisted, also, that women do plow even when male labor is available. She did not offer a rationale for this behavior, seemingly at odds with the one just expressed for taking advantage of available male labor.

Several women and men who were working at the *minga* joined the conversation and agreed with Valentina. According to all of those present, no agricultural tasks or domains are the exclusive responsibility of women or men in Chanchaló. Everyone insisted that women do plow. When I asked about applying agrochemicals—a labor domain reportedly avoided by or closed to women elsewhere in Ecuador (Blumberg and Colyer 1990)—the answer was that women apply all types of chemicals, "the same as men." There are very few trees left in Chanchaló, but I asked about clearing land. The group insisted that women do this, as well. Later I observed a group of women felling tall eucalyptus trees together with men. I also observed many women spraying pesticides.

Because I never saw a woman plowing, I interpret Chanchaleños' insistence that women do plow to mean that women's plowing would not be considered inappropriate behavior, that it is both conceivable and possible that women could plow. It is possible that some women do so, at least on occasion. However, I must conclude that land preparation is the one phase of agricultural production in which there are complementary female and male tasks such that in the overwhelming majority of households, women never plow but usually sow.

Valentina herself puts in full agricultural days, but some of her time is spent supervising the labor of her family. Like Clemencia, Valentina was ill during the wet season and continued to work in spite of her illness, which was not as severe or as protracted as Clemencia's. However, she spent more time doing housework, light agricultural labor such as picking beans, and taking rest breaks while she supervised her children's work than did Clemencia. She also supervises, in addition to working in the field, when she is not ill. Valentina does not milk or pasture animals, assigning those tasks to her children. The children also assist her in most domestic duties, although Esteban cleans the house and yard regularly. Both male and female children perform housework and look after Valentina's grandchildren.

In Valentina's household, as in Clemencia's, both personal preference and individual abilities, as well as the amount of labor available, influence the division of labor. Clemencia does not market products whereas Valentina does, for example. Clemencia abhors haggling whereas Valentina relishes it. Valentina is also good at it, whereas Clemencia puts her confidence in Alejandro's ability to get a good price. Alejandro does not haggle much, operating on his stated assumption that "all of the buyers offer the same thing so it doesn't matter who buys the crop." After following Valentina around the market, I would not agree with Alejandro's view, but Clemencia is satisfied that Alejandro does well and that her input is not needed. When these two households are considered together, domains of women's labor and decision-making are expanded to include marketing.

In neither household do women and men share all tasks. On the other hand, in neither household is anyone excluded from participation in a domain of labor or decision-making because of gendered exclusivity in ownership of resources, including knowledge, or because of beliefs that only one gender is physically or emotionally able to perform. Perhaps this lack of exclusion is reflected in statements that men and women do "the same" work. Considering the fluidity in the division of labor observed in Clemencia's household, and the complementarity based upon ability rather than individual ownership observed in both households, I find this a justifiable interpretation. I suggest, also, that statements about the "equal" work of men and women reflect an egalitarian valuation of women's and men's labor and abilities, together with a fluid gendered division of labor, rather than the absence of labor complementarity within a given household.

### Experience with Development Organizations

Valentina wants to learn about new agricultural techniques and is willing to try even high-risk innovations if the potential return is sufficient. Although the women's association in Chanchaló is production-oriented, none of the institutions that regularly supply the group with information and assistance have offered production-oriented help. From FUNDAGRO and the Roman Catholic diocese in Latacunga, Valentina has learned about health, nutrition, craft production, and organizational skills—information considered useful by national-level organizations that expect rural women to be homemakers.

She has not been offered information concerning livestock production. Thus, when a Peace Corps volunteer discussed with her the advantages of castrating male piglets, Valentina had no previous knowledge of the procedure. Against the advice of the volunteer, a newcomer whose expertise had yet to be tested in the community, Valentina decided to have a nearly adult hog castrated. When the pig died in shock, Valentina concluded that both the procedure and the volunteer were useless. She was so angry at the loss of her investment that she threatened to use her social influence against the hapless volunteer. But Valentina is, in her own way, community-minded. She calmed down and did not interfere with the volunteer's work. In addition to the animal, what had been lost was Valentina's personal access to potentially productive innovation. Had the extension efforts of FUNDAGRO in livestock management, which have been offered to the community for five years, been targeted to women, Valentina might have had the knowledge she needed to evaluate the volunteer's recommendation.

Although Valentina may be less likely to consult her husband in matters of economic decision-making than Clemencia, Valentina's problem is not that her husband receives knowledge he does not share with her. Rather, her husband does not participate in FUNDAGRO activities. In many households in Chanchaló, either wife or husband participates in local production associations, but not both. Thus failure to target all producers regardless of gender has excluded half the population served by FUNDAGRO from production-oriented assistance. The assumption by many development professionals that development benefits extended to men will be disseminated intact to their wives is not warranted. Studies of information transmission have demonstrated that women and men often glean different information from a single source (see discussion in Mehra 1993). In Chanchaló, even husbands and wives who share all received knowledge will not have the benefit of women's cost-benefit analysis based upon their own direct access to information sources.

## Summary: A Land-Rich and Influential Matriarch

Valentina has used her considerable social talents to advance the women's association's social and economic goals and to make economic deals advantageous to her own household. She has used her political talent to build individual influence in her community and beyond. She has applied her own labor and that of her family to the acquisition of land. Valentina's husband acquiesces in her assumption of greater economic authority within the household. Where Clemencia and Alejandro are evenly balanced in terms of force of personality, Valentina and Esteban have forged a successful partnership with asymmetrically powerful but complementary personalities: hers more intense and overtly bossy, his more complacent. Both Valentina and her husband seem satisfied with her relatively independent management style. This pattern has proved materially successful for Valentina and her family; they have accumulated a relatively large amount of capital in the form of land.

## Marina

Marina is a charismatic young woman with a wide smile and flashing eyes, whose gaiety and wit considerably enlivened my stay in Chanchaló. I spent many late afternoons on her front porch watching the sun set behind the magnificent Western Cordillera across the Valley of Salcedo and sipping oregano tea, enjoying family life with her parents, maternal grandfather, younger sisters, and also with Alejandro and other married siblings who dropped in frequently with their own children. Marina was introduced in chapter 1, where she remarked on women's economic inequality and vulnerability to male violence in the United States compared with women's equal economic valuation and freedom from violence in Chanchaló.

Although only twenty-one and an unmarried daughter in her parents' household, Marina already has become an independent agricultural producer, working the land she has inherited. She is also a wage laborer, working for Alejandro and Clemencia and also for Clemencia's parents. Marina was one of the three women from Cotopaxi Province who attended the horticulture and community-organization courses in the United States. She was elected president of the entire Ecuadorean USAID scholarship class.

Marina is, like her father, brother, and sister-in-law, a community activist. Not only does she actively participate in the women's association, but she is also one of two female members of the quesería. Marina participated equally with male members in the construction of the quesería. She also presents informative programs to the members and spoke along with development-agency dignitaries at the inauguration of the new quesería building. What kind of family has reared this independent and highly competent young woman? What are her goals? What are her prospects?

### Family, Tradition, and Traditional Reciprocity

Marina and her two younger sisters live with their parents, who have six living children between the ages of thirty-eight and fifteen. The family share a

*Egalitarian partnerships in generation: this couple has helped both daughters and sons to achieve economic goals.*

three-room cement-block house furnished sparsely and without appliances. The small plot surrounding their house, however, is a work of horticultural and topiary art. Marina's father, Rodrigo, planned and implemented a marvelous garden, comprising fruit and medicinal trees, myriad varieties of flowers, experimental vegetables such as asparagus, and sculpted hedges.

Having bequeathed one hectare to each of their children, the parents have retained only two for their own use. Marina produces, processes, and markets her own crops on her own land. She has her own savings account at the Cooperativa San Francisco in Salcedo, where loan rates are more favorable than at the banks. However, much of her income is pooled for household expenses. She and her siblings also provide labor for their parents' agricultural production.

Marina is a highly literate woman with little formal education (six years at the local grammar school). She dresses in jeans and T-shirts as well as in the more traditional skirts for working in the country. Although Marina braids her long hair for convenience when working, she wears it loose and curled for trips to town. And she dresses to kill for special occasions, wearing party dresses, high heels, modern jewelry, and hair ornaments.

For all her modernity in dress and experience of urban and North American lifeways, Marina is also concerned about the erosion of what she considers to be valuable components of her own indigenous culture. She is keenly interested in preserving the heritage of her community's pre-Hispanic language, which she studies with her ninety-year-old paternal grandmother. Although both of her parents know Quichua, Spanish is spoken in their home.

While interested in learning what the world outside her community has to offer in terms of economic development and cultural diversity, Marina is mindful that Ecuadorean national society has not been kind to her people. She does not want anyone to forget that, according to Chanchaló's elders, the sources of strength and survival for indigenous communities historically have lain in traditional forms of economic cooperation and social solidarity:

You remember what granddaddy said about how we helped one another on the hacienda? He always says we had to help one another to survive. Well, we have always done that. Daddy says that's why we were able to organize the strike and establish the community. [Rodrigo was a leader in the strike and community foundation.] We had solidarity before we had a community charter.

Collaboration is important now, too. We have to help ourselves. It's important for people to support groups like the quesería and the women's association. So we won't have to go to the banks. And even the cooperatives charge pretty high interest. We need the production associations because they *make* money for the members. They help if someone is ill, too.

In the women's association the members work well, but the young people don't always understand that we need to work together. We need more unity, we need to be more responsible, more punctual.

Some women don't show up for every meeting or every *minga*. That's okay. Women have a lot of work to do. And sometimes their husbands can't manage by themselves. Well, you see, only one person from each family belongs to an organization like the quesería or the women's association. Because only one person will be free to do the organization's work while the other one sees to the farm. But sometimes there is just too much work and not even one person can attend a *minga*.

But we are doing well. We have twice as many members as when we started seven years ago. We have twenty-eight now. Sometimes more. The women are pretty well organized, but we could do better.

In Marina's case, traditional forms of economic cooperation include providing labor for her brother's agricultural production. Marina is paid the same wage as any other laborer for her work in Alejandro and Clemencia's fields. The difference between working for an extended-family member and working for wages outside the family is that family members are mutually obligated to supply labor or other resources even if the opportunity cost of doing so is relatively high.

Marina helped me with my research on an informal basis, formulating questions for the NSF/FUNDAGRO survey instrument, mapping the community, introducing me to people, and supplying me with a great deal of information about community-development institutions. I insisted that she accept payment for some of her time, although she was reluctant to do so. Marina could earn twice the daily wage for a morning of research assistance. Nonetheless, at times she opted to work for the family. For example, she helped Alejandro and Clemencia get their potato harvest in when they needed all the hands they could mobilize to avoid leaving potatoes to waterlog during heavy rains. Marina did not tell them of her alternative opportunity.

Marina has no plans for imminent marriage. She hopes to become married eventually but is not interested in any of the local men. Although impressed by an attractive professional mestizo she met when applying for her USAID scholarship, Marina suspects this man is not marriage material. She is not daunted by differences in ethnicity and socioeconomic status. However, this man is rumored to be encumbered with both a fiancée and a married mistress. Marina and Clemencia refer to men who deceive their wives or fiancées as *bandidos*. Marina says she wants *un hombre de confianza*, a "reliable" man like Alejandro.

## Family Cooperation and Individual Autonomy

Marina has been an independent member of extrahousehold organizations for several years. All political and economic organizations are open to women, and her family have encouraged her to participate in the quesería as well as in the women's association and the comuna. Although her mother organizes labor on the parents' land and in the house, neither of Marina's parents attempts to restrict her movements or her social interactions. One day when I was looking for Marina, her parents told me three likely places to look for her, but no one was certain of her whereabouts. It was late on Sunday afternoon and many people had not yet returned from market day in Salcedo. When Marina returned after dark, we learned that she had gone from Salcedo to visit her sister in another community. No one was concerned for her safety.

The idea of chaperoning unmarried young women is foreign to Chanchaló. Marina says that among her friends, no one is socially restricted by parents. She maintains that when young women give parental restriction as an excuse for not joining the women's association or for missing work parties, they misrepresent their personal freedom. Marina points out that these same young women are free to travel alone to Salcedo and elsewhere outside the community, and to interact with anyone inside the community.

Marina's parents have not only accorded her personal freedom, they have also encouraged her to take advantage of available opportunities to obtain knowledge, skills, and experience of life outside the community. Marina says that her father, especially, has always encouraged her to pursue such opportunities. Marina's parents have also agreed to contribute resources to help her do so.

Marina's mother, María, is seriously ill and currently does not participate much in extrahousehold activities. She does, however, quietly organize the household very well. María watches over Clemencia and Alejandro's mischievous brood, who are frequently at her house. Another grandchild, three-year-old Beto, has come to live in the household. María felt that Beto's mother, her daughter Cecilia, had too much to cope with trying to manage both Beto and a new baby on slim resources. The baby was born prematurely and was so small the family were afraid she would not survive. She has been ill several times during the first months of her life and María felt that separating the baby from a three-year-old's childhood diseases might help her to become healthy and grow well. Cecilia also has an extremely heavy workload, as she is helping to construct her family's new house as well as doing agricultural work. One day as I was cutting through a field near Cecilia's new house, I observed the frail-looking young woman digging a latrine while her husband cared for the baby. Observing Cecilia run between their two houses sheltering the baby from a freezing downpour, María sighed "my poor daughter."

María tolerates her husband's obsession with flower gardening, which absorbs a great deal of his and her younger children's labor, because "it keeps him calm." María keeps the entire household calm and flourishing. Her nurturing has been an important component in cultivating a household environment where cooperative individualists like Alejandro and Marina could thrive.

María says that she and her husband have a better life than her own parents, because her generation no longer have to work for the hacendado. She points to her father's house across the road, a small adobe and thatch affair, and says, "Now *they* had a hard life. They worked all their lives and have little because it was all for the hacendado." (María supplies her father, aged eighty, with produce from the land she has bought with her husband.) María is optimistic that her own children will have a better life than she has had.

*A Vision of Personal and Community Development*

Marina shares her mother's optimism, but her parents' best efforts alone cannot enable her to achieve the kind of life she wants. Marina envisions a future of contribution to her community through continued participation in programs such as the USAID scholarship. She wants to help extend these participation opportunities to others, as well. However, Marina is handicapped by her lack of formal education and may not be eligible for many future scholarships.

Like Clemencia and Valentina, Marina is a farmer whose production needs are not addressed by local development efforts. Like Clemencia, Marina is willing to devote considerable time and material resources to her community's economic-development efforts. Unlike the other women, Marina wants to become a development worker. She hopes she will be able to learn enough through scholarship programs to work as a paraprofessional extensionist. A consultant at USAID investigated international opportunities for Marina to receive training, but current prospects are severely limited.

According to researchers who analyze agricultural technology development and extension in the sierra, Marina would be an ideal extensionist (Garrett and Espinosa 1988). Having observed interactions among professionally educated extensionists (both mestizo and indigenous) and small-scale indigenous farmers, they recommend that positions be created for both male and female indigenous paraprofessionals who lack formal education. These researchers find that most indigenous farmers would be better served by local women and men who have a more immediate understanding of farmers' constraints than professionally trained individuals who represent the socioeconomic elite among indigenous peoples. Although Marina is exactly the kind of farmer who could serve her community well, she is more visible to international institutions working in her region than she is to the national extension service. In an environment of institutional cutbacks and retrenching, national agricultural development programs have little outreach representation in the region.

Marina's best hope for becoming a paraprofessional extensionist may lie in her direct interactions with the young student-professional extensionists completing their required year of rural service in collaboration with the FUNDAGRO dairy program in Salcedo. She has asked them for help in managing the diseases and pests that plague the family's experimental fruit trees and asparagus plot. They are aware that she seeks out opportunities for farmer training and completes any available short courses. The student extensionists say that they will be glad to help Marina apply for a paraprofessional position should opportunities develop in the region.

*Summary: Young Ambition*

Marina is the unmarried child of a middle-income family who have helped her to participate in several informal agricultural training courses, the most intensive being the USAID-sponsored scholarship. She has inherited a small amount of land and is a competent farmer as well as an active community organizer. Like other young women in her community, Marina enjoys considerable personal autonomy, going where she pleases and choosing her own company. She has joined a predominantly male production association organized by a development agency and has become a leader in this organization. Against long odds, Marina is ambitious to use her agricultural and organizational skills to become an agricultural development worker.

## Susana and Nicolás

Susana is an elegant and vivacious twenty-three-year-old woman, a full-time farmer and mother of Marisela, aged three. She has been married to Nicolás for five years. I met Susana at the Chanchaló community center, where Ministry of Health workers were offering the first free vaccinations for children under five. She was dressed in an individualistic version of country working attire: white painter's pants and a pink turtleneck sweater, with a heavy crocheted pink-and-white shawl draped around her waist and hips. Her shoulder-length permed hair was tied back with a knitted scarf; fluffy bangs framed her eyes. She wore large, dramatic gilded earrings. Susana was the only woman in the crowd not wearing the usual working costume of wool skirt, shawls, felt hat over waist-length braided straight hair, and small, delicate earrings.

While Nicolás played with and comforted Marisela, who was afraid of the doctor and his needle, Susana and I interviewed one another and became friends. She initiated our lengthy conversation. For every question I asked, Susana asked at least one. Then she asked to see my interview notes, helping me with Spanish spelling and ascertaining that I had recorded her exact words. She asked the English equivalents of several words and we made a game of trading Spanglish puns and wordplay. This game developed into regular but very informal English lessons, which provided a format for exchange of information on numerous topics.

Susana and Nicolás are recently returned migrants who have lived in urban areas from their early teens. Susana grew up in Chanchaló and neighboring Chanchalito; Nicolás's family lived in Sacha, a predominantly indigenous community about one hour's drive from Chanchaló. Both moved first to Salcedo, where they attended high school. Nicolás graduated; Susana dropped out after two years because she did not like school. After graduation Nicolás served one year in the army at a post in Amazonian Ecuador. Following their marriage they worked in a cheese factory near Quito for three years. Although Susana and Nicolás lived in urban areas for so many years and have adopted urban (or blanco/mestizo) dress, neither they nor their neighbors consider them to have become blanco. They participate in community social and economic reciprocity networks—an important measure of indígena status among Chanchaleños—although they do not give as much time as Clemencia, Valentina, Marina, and Alejandro.

The couple are generally considered poor. Their income is derived from Nicolás's part-time work in the quesería as well as from commercial agriculture. Their two-room, dirt-floored house was given to Susana by her parents, who have moved to Salcedo. Susana has also been given about one-half hectare of land next to the house. She and Nicolás have bought an additional one-half hectare and they sharecrop small plots with both Susana's younger brother and Nicolás's family in Sacha.

Although they own shabby upholstered furniture and matching pieces of china and glassware, considered luxuries in Chanchaló, Susana and Nicolás struggle to make ends meet. The luxuries were purchased while they lived near the city or were received as wedding presents from urban friends. Now that they are trying to survive on a small land base together with Nicolás's daily wage of one dollar and Susana's occasional craft production, they sometimes cannot produce or purchase enough to eat. They do not go hungry, because Susana's parents and local extended family give them food. Unlike many children in Chanchaló, Marisela has achieved normal weight for her age by international standards. But without this extrahousehold social and economic network, they would face hunger at times.

## Social Life

Susana's public roles differ from those of her cousin Marina, Clemencia, and Valentina. Susana is not a community activist, although she joined the women's association during 1993. Her mother is one of two women members of the quesería; Susana substitutes for her mother in the group's labor rotation.

Unlike Clemencia, Alejandro, and Marina, Susana participates enthusiastically in an additional expression of social solidarity: the community's annual celebration of its political founding and spiritual tradition. Where Clemencia and Alejandro do not enjoy the traditional three days of ritual performance, drinking, and dancing in honor of San José de Chanchaló, Susana exuberantly dons her best party clothes, dances with everyone, and drinks many men under the makeshift bleachers. She does not stop until she can no longer

stand up, at which time she retires for a siesta so that she can continue refreshed for the duration of the festivities. Women participate equally with
men in the festivities, holding ritual office as well as enjoying the party. Susana is admired for the gusto with which she embraces the festive tradition.

Clemencia and Alejandro consider such extended drinking to be a waste of
energy for all and of money for fiesta sponsors and those who cannot afford
to purchase special treats but feel they must do so. They enjoy a good party,
such as the fifteen hours of drinking and dancing that helped to inaugurate
the quesería, but consider the annual three-day fiesta both excessive de-
bauchery and an inhibition to the kind of economic and spiritual development they consider to be positive and progressive. Susana, in contrast, thinks
that the concentrated burst of ritualistic excess is perfectly suited to life in the
country, where concentrated hard physical labor is the rule most of the time.
She was telling me how much she enjoyed dancing with my husband, who
visited during the fiesta, and laughing at herself:

Of course I can't remember his name. I can't remember much at all. We drank so
much. I loved it. Did you?

You see, once a year we forget all our worries and drink and dance all we want for
three days. The fiesta is for the whole community and anyone who wants to visit.
Everyone joins in and honors San José and Chanchaló. It's good to remember the community. We love to dance. People in your country don't dance enough. Well, for three
days, little work and no worries. If you get drunk and fall down, someone will take you
home and you sleep. Then you get up and drink and dance some more. Okay. Then it's
over and everybody goes back to work.

Traditional social reciprocity remains important to Susana's mother, Carmen, who continues to practice traditional social and economic reciprocity although she no longer lives in the community. Carmen was *prioste* (literally
"page," refers to a host) for the 1993 community fiesta, an office of ritual
sponsorship that requires both considerable time and material resources as
well as high social status. Performance of this office is considered a gift to the
community; Carmen was proud to be able to give this gift. An herbal healer
who treats campesinos at her home in Salcedo, Carmen is not wealthy. Susana's father is a bricklayer of moderate means. Yet her parents have invested
considerable resources in Chanchaló's economic development and a traditional form of social solidarity. Susana is an enthusiastic supporter of her family's
continued involvement in traditional social activity.

## The Working Day

Susana's working days are much like Clemencia's in that she generally
puts in a full day on the farm and also contributes time to the women's association. Since Nicolás "helps out" (Susana's term) with her farmwork, Susana

occasionally helps him at the quesería. On the day of the quesería's first cheese-making in their new factory building, Susana was on hand. For five hours in the morning, she and Nicolás performed together all of the tasks involved in cheese-making. They washed equipment in boiling water, heated milk in a huge cauldron until the curds were firm enough to place in molds, molded and pressed cheeses, packaged them for sale, cleaned the equipment and work area, and took the cheeses to retail merchants in Salcedo. Nicolás dealt with the retailers alone while Susana went to the indoor food market and bought small quantities of shredded pork, peppers, tomatoes, and bananas. All the other tasks were performed by both wife and husband.

Nicolás is the only paid employee of the quesería, working mornings five days a week. Susana does not always help him, but she did on this particular day because there were many other activities going on around the cheese-making, as members put the finishing touches on the quesería building in anticipation of its official opening two days later. Nicolás felt that her help would be needed to manage the cheese-making in time for afternoon distribution to retailers.

When they returned from Salcedo, Susana cut pasture grass, picked dry maize stalks, and shelled hard maize to feed to the animals. She explained that the maize crop had been hurt by excessive rains following upon drought. She showed me the stunted plants that had been hardest hit by the rainfall fluctuation, and the vertical gullies where valuable topsoil had run off between plants on the more steeply sloping portion of the maize field. She said:

This land is mine. My parents gave it to me. My brother has half of this field and I have the other half. He stays with me sometimes instead of with my parents in Salcedo, and he helps with the work when he is not in school. We won't have enough maize to sell this year; my brother and I will share it.

Look at these gullies. That's where the water runs down the hillside during the worst rains. We try to stop it, but we can't. Erosion is terrible here. Marina told me about her course in the United States. She learned about contour plowing and other ways to stop erosion. We do the contour plowing, you can see. It helps, but it doesn't always stop the water.

And look at these worms in the maize. We have to fumigate against them, too. The worst problem is the water and the worms are very bad, too. This isn't a good year for maize.

It was bad for the garlic, too. Up there I had a garlic patch, but the virus ruined the garlic. I lost it all. That was bad because the plants were very expensive. I wanted to plant it because I can make a lot more money from garlic than from anything else and I don't have much land. The land is resting now. I planted pasture there. I'm going to try garlic again after the land has rested enough.

While Susana tended to the farm animals, Nicolás tended to the house and Marisela. He took laundry down from the clothesline and ironed clothes while he watched a soccer match on TV. He made beds and straightened the house. When the soccer match was over he scouted the neighborhood for Marisela, who had been roaming the countryside with a band of children of all ages. While Mari played in the patio with her friends, Nicolás cranked up the sound on the stereo; as the music wafted into the maize field from speakers strung up on the front porch, he joined Susana in the field.

After they had completed their work in the field, Nicolás prepared the evening meal, a treat of fried fresh maize with peppers and onions, the shredded pork bought that afternoon, and potato-based soup, while Susana and I engaged in an English lesson. We used photographs of her family and mine to illustrate kinship terms, while three-year-old Mari provided correct answers for questions about verb forms and pronouns. After dinner, Susana crocheted a shawl and Nicolás played with Mari while the family watched their favorite soap opera. Susana sells around two shawls a month; depending on prices and output, income from her craft production can equal half the amount Nicolás makes at the quesería.

On most working days, Susana is in the field by 7:30 in the morning and works until 4:00 or 5:00 in the afternoon. Nicolás does the milking (which Susana dislikes as much as Clemencia does) and often gives Mari her breakfast. If she is working in fields near the house, Susana will feed the animals three times a day. She feeds only twice daily when she is working on sharecropped land in Sacha.

Marisela is a free spirit who accompanies her mother to the fields, plays near the house in the company of Susana's younger brother or Nicolás, or takes off to play with friends or visit neighbors while the adults work. Susana could take advantage of free day care and meals for children provided by the Ecuadorean state but says that Mari prefers to go to the fields with her, and Susana prefers it as well. Mari is as lively, curious, and intelligent as Clemencia and Alejandro's children and can always manage to find entertainment and food in the neighborhood. Mari often goes out for lunch.

Susana will usually be joined by Nicolás following the morning's cheesemaking unless other quesería business or a soccer game takes precedence. Nicolás is both a regular player on Chanchaló's team, which plays other Cantón Salcedo teams on Sunday afternoons, and a fanatical fan of several Ecuadorean teams including his favorite, Quito's Nacional. In his opinion, the crops will not fail while he lends support to the teams that need him.

## Why the Country, Not the City

The freedom to schedule his own working time is one of the attractions that drew Nicolás to Chanchaló. A small, wiry man with a smiling open face, Nicolás is well respected by the quesería members who employ him and is expected to become a community leader if the couple stay in Chanchaló. He says they returned to Chanchaló because that is where they have property and can work for themselves:

In the city we had to work all the time. Every day, all the time. We liked the work and we liked the city. The weather is warm there, really nice. And we had a lot of friends. But life is better here. You see, even if you have to work all day every day, it isn't as hard if you are working for yourself. It just isn't as hard. And if I want to do something else for a while and then finish later, I can do it. So long as all of the work gets done, I can decide when to do it. Well, I can't do that in the city. We had more money when we worked in the city, but it wasn't worth it. Life is more peaceful here. Truly, I love it here.

Susana echoes some of these sentiments; she, too, enjoyed the urban climate and work. She also prefers life in Chanchaló, but for different reasons:

I love the country. There is no crime here. People lock up their houses—I lock my house, too—so nothing will be stolen but there is no danger here. In the city there is danger.

Two things I like best about living in Chanchaló: family and farming. I love my grandfather very much, and my cousins. My mother's family live in other places, all over the country. No one in Chanchaló. But my father came from a big family, and I have lots of aunts and uncles and cousins here.

Working in the cheese factory in the city was okay, really, but what I like best is farming. Maybe that surprises you. Most people who aren't campesinos think that life is harder in the country than in the city. In the country you have to work all night sometimes if you have a sick cow or pig. Or maybe you have to work in the cold rain. You can't decide when you want to work; you have to work when it's time for the harvest or when the plants need fumigating or whatever. Sometimes you can't wait even one day or you won't have anything. And sometimes you don't get much for it, no matter how hard you work.

You probably think I'm crazy. Sometimes I think I'm crazy, or as you say in English: "nuts." But I am very happy that my parents gave me the land so we could live here.

## Agricultural Production and Resource Control

Within the constraints of her small land base and limited labor supply, Susana is an enterprising, risk-taking commercial farmer. She and Nicolás invest in high-input, high-technology production. They produce potato, maize, beans, barley, and several kinds of pasture. All crops are grown for sale as well as for home consumption. The couple earn 80 percent of their cash income from agriculture and animal production. Approximately two-thirds of total household income, including the subsistence value of production, is derived from commercial agriculture.

Susana's goal is to intensify yields and profit on a small base. To this end, she applies agrochemicals approximately every two weeks per crop during the dry season. This is a relatively high level of agrochemical usage. Unlike Clemencia, Susana sprays pesticides regularly as well as applying chemical fertilizer. She participates in all other agricultural tasks except driving the rented tractor during land preparation. Nicolás also participates in all agricultural activities, but Susana puts in more time.

Susana has greater decision input than Nicolás in many production domains. She says that she and Nicolás always discuss crop choice, agrochemical and other input selection, and other investments in production, but that the balance of decision-making is usually up to her, as she has more farming experience than he. Susana considers their situation unusual, as most men in Chanchaló have as much agricultural knowledge as their wives. She says that from the age of twelve, Nicolás has evidenced less interest than she in agriculture. He likes country living but does not consider himself an equally expert farmer and is content to follow her lead. Nicolás agrees with this assessment.

For example, as Susana stated, she has experimented with garlic production. Garlic potentially offers the highest return from a small amount of land and is suitable for Susana's land at the relatively low altitude of around 3,000 meters. It is also expensive to produce and extremely risky, as it can fall prey to a number of diseases untreatable locally. Although the decision to risk the investment in garlic was consensual, Susana originated the plan. She wants to try again to produce the potentially lucrative crop after the land has rested sufficiently. Nicolás says that he will agree with whatever Susana wants to do on the land, even if great risk is involved, because she is the more knowledgeable farmer and does more work on the farm:

We talk about everything before we decide about the crops. But if we disagree at first, later we will do what Susana wants. I agree because she knows more about farming than I do. She's more interested in it. She always has been. She learned a lot from her parents and she learns from Marina and Alejandro, from many people. And she does more work than I do on the farm. So I will agree with her.

Although Susana is short on land, she is long on social networking, and she has turned this advantage into potential profit as well as a security net. For example, she is caring for a neighbor's pig that she feeds partly with whey left over after Nicolás's cheese-making. She will receive a share of the piglets due later in the year. Susana is also breeding chickens, rabbits, and guinea pigs for sale and home consumption. Milk sales provide an important source of regular income. Susana feels that diversified crop and animal production offer the best chance of making a living and increasing her productive base.

*Marriage and Economic-Decision Processes*

Susana and Nicolás fell in love when she was twelve and he was fifteen. They married and produced Marisela while Susana was still in her teens. They are negotiating their way through a mutually chosen but sometimes difficult adjustment to rural life, a process that includes economic-decision conflict. Conflict arises concerning Nicolás's contribution of labor to the family's agricultural enterprise. Considering their contrasting views of the exigencies of agricultural work, this is not surprising. Nicolás feels he has the freedom to schedule farmwork around his leisure activities, so long as enough work gets done to support the family. Susana is convinced that successful farmers schedule recreation around the climatic and other exigencies related to particular crops, with the notable exception of very occasional and important fiesta weekends. We have seen that Susana likes to play as much as Nicolás; she, however, is generally willing to defer play until she is satisfied that crop and animal production are proceeding on schedule. Susana also is more concerned with the ultimate accumulation in land that could be achieved by increasing their total amount of work. Nicolás has to be prodded to keep this goal in mind.

At times tense arguments result from their differences. Although I removed myself from the immediate scene of such interaction, both the tension and the subject matter were obvious even from a moderate distance. Most arguments I skirted in this manner dealt with Nicolás's work habits. According to Susana:

Nicolás helps me with the farm in the afternoons after he returns from the quesería. He cleans the house, washes clothes, cooks, and takes care of Mari, too. He does everything. Nicolás really is a very good man. He works hard. You know he works faster and better than anyone. He can do as much as two people. And most of the time he helps me. Nearly every day.

But sometimes he just takes off. We're not like Clemencia and Alejandro: we can't afford to pay workers, and we don't have many siblings to help. You can say that we have only ourselves. Sometimes I don't know where he is when I need him. Then we have trouble. He doesn't do it as often as before, when we first came here.

Another area of potential conflict is Nicolás's greater decision input in household expenditure. As in the other households profiled, income from all lands, crops, and animals is pooled. Nicolás's wage and the daily milk money provide for daily expenses. Income from crop and animal sales pays debts and is banked, although the couple have only meager savings. Susana shops for food and for personal items for herself and Marisela. Nicolás has bought large items like the stereo and television set.

Nicolás is an experienced bookkeeper and marketer, and Susana has grown accustomed to his keeping accounts and dealing with vendors. Now she worries that he sometimes spends too much, and they are often not able to stretch their income to meet many needs. Because Nicolás has responded positively to her recent requests to decrease spending, she is hopeful that he is changing his expenditure patterns. She has not attempted to increase her participation in direct consumption.

Well, I don't manage the money. Most women do, but I don't. When we lived in the city, Nicolás did the buying except the food, and he is good with accounts. I'm not. I hate it.

We have a problem because we need to save for investment, you know, to buy chemicals for the crops or medicine for the animals or something else. Sometimes Nicolás doesn't think about what we will need for the crops when he buys things that we use in the house. He buys things for Mari and me, too. Maybe I should keep the money. I don't know. I told him we shouldn't be buying anything unless we talk about it first. Well, now he buys only what we talk about. We'll see how it goes.

Susana and Nicolás have not managed to reach consensus concerning labor priorities, nor has either of them emerged as dominant in all economic-decision areas. Although Susana prevails in most productive decisions and allows that Nicolás contributes a sufficient amount of agricultural labor, she is not comfortable with his occasionally capricious work habits. Although Nicolás manages the expenditure of household income more directly than Susana, he has apparently accepted her request to modify his spending habits. Serious economic negotiations are an almost constant fact of life in the household.

In spite of the seriousness and frequency of these negotiations, and the fact that negotiation can escalate into draining arguments which neither wins, Susana does not feel she is fighting with Nicolás. Rather, she views these discussions as part of the difficult job of trying to direct his considerable energies, just as most women in Chanchaló shoulder considerable responsibility for the organization of household labor:

Sometimes we quarrel. I hate it. But I have to argue so that Nicolás will understand what we have to do to be successful on the farm. For me it is hard. For him, too. Nicolás hates fighting, too. Maybe he hates it more than I do. He's very gentle. Really, I don't struggle against Nicolás. I am struggling against being poor. We are struggling together against being poor.

Nicolás and I did not discuss the patterns or seriousness of intrahousehold conflict. Although we talked privately on several occasions, Nicolás did not mention any areas of conflict. He remained somewhat shy with me, and I felt that questioning him concerning intimate or emotionally loaded subjects would be counterproductive and perhaps offensive. I never observed a statement or action that would contradict Susana's conclusion that Nicolás is a hardworking and gentle family man.

### Summary: Egalitarian Conflict

This young couple are negotiating for mutual accommodation of one another's priorities and preferences. They listen to one another, and both respect the abilities and work of the other. Their decision process is ultimately consultational and egalitarian, if more confrontational than that observed for Clemencia and Alejandro. Although the couple have not achieved a mutually satisfying pattern of compromise on all issues, neither Susana nor Nicolás dominates the decision process. Neither expresses dissatisfaction with the partnership. They enjoy life together, intensely, in work and in play. Both are doting parents who want to rear a family in the country. In Susana's view, they fight primarily against poverty rather than against one another.

## Beatriz and Luis

Beatriz and "Lucho" are prospering. They have bought nine hectares of land since their marriage seventeen years ago. Although they are only thirty-three and thirty-four, they have accumulated much more property than Clemencia and Alejandro. They have built three houses, two in the country and one in Salcedo, where their teenaged daughters live during the week while attending secondary school. One of the houses (in which I lived) is not yet finished, lacking a fourth wall for one of its four rooms, but is equipped with concrete and wood flooring, a kitchen range, and metal and plastic dining table and chairs. The walls for a second story have been partially raised. My rent for nine months was the installation of a bathroom. Beatriz and Lucho do not have indoor plumbing in the very modest two-room house they occupy. They do have a refrigerator (a luxury owned by only a very few families), a television set, and a stereo. Beatriz and Lucho do not own a vehicle. They have saved three-quarters of the amount they need to purchase a tractor (a huge amount considering their income), which will earn rental income as well as serving their own production. All of the family's income comes from agriculture.

Although they are relatively uneducated, Beatriz and Lucho are firm believers in the power of education to better the lives of their daughters. They encourage the girls to do well in school and will try to secure university education for them. Fifteen-year-old Nancy wants to be a physician. She is an outstanding student and hardworking part-time farmer. Grimanesa, aged thirteen, is less serious than her older sister. She dreams of working in the United States. Her parents think this is a terrible idea but asked me if I would help her. They say she is determined to go and they will not try to prevent her.

*Intergenerational Conflict and Cooperation*

Beatriz and Lucho incorporated me into their family life on a daily basis. As I was renting from them and lived just down the dirt road from their house, we saw a great deal of one another. In addition to allowing observation of their own family life, Beatriz provided an invaluable source of information covering a three-community geographical area: she loves to gossip. Beatriz is genuinely and cheerfully sympathetic to the plights of others, and she could always elicit a well-embroidered tale. Many of these I listened to in her company and she repeated others for family entertainment. I became friends with their teenaged daughters as well as with the adults. Their infant daughter, Kati, is my goddaughter. I also became acquainted with their large extended families, who live in several rural communities as well as in Salcedo.

This large and closely collaborating network of fictive kin watched over me with constant kindness. I spent many evenings laughing and singing with the family. Hours spent with them melted away, and I always left feeling refreshed, very glad they were my local family. Beatriz literally clucked over me like a mother hen while teaching me how to light fires, burn trash, keep a clean house and patio, and dress appropriately for public occasions. Feeling sorry for me because my hiking boots were so ugly and no good for dancing, she offered me her own tiny high-heeled pumps so I would not feel out of place at a fiesta. She took me on long walks, gathering vegetables, fruits, and herbs, pointing out medicinal uses for numerous plants and advising me on the best ways to cook foods. When I was ill, she sent me home to bed and brought me herbal remedies every day until I recovered. Lucho walked around their property every evening, checking on the animals, including me. If I had not seen him during the day, he always called in to see if I needed anything and to share the latest news.

Beatriz and Lucho also incorporated me into their economic reciprocity network. We loaned one another money. When my Fulbright check was late (a common occurrence), Beatriz paid for my gas and electricity. When they were short of cash and I was solvent, I paid for pesticides needed immediately for the maize and potato crops. We exchanged food and other small gifts on a regular basis. As I was walking home in the afternoons, I often saw Lucho watching for me from the roof of my house, calling out "¡Hola, vecina!" (Hi, neighbor!) and holding fresh trout or some other treat that would then become that evening's dinner.

Nancy and Grima taught me important survival skills, as well as helping me to understand the complicated existence of young women who live in both town and country and whose futures promise to be so different from the lives of their parents. Nancy is an extremely mature, responsible young woman who can not understand why her parents will allow her to enjoy the social freedom described by Marina in the country but will not allow her to attend parties in town. Although she and her younger sister live unchaperoned in Salcedo during the school week, Beatriz's younger sister lives in town and drops in frequently; Beatriz, Lucho, and other relatives keep an eye on the girls on market days and other days when they are in town. Nancy says they are always being watched in Salcedo.

It's terrible. My friends ask me to parties, and Grima, too. They are very fine people, and my parents know them. Mom says that if I were a boy, I could go, but that it isn't proper for a girl to go to parties in Salcedo. It's the same with Norma. [The daughter of Beatriz's older sister, Norma is a sixteen-year-old young woman who also lives in Salcedo while attending school.] My aunt and uncle let her brother do anything he wants, but Norma can't do anything. Why is that? Why is it that in the country girls and boys can do the same things, and a girl can walk around with anyone she pleases, but not in town?

I reply that I don't know the answer and ask what reasons her parents have given:

Well, it's Mom who says no. She says that people in town don't respect a girl who goes to parties or walks around with boys. She says that town boys are different from country boys: they don't respect girls. Some of the town boys are pretty terrible, but some of them are nice to me and to the other girls. I don't have a boyfriend anyway. I don't want a boyfriend. I don't want to get married for a long time. But I like parties and I really like my friends in town. I know girls in the United States go to parties. Did you go to parties when you were in school?

I answer that I did go to parties. Before I can continue, Nancy cries that she is terribly unhappy and pleads with me to intercede with her mother. I reply that her mother must have good reasons for wanting to protect her, and that I cannot interfere. Nancy philosophically accepts the collusion of the adults, but remains unconvinced that she needs to be protected from the urban male universe.

Beatriz's version of this intergenerational conflict is consistent with Nancy's. She is so vigilant that she tries to chaperon Nancy even in the country if she suspects that town boys will be around. When Nancy and I left for the annual fiesta of a neighboring community earlier than the rest of the family, Beatriz pulled me aside and told me to stay with Nancy at all times. She said that a certain young man from Salcedo had visited Nancy at their house in the country earlier in the week and had said he'd be at the fiesta and asked if Nancy would be there. Beatriz said:

Nancy is very serious. I have confidence in her. But I don't want her walking around with a boy from Salcedo. She doesn't understand that town boys aren't like her cousins and the other boys around here. She doesn't understand that town boys are dangerous. They don't respect the girls. We want the girls to have a good education so we have to send them to town to school. But I worry about them all the time. Grima isn't serious like Nancy. The boys have already started coming around to see her, too. You stay with the other one. She can go anywhere she wants, but you stay with her.

Beatriz and Lucho are proud, affectionate parents who have created a cheerful and loving atmosphere barely ruffled by occasional conflict between generations and between the ways of doing things in town and country. By their own choice, Nancy and Grima arrive home as soon as school ends every week and often spend a night or two at home during the week, as well. Nancy and Grima say that they prefer life in the country, although they would like to add to it the social activities their parents forbid. They appear to be eager to rejoin the family and clearly enjoy busy, laughter-filled weekend days on the farm. Nancy is resigned to leaving home in a few years to pursue her university and professional careers, but the thought of leaving her family saddens her greatly. She says she may have to take her baby sister along for company.

The parents also enjoy an affectionate marriage. The following discussion will illustrate many ways in which Lucho depends upon his wife to keep the family enterprise running smoothly. However, when Beatriz went to Salcedo for the birth of their baby and Lucho had to spend time on the farm to see to crops and animals, he did not lament the absence of her work or skill; rather, he lamented the absence of her person. On his evening walkabout, Lucho came to my door to tell me that the baby had been born:

I am sad tonight and happy, too. The baby came last night, two weeks early. She is fine. But Beatriz is ill. She doesn't feel well at all. The birth was fine, but she doesn't feel well. I could help her, but they won't let me stay with her in the hospital. They don't want me to see her. Everything's a mess. The hospital is on strike and they don't have enough people working there. I am very sad because I cannot be with her.

Tomorrow she will leave the hospital and stay in our house in Salcedo for a month. It's always a month for a new baby. She will have to stay in bed for a month. She can't come home to the country because it's too cold for the baby. So she will have to stay in town. Her sister and the girls will stay with her. But I will have to stay here most of the time and take care of things. This makes me very sad. I want to be with her.

Lucho sorely regretted his inability to care for his wife during her recovery, a husband's traditional responsibility and pleasure. A number of women and men in Chanchaló described a husband's typical duties following the birth of a baby. Regardless of her health, the mother spends at least a month in bed following the birth. During that time, the husband performs all work, domestic and agricultural, and cares for mother and child. Both men and women remembered this time as a good one, even though the men are working for two. Susana spoke of how well Nicolás took care of her and the baby following Marisela's birth. She said that Nicolás is a good cook and housekeeper, and he managed well so she didn't have to worry about anything. An older, politically powerful father of a new baby described his motivation to care for his wife:

Women need to rest after they have babies. Women work as hard as men in the fields. *Ellas tienen la fuerza* [they are strong].[6] Women aren't weak. That isn't the problem. The problem is that it is possible that they will die when children are born. Yes. It is very serious.

So we take very good care of them. We like to do it. See, they don't have to do anything but just stay in bed with the baby. For at least a month, sometimes more. My wife is out of bed now after one month. She is in good health. I cook good food for her—vitamins and proteins. I made special tea with many herbs, this was to help her milk come and to help her be well. She liked it. She said I did a good job for her and the baby and the other children.

Perhaps Lucho was saddened by having to miss this important time of nurturing both the new life and his wife's health, as well as by having to miss his wife's company. Lucho is a gregarious, light-hearted, universally liked and respected man who has never met a stranger. He finds intense personal enjoyment in rainbows, birdsong, moonlight, and other features of his landscape as he goes about his daily business. Yet during the six weeks Beatriz remained in Salcedo, Lucho was relatively silent and withdrawn when at home on the farm. His main topic of conversation was how much he wanted to be with Beatriz. Whenever possible, the girls looked after the farm so that Lucho and Beatriz could be together. As soon as Beatriz returned, Lucho became his regular, boisterous self and the couple returned to their constant, often flirtatious and bawdy, teasing and joking. These affectionate exchanges appear to express a deep and mutual commitment.

## Public Life and Community Development

Although Beatriz and Lucho are public-spirited people, their participation in public affairs differs from the pervasive commitment evidenced by

Clemencia, Alejandro, and Marina. Beatriz and Lucho are primarily interested in securing public services for their community: clean water, health services, a paved road, and telephone access. Although their current residence is located in Chanchalito, just across the *quebrada* (ravine) which marks the western boundary of Chanchaló, Beatriz and Lucho own land in both communities. Chanchalito is much smaller than Chanchaló and only recently achieved sufficient population to become legally incorporated as a community. As its name suggests, it was until recently perceived as a smaller and less formally constituted adjunct to Chanchaló. The president of the new community no longer lives there; Beatriz and Lucho state that both political organization and collaborative spirit are less well developed than in Chanchaló. However, they have not petitioned to join the production associations of Chanchaló.

Lucho is president of the local four-community water board, an important position in communities whose residents depend on agriculture for their livelihoods and on the water board for distribution and maintenance of limited irrigation and drinking-water supplies. The state officially owns all water supplies and determines where large modern irrigation networks will be built and how water will be distributed regionally. The state is more responsive to the needs of large landowners than to campesinos, however.

Lucho's water board cannot enforce legally granted access to irrigation water when access is challenged by large landowners whose armed thugs patrol the canals and divert water from campesino supplies. Nor can the board gain improved storage and transport conditions for drinking water that is often heavily silted following an eighteen-kilometer journey from source to storage tanks. During the wet season, silted water clogs the filters in the tanks, and people are regularly without water for days at a time. It is the responsibility of the water board to determine distribution rights within the four local communities who share a single water source and to ensure that all users participate in the quarterly cleaning of the canals. The board presidency is perceived locally as a highly responsible and influential position.

Lucho and Beatriz also participate actively in support of the Rural Social Security network, a health insurance and service organization that is being threatened by the national government's plan to privatize it. Lucho and Beatriz attended numerous meetings and rallies in support of maintaining the system as a government service. The government responded positively after campesinos mounted a series of protests, but Lucho explained to me that the system will eventually be privatized and thus become unaffordable to most campesinos; in his view, they have achieved a delay in privatization rather than a commitment for continued support.

Lucho also spearheaded a (currently unsuccessful) drive for telephone service. He attempted to interest his neighbors in petitioning the government for a paved road but was discouraged when he was told that only the community's president could submit such a petition. The absent president was not interested.

Unlike Clemencia and Valentina, Beatriz does not participate in campesino politics through the Casa Campesina. Nor is she interested in starting a women's organization, as Clemencia and Valentina were. Beatriz says she is more interested in working for her own family. She does not think she needs the security net provided by a production association. Using words echoed by her brothers, Beatriz puts her faith in family economic collaboration rather than in communitywide production associations:

In my family we collaborate. If someone needs a loan to help buy a truck or a tractor, we help out. They always pay us back. You know that Raúl and Eduardo have tractors. Well, they got help from the family. We helped. Now we are trying to save for a tractor, and they are helping us, too. It's the same with the children's school fees or if someone needs an operation. We help one another. Also, we work harder than some other people. That is how we are able to buy things and to educate our children.

I asked if she or members of her family belong to production associations in Chanchaló. Beatriz replied:

We don't belong to the production associations in Chanchaló. Some of us live in Chanchaló, some in Chanchalito, some in Palama. Only Chanchaló has those associations. Besides, it takes money to join a cooperative or a production association. Adolfo could join, but he said he'd rather invest in a truck so he could make money hauling and taking children to school. He'd rather be independent. Raúl says the same. Rubén joined in Palama, but that association failed.

Of course some in the family don't always share, like Eduardo. You know he has that camera that you gave to all of us. Well, he won't let us use it. Keeps it for himself. And Adolfo is greedy. Pah! Adolfo, always a greedy boy. But we always know we can get help.

In sum, this family includes a well-respected community leader, but the female household head directs her organizational skills primarily to household labor and accumulation. She is not interested in nurturing the community, as Clemencia does, or in gaining political influence for herself as Valentina has done. She does not share Marina's conviction that interhousehold economic cooperation helped indigenous communities to survive centuries of virtual enslavement on the haciendas and is a key component of future survival. She is both more materialistic than the other women profiled in this chapter, and less convinced of the value of community social solidarity.

## Managing People and Money

Beatriz has been enormously successful in household organization and ac-cumulation. She, like Valentina and like Marina's mother, manages the as-signment of household labor. She is more successful than Susana in husband organization, perhaps the result of having an additional twelve years for per-fecting the art. Lucho cheerfully submits to Beatriz's brand of household man-agement; he maintains that the family owes its economic success to the fact that Beatriz is *bien organizada* (well organized, a good manager).

Although Beatriz has to prod Lucho out of bed on cold early mornings, and sometimes cannot rouse him until the rest of the world has been working for an hour or so, he works energetically and efficiently once he is resigned to it. Beatriz finds Lucho's laid-back approach to life entirely tolerable, laughing af-fectionately at her sleepyhead while her earnestly capitalizing brother-in-law voices disapproval. She tells me that after seventeen years of marriage, she knows the day's work will be done. Lucho may not arrive back from the field until after nightfall, but he likes working in the evening and she does not mind his late hours.

Although Lucho holds an important public office, it is Beatriz who iden-tifies and locates the documents required to do business with public utility companies. It is also Beatriz who interviews loan officers in the local banks and savings-and-loan cooperatives. She is working to arrange the best terms for the family to borrow the remaining money they need to purchase a trac-tor. This purchase is critical to the family fortunes; they will be able to make a great deal of money by renting out the tractor if they can only manage to buy it.

Beatriz is unilaterally in charge of managing the household's saving, bor-rowing, and expenditure. She negotiates informal loans as well as formal ones. Beatriz makes certain that the family gets a good deal. When Lucho told me I could rent their house if I would install a bathroom commode, Beatriz said the rent would be a commode, lavatory, and shower. As noted above, I installed a complete bathroom. As described in chapter 1, Beatriz weighs Lu-cho's opinions when deciding how much to spend for agricultural inputs; the decision, however, is hers. And she is deaf to any request that would interfere with their long-term financial goals. He can ask, he can plead, he can tease; I have seen him do all these things, but I never saw him make any purchase Beatriz had not approved.

Beatriz sells the family's agricultural products, and she makes sure they get a good deal from market intermediaries. I observed her negotiation for the best price she could obtain for high-quality potatoes, and her refusal to sell at the price several intermediaries had agreed among themselves to offer. She walked away and did not return for an hour or so. The buyers believed her insistence that she would not sell at their price. When she returned to the market, Beatriz agreed to sell to a buyer who raised her price "on quality." Beatriz's method is less folksy than Valentina's. She employs no back-patting or joking with buyers. Her refusal to take an unacceptable deal is just as effective.

Beatriz and Lucho cooperate economically with both of their extended families. They engage in labor reciprocity with both families. They also sharecrop with Beatriz's mother. I observed one negotiation regarding the produce from a sharecropped field of maize and pasture grasses. A woman neighbor wanted to buy pasture. As she and Beatriz negotiated the price, the buyer's husband stood a few feet away and listened to the conversation. Then he walked around the field, handling the grass and looking at a few ears of maize. When he returned, Beatriz demanded if he didn't think it a fine crop of pasture and her price a fair one. He hesitated and mumbled his agreement. She then asked me if I didn't think it a fine crop of pasture and her price a fair one. I seconded the neighbor's husband. As she started in on her daughter Nancy, the neighbor good-naturedly capitulated to Beatriz's second price. The sale was divided into equal shares for Beatriz and her mother.

Nancy has a share in this arrangement, as well. She cares for her grandmother's six cattle, grazing them on sharecropped pastureland that she and Beatriz plant and cultivate. In return Nancy is accruing ownership rights. Cattle are considered a form of savings, and Nancy (like Marina) has her own "savings account." Milk income is pooled in the household, as is agricultural income.

Beatriz is training her daughters to manage both agricultural production and money. It was her idea that Nancy should earn a stake in cattle and pasture production. She wants her girls to have individual savings. Nancy also is deputized to hold on to the physical money supply during outings or shopping trips if Beatriz does not go along. Although Nancy dotes on her father, she will not give him "lunch money" (enough to enjoy a few drinks with friends) if Mama has said no. Mama does not always say no, as she wants Lucho to "enjoy the life" on election days, fiesta days, and other occasions. As Nancy says:

Daddy works really hard. He's always happy and singing, but he really works very hard. Every day. Well, sometimes he needs to relax. Then he likes to drink *trago* [cane alcohol] or rum or beer with Mama or with his friends. Sometimes Mama says not to give him very much money, because some of his friends drink too much.

*Mother and daughter harvest potato during the school holidays.*

Beatriz is also *bien organizada* in terms of her family's health. Like Clemencia, she takes her young child to the public hospital in Salcedo for vaccinations "so she will grow well." Unlike Clemencia, she maintains a clean cooking and eating environment. Clemencia cooks on a dirt floor rather than on her countertop. Her children eat on the floor amid cats, dogs, flies, and other creatures; although she boils the drinking water, the children drink from an outdoor tap when no one is looking. In contrast, Beatriz cooks on her countertop, always boils water for a full ten minutes, and has her family sit on a bench to eat. Mother and children are seldom ill. Both women feed their children an adequate supply of calories and protein. Nonetheless, Clemencia's two-year-old is chronically ill and underweight. Having no health problems to counteract the positive effects of an adequate nutrient supply (in this case to the mother, as the baby is nursing), Beatriz's baby is growing at a rate favorably comparable to those of children in the United States. Everyone says Kati is the largest baby ever seen in Chanchaló.

*The next generation: girls are nourished and educated equally with boys.*

This family avails itself of private medical care and birth control technology in Salcedo. Soon after Kati's birth, Beatriz consulted me about family planning. She had stopped receiving birth control injections after thirteen years, only to have an immediate and unwanted pregnancy. She brought Nancy with her for this consultation:

We need to know about the best medicine for family planning. I know you don't have any children. How did you manage that? Nancy needs to know about this, too. I can't take the injections any more, because they make patches on my skin, see? And I think that maybe they make my chest hurt, too. So what should I do? I really don't want any more children because it is so expensive to educate them and everything. We didn't think we could afford three, and now we have three. We can't afford any more.

I told her about the doctor I had recommended for Clemencia. Unlike Clemencia, Beatriz was receptive to the idea of sterilization, for either herself or for Lucho. She said it might be expensive, but not as expensive as having another baby. She was confident she could raise the money and convince Lucho of the necessity for one of them to have surgery. She said there was no hurry, but she needed to know how much money they would need to obtain sterilization so that she could begin to save for it.

Beatriz's role in budget management is similar to that of Clemencia and Valentina: she has at least an equal say in decisions concerning major expenditures and ultimate veto power corresponding to her greater responsibility for stretching income to cover expenses. Like Valentina, she enjoys bargaining and is good at it. Her greater-than-equal role in financial decision-making has the full support of her husband, who credits her with the family's ability to accumulate considerable savings. Lucho does not mind being organized and having his expenditure somewhat restricted. He teases his wife about how hard she has to work to manage him. He is extremely proud of the results.

## The Working Day

Beatriz is a full-time farmer who performs all agricultural tasks in spite of having a new baby. She not only puts in full days in the fields but also performs even the one task considered dangerous by some women: the spray application of pesticides. She usually takes the baby with her to work, bound to her body in a shawl.

On a day typical of many, Beatriz rises early, makes breakfast, cleans the kitchen, dresses the baby, and milks the three cows currently giving milk (of their nine cattle). She washes clothes at the outdoor sink so they will have the entire day in which to dry. She then rouses Lucho and leaves the house to pasture the animals in a nearby field. By the time she returns, Lucho is up and has straightened the house; he is playing with the baby.

They leave home together but do not work in the same field. Lucho has promised to help his father harvest potatoes in Chanchaló; his brothers will also be at the harvest. Beatriz's first task is to examine some of their own potato plants that have been infested with late blight in a field near the house. She determines the amount she will need to spray and returns to the house to mix the chemical preparation and to fill the *tanques,* a two-tank backpack sprayer she will use (without benefit of protection for her face or hands). For this operation, she avails herself of the help of her nephew, whom she recruits by hollering loudly enough to reach his house one-half kilometer away. She explains to me that as the plants grow, they require more pesticide for each application. These plants are riddled with "white worm" as well as with fungus, and she is using a combination of chemicals that should prove effective against both. She offers to pay her nephew to help with the spraying and he agrees, saying he'll first make sure his mother doesn't need him at home.

Beatriz returns to the field alone, hands the baby to me, and begins spray-

*Washing clothes by hand with piped-in water.*

ing the potatoes. The baby sleeps most of the morning, but she awakes once and becomes restive. Beatriz stops working to nurse the baby. She works alone for an hour and is then joined by her nephew who has returned with his own sprayer to help her complete the job.

We all go home for a hearty lunch. Beatriz includes more meat in her family's diet than most other women. Today's lunch includes canned tuna and rice, a favorite with all of her family, prepared with a rich egg sauce and green peas. She also prepares a side dish of sautéed corn. There are sliced tomatoes for garnish and mandarin oranges for dessert. It is not unusual to find a chicken in Beatriz's soup, usually on Sunday. She also frequently prepares Lucho's favorite: roast guinea pig with potatoes in egg sauce and fava beans. On this occasion, we leave the kitchen well fortified for the afternoon's work.

During the afternoon Beatriz performs a circuit of all of the family's property. She checks maize plants for worms, finding too many. She collects edible ears as well as squashes and lupines that are interplanted with the maize. These she folds into a second shawl, carrying them on her back while the baby nestles against her chest. I offer to carry the baby or the produce; she hands me the baby and enjoys laughing at my attempt to imitate her expert construction of a shawl baby carrier. She weeds potatoes in a different field from those she sprayed earlier. Nancy and Grima arrive home from school and help with this task.

As the afternoon draws to a close, we return to the house. Lucho is just arriving home from the potato harvest. He has collected the cattle and brought them home for the evening. He does the evening milking while Beatriz prepares dinner. She repeats the luncheon menu, as everyone likes it so much. As a special treat, she adds *chochos,* lupine beans marinated in oil with tomatoes and onions. Nancy brings in the laundry while Grima helps her mother in the kitchen. Lucho does not cook as long as one of the women is at home to do it. The very idea of her father cooking sends Grima into peals of laughter. After dinner everyone enjoys bathing the baby. When the baby has been dried and wrapped in layers of swaddling and a knitted woolen suit, Lucho turns on the stereo and dances her around the room amid much giggling from the older girls. Then the family all curl up on one of their two beds and settle in for Friday evening's soap operas on TV.

## Managing Agriculture

Beatriz and Lucho practice progressive, high-technology, commercial agriculture. They try to conserve soil by practicing contour plowing with a rented tractor. They apply heavy doses of several agrochemicals. Their diversified commercial production has included garlic and other vegetables, although they no longer risk garlic cultivation. They pay to truck some of this produce to a nearby provincial capital for sale, where the products bring a higher price than in the local Salcedo market. Their investment in production and marketing has yielded both high-quality products and higher prices than their neighbors have been able to obtain.

Beatriz is a full consulting partner in all agricultural decisions. In a manner similar to that detailed for Clemencia and Alejandro, she and Lucho reach consensual decisions concerning how their land is to be used and the level of technology that is most efficient and productive. It is up to Beatriz to decide if they can afford this level of technology, and to manage the household's pooled finances so that they will be able to afford it in the future. She also, on her own, manages the recruitment and supervision of paid labor, as well as the deployment of expensive agricultural inputs. The family's success is indicative of the quality of her management.

## *Summary:* Bien Organizada *for Success*

Beatriz's effective management of household labor and finance has resulted in considerable capital accumulation for her family. Neither she nor her husband has inherited any land. By virtue of their work and her management, they have been able to buy a relatively large amount of land, to construct houses, to pay for their children's education, for health care, and some household luxuries. They have saved a great deal. In the last letter I received from Beatriz, she asked me for the second time to help them buy that tractor. (In contrast, Clemencia wrote about progress of the community's cooperative associations and asked for help in locating buyers for traditional crafts produced by the women's association.) Beatriz has devoted most of her energy and skill to her own family's accumulation, and she has secured their cooperation. It is not surprising that Lucho says he doesn't argue with success.

## Conclusion

The women introduced in this chapter are full-time farmers and full decision-making partners in their households' agricultural production. Women perform these roles on commercial farms of all sizes and levels of technology. They are landowners. They also have equal access to the income derived from production on all household lands. Women control their own labor and organize that of their children and, in some households, of their husbands. All have as much personal autonomy and control of biological reproduction as their husbands. Most cooperate economically with their parents or siblings, bringing into their households greater access to valuable productive resources. Some also give considerable time and expertise to extrahousehold communal organizations devoted to economic and social development; these women have become respected community leaders.

Among the households described, none is patriarchal. Economic-decision processes within the households vary according to both personalities and the personal relationships forged during marriage. Yet the term *egalitarian* can be applied to three of the four partnerships profiled. Although women may have accepted greater responsibility for mobilizing household labor or material resources, in most households most decisions are jointly taken. Both partners have the opportunity to voice their goals, preferences, and misgivings. Neither partner always determines the ultimate action. Even the young Susana, who struggles to motivate her husband to prioritize agricultural labor and reduce his spending, feels she is making headway in directing her husband's energy and expenditure toward jointly held objectives. In the one household where a single partner appears to have greater influence, the more influential partner is female.

All of the husbands in this sample voiced respect for their wives' work, knowledge, and acumen. Two expressed admiration for their wives' strength of will or character. Fathers expressed and provided support for their daughters' personal development goals, even though these took the girls away from home, in one case to the United States. Husbands who have spent considerable time away from their homes were as likely to admire their wives' skills and determination, and to share decision processes equitably as those men who have never lived outside their communities. Husbands' working within mestizo business hierarchies, serving in the mestizo-dominated military, and living in urban environments where men idealize machismo and the male control of women's bodies and household livelihoods have not produced indigenous patriarchs among these families.

On the basis of these five case descriptions, it appears that household participation in development processes has not marginalized women from control of economic resources. Neither agricultural commercialization nor exposure to mestizo patriarchal institutions appears to have disadvantaged women. Post-hacienda restructuring of landownership in accordance with national law does not seem to have resulted in unequal ownership of, or access to, land for women. The presence in the community of male-oriented production organizations does not appear to have reduced women's access to income earned by men. Rather, observation of women's roles as full-time, decision-making farmers, together with their experiences and statements concerning agricultural development programs, suggests that planned development processes should be opened to women.

FOUR ✸ **Women's Work**

*Production and Reproduction in Cantón Salcedo*

THE WOMEN PROFILED in the previous chapter are full-time farmers who cooperate with their husbands and other family members in a fluid division of household productive and reproductive labor. Their agricultural labor is valued equally with that of men in terms of wage rates and in terms of voiced appreciation by husbands for the energy, knowledge, and skill contributed by wives to the household enterprise. In contrast to the model of small-scale highland agricultural production dominant in development institutions, women's dedication to farming does not appear to vary greatly according to household wealth or the amount of household and hired labor available. Nor do child care and other reproductive responsibilities appear to determine the level of women's participation in agricultural labor. In this chapter, quantitative information from the NSF/FUNDAGRO household surveys (see appendix A for a full description of the NSF Child Growth Project and household surveys) will be analyzed to determine whether these patterns are representative of indigenous farming communities in Cantón Salcedo. Case descriptions from surveyed households and from my ethnographic sample will be provided to illustrate the range of variation in women's agricultural labor.

## Production and Reproduction in the Ecuadorean Sierra

*Relevance of a Quantitative/Qualitative Approach*

Both the study of gendered economic processes and the equitable and efficient targeting of decreasing agricultural-development aid to actual producers require knowledge of women's productive and reproductive work. In Ecuador, as elsewhere in Latin America and the developing world, there are conflicting macro- and microlevel reports concerning women's participation in agricultural production. Census and other national-level data often report dramatically lower levels of female participation in agricultural production than are indicated in ethnographic and other local-level analyses (Rogers 1980). A number of researchers have concluded that census data are unreliable, underreporting women's participation because (1) women's participation may be seasonal or informal; (2) respondents are usually asked to list only one occupation and women often choose their reproductive role, describing themselves as housewives; (3) production for household use is not defined as economic activity; (4) respondents answer dishonestly in order to conceal women's income or culturally proscribed behavior.[1] In Ecuador, the 1990 census reports that only 13 percent of the agricultural economically active population is female (Mardešic 1992, 164). For Salcedo, this rate rises to 33 percent (INEC 1990a, 242).

Microlevel analyses, however, indicate that rural women in Salcedo and throughout the sierra are likely to be full-time farmers. Development analysts widely report the "feminization of agriculture." Buvinić (1980) reports that 80 percent of "subsistence" farms in Cantón Salcedo are operated by women (at that time census figures put the female percentage of the agricultural workforce at only 7.5 percent). Chiriboga (1984) also concludes that women are largely responsible for production among Salcedo smallholders. Among smallholding potato producers in Chimborazo Province, over 90 percent of surveyed women work year-round on family farms, averaging forty hours per week (Hamilton 1992). Ethnographic accounts from throughout the sierra confirm that indigenous women are likely to be farmers (Belote and Belote 1977, 1988; Stark 1984; Poeschel 1988; Alberti 1986; Weismantel 1988).

Several reports suggest that the proportion of women's labor devoted to agricultural production is likely to be conditioned by household wealth, demographic variables including the age of the woman and motherhood of young children, and most important, the presence or absence of adult men in the household. The feminization of agriculture is generally attributed to the interaction between poverty and temporary male outmigration (Garrett and Espinosa 1988; Barsky 1984; Balarezo 1984; Chiriboga 1984). On the smallest, poorest, or "subsistence" farms, families often cannot make a living by farming; even those whose land base could be made more profitable through investment in modernized inputs and improvements often conclude that farming is not likely to prove an advantageous investment of all household labor (Preston 1980). The lack of well-paying local nonagricultural employment means that some household members will leave home to work. Urban wage differentials for men and women are such that male labor can be more profitably invested in off-farm work than female labor (Faulkner and Lawson 1991). Thus, adult men are more likely to work away from home.[2]

Researchers are agreed that male outmigration increases women's responsibility for agricultural labor; women must either perform more labor themselves, pay for it, recruit it through kinship and other reciprocity networks, or organize work parties (Blumberg and Colyer 1990, 252). An insufficiency of male labor, owing to outmigration or poorer households' inability to supplement household labor, is considered by most analysts to be the primary reason women are heavily involved in agriculture: "a general principle is that the feminization of agriculture is a consequence of poverty" (Garrett and Espinosa 1988, 204). Acceptance of this "general principle" by development planners contributes to the exclusion of women from technical-assistance programs targeted to small-scale commercial—as opposed to subsistence—producers (de Janvry and Sadoulet 1990). The view that poverty forces women into the fields has an inverse corollary: household wealth removes that economic imperative and with it women's participation in field labor associated with commercialized production on larger farms (see Deere and León 1982). In sociocultural contexts where labor is viewed as an entitlement to the means and fruits of production, wealthier women's decreased involvement in field labor can result in reduced access to household economic resources (Bourque and Warren 1981).

An alternative pattern is suggested by Alberti (1986), who finds that indigenous women of all socioeconomic levels are likely to be fully engaged in agricultural labor in Chimborazo Province. Alberti's findings must be considered suggestive only, as she points out, owing to her small sample size. A rural-reconnaissance survey that produced similar findings for Chimborazo Province must also be considered suggestive, given the nonrandom nature of the sample survey (Blumberg and Colyer 1990). My own previous work, which also found that indigenous women of all socioeconomic levels are full-time farmers in ten Chimborazo communities (Hamilton 1992), is based on a larger representative sample but lacks qualitative information with which to contextualize reported variation in levels of wealth. Allowing for regional and ethnic variation, contrasting patterns reported in these studies point to the need for analysis of interactions among household wealth, male outmigration, and women's agricultural labor in a population for which both probabilistic sample data and qualitative information are available.

Reproductive constraints associated with the household's developmental cycle may influence women's involvement in productive labor (Buvinić 1990). Periods of pregnancy, childbirth, and lactation may limit women's productive labor time, as well as their ability—or perceived ability—to perform certain tasks. Although Ecuadorean cases suggest that husbands and older children are likely to share child-care responsibilities (Stark 1979) and that women are likely to take small children to the fields with them (Hamilton 1992), the number and ages of a woman's dependents may affect her ability to work.

Microlevel reports differ considerably concerning productive domains (such as crop versus livestock production), activity or labor domains (such as land preparation or marketing), and specific tasks (such as planting following men's plowing during land preparation) likely to be performed by women. Kristi Anne Stolen (1985) finds that women in Machachi are likely to execute all production tasks except plowing, for which they must depend upon males. Similarly, Louisa Stark (1984) finds that in the northern sierra, both men and women participate in all household productive activities such as land preparation or clothing manufacture, but that men and women execute different or "complementary" tasks within domains, such as men plowing while women plant. Rae Blumberg and Dale Colyer's rapid rural appraisal finds that indigenous women participate to some degree in all "main crop tasks" except plowing and chemical applications (1990, 252). Andrea Allen observes that women in Chimborazo participate in neither application nor purchase of agrochemicals (personal communication).[3]

With respect to the management of productive domains, Blumberg and Colyer report a general pattern of "men's activities being concentrated on crop production and women devoting relatively more time to livestock raising activities." This division is refined by the observation that, concerning crop production, men "generally do the heavier field work, such as land clearing and plowing, with women being more involved in planting, weeding, and harvesting crops" (1990, 250). Garrett and Espinosa also report distinct male and female "enterprises" in smallholder households but do not refine their analysis to include women's roles within male enterprises. They conclude that women are likely to be involved in kitchen gardens and small-animal production (1988, 208–9).

From most of these reports a picture emerges of the relatively inclusive participation of indigenous women in agricultural production. However, certain critical tasks, predominantly plowing and agrochemical application, must be performed by men. Men may be more intensively involved in cropping and thus bear more responsibility for crop production than women. Women may be more likely to bear primary responsibility for livestock production, especially small-animal production. Development programs that only offer production assistance to women for small-animal projects are based on the assumption that these patterns apply throughout the sierra.

Yet reconnaissance survey teams preparing preliminary reports to aid in the design of agricultural development projects observed sierran women participating in *all* crop production tasks in three provinces, including mixing chemicals for fumigation (K. DeWalt and Uquillas 1989). Belote and Belote observe that, even within a traditional division of labor based upon sexual complementarity, most Saraguro men's and women's tasks are flexibly interchangeable (1988). Ruthbeth Finerman agrees that Saraguro women regularly expand their traditional duties to take full charge of agriculture and pastoralism when men are gone; she finds, however, that men are less likely to perform women's domestic duties (1989). Weismantel describes a similar pattern of flexibility in Cotopaxi Province, where women perform all agricultural labor in their husbands' absence (1988). Allowing for regional and ethnic variation, these contradictory findings suggest that studies of rural women's work in the region should describe both the range of women's agricultural activities and the division of household productive and reproductive labor.

## Research Questions and Samples

Information from Chanchaló and two additional indigenous communities of Cantón Salcedo will test the applicability of contrasting models of women's productive and reproductive labor for a more recently studied population of indigenous agriculturalists. I shall examine (1) the amount of time women devote to agricultural production;[4] (2) whether the amount of time women devote to agricultural labor is conditioned by household wealth, male outmigration, the age of a woman or of her children; (3) the range of women's participation in agricultural activities and the gendered division of reproductive labor; and (4) the material and ideological valuation of women's labor.

The NSF/FUNDAGRO Household Surveys were conducted during three seasonal rounds beginning in August 1992 and ending in July 1993 (probabilistic sample–selection criteria described in appendix A). The quantitative information presented in this chapter comes from the survey's first and second rounds. Information on the range of women's agricultural activities was collected during the first round, when 108 female and male household heads (conjugal pairs) participated in the survey (appendix A). The sample size was reduced to 80 during the survey's second round. Difference of means tests indicate that the samples available for analysis do not differ in terms of socioeconomic status, male outmigration, and household demographics across rounds (Hamilton 1995, 286–88; appendix 1). Analysis of the amount of time women devote to household agriculture is based on the survey's second round.

The communities of Chanchaló, Sacha, and Cumbijín resemble one another in terms of level and distribution of wealth and services, the importance of commercial agriculture to household economies, and household demography. As male outmigration is higher in Sacha than in Chanchaló, the three-community sample more closely resembles many other sierran smallholding populations than does Chanchaló (see appendix A).

## Women Are Full-Time Farmers

### Measuring Agricultural Labor Time

The women introduced in chapter 3 work full days on their families' farms. In the three-community sample, as well, most women are full-time farmers. Women interviewed during the second round of the household survey (N = 80) provided both twenty-four-hour recalls of primary and secondary activities and their estimated average weekly time expenditure in agricultural production. Women work an average of forty-seven hours per week in agriculture (SD 15). On the day before they were surveyed, women worked an average of eight hours in agriculture—six in crops, two in animal care. Thus, both estimated weekly average and twenty-four-hour-recall measures indicate that most women work full eight-hour days in agriculture, six days per week.

The amount of labor a woman devotes to agriculture does not appear to be conditioned by household wealth, the absence of her husband from the farm, her age, or her child-care responsibilities. (Results of a least-squares multiple regression analysis testing the effects of these variables on women's agricultural labor are presented in appendix B, table 1; see also table B.2.) The relatively small size of the sample available for this analysis suggests caution in interpreting results. However, statistical results are consistent with qualitative information. Discussion of the interaction of these variables will include observations from my ethnographic sample together with qualitative information collected from survey participants in Sacha and Cumbijín.

## Wealthy Women and Older Women Work in the Fields

I observed the most economically secure women, including the fifty-eight-year-old Rosa, working full days and doing the most arduous tasks. Rosa and her husband own more land, household goods, and machinery than any other family living in Chanchaló. Informants placed them in a category by themselves as the wealthiest family in the community. They regularly employ agricultural laborers. Yet, Rosa puts in a rigorous day in the fields (see chapter 1). She utilizes the family's truck, tractor, and household appliances to accomplish greater output rather than to reduce her working hours.

Rosa and her husband, Rosalino, have most of their landholdings in the *páramos,* some of it near 4,000 meters, the highest land that is cultivated in Chanchaló. Despite the cold high winds in this environment, Rosa works daily alongside her husband and paid workers, whatever the task. I observed her digging potatoes with hand tools, a backbreaking endeavor. While her husband grumbled about how such hard work has worn them out before their time, Rosa just kept on digging, pausing at times to straighten up and enjoy the view of range after range of the Western Cordillera receding in the distance across the inter-Andean valley.

Two-thirds of the way through her grueling day, she turned to wave to me in an adjoining field, spreading wide her arms to encompass the scene, a radiant smile on her face. She called out that she wanted me to take a picture of this magnificent landscape and of her in her fine potato field. I did not have my camera and thus could not record on film the tremendous vitality of this woman who embraces the hardest agricultural fieldwork although her family does not need her labor to survive, or even for an additional measure of comfort.

When I asked her why she continues to work so hard, Rosa appeared surprised by the question. "I like to work. And I am a farmer. What else would I do?" Although she does not identify material needs that necessitate her continued labor, I know that Rosa is ambitious for her children. She and her husband are educating their young-adult children at least through secondary school. They have helped older children secure nonagricultural livelihoods. And although they make money by sharecropping their land with Clemencia and other children living in Chanchaló, they have also given the use of several plots of land, as well. Rosa has a large family. It is possible that she works because she wants to maximize household production per the cost of labor, even though she can enjoy a considerable measure of comfort and security without contributing her own field labor. I suspect that Rosa has a material motivation for her intense agricultural labor, as well as the personal satisfaction she evidently derives from her work.

I observed women older than Rosa also executing difficult tasks and working regularly in the fields. I watched Cleotilde, whose age was estimated by informants to be around seventy, sprint up a steep slope while carrying a heavy load at the end of her morning's work in the fields. She was winded when she reached the top, but her pace never slowed. I also observed poorer elderly women who work more slowly and with less apparent energy than Rosa or Cleotilde; I am certain their labor is needed for survival.

I observed one woman of fifty-eight who, owing to ill health, works only intermittently in the fields. María is content to turn the fieldwork over to her children. She is content, also, to live in a smaller, more rudimentary home than Rosa. She and her husband have not educated their children beyond the sixth grade. María's husband is in vigorous health but prefers to tend his beautiful flower garden and to participate in community affairs rather than devote his days to the ardors of fieldwork. Having given their children their full inheritance, María and Rodrigo have kept only a small amount of land and are semiretired from agricultural work. María's delicate health does not prevent her from putting in a full day doing housework, caring for animals, cooking, and looking after several grandchildren.

I would not conclude that all women of nearly sixty would have Rosa's seemingly endless energy and considerable enthusiasm for fieldwork. I would conclude that, barring ill health, women may expect to continue working in the fields through middle age even if their families do not need their labor to survive.

At thirty-five, Alegría is younger than Rosa but also is considered wealthy. Alegría and her husband, Rubén, no longer live in Chanchaló, although they farm fifteen hectares in the community together with Alegría's father-in-law. Alegría and Rubén live in neighboring Palama, where they have bought land. They also own a sixty-hectare cattle ranch in the Amazon basin. In addition to owning more land and productive assets than others in Chanchaló, Alegría is also better educated, having graduated from high school. Yet Alegría also puts in full days on the farm.

During a typical day, she rises at 5:00 A.M.; prepares breakfast for her husband, father-in-law, and two school-aged children; tends to the feeding, health care, and milking of animals; leaves for eight hours in the fields, where she works alongside her husband, father-in-law, and several hired hands in all phases of agricultural production (see chapter 1). Following her fieldwork, Alegría returns home to check on the animals and do laundry or housework while her husband prepares dinner. After dinner, both parents join their children to supervise schoolwork or enjoy their favorite TV soap opera. Alegría and her husband own a truck, which she often drives home from the fields so that she can tend to animals closer to home while her husband continues fieldwork. She says the truck is a big help because she has at least ten hours of work a day to put in on the farm, and her day would be even longer if she had to walk or ride a burro to the fields as most women do.

When I asked Alegría why she works so hard when her family is not poor, she replied that her work isn't hard and that she likes it. Thinking that her work looks extremely hard to me, I asked what she would consider to be difficult work. Alegría paused and replied, "It would be hard if I didn't have a good man to help me. It would be harder if we didn't have a tractor." I point out, "But a tractor can't dig potatoes or cure a sick calf." Her response was: "That's for sure. Well, if you want to know what hard work is, you should ask my cousin. She works in an office and has to do what other people say all the time and doesn't make very much money. It seems to me that is very hard work. But the work that we do here is not hard."

The pattern observed in Andean mestizo communities by Deere and León (1982) and others, and in an Andean indigenous community by Bourque and Warren (1981), in which women from wealthier smallholder households participate less in agricultural field labor than poorer women, does not apply to Chanchaló. Full-time female farmers are found at all socioeconomic levels. Implications of this pattern for women's control of economic resources in wealthier households will be addressed in chapter 7.

*Mothers of Very Young Children Work in the Fields*

Piedad is another relatively wealthy woman who works hard in the fields; she is also the working mother of a young child. Piedad and her husband are generally considered to be among the most successfully enterprising farmers in the neighborhood. They have amassed enough capital to buy both a truck and a tractor; they live in a two-story house and send their teenaged children to town to school. Piedad's daughter, Jessica, was nine months old when I met the family on my first day in the community. As I watched Jessi grow from an infant to a toddler, her mother never missed a working day in the fields. She wrapped the baby in a shawl and carried her nestled into her chest until the little girl could walk. Then Jessica would amuse herself in the field while her parents worked and watched out for her. Beatriz also carries her baby to the fields (see chapter 3). Both of these women perform all production tasks, including the spraying of agrochemicals, with their babies either tied onto their bodies, playing on blankets nearby, or under the care of teenaged children.

Child care is a family affair rather than the exclusive responsibility of women. When mothers and fathers work in different fields, it is not unusual for fathers to take the children who are no longer nursing along with them.

*A father shares child-care duties in the field.*

Fathers working around the house often are in charge of children. In many families, older children or teenaged relatives remain in the house and take care of younger children. Clemencia trusts her ten-year-old son to make sure that two-year-old Milton stays out of mortal danger; at ten, Diego is a responsible, if occasionally mischievous, babysitter. Susana's twelve-year-old brother often supervises three-year-old Marisela. It is not unusual to find that a woman's teenaged sibling, cousin, niece, nephew, or affinal relative temporarily serves as babysitter or has come to live in the household.

The communities have intermittent access to government-supported day-care facilities, where children are supervised and given meals by local young women. These facilities closed during the time I was in Chanchaló, owing to national restructuring policies. Approximately one-fourth of surveyed mothers took their children to the day-care facility; most of these mothers took their children to the fields with them when the facility was closed. A little more than half of surveyed women reported taking their children to the fields with them when the facility was closed, as opposed to 41 percent when it was open. During both time periods, a little less than half reported leaving their children with a relative.

Children of all ages roam freely through the community. Women in Chanchaló can be heard calling their children to return from their wanderings as far away as my house in Chanchalito, across the small ravine marking Chanchaló's western boundary. They often deputize a child going down the road to carry a message to their own absent offspring. Parents say they are not concerned about their children's roaming, as neighbors can be counted on to track their progress through the fields and even to feed them should they show up at mealtime.

Women's child-care strategies vary, depending on the availability of husbands, older children, and other relatives who serve as caretakers, as well as the availability of state-supported day care. Whether mothers take their children to the fields or leave them at home or at the day-care center, having very young children does not decrease women's work outside their homes.

## Women Work as Many Hours with Husbands Present or Absent

Women's workloads are generally expected to be greater in households where men are away from home working for wages. Although the expected pattern is logically compelling, women in Chanchaló maintain that they work just as much in the fields when their husbands are home as when the men are away. As Chanchaleñas see it, the difference is that more overall agricultural work gets done when the men are around, including work that does not have to be done on an immediate or daily basis. Some families can hire or

agree to exchange future labor in order to compensate for a husband's temporary absence.

Mariana's husband works in Quito several months during the year doing
construction. He is also a member of the cattle and fish production cooperative and must report for labor rotations in the *monte*. Thus, he is likely to be
away—at least during the week—for about half the year. Mariana's daily
schedule is much the same whether her husband is at home or away. Like the
women profiled above and in chapter 3, whose husbands are working full-
time on the farm, she puts in about eight hours in the fields daily when her
husband is away. Mariana grows high-altitude crops including melloco, oca,
and fava beans as well as potatoes, barley, and wheat. She climbs the one-to-
two-hour trip to the *páramos* with her nursing baby on her back. She sometimes travels to nearby Palama, where she owns a one-third hectare plot; she
works this land together with her sister, producing the maize she cannot grow
at higher altitudes. Mariana's days in the field are much like those of Alegría
and Rosa, who also travel to the *páramos* to work. Mariana sold her few animals during the time I was in Chanchaló; at least temporarily, she did not devote as much time as Alegría and Rosa to animal care. However, she has no
truck, so her trips to work are arduous, as well as more time-consuming. She
also has four children under the age of eight and no husband at home to help
with child care.

When Enrique is present, he accompanies Mariana to the *páramos* of
Chanchaló or to Palama; she puts in the same full agricultural days when Enrique is at home. Mariana says that her round of activities is determined by
the needs of the crops, not by her husband's presence or absence:

Well, I have to do more housework when my husband is in Quito. And I don't have
anyone to help with the children. During the day they go to school and to the day-care
center. And they can go to my in-laws' house. But I have to take care of them and the
housework when my husband is in Quito.

But the work I do with the crops does not change when he is not here. I work all
day—every day—whether he is here or not. There is always something I have to do—
every day—with the crops. It is true that we do more work and better work when he is
here. He sharpens the tools very well. He cleans the ditches. I don't have time. And he
works very hard in the fields.

Although the family are considered poor by informants, living in a one-
room adobe house and currently cultivating little more than one hectare of
land, they invest earnings in productive activities, including occasional hired
labor as well as cooperative membership. Both Enrique's wages and their
commercial agriculture provide money for these expenses. Although they
hire help at harvest time, Mariana says they also decrease production during

years when Enrique expects to be away for relatively longer periods of time. Because Enrique has found well-paying work in construction this year, they have planted less during the current cropping cycles than in some previous years. Less total household agricultural labor and production occur when her husband is absent, but Mariana's agricultural labor does not increase.

## A Part-Time Farmer

All of the women in my ethnographic sample and all of the women in the probabilistic sample from Chanchaló are full-time farmers. Among the few women in other communities who are not full-time farmers, is Nely of Cumbijín. Nely moved to Cumbijín from Salcedo twenty years ago when she was fifteen. She has six children, aged from eleven years to nine months; she is breast-feeding the baby. The family are poor, living in a one-room house with a television set and not much else in the way of amenities. They do not own land but rent between one and three hectares for agricultural production. During our first-round survey, they did not have enough to eat (only about two-thirds of the calories they need [FAO 1973]). Their baby is seriously undernourished.

Although Nely does most of the household's animal care, she only works in the fields when the family needs her labor for harvesting and weeding. She also sells onions produced on the farm occasionally, but she does not market crops regularly. Nely says she "helps out" with agriculture. At the time she was surveyed, Nely worked afternoons in the fields following mornings devoted to housework and animal care.

## A Nonagricultural Wage Laborer

One woman in the probabilistic sample does not participate in agriculture; her household does not farm. The stark poverty of this family from Cumbijín contrasts with the relative security of even a poor Chanchaló household like that of Susana and Nicolás. Susana can count on the help of extended family during hungry times and can develop economic opportunities in cooperation with friends. The family of Transito, however, goes hungry. During the period of our survey, Transito's family had less than half the calories they need. No one gave them any food. Transito says: "We have nothing. Neither land nor animals." The family also does not have a home. They work for the state as custodians. Transito is the elementary school janitor; she, her husband, and four children live in the school building.

Transito is a mestiza from Guayas Province on the Ecuadorean coast. All of her relatives still live there. She has lived in Cumbijín for six years apparently without establishing a mutual-aid network. It would be pointless to speculate on the reasons for this family's economic isolation beyond the fact that they are coastal immigrants with no kinship ties in the community and no material resource base from which to establish reciprocity. I cannot help thinking that had they moved to Chanchaló, they might have been encouraged to exchange labor for the measure of security provided by the production associations' credit funds. Although Cumbijín is developing production associations, I have been told by development workers and members of other communities that Cumbijín is less friendly to outsiders than Chanchaló.

## Range of Women's Productive Activities: Equal Work for Women and Men

Nearly all women report that they work in all phases of agricultural production, not only during times of peak activity such as harvesting (see table 7). Women interviewed during the survey's first round (N = 108) were asked to rank their participation in each activity relative to that of their husbands. The percentages displayed in table 7 refer to the number of women who ranked their participation as equal to or greater than their husbands'.

Nearly all women reported equal participation in *siembra* (sowing, planting). Women were not asked if they participate in land preparation. As observed during land preparation at the women's group *minga* described in chapter 3, a gendered division of labor characterizes the participation of women and men in the overall process of land preparation, which includes opening the ground, turning the soil, and sowing or planting. During all land preparation activities I observed, men drove the draft animals or tractor, while

*Table 7. Women Report Equal Participation in Agricultural Production, Cantón Salcedo, 1992*

| Household Production Activity | Percentage of Women Reporting Equal Participation |
|---|---|
| Planting | 96% |
| Cultivation | 99% |
| Harvest | 98% |
| Marketing | 69% |
| Animal care | 96% |

*Source:* NSF/FUNDAGRO Household Surveys, round 1, August–October 1992 (N = 108).

   *Notes:* By "equal participation" is meant "participation equal to or greater than husband's participation."

women did not, although women participated with men in hand-tool preparation of soil. Although women were more likely to plant than men, men also participated in planting.

I do not have a reliable measure of the level of mechanical technology for surveyed households; surveyed men were asked whether they own equipment such as tractors, not whether they use agricultural machinery. Among the five households described in chapter 3, four households use rented tractors. Most households apply either machinery or draft animals to the task of land preparation; some households supplement this technology by hand hoeing to refine the soil.

Nearly all land in Chanchaló has long been cleared of forest. This is true of other surveyed communities, as well. When trees are cut in Chanchaló, it is generally to provide fuel rather than to clear land. Both women and men cut trees.

Women and men perform the same tasks within most other agricultural activities, such as weeding and harvesting; over 90 percent of surveyed women reported that they and their husbands contribute an equal amount of work to these activities. Nearly 90 percent also reported equal participation in the processing of agricultural products. Although 10 percent of surveyed women devote more time than their husbands to processing, this percentage is smaller than might have been anticipated considering reports from other Andean communities, where processing of tubers and grains (that is, the bulk of household production) is more of a female specialty (C. Allen 1988; Harris 1985). There is remarkably little regularized specialization by gender in household agricultural production. Women work with all crops and with all animals, as well as in all phases of agricultural production.

Men were not asked if they market products; I cannot compare the fact that two-thirds of women market household products with a comparable percentage of men. Considering the fact that some women establish the price they will accept and leave the actual market negotiation to their husbands, I suspect women's involvement in marketing may be somewhat underestimated in the survey. In households I observed, two-thirds of the women (such as the adroit bargainers Valentina and Beatriz) handled most of their household's selling. Although I would not conclude that marketing is a female specialization in households where women participate, I would conclude that most women are at least equal participants in household marketing.

## Agrochemical Use and Women's Freedom to Choose

Over two-thirds of women in pesticide-using households (84 percent of the sample) apply pesticides, using backpack sprayers without protective clothing, masks, or gloves. A slightly larger percentage use and apply chemical fertilizers. These findings contradict patterns reported elsewhere in Ecuador and the Andes. A widely applied Rapid Rural Appraisal conducted among indigenous small-scale producers in Chimborazo Province (see Blumberg and Colyer 1990) concludes that even women who perform most other agricultural activities do not work with pesticides. It may be that sensationalized reporting of fetal death resulting from pesticide exposure in a pregnant worker during the late 1980s (see Dinham 1993) influenced behavior reported in the Chimborazo survey. Anecdotal evidence from similar communities in Chimborazo suggests this connection: in 1988–1989 women of child-bearing age reported avoiding pesticide use because of dangers to fetal health. Lacking access to family planning, these women viewed themselves as potentially pregnant most of the time (Andrea Allen, personal communication). It may be that with the passage of time since the sensationalized reporting of this fetal death, women have become more amenable to working with chemicals, or that with increasing use of pesticides on small farms (Zuloaga et al. 1990) their labor has become more necessary. It may be that practices in Salcedo and in the Chimborazo communities differ.

Elsewhere in the Andes indigenous beliefs concerning women's physical or emotional frailties, especially those related to biological reproduction, are reported to exclude them from participation in some productive activities, often those activities that add most value to a crop (Bourque and Warren 1981; Larme 1993). In direct contrast to this pattern, women in the study population are said—by both male and female informants—to be *fuerte*, a term that refers both to physical strength and heartiness and to strength of character. No one in Chanchaló considers women unfit to handle pesticides.[5]

It is widely believed in the study area that viruses and other pathogens travel on the wind from as far away as other countries. Spraying powerful chemicals is thus a potentially dangerous activity for anyone, male or female, who is particularly susceptible to airborne disease. Some women, including Clemencia and Mariana, expressed a preference for avoiding the spraying of pesticides for health reasons. One man expressed the same reluctance: "Fumigating is very bad for me. I have been sick all during the rains with this flu. I can't get better. My wife says she and the boy should do the fumigating. So that's what we do. Once a month for some of the potatoes; once every two weeks for others. When I get better I will fumigate, too."

Women and men may feel constrained to perform disliked tasks if their labor is needed, but they enjoy equal freedom to negotiate with other household members in an attempt to avoid those tasks. We observed Clemencia's ability to avoid spraying pesticides, an activity she felt would contribute to extant respiratory distress. Mariana fears that exposure to pesticide fumes is bad for her skin. Both of these women prefer that their husbands or hired labor apply pesticides. Clemencia will occasionally pitch in when her health allows to "do a little fumigating." Mariana's household produces less and she has been able to avoid this labor domain altogether. Both apply chemical fertilizers, which do not require spraying.

I interpret the percentages reported above as reflecting women's judgment regarding activities in which they regularly participate. Clemencia occasionally does some fumigating, yet on the survey she characterized her participation as *ninguna* (none). In observing individual households and in the communities, I found no evidence that women had exaggerated their participation in the full range of cropping and livestock activities.

## Gender Ideology and the Division of Labor

*"Somos iguales"* ("we are equals" or "we are the same"). Colleagues studying nutrition in Sacha received this answer when they asked women and men to describe their work. Observation of work and measures of energy expenditure confirmed that women and men share physically taxing productive labor in an equitable manner (Leonard 1995; P. Berti, Leonard, and W. Berti 1995; P. Berti 1996). In Chanchaló, as well, informants stressed the uniformity of men's and women's agricultural work, using the same term.

Do men and women do the same agricultural work? Certainly both men and women participate in all phases of agricultural production. Although women are less likely than men to apply pesticides, this activity is not closed to women. Although some women do not market their households' products, this activity is also open to women. No labor domain is exclusively female or male. Only one task within one labor domain—plowing with machinery or draft animals—is a male specialization. To some degree, animal care is a female specialization; nearly one-fifth of surveyed women reported greater involvement in animal care than their husbands, while only 2 percent reported less involvement. However, in most households, both men and women feed, milk, and care for the health of animals.

Taking the research population as a whole, then, it would not be inaccurate to say that men and women do much the same agricultural work. Within a given household, and to the degree that the total labor supply makes specialization possible, it is quite likely that household heads specialize in those labor domains for which they are particularly skilled, such as marketing, or for which they have a preference. However, this division of labor is neither rigid nor, with the exception of plowing, determined by gender. Although

*The two-headed household in action: wife and husband share the work and the rewards of agricultural production.*

most women regularly milk cows, we observed Alejandro and Nicolás do the milking in their households. Both of their wives prefer to avoid that task. When these men are not available, their wives do the milking. Beatriz and Lucho do not express a preference regarding milking, and one is as likely as the other to perform the task. Both of these patterns are frequently repeated among the households I observed: (1) a mate will substitute for an absent partner in tasks regularly performed by the absent partner; (2) both partners routinely perform a single task, either jointly or alternately. Both flexibility and expediency characterize the division of agricultural labor within individual families. It is not surprising that local people perceive that women and men do "the same" work.

*Igual* also means "equal." In Chanchaló, equality with reference to agricultural labor involves both material and ideological valuation. Both agricultural workers and employers unanimously reported to me and to the survey that women and men receive an equal wage. The agricultural wage varies both by employer and by task, with more physically demanding labor such as digging potatoes bringing a higher wage, although both variations tend to be small. Both women and men are employed in all phases of agricultural production.

When I asked informants if there were any tasks that only men or women could perform *well,* I was told emphatically—by both men and women—that men and women are *igual* in ability. For example, when I persisted in asking if women could drive oxen, the unanimous response from both men and women was that women drive oxen as well as men. When I remarked that I had never seen a woman drive oxen, I was told that women do drive oxen. Although managing the team is clearly a male specialty, no one remarked that it would be improper or foolish for a woman to attempt this task. The feeling seemed to be just the opposite: an insistence by informants of both genders that neither gender owns exclusively the strength or expertise to manage any particular agricultural labor domain or task. What interests me most about the disparity between my own observation and local knowledge with respect to women's plowing is not that the disparity exists—behavioral observation proved remarkably consistent with local perceptions in all other areas of household labor—but that the basis for the disparity appears to be an ideological stance favoring the *absence* of gendered boundaries in the division of labor and skills.

This insistence on the absence of gendered boundaries for agricultural labor roles is at variance with cultural norms recorded for many other Andean farming systems, in which the gendered division of labor may be fluid in practice, but in which the *perceived* roles and abilities of men and women differ. In many studies of Andean farming systems, compelling descriptions of traditional gender ideology and behavior delineate a dualistic cultural landscape, in which women and men are believed to occupy highly differentiated but equally vital—that is, complementary—roles in their families' and communities' agendas for economic, social, and even cosmic perpetuation.[6]

These studies report that women and men operate in perceptually gender-bounded arenas of labor and knowledge. Although both women and men may actually participate in productive domains associated with the opposite gender, even to the point of performing essentially the same labor, these domains remain conceptually separate.[7] In some farming systems, the perception is that women specialize in animal husbandry, whereas men concentrate on crop production (Fernández 1988), or vice versa (Belote and Belote 1988). In other systems, women and men are differentially associated with the labor and products of particular ecological or physical production zones (Harris 1978, 1980, 1985). Even if both women and men work with all crops and animals, complementary essential tasks within crop or livestock production may be perceived as being female or male work. A frequently reported belief is that men may open the earth, but women—inheritors of a tradition that associates female deities with agricultural fertility and the well-being of the earth—must sow the seed or else crops will not thrive.

In systems characterized by gender complementarity, households need the labor, skill, products, and power associated with both women and men to survive and prosper. The observed equal valuation of women's agricultural labor is explained by researchers as resulting from their separate-but-equal contribution to the household economy (Lambert 1977; see Hamilton 1995, 333). Indigenous informants, also, make strong statements regarding the propriety of maintaining distinct gender roles in household production and the necessity of obtaining the unique contributions of both women and men for household reproduction (C. Allen 1988). Among the minority of observers who find that women and men do not enjoy equal valuation for agricultural labor, gender specialization is seen as a source of gender inequality (Bourque and Warren 1981).

In Chanchaló, women and men do not have culturally defined complementary roles in agricultural production, yet their work is valued equally. Men's and women's work is perceived as "the same," rather than as separate; it is also perceived as "equal." As I was not able to uncover evidence of pre-hacienda labor relations in Chanchaló, I do not know whether culturally constructed complementary roles once characterized household agricultural production in the traditional manner. Local people insist that women and men did the same work in the fields of the hacienda; it is quite possible that hacienda labor patterns drew women into particular activities or tasks within agricultural production that had been traditional male specialties. However, as women no longer plow with oxen as they did on the hacienda, it is also possible that household labor patterns have not been affected profoundly by hacienda structures.

## Reproductive Labor: A Family Affair[8]

Although women are generally considered to be the managers of food procurement and preparation for their households, their husbands often bear much of the responsibility for daily food preparation. Although women are more likely to care for the youngest children, their husbands often share child-care responsibilities. Although women are more likely to treat medical problems within the household, their husbands share knowledge of medicinal herbs and other treatments. Responsibility for household cleanliness is also shared between women and men (see chapter 3). To some degree, then, women specialize in reproductive labor. However, the same sort of flexibility and fluidity in task-sharing and task-substitution is found regarding the work of reproducing the household as that observed regarding agricultural production.

The realm of food procurement, preparation, and distribution within the household is, in many Andean settings, managed by the female household head (C. Allen 1988; Harris 1985; Weismantel 1988). Even in communities in which women may not participate equally in production of food crops for sale, it remains a feminine responsibility to ensure that the household retains enough of its production to feed the family (Bourque and Warren 1981). In Chanchaló, women are more likely to shop for food, and they also have at least an equal say in decisions concerning how much of the household's total production to keep or sell. However, handling food and thinking about food quality are not female specialties.

In most households men are as likely to prepare food as are women. Within my ethnographic sample of ten households, eight husbands do the cooking as frequently as their wives, or, on a regular basis, they participate equally in joint food preparation. Men also appear to be knowledgeable regarding nutrients and problems associated with undernutrition. When discussing cultigens, men are as likely as women to describe nutrient content and to suggest the best ways of preparing plants for human consumption. When discussing the community's development needs, men are more likely than women to emphasize lack of protein and vitamins in the local diet and to suggest ways agricultural change could help solve this problem. Men are also as likely as women to ask about food consumption and preparation in the United States. Several men remarked that they particularly enjoy cooking.

In the previous chapter we observed fathers caring for their young children, older children tagging along with or working with their fathers, and men cleaning houses and patios, washing and ironing clothes. There are no tasks within these domains that women perform exclusively. In all of the households I observed, men and male children perform child care and housework on a regular basis. All of my male informants say that they perform all domestic duties when their wives are absent. Several husbands express pride in their ability to manage food preparation, child care, laundry, and house cleaning while their wives were abed during the month's convalescence following childbirth. I also observed men teaching their male and female children to cook and do laundry.

I have emphasized the lack of behavioral and perceived gender complementarity within agricultural labor domains in Chanchaló. When reproductive labor is added to the discussion, a degree of specialization by gender emerges, but fluidity in task performance by women or men remains. As with agricultural labor, both men and women say that whoever is most immediately available will perform any domestic task that needs to be done. Collins aptly summarizes the division of productive and reproductive labor characteristic of Chanchaló as well as Southern Peru: "Perhaps the best way to describe the variety of arrangements that exist is that expediency rules, and as long as both spouses are working and cooperating, the actual division of labor is of minor importance" (1988, 140).

## Conclusion

The quantitative and qualitative information presented in this chapter demonstrates that models of household production and reproduction predominant in development institutions and in Andean ethnography do not characterize Chanchaló, Sacha, and Cumbijín. Both state and private development institutions base much of their agriculture policy on the assumption that the "feminization of agriculture" is a result of poverty and male outmigration. In these communities, however, neither women's status as full-time farmers nor their participation in particular labor domains can be considered a "household strategy," determined purely by the collective needs and assets of the household. Although gender bias in regional labor markets does result in the investment of off-farm labor by men rather than by women, women's agricultural work is not determined by the absence of their husbands. While wealthy women with access to hired labor work full-time in the fields, a poor woman's family tries to get along without her full-time fieldwork. Women are full-time farmers on farms of all sizes.

The gendered division of productive and reproductive labor observed in

Chanchaló also is not addressed by development agendas that target technical assistance for commercial agriculture to men, and small-animal or household-garden projects to women. Although household gardens and small-animal production seem to development planners to be a natural outgrowth of women's reproductive responsibilities, local women's productive work is not limited to these arenas. Moreover, Chanchaleñas do not consider household gardens to be a worthy investment of productive labor. Local women are targeted by both public and private institutions to receive technical assistance in the areas of nutrition and family health. Many women have become impatient with programs addressing only their externally perceived reproductive roles.

The model of traditional Andean gender complementarity in household production and reproduction, convincingly presented in several ethnographies, also does not fit Chanchaló. There are no "separate-but-equal" spheres of activity for women or men, either in practice or in people's perceptions. Egalitarian valuation of labor is based, rather, on the perception that women and men do the same work, and do it equally well. In Chanchaló women and men can share productive domains, labor domains, and individual tasks—crossing gender boundaries preserved in ideology if not in practice elsewhere—without sacrificing egalitarian valuation of women's work. In fact, informants' statements suggest that the concept of gender egalitarianism per se may carry an intrinsic value within local ideological constructs. (This suggestion will be further explored in chapter 6.)

Indigenous women in Chanchaló, Sacha, and Cumbijín inhabit a world of work in which their labor is relatively undifferentiated from that of men. They believe that this lack of differentiation sets them apart from their own national society and from mine, where women and men do not have equal access to many forms of employment and do not receive equal pay for equal work. It also sets them apart from the many societies in which women are not able to control their own labor within household production or to share reproductive responsibilities with their mates. The fluidity in task-sharing by women and men, gender-egalitarian division of the household labor burden, and equal valuation of women's and men's work observed in Chanchaló indicate that intrahousehold labor relations are egalitarian.

FIVE ☀ **Women's Control of Household
Economic Resources**

*The Range of Variation in Cantón Salcedo*

---

MOST WOMEN IN CHANCHALÓ, Sacha, and Cumbijín are full-time farmers whose agricultural labor domains do not differ from those of men. For a study of gender and agricultural development, the implications of this division of household labor go beyond simply understanding how the work gets done, or women's share of household labor. We have seen that the household labor load is shared in a gender-egalitarian manner and that, in Cantón Salcedo, women's work is valued highly in both household and community. Unless these full-time laborers participate equally with their husbands in the management of the agricultural enterprise, however, gender relations cannot be characterized as egalitarian, but must be considered patriarchal (Deere and Léon 1982).

The gender-egalitarian control of land, labor, agricultural technology, and incomes observed in my ethnographic sample from Chanchaló (chapter 3) is not sufficient evidence from which to conclude that intrahousehold relations of production are gender-egalitarian in Cantón Salcedo. In chapters 5–7, quantitative evidence derived from the randomized, three-community-sample household surveys will be analyzed, together with structural and cultural institutions that influence patterns in resource control. First, I shall present

descriptive statistics and brief case examples that delineate the range of variation in women's control of land, incomes, and agricultural technology in the
three communities (chapter 5). Then the discussion will turn to an analysis of
gendered land inheritance and ownership structures, gender ideology, interactions of tradition and change with respect to structural and cultural institutions, and women's access to social and political institutions outside the
household (chapter 6). This discussion is intended to contextualize processes
within the household, both by looking at the cultural and structural bases for
those processes and by broadening the discussion of gender status to include
social and political domains beyond those encompassed by household
economies. I shall then address the impact of economic change in determining observed variation in women's control of economic resources (chapter 7).

For development planners and students of gender and development, resource dynamics within households have even more far-reaching implications than the gendered division of labor. I have been in the company of development professionals who, observing Chanchaleñas at work in the fields
with their husbands, assume that women are merely "unpaid family labor" in
market-oriented small-scale agriculture. They maintain that, even if women
do much of the agricultural labor, their husbands make all important production decisions. As development assistance will be offered to the household decision-making partner who has authority to commit resources or to veto participation in projects, these development professionals expect to work with
groups of men. Knowledge of women's access to productive resources and
management roles in small-scale commercial agriculture can facilitate the equitable and efficient targeting of development benefits. Such knowledge will
also contribute to theoretical discourse concerning the effects of household
participation in commodity and labor markets on women's control of economic resources.

The five women introduced in chapter 3, together with their marriage
partners, exemplify egalitarian, cooperative patterns of intrahousehold resource control. These women hold land equally with men, both through gender-egalitarian inheritance and through joint purchase with their husbands.
They participate equally in decisions concerning the use of all household
lands. They control their own labor and the labor of their older children;
some of them also organize the labor of their husbands. In those households
employing hired labor, women supervise labor either independently or jointly
with their husbands. Most of these women bear greater responsibility than
their husbands for the management of household finance: they keep accounts, keep their households on track regarding jointly determined investment priorities, and disburse household subsistence funds. As guardians of

the household purse, they have final approval of expenditure for agricultural inputs. These include hired labor, machinery rental, and agrochemicals—all of them major productive investments. These women also bear greater responsibility for decisions concerning the disposition of household production for use or sale. In sum, they are full partners in the management of their households' agricultural enterprises, both market- and subsistence-oriented, as well as of household consumption and capital accumulation.

I shall present in this chapter quantitative evidence of the degree to which these five women typify women's control of household economic resources in Chanchaló, Sacha, and Cumbijín. I shall report measures of women's participation in each of the following economic-decision domains: land use, finance, agricultural technology, and product use. Variation will be illustrated with brief case examples detailing decision processes and providing socioeconomic context.

Quantitative information was collected by the NSF/FUNDAGRO Household Surveys, during the survey's first round, August–October 1992. The sample includes 108 households in which both female and male household heads were interviewed. Information concerning control of individual income sources is derived from interviews with male heads, 99 of whom gave complete information on all listed incomes and control of them. Additional information concerning women's control of agricultural technology is derived from the survey's third round; the sample available for analysis includes 60 households in which both husband and wife provided relevant information, 86 percent of households remaining in the survey.

## The Big Picture: Women Manage Economic Resources

Most women in Chanchaló, Sacha, and Cumbijín report equal or greater participation than their husbands in areas of decision-making that profoundly affect household productivity and capital accumulation (see table 8). More than four-fifths of surveyed women state that they have at least an equal say in deciding how to use household lands and in managing the household's pooled financial resources. More than two-thirds have an equal voice in determining agricultural technology levels, including the use of environmentally sensitive agrochemicals. Although surveyed women were not asked if they manage labor, ethnographic observation has shown that women such as Alegría, Valentina, and Beatriz recruit extrahousehold labor from kinship networks or the local wage-labor market and are often responsible for assigning their families' agricultural tasks, as well. Women are equal partners in the management of household economic resources.

*Table 8. Women Report Equal Control of Household Economic Resources, Cantón Salcedo, 1992*

| Resource Control Domain | Percentage of Women Reporting Equal Control |
|---|---|
| Land use | 84% |
| Financial management | 88% |
| Product use | 89% |
| Technology selection | 71% |

*Source:* NSF/FUNDAGRO Household Surveys, round 1, August–October 1992 (N = 108).
   *Notes:* By "equal control" is meant "equal or greater than husband's control."

## Managing Land Use

Women's reported equal participation with husbands in determining the use of all household lands is consistent with decision processes described in chapter 3. All of the women profiled there and the remaining women in my ethnographic sample participate equally in this decision domain. I shall review the participation of women already introduced, provide an additional example from my ethnographic sample of women's equal participation in land-use management, and then provide profiles of two surveyed women who do not make land-use decisions.

Among the women profiled in chapter 3, Clemencia participates equally with Alejandro in decisions concerning the choice of crops in which their land will be invested. In making her recommendations she considers soil, rainfall potential, pricing trends, resistance to disease and pests, labor and other input requirements, and benefits to be derived from crop-rotation patterns. She and Alejandro both report that her recommendations carry equal weight with his, and that neither partner always determines the ultimate decision.

Susana decided to experiment with growing an expensive and risky, but high-value crop. Nicolás says the choice was hers because she has more knowledge than he concerning many crops. Although the crop failed, Nicolás also says he will support Susana's plan to try again. She will decide when the land has "rested" sufficiently to be productive again.

Beatriz and Lucho agreed on an estimate of their household's need for pasture. Beatriz suggested they could produce enough for sale, as well, if they could access additional land. She negotiated a sharecropping arrangement with her mother that would provide enough land to produce sufficient pasture for her own and her mother's cattle and for sale. All of these women own land, either inherited or purchased jointly with their husbands. All of them are engaged in high-input, modernized production; most of their household production is sold in local commodities markets.

Among the remaining women in my ethnographic sample, Dolores also participates equally in household decisions concerning sharecropping arrangements. In her case the decision involved sharecropping out land rather than adding land to production. Dolores and her husband, Julio, are full-time commercial farmers; their six hectares have been jointly purchased. They are investing in private education for their three children, who will not have much land to inherit, and in hired labor to manage high-input production of vegetable crops as well as traditional Andean crops. Julio feels that, relative to other forms of employment, "farming is no good" for himself or for his children, but he lacks education and remains in Chanchaló working on the farm. Julio is a very enterprising individual, always looking for a way to earn an extra few sucres.

Julio thinks that with the children away and the necessity to employ labor on the farm, the family might be better off renting out some of their land. He asked Dolores's opinion regarding the profitability of his suggestion. She calculated the opportunity costs of renting out each of their several small parcels with differing elevations, soil mixes, levels of erosion, and distances from the house. Dolores chose a parcel relatively far from their house, which is suitable for most crops; she did not want to rent out land at a lower elevation near the house on which she wanted to continue growing melloco and oca for sale and home consumption and vegetable crops for sale. At the lower elevations, these crops require shorter growing seasons and have been bringing relatively high prices. She is hoping to bring in two harvests of melloco during the current year; only one would be possible at a higher elevation. Although the lower-elevation parcels might bring in more sharecrop income than the higher parcel, the opportunity cost would also be higher. She also recommended a likely prospect for the sharecropping arrangement. Julio agreed with her evaluation of both opportunity costs and the reliability of the potential sharecropper and set out to negotiate the deal.

These egalitarian land-use-decision processes represent 84 percent of the survey sample, according to women's reports. Surveyed male household heads were not asked who participates in land-use decisions; husbands of the women profiled in chapter 3 state that they rely on their wives' expertise in joint land-use decisions. In order to describe households in which the female household head does not participate equally in land-use decisions, I had to look outside my ethnographic sample. I shall introduce two surveyed women with whom I am acquainted.

*Women Who Do Not Participate Equally in Managing Land Use*

Marta is a full-time middle-income farmer who has inherited one hectare of land and has purchased another two hectares with her husband, Amable. She and her husband are both twenty-nine; they have three young children. Neither has been educated beyond the sixth grade. Marta and her husband practice high-input agriculture from which they derive all their cash income. Marta engages in all agricultural activities, including the application of agrochemicals. She regularly markets the household's agricultural products.

Marta also is an economic decision-maker. According to both Marta and her husband, she manages the household's income, including the arrangement of production loans. She participates in decisions concerning the amount and type of agrochemicals to be purchased. Marta also has an equal voice in deciding how much of the household's production will be sold and how the remainder will be used in the household.

Yet this full-time, landed farmer reports that she does not make land-use decisions, preferring to leave this area of decision-making to her husband. Marta says that she and Amable discuss what they will plant. She contributes her calculation of expected expenses and then the decision is finalized. But she says that she leaves the final choice to him, as he "knows more about the crops" than she does.

Amable is active in all of the FUNDAGRO-affiliated organizations and often visits the FUNDAGRO office in Salcedo. He is also a brother of Alejandro, who has gained considerable knowledge of higher-input agriculture through volunteer activities outside Chanchaló. The two men exchange information on a regular basis. Perhaps Amable is the more knowledgeable partner concerning modernized production. Perhaps if Marta had access to information and inputs through agricultural development activities directed to women, she would be more able or more interested in making land-use decisions. Considering her equal participation in all other aspects of household productive and financial decision-making, as well as her own and Amable's statements, I do not think she is being denied equal participation in land-use decisions.

Structural inequalities within the household may constrain the female farmer's decision input in the case of Blanca and David. Blanca is a full-time farmer who participates in all phases of agricultural production, including chemical applications and marketing. Yet she does not participate equally in decisions regarding land use, inputs, or product use.

Blanca and David practice high-input, modernized agricultural production, from which they derive all of their income. Blanca reports that land-use decisions are made by David and his parents; they own all of the land accessed by her household. Two hectares of sharecropped land come into the household through David's parents; he has inherited one hectare. Blanca does not own land independently, nor have she and David purchased land together. In addition, Blanca has minimal education, whereas David has completed three years of technical university study. Expensive inputs, such as tractor rental, are also accessed through David's parents, who own a tractor and allow the couple to use it in exchange for David's labor. It is possible that David's technical knowledge, as well as his independent access to the means of production, have accorded him a greater role in productive decisions.

Blanca is a shy woman who did not want to elaborate on her role in productive decision-making. She simply said, "My husband and my in-laws make decisions about the crops." Regarding her participation in the management of household finance, she said that she does participate equally in decisions regarding saving and expenditure of cash income from all household production.

Blanca cooperates economically with her parents and decides independently how much of her labor will be applied to obtaining food and income by working with them. She and David sell nearly all of their own production, relying on her labor exchange and purchases to secure food. Blanca's labor brings a steady stream of produce into the household. During their lean times, Blanca's mother generously supplies the family with more than a sufficient quantity and diversity of foods. Blanca's two young daughters are not undernourished.

Blanca is not marginalized from economic decision-making. She controls her own labor and has an equal voice in household finance. Although she reports that her husband decides how much of their crops to sell, she also states that his decision reflects her assessment of the amount of food they will need and how much she will be able to supply by working with her parents. In Blanca's perception, her decision-making is related to household consumption rather than production.

My knowledge of these two women and their households is not sufficient to offer more than suggestions regarding the bases for their unequal participation in land-use decisions. In Marta's case, the only observed structural inequality that might constrain her participation is her husband's greater access to technical information and inputs through agricultural development projects directed to men. In Blanca's case, structural inequalities include the ownership of land as well as information and inputs. I do not have sufficient knowledge of these households to suggest an ideological basis for unequal participation. Because Marta participates equally in all other productive decisions and attributes her husband's greater input into land-use decisions to his greater expertise, I do conclude that her unequal participation is voluntary. Blanca's social reticence inhibited her communication with me; I do not know whether her shyness contributes to her unequal participation in productive decisions. She gave no indication whether her unequal participation is voluntary or not.

### Variation in Land-Use Management

Among the women who manage land use equally with their husbands are women from affluent households and women from poor households, women who own land independently and women who do not, and women of all ages. All of these women do own land jointly with their husbands. All manage resources in households engaged in highly commercialized agriculture. Their decisions are not limited to particular crops or to crops destined for home consumption. Women who do not manage land use equally include those with and without land; their households, also, engage in market-oriented agriculture.

## Managing Household Finance

Women's equal or greater control of household finance described in chapter 3 is confirmed by both male and female household heads included in the survey sample. Nearly 90 percent of women report at least equal participation in the management of household income. Although women were not asked to identify household members who manage income from all sources, men were asked to provide this information. Table 9 shows that husbands credit their wives with the management of both agricultural and off-farm cash incomes (most off-farm income is earned by husbands). Income from all sources is pooled and under women's management, either independently or jointly with their husbands, in the overwhelming majority of households. Even income earned by temporary migrants is managed by their wives in nearly three-fourths of households reporting such income.

### Responsibility and Authority in Household Financial Management

Although financial decision-making is perceived to be a joint process by both women and men, both also say that women tend to bear greater responsibility for decisions regarding investment of household funds, including production expenditures, as women are regarded as the guardians of household income. Women are both keepers of the purse for current expenditure and overseers of household accumulation. Income from all sources (including all

*Table 9. Men Report Gender-Egalitarian Management of Household Cash Incomes,
Cantón Salcedo, 1992–1993*

| Income Sources | No. of Households Earning Specified Income N | Percentage of Earning Households in which Wife Manages Income[a] |
|---|---|---|
| *Agricultural Production* | | |
| Crops (potato, grains) | 93 | 92% |
| Milk | 70 | 93% |
| Animal sales | 69 | 89% |
| *Services and Commerce* | | |
| Transportation | 13 | 100% |
| Commerce, retail | 5 | 100% |
| Commerce, wholesale | 1 | 100% |
| *Labor Market* | | |
| Wage labor, local | 23 | 93% |
| Salary, local | 7 | 100% |
| Wage or salary earned during temporary outmigration | 14 | 73% |
| Remittance | 4 | 100% |

*Source:* NSF/FUNDAGRO Household Surveys, Cantón Salcedo, August 1992–July 1993 (108 male household heads).

   *Notes:* N = 99 male household heads who reported income amounts.

a. Individually or jointly with husband.

crops, animals, and wages) and earned by all household members (including
migrant husbands) is generally managed by the female household head. Both
women and men say that women have the authority to execute this responsibility (see Poeschel 1988; Alberti 1986). Management of household consumption and accumulation is something of a female specialty in the research communities.

Most of the women presented in chapter 3 exemplify the pattern summarized above. In the households of Clemencia and Beatriz, women and men
propose their agendas for household consumption and accumulation in an
egalitarian fashion; the agendas are revised and the household's policy is
renegotiated regularly. Women and men have equal say in deciding on their
household's ultimate goals; women bear greater responsibility for stretching
income to cover needs, keeping accounts, doling out money for subsistence,
and marking a portion of proceeds for savings toward long-range accumula-

tion goals. We observed Clemencia weigh her husband's desire for an expensive household luxury against probable income in a year of low agricultural yields. Her husband expressed appreciation for her ability to maintain a long-range view, to calculate short-term production needs and expenses, and to manage accounts. In Clemencia's view, both she and her husband try to accommodate one another's desires regarding large expenditures for household goods, children's education, and family planning, among other areas of household financial planning.

Beatriz and her husband also have an equal say in determining the household's ultimate accumulation goals. Beatriz exerts a somewhat heavier hand in controlling daily expenditure, as her husband will try to wheedle money for impulsive large expenditures he perceives to be bargains and for his own pleasure. She has to remind him of their agreed-upon investment requirements, but he eventually accepts her decisions.

The matriarchal Valentina perhaps exerts a greater influence over her household's budget and accumulation goals than does her husband. It was she who decided, over her husband's misgivings, that their children should work on the farm rather than attend secondary school. This decision has had a major impact on household production and consumption for several years and will continue to affect the children's earning power into Valentina and Esteban's old age, when they will expect their children to contribute to their economic well-being. Valentina is the only woman among my ethnographic sample whose husband hinted that she may maintain a separate stash alongside the pooled household subsistence fund.

Young women living with their parents control their own income while also contributing to household subsistence. Both Marina and Beatriz's daughter Nancy have individual savings accounts. Marina, a full-time farmer, contributes a considerable portion of her agricultural income to the household subsistence fund. Nancy, a student in a more affluent household, earns less and banks most of it. These young women defer to their mothers' role as primary manager of the household budget while maintaining the freedom to pursue individual accumulation goals.

Financial management includes negotiation outside the household as well as within it. All of these women, including the young Marina, balance their households' needs and assets against lending institutions' terms, making recommendations regarding whose loans to secure. In addition, Valentina and Beatriz also handle interactions with lending institutions for their families. Known as shrewd bargainers, they have emerged as their families' financial negotiators. All of these households depend on agriculture for most or all of their income. What happens to a woman's control of household consumption and accumulation when the bulk of household income is earned by her husband working away from home?

## Managing Men's Wages

Mariana's husband, Enrique, is absent for several months each year, returning home about once a month during this period. He earned a high wage during 1993; his work in construction netted the household as much in one month as their agricultural sales during the preceding three months. Yet Enrique continues to rely on Mariana to manage his salary as well as the production earnings. Often he turns over his entire salary, accepting her decision regarding how much of it should be spent for his living expenses until the next payday. She reports greater-than-equal participation in decisions regarding use of household funds for all "big-ticket" items, in her case related to agricultural production. Mariana explains her role in budget management and accumulation:

My husband is very good about bringing home the money. I know his salary and what he spends in Quito, and he spends very little on himself. So you might think I have a lot of money to spend, but I don't. We wanted to join the cattle production cooperative. That costs a lot and we had to pay it all at one time. Plus we are saving to buy land. So we have nothing in the house. No TV, no stereo. I'd rather have land. Land makes money. Enrique says the same. Well, I decide what we can spend. My mother taught me how to get along on very little. She had ten children.

## A Woman Who Does Not Manage Household Finances

Among the ten women in my ethnographic sample, one reported less than equal participation in household decisions regarding consumption. Susana stated that she had voluntarily accorded greater decision authority to Nicolás regarding purchases but was having second thoughts about his ability to keep jointly established accumulation goals in mind when deciding whether the family could afford luxuries for the house and their personal enjoyment. Susana is a landholding equal partner in all household-production decisions; agricultural production earns most of the household's income. As she dislikes keeping accounts and "buying and selling," she would prefer that Nicolás handle big-ticket market interactions. She currently depends on his good intentions—over which she has been able to exert increasing influence—to curb spending.

According to survey interviews, Nicolás's perception of his own and his wife's control over income derived from agricultural and off-farm sources changed during the time I was in Chanchaló. In the early fall of 1992 Nicolás reported that he controlled his own wage earnings while Susana had an equal voice in income derived from dairy and livestock production. He did not report who managed crop income. By March 1993 Nicolás was reporting equal participation by Susana in decisions regarding income from all sources, including his own wages and the sale of pasture grown on land owned by his father. This pattern was repeated during the third wave of the household survey in June 1993. Although both Susana and Nicolás perceive that she has gained a greater voice in financial management, Susana does not aim to increase her role in direct consumption. As incomes are pooled and Nicolás has begun to respect Susana's desire that they discuss purchases before he makes them, Susana has settled for a less inclusive role in financial management than most other women enjoy.

## An Andean Pattern of Financial Management

Women's control of household consumption and accumulation in Chanchaló is not unique within indigenous communities in Ecuador. Most ethnographic studies report that income is pooled and that women have equal participation in establishing household accumulation goals and greater-than-equal participation in managing daily expenditures, even in households that are heavily dependent on migrant males' wages (Poeschel 1988; Alberti 1986; Barsky 1984; Belote and Belote 1988). However, Weismantel reports that some Zumbagua men no longer feel obligated to turn their wages over to their wives, with the result that women may have access to their husband's cash earnings only when the men are at home (1988). Although they do not see women's control becoming eroded in households that have been integrated into wage markets for many years, Poeschel, Linda Belote, and Jim Belote fear that women eventually may lose control as households come to depend more on wages earned by migrant men.

## Managing Agricultural Technology

Two-thirds of surveyed women report equal participation in decisions concerning selection of one of their households' most expensive and essential technologies: chemical pesticides.[1] This level of access to technology selection applies to other inputs, as well, but I will limit discussion to pesticides. These hazardous chemicals are viewed by many farmers as their most critical input; virulent fungi, worms, and other "pests" threatened potato crops during 1992–1993. Farmers consistently cite the fungus late blight as a serious, potentially devastating, production problem and most aim to apply as much pesticide as they can afford (Hamilton 1994). Pesticides tend to be applied on crops or particular varieties that are destined for market, rather than on those intended primarily for household consumption. Both men and women conclude that choice of pesticide is based on their joint evaluation of the efficacy and cost-effectiveness of products. Women are primary decision-makers concerning how much of this expensive input their households can afford to buy. While men usually make the purchases, their wives must approve both outlay and the negotiated sale.

Both women and men state that the relative influence of either partner in pesticide-decision processes is based upon *expertise* concerning pesticides, crop requirements, and economic valuation of the crop, and upon *responsibility* for the budget and/or for the application of the chemicals. Neither women nor men unilaterally own this expertise or responsibility. Both women and men apply pesticides. As information concerning pesticides currently comes from chemical companies and agricultural supply stores, women and men are equally well informed; sellers do not discriminate on the basis of gender. Although women may have to manage the production budget, they rely on their husbands to participate in a collaborative decision process resulting in the best product for the best price.

Alegría and Rubén apply pesticides to their potato crops at least once a week during the rainy season, a level of agrochemical usage as high as any in Ecuador. Rubén is eloquent on the subject of the need to "industrialize" agricultural production. He also becomes expansive when discussing his wife's managerial skill. He says that Alegría is *bien organizada* and that her managerial ability pays off in cost-benefit analysis regarding inputs. Although the household hires a great deal of labor and Rubén also works on the farm, Alegría applies pesticides frequently.

Rubén states that he relies on Alegría's good judgment concerning both choice of chemical and frequency of application. I observed the selection process in which Alegría and Rubén examined plants that had been recently sprayed. They discussed the effectiveness of the product used and whether they should intensify application or opt for another product. He agreed with her recommendation to switch products rather than increase the level of application. This plan was carried out and proved effective.

Beatriz and Lucho apply pesticides every two weeks, and they would apply more often if Beatriz felt they could afford it. Beatriz mixes and applies chemicals. I observed Beatriz not only discuss with Lucho the best choice of pesticide but also negotiate the loan that would make its use possible. She also regulates expenditure for all inputs, balancing their need for agrochemicals with saving for the ultimate input: a tractor that will earn considerable rental income. Beatriz occasionally must veto her husband's suggestion to stock up agrochemicals at "bargain" prices. In her view, they cannot afford to invest in storable pesticides unless the savings are substantial; her criteria for the constitution of "bargain" prices are more stringent than her husband's.

Among the women in my ethnographic sample, all participate in decisions regarding selection of pesticides and other agrochemicals. Even Valentina, Mariana, and Clemencia, who do not regularly apply chemicals, participate in selection. Clemencia (whose reportedly full participation in the selection process regarding both agrochemicals and alternate technologies is described in chapter 3) responded to the survey that she does not participate equally in the selection of pesticides. When I asked her to clarify her survey response, she replied that the products she prefers are not locally available, whereas the products with which Alejandro has experimented are sold in Salcedo. She feels that if her choice is differentially constrained by the market, her participation cannot be equal with that of her husband. To my knowledge, she is the only surveyed woman who has studied pesticides not available in Ecuador. I expect that she is unique in placing this interpretation on the survey question.

With the exception of Clemencia's, I have not observed the one-third of households in which surveyed women report they do not participate equally in the selection of agrochemical inputs. However, I can offer some insights into their likely production profiles based on multiple regression analysis (reported in appendix B, table 3). Results indicate that women who do not participate equally in decisions regarding pesticides are likely to be those who do not apply the chemicals and whose households use smaller amounts of pesticides. Clemencia's explanation of this phenomenon is that in households where a small amount of the budget is allocated to pesticides, women may not feel the need to "bother" with controlling the amount purchased; further, if women do not work with pesticides, they may not have a compelling interest in discriminating among the varieties of products available (Hamilton 1994). All informants agreed that, although relevant labor is not a *requirement* for participation in decision processes, both men and women are expected to participate in decisions regarding any productive domain in which they work.

Variables that do not appear to affect women's equal participation in pesticide selection include the size of the household's land base, women's independent ownership of land, and husband's absence from the farm. In contrast with the expectations of many development professionals, women are equal partners in decisions regarding agricultural technology on farms of all sizes and among market-oriented producers utilizing *higher* levels of technology, independent of whether their husbands are absent from the farm.

## Women Who Do Not Manage Production

Only two surveyed women report unequal participation in all areas of both agricultural and financial management: Transito, whose household does not engage in agriculture, and Nely, the part-time farmer from Cumbijín. It is not surprising that a woman who only "helps out" occasionally in agriculture would have little decision input. Susana's husband, who also "helps out" with agricultural production, also has less decision authority than the full-time and more experienced farmer in his family. Moreover, both women are immigrants from mestizo-dominated urban areas. (Contrasting patterns in mestizo versus indigenous gender ideology and resource control within the household will be discussed in chapter 6.)

## Conclusion

Women's equal participation in control of household economic resources characterizes the overwhelming majority of households in Chanchaló, Sacha, and Cumbijín. Women are full partners in decisions affecting all household lands and all crops. Women's management of household financial resources impacts agricultural production as well as household consumption and accumulation. Women are at least equal partners in technology selection and in decisions regarding trade-offs among expenditures for varying agricultural inputs. Thus women's equal participation spans the full range of agricultural and financial decision-making within their households. Women's equal participation in the management of household economic resources occurs in households that are both affluent and poor, where men are and are not present on the farm, where families are just beginning or have matured. Women manage resources on highly commercialized, high-technology enterprises.

Both the prevalence and the socioeconomic and demographic distribution of gender egalitarianism in control of economic resources indicate that household economies are not patriarchal in these communities. Clearly, if development professionals seek to identify decision-making partners in small-scale commercial agriculture, in Cantón Salcedo they must include indigenous women. On the basis of representative case descriptions and reports from male and female survey respondents, participation by households in commodities and gender-biased wage markets does not appear to have marginalized women from control of productive resources or incomes earned by men.

SIX  The Power of Balance

*Structural and Ideological Foundations of*
*the Two-Headed Household*

IN CHANCHALÓ, women and men share control of their households'
most important economic resources in an egalitarian manner. Women's authority over productive resources has not been eroded by forms of economic
change that elsewhere have marginalized women in many smallholder production systems and that are thus widely viewed as inevitably detrimental to
indigenous Andean women. Women's agricultural labor and expertise are
valued highly in household and community. This valuation does not depend
on gender complementarity in household production, viewed elsewhere as a
probable basis for the precarious survival of egalitarian forms in some modernizing Andean communities. As these gender-and-development paradigms
do not explain resource control patterns observed in Chanchaló, we must further examine the local structural and cultural contexts in which household
economies are embedded.

In this chapter, cultural constructions of gender, household, and household headship will be delineated. Women's ownership of land throughout the
three-community sample will be quantified, and inheritance patterns will be
described. Ideologies of gender and household, together with kinship and inheritance structures, exhibit some features identified elsewhere as traditional

for indigenous Andean communities. These patterns will be placed in pan-Andean context, and their derivation from tradition versus cultural and structural integration into mestizo society will be addressed.

Some of the ways women are valued in Chanchaló derive from their performance as community actors and from the community's remembrance of hacienda life. I will discuss women's participation in community political and social organizations, and an ideological commitment to social solidarity that I believe is relevant to household processes. Some of the ways women are valued in Chanchaló are expressed in attitudes toward violence and biological reproduction. I will also evaluate women's control over their own bodies.

## *Dos Cabezas:* Cooperative Decision Dynamics

Both men and women in Chanchaló emphasize the importance of cooperative decision-making within the household. Rosa's reference to *dos cabezas* (two heads) was an expression commonly heard in discussions of economic resource control. When asked during the household surveys who manages incomes, an overwhelming majority of both men and women responded *los dos* or *ambos* (both household heads). The phrase most commonly used by men in answer to questions regarding who owns crops and who makes economic decisions is *La Señora y yo* (my wife and I). These practices reflect both observed patterns in resource control and a strong and culturally legitimated preference for dualistic household headship. Dualistic, cooperative, and ultimately egalitarian patterns in the distribution of authority within the household are encouraged by cultural norms underlying Clemencia's summation of decision-making in Chanchaló (and many similar statements recorded in chapter 3): "Women do not make decisions. Men do not make decisions. Women and men make decisions together. Both participate or there is no decision, there is no action."

Within most households profiled in chapter 3, a dynamic balance is maintained between two decision-making partners. When spouses disagree concerning the disposition of economic resources, neither wife nor husband always prevails concerning a given resource or within a given household. My own observations and men's and women's reports suggest that the spouse with greater knowledge, past success, or stubbornness tends to prevail in particular decisions. In the household I have characterized as matriarchal, the matriarch possesses liberal quantities of all of these commodities.

Although most households' *dos cabezas* do not occupy dualistically distinct productive and reproductive spheres, the concept of dynamism through dualistic power-sharing is strong. "Collaboration" among equals is viewed as critical for doing the best work and for making the best decisions, those that advance the household's jointly determined long-range goals. Although not ascribed according to gender, the varying and perhaps complementary strengths of both household heads are valued.

Clemencia pushed for investment in secondary education for her children, and for family planning—long-range goals she considers important for her family's future success. She convinced her husband, who voices appreciation for Clemencia's long-range perspective, to adopt these goals. Alejandro has made personal sacrifices to help achieve them. Alejandro pushes for the maintenance of certain standards of child discipline, which Clemencia has accepted. She relies on Alejandro to enforce these when he is at home. She also relies on Alejo to use his temperamental edge to advance the family's fortunes in local commodities markets, where one of the household heads must negotiate with buyers.

In Valentina's household, these patterns are reversed. The female household head disciplines the children and negotiates with market intermediaries. It is she, rather than her husband, who is more committed to the imposition of behavioral standards for children and more enthusiastic concerning market interaction. She is also the toughest bargainer in her household, whether negotiations involve market intermediaries, political contacts, or spouse. When Valentina failed to adopt her husband's proposal to educate their children, Esteban apparently gave way with good grace. It is my impression that he appreciates the household benefits of his wife's toughness as well as the more peaceful nature of household relations when he and Valentina do not operate at cross-purposes.

In these and other profiled households, the varying skills and personalities of both male and female heads have contributed to household material accumulation and social standing in the community. The contributions of both heads are valued by their mates. Although there is no cultural proscription inhibiting any man or woman from individually performing or employing all work necessary to economically reproduce a household alone, most Chanchaleños agree with Rubén's opinion of the single life, imposed on his father by his mother's death: "It is no good alone."

## The Power of Balance: Ideologies of Household Formation and Gender

Throughout the Andean culture area, ethnohistorians and ethnographers have found evidence for a tradition in which cultural norms prescribe that households have two equally powerful heads: one female and one male. Both balance and dynamism must characterize relations between these two heads if the household is to prosper. The desired balance of power is maintained in households where neither head controls a greater share of material, social, or spiritual resources. Dynamism is achieved by a continuous and egalitarian shifting of the balance, as neither head controls all decision domains. The perception that maintaining this dynamic provides the push enabling the household to move forward in time, to grow and mature properly, can be called the "power of balance."

Belief in the power of dualistic headship to both nurture and guide households is strong in Chanchaló. However, the power of balance is not encompassed by—nor can it be encapsulated in—the view that "two heads are better than one" in matters of intrahousehold decision-making. Although Chanchaleños do embrace the idea that the sum of two heads' experience and dedication to family survival is very likely to yield better decisions than any single head can provide, the power of balance lies in the vibrant tension inherent in dualistic power-sharing.[1] I will propose an interpretation of this cultural basis for observed balance in gender relations that borrows heavily from the work of several Andean ethnographers, summarized below.

It seems clear to me that both men and women in Chanchaló place a high value on preserving egalitarianism in gender relations. However, the many statements reported in chapter 3 attesting to the salience of this value do not reveal the derivation of the strong belief that power-sharing is both essential to household survival and, simply, the right and proper form of household headship. Perceived material correlates of this high valuation abound: Chanchaleños are quick to attribute household economic successes to collaborative work and management. In chapter 7 I shall test the material evidence that their perceptions reflect a positive association between dualistic control of household economic resources and measurable household accumulation. I have no doubt that material and ideological bases for the perpetuation of dualistic authority are mutually reinforcing.

Yet I always came away from discussions in which men and women passionately affirmed ideals of dualistic power-sharing with the strong impression that even more was at stake than the household's material welfare. The belief that household headship must incorporate equally powerful female and male parts cannot be accounted for by the importance of traditional gender complementarity or parallelism to household production and reproduction. Although women specialize in labor and financial management, and individual couples practice their own forms of complementarity, cultural rules do not specify distinct productive and reproductive roles for women and men. I was left with the need to delineate an unvoiced—yet apparently fundamental and deeply felt—principle underlying Chanchaleños' commitment to dualistic power-sharing and the importance of the female-male dyad to concepts of headship.

Based on ideological patterns identified in other Andean communities, I offer the following interpretation of gender-ideological fundamentalism in Chanchaló. Dualistic headship is perceived by Chanchaleños to be different in kind, as well as in the quantity of ruling partners, from unitary headship. The two-headed household is conceived to be a distinct organism, separate from the individuals that comprise it, and greater than the sum of its parts. Where there is collaboration between female and male equals, the household is conceived as an organic entity equally female and male in constitution and thus more securely and enduringly nested into the Andean nature of things than would be possible with unitary headship. The two-headed household is viewed as both more dynamic than units powered by only female or male heads, and more dynamic than any unit in which female and male parts are locked in asymmetrical power relations.

## Fundamentalism in Andean Gender Ideology: Without Female and Male, Nothing Can Go Forward

Traditional Andean views of gender parallelism or complementarity ascribe differing attributes to women and men, as well as differing productive and re-productive roles within their households. The products, expertise, and power associated with both female and male heads are required for the household enterprise to succeed. A sort of gender-ideological fundamentalism emerges as central to the maintenance of both balance and dynamism. Women are believed to embody separate and indispensable creative principles; therefore women should dominate conceptually separate and indispensable economic spheres. Most ethnographers conclude that women and men derive equal economic and social benefit from traditional complementarity systems; others find that separate cannot be equal.

It is not necessary for the gendered division of labor to be complementary or parallel, in practice, for the interdependence of male and female to be considered essential to the survival of the household. Describing a Quechua community in Peru, Catherine Allen reports that, although any person can perform any task, people frown on an individual of either gender who does everything, who is self-sufficient. Maintaining the functioning pair, the unity of male and female parts, is considered the proper way to ensure the survival of the household and Andean way of life.[2] Allen summarizes: "Thus, while each man or women is a complete individual with both male and female qualities, the two unite to form another individual of a higher order: a *warmi-*

*qhari* ["woman-man" or "wife-husband"], nucleus of the household" (1988, 85).

Olivia Harris has described the ideologically superordinate position of the male-female unity among the Laymis, a Bolivian Aymara group (1978, 1980, 1985). Harris constructs a model of gender parallelism in which symbolic dyadic unions—essential for the dynamism of cosmic creation and continued human economic and biological fertility—are reflected in dualistic patterns of resource exploitation and control within the household. Thus, as the household needs the labor, expertise, and biological apparatus of male and female to reproduce itself, so it also needs the productive resources of two ecological floors at differing altitudes and the products of these zones. All dualities have a male and a female component: women exploit one ecological zone and control its productive base, men another.[3] Within every dyad, one component is symbolically female and the other, male.

Summarizing ethnohistorical evidence for the ideological basis of Andean women's independent control of economic resources and political power before the Conquest, Irene Silverblatt concludes that, within the indigenous Andean worldview, every creative principle must have a male and a female component (1980, 1987). Without the interaction of two entities or halves, each endowed with female or male value, nothing can be created. In Andean mythology, the creation of the primordial universe depended upon this dialectic or dynamic. The creator god of the Andes, Viracocha, embodies both male and female sexual elements. From Viracocha were descended parallel lines of female and male deities, and from them were descended female and male humans (Silverblatt 1980, 159). Silverblatt also describes parallel forms of engendered political and religious organization that were elaborated during the Inca empire by both elite and nonelite classes. Not only were female deities related to agricultural fertility worshipped throughout the empire, but Inca legend also accorded to female figures important agricultural innovations: the introduction of maize, irrigation, and terracing (Murra 1980, 16). Thus the presence of a critical female component distinguished pre-Conquest Andean concepts of both fertility and productivity.

Whereas Silverblatt emphasizes the dialectic between female and male forces that allows the creative principle to operate in Andean myth, both Harris and Allen emphasize the overarching importance of the whole, or unity, created by each dyad rather than opposition between the two parts. Harris maintains that neither man nor woman always predominates, in symbol, ritual, or practical economic and political affairs. If men represent the household in public affairs, the domestic economy is controlled by women. Within the domestic economy, "the predominance of the woman is relative and to be understood in terms of the overall mutuality of the relationship" (Harris 1985). Within the public domain, men vote in communal organizations, but issues are raised and then taken home for discussion before being voted on. Allen presents similar findings in a cogent passage:

Although men talk with bravado, they avoid making commitments they have not cleared with their wives in private. The most respected men in the community have strong-minded, capable wives. *Runakuna*—male and female—state categorically that men cannot fulfill their civic and religious *cargos* without their wives' support. Moreover, they say this is as it should be. The interdependence of men and women is accepted as the natural state of things; single adults are considered not only unfortunate, but unnatural as well. (1988, 79)

### Fundamentalism and Change

Whether it is women's control of separate and critically important resources and roles that is being considered, or the ultimate sharing of responsibility and authority in traditional Andean households, intrahousehold relations between women and men are considered egalitarian by these ethnographers of traditional Andean communities. Ecuadorean ethnographies present similar findings, extending the geographic and ethnic boundaries of this pan-Andean phenomenon (Belote and Belote 1977, 1988; Stark 1984; Poeschel 1988). Spanning a time period from the early 1960s to the mid-1980s, the two-headed household is observed in Ecuadorean communities that, like Chanchaló, have become integrated into wage and commodities markets. In all of these settings where intrahousehold power-sharing has been observed, kinship and inheritance structures affording women equal access to the means of production have survived varying attempts by colonial and republican governments to increase the patriorientation of households through national inheritance and land-tenure laws favorable to male household heads (to be discussed below). It is my contention, shared with other ethnographers, that the survival of ideological and structural bases for gender egalitarianism are linked (Belote and Belote 1988; Alberti 1986).

Although gender complementarity (an inherently dualistic construct) does not influence the division of productive labor or resources in Chanchaló, dualistic concepts of resource control and power-sharing within the household are vividly present. Chanchaló appears to have retained a fundamentally Andean way of perceiving household survival and prosperity as dependent on the contributions of two equally powerful heads, *without* having retained the perception that those two heads represent separate-but-equal powers, products, or decision domains. The discussion will now turn to the perceived distribution of human resources in Chanchaló—an instrumental model of noncomplementary, egalitarian gender ideology at work. Women and men are perceived as being endowed with certain forms and measures of human capital, which are related in no small way to gendered access to social and economic capital. Of what are they made, these women and men who balance power?

## Constructing Gender: Concepts of Strength in Women and Men

The high valuation of women's work and economic management expertise that contributes to egalitarian wage scales and intrahousehold gender relations is embedded in concepts of gender that accord women the possession of physical, emotional, and moral attributes associated with *fuerza* (strength or force). Although I am certain that women are to some degree characterized by their differences from men, the possession of strength, an admired quality, is not determined by gender. Nor, to my knowledge, are women regarded as possessing consistently distinct varieties of strength that are absent or underdeveloped in men. "Strong" women were admired in much the same language, and often in the same context, as "strong" men.

In delineating forms of strength that were attributed to women in my ethnographic sample, I refer to statements made by husbands, friends, and neighbors regarding the character of individual women; statements regarding women's perceived strengths expressed by many Chanchaleños not included in my ethnographic sample; and observation of behavior. I did not systematically interview informants concerning strengths or weaknesses associated with either gender, or the characteristics of a "good" woman or a "good" man. Following this catalog of attributes, I will contrast concepts of strength in Chanchaló with constructions of gender in Ecuadorean mestizo coastal and urban areas, and in two indigenous Peruvian communities.

In a community where most people earn most of their income agriculturally, and much of the work is done manually, physical strength and endurance are highly valued attributes. Women are generally regarded as capable of performing all physical tasks; most women perform all agricultural work except plowing. Individual women and men are praised for exceptionally hard work well executed and for having a reputation as a particularly hard worker. A gender-blind work ethic is pervasive in Chanchaló. Tiny, frail-looking women are praised for being physically *fuerte* (strong, hearty).

When I asked a farmer what he paid the women and men working in his fields, he replied that he paid an identical wage to workers of both genders. This was early during my fieldwork and I must have appeared skeptical. I had been impressed by the striking account by Bourque and Warren (1981) of the unequal valuation of men's and women's work in a traditional Peruvian community and I knew that unequal wage rates characterize Ecuadorean urban areas. "Why are you surprised?" he demanded. "Look at how well those women work. You can see they are harvesting as much as the men." I did look, and during the five hours I observed his operation, women who appeared to weigh less than ninety pounds, carrying at least fifty pounds on their shoulders, deposited an equal or greater amount of produce than their male counterparts.

Women such as Clemencia and her mother, Rosa, are praised by their husbands and friends for their hard work. Although Rosa is the richest woman in Chanchaló, she is also among the hardest working. I never heard anyone express envy of Rosa's wealth. In the view of her neighbors, she has earned it. Similar expressions of admiration for hard or enduring physical work successfully applied to household accumulation were voiced concerning men. Eduardo is generally considered to be an enterprising farmer whose endurance has contributed to his rapid accumulation of material goods: "He works through the night many times. He pays attention to everything. That's why he has so much." Several people voiced confidence in the ability of the hardworking Susana to overcome poverty. The endurance and motivation required to put in long hours are admired in both men and women.

Emotional and moral strength are also admired in Chanchaleñas, both within their households and in the community. Women and men considered *seria/o* (serious, reliable, earnest) are admired. Seriousness may be expressed through demeanor or work. Rosa is praised for the dignity with which she represented Chanchaló in a regional religious celebration; Clemencia is admired for the seriousness of purpose evident in her work with the Women's Production Association. Both mother and daughter are described as *muy seria*. A related concept is the quality referred to as *sentada*, meaning settled or judicious, the opposite of flighty. Women praised for their long-term vision are sometimes described in this way. Both of these terms were used by Rosa's husband, Rosalino, in praise of his wife. Alejo also expressed gratitude for Clemencia's ability to envision long-term processes; she used the term *sentado* to describe him, as well, when characterizing her husband's steadfastness.

Alejo also admires Clemencia's resolve. He described her determination to work through illness and in so doing to help others as well as the household. He associates determination with strength in his description of "my Clemencia" as *muy decidida, muy fuerte*. Alejo is confident that once Clemencia sets her mind to something, she will accomplish it regardless of the difficulty, and the pride in his voice is as revealing as his words.

The ability of some women to channel their determination into efficient administration of household labor and capital is considered a form of strength. Women such as Alegría and Beatriz are described by their husbands and friends as being *bien organizada,* implying both resourcefulness and firmness. The resolve of these women is primarily manifested in managerial skill and rigor: relentless guarding of household capital accumulation, negotiating loans, accomplishing much with slim resources, eliciting the best work from family members and hired laborers. Possessing the firmness required to run a tight ship is considered an attribute of character with which some individuals are better endowed than others.

Individuals who possess firmness as a leading and generalized characteristic of their personalities are described as *tener mucho carácter* (having a strong character). Neither Beatriz nor Alegría is so described, although they effectively manage their households. Valentina, however, is so described by several informants of both genders. Valentina's local political leadership and ability to influence highly placed mestizos in national religious and development organizations are partly responsible for this characterization, often made in conjunction with a positive evaluation of her political skill. This phrase is also used to describe Marina's father, Rodrigo, a respected elder or *gran viejo* who was a leader in the rebellion that established Chanchaló. Valentina is well liked by both male and female Chanchaleños. Having a strong personality is considered a positive trait in Chanchaló, appropriate for public leaders of either gender.

The opinion of friends that Doña Valentina is a force to be reckoned with in her own household probably also contributes to her perceived force of personality. Her husband, Esteban, does not suffer ridicule for having a wife who is considered an authoritarian household head. In Chanchaló, authority within the household is not perceived to be a limited good. To my knowledge, weakness is never imputed to men who have strong wives. It is my impression that men such as Alejandro and Esteban derive respect for having chosen such strong women, women who can make things happen, get themselves elected to regional posts, and even win a scholarship to study in the United States. Their wives' prestige appears to enhance that of the entire household.

Among other characteristics admired and associated with strength is having a strong head, both for thinking and for drinking. Marina and her brother, Alejo, are both considered extremely intelligent, as is Clemencia. Their intelligence is perceived as wide-ranging and useful to the community. Marina and Clemencia both won scholarships, against stiff competition, to study in the United States. Local admiration for this feat is widespread. Alejo has been elected president of the quesería for multiple terms and is being encouraged to run for president of the Casa Campesina in Salcedo. Among the attributes said to qualify Alejo for leadership positions are his mental acuity and good judgment. It is often said in the community that "people in that family are smart." People in Chanchaló want smart representatives in political and other institutional bodies.

Having a strong head for alcohol is also considered a positive characteristic among many Chanchaleños, who appreciate both women and men who participate unreservedly and with aplomb in the drinking and dancing central to community fiestas. Everyone enjoyed watching Susana outdrink many men during the fiesta of San José de Chanchaló. Cries of "¡Viva!" accompanied her exuberant dancing. The politically successful Lucho is admired for both the enthusiasm and the capacity of his periodic hedonism.

Chanchaleños are well aware of the stereotype of the lazy, drunken Indian popularized in mestizo society; they are quick to point out that the stereotype does not apply to a hardworking, collaborative community such as theirs. They, and outsiders familiar with the community, hold that alcohol consumption is moderate in Chanchaló. Maintaining moderation, rather than abstinence, is an ideal that seems reasonable to most people in Chanchaló, and an ideal that is embodied in both women and men. The minority of individuals who disapprove of ritualized excess, including Clemencia and Alejo, do not confine their disapproval to women.

## Absence of Complementarity in Gender Attributes

Chanchaleños admire strong minds and bodies, strength of purpose and strength of personality in both women and men. They admire a woman who participates in public ritual with style, whether it is the gracefully dignified Rosa or the ebulliently intoxicated Susana. They praise and support a woman who executes public office in a way that benefits the community; women consistently reelect Valentina and Clemencia in recognition of their political skill and community values. Some Chanchaleños may be a bit in awe of a commanding woman such as Valentina but express admiration of her toughness. The more domesticated managerial rigor and cleverness of *bien organizada* women are also appreciated, both within and outside their households.

Most of these strengths are shared with men. The exception, within my experience, is the attribute *bien organizada*. I never heard a man so described. I did hear provincial governments and other institutions described as more or less *bien organizada*. Administration of household labor or capital and administration of public institutions may be perceived as involving some of the same skills and commitments. In any case, as the discussions of household financial management and labor allocation have indicated, administering household money and personnel is often regarded as a female specialty. It is not surprising that women would be more likely to be characterized as more or less *bien organizada.*

## *Absence of* Marianismo

In mestizo Ecuador, as elsewhere in mestizo Latin America, cultural constructions of gender differentiate the moral and spiritual attributes and roles of women and men. The term *marianismo* (marianism) is often used by analysts to identify "the cult of feminine spiritual superiority, which teaches that women are semi-divine, morally superior to and spiritually stronger than men" (Stevens 1973, 91). Although the movement is not religious, the figure of the Virgin Mary provides "a convenient set of assumptions around which the practitioners of *marianismo* have erected a secular edifice of beliefs and practices related to the position of women in society" (92). These beliefs include "the sacredness of motherhood" (99) and veneration for the differential ability of women to abstain from the temptations of the flesh. In practice, women may gain "respect and influence from their adherence to a chaste, home-bound . . . existence" (Jaquette 1986, 253). Women have also employed an idiom of maternalism to legitimate social and political movements throughout Latin America (Safa 1995b; Martin 1994).

In Chanchaló, a contemporary Roman Catholic variation on this theme is occasionally preached by circuit-riding priests. On Easter Sunday, parishioners gathered for an outdoor mass in honor of the Virgin of Cisne, patroness of neighboring Palama, where the only local Easter mass was held. The priest exhorted the faithful to give up their devotion to the miracle-working Virgin in her location-specific visionary incarnations (see chapter 3), and to concentrate instead on the role of Mary as the Mother of Christ and manifestation of ideal motherhood. He then described the "good" woman as "dignified, pure, a good mother, and strong in the church." The good woman was exhorted to serve as a moral example for her entire family and to teach Christian values in her home. The priest emphasized the independent role of the "new" woman in providing moral guidance to her family and exhorted the "new" man to be a good father and to provide for his family. In the "new" church, women are not expected to condone or make spiritual restitution for the moral lapses of their husbands, a feature of the secular marianismo tradition.

Through several feminine orders, the Roman Catholic Church also provides social outreach to women's or "mothers'" groups in Chanchaló and other rural communities in Salcedo. The sisters offer information and material assistance in the areas of health, nutrition, and interpersonal relations. The role of women as primary health-care providers, nurturers, and socializers of children is emphasized. Women are encouraged to provide a moral center for their families. This is an important role in mestizo Ecuador, where having strong families is generally considered critical to individual and collective welfare.

Beliefs and practices associated with secular marianismo are both prevalent and culturally salient in mestizo Ecuador. In Salcedo, as in every other Ecuadorean town, a gleaming white statue of Everymother adorns at least one prominent public area. Salcedo's *madre* holds a babe at her breast while a toddler clutches her legs; she appears serene. In a nearby town, the sculpted representation depicts a muscular and fiercely determined woman protecting her children from an unseen menace. All of these public *madres* feature a woman feeding, comforting, or protecting her children. Public parks, where families take their children on Sunday afternoons, are favorite locations for these statues, as well as public thoroughfares and plazas. Public funds have provided many of these expressions of institutionalized appreciation for women's sacrifices to family.

Mestizo society can be categorized broadly as patriarchal: with notable exceptions, men tend to enjoy greater control of political power, wealth, and many social institutions. However, within the family, women can exert considerable influence over husbands as well as children and derive considerable respect for their embodiment of marianismo ideals. Teachings of the "new" church notwithstanding, mestizo men have been heard to make remarks such as "We men are animals. We can't control ourselves. Women are different. They can control themselves. We're not responsible for what we do." Women are expected either to counteract or to indulge male moral imperfection within their families, depending on the perspective employed regarding the improvability of men. In either case, women are generally expected to exert a moral influence in their homes. It is not an exaggeration to say that in many mestizo families, mothers are *revered* for their effective execution of this role.

Notably absent in Chanchaló is any association of women's strength with motherhood or with a spiritual tradition that casts women in the role of maintaining family religious morality. Neither religious teachings nor secular mestizo marianismo ideals have influenced cultural constructions of gender in Chanchaló. Women do not have a gender-specific role as religious or moral teachers within their families.

Moreover, mothering and fathering do not appear to be rigidly differentiated. Women are not perceived as privileged or even primary socializers or protectors of children. Once children are off the breast, women may not even be perceived as being the primary nurturers within their households. Women are not more tender with children than men, nor are they more responsible for enforcing discipline. "Mothering," as it is conceptualized in mestizo society, is not a female specialty in Chanchaló.

Although many analysts expect that cultural patterns sanctioned by politically and economically dominant classes will define values among subordinate groups, cultural hegemony is not observed with respect to ideals of womanhood. Indeed, many people in Chanchaló voice disapproval of gender relations in mestizo Ecuador. Although behavior within many mestizo families may not reflect marianismo ideals, it is not an exaggeration to say that gender ideologies are almost perfectly reversed in the two sociocultural traditions.[4]

## Women's Bodies and the Body Politic

In many ways Chanchaló, Sacha, and Cumbijín are highly integrated indigenous communities, in both cultural and political-economic terms. Following hundreds of years of economic servitude to politically authoritarian landowners representing national culture, and facing rapidly increasing incorporation into wage and commodities markets following liberation from the haciendas, many indigenous institutions have changed or disappeared. Most people no longer speak Quichua, even at home. Distinctive ethnic clothing has been replaced by generic indígena-campesino dress. It is possible that indigenous female deities have been syncretically submerged into a generalized association of the miracle-performing Virgin with powerful features of the landscape. If parallelism and complementarity characterized past gender ideology and division of household labor, these features have been eradicated. The state has mandated certain forms of local political organization for indigenous communities emerging from hacienda control.

### Social Ideology: Support for Collaboration and Nonviolence in Households

Social organization in Chanchaló, however, embodies fundamentally traditional features. Many Chanchaleños associate their indigenous social traditions with both physical survival and ethnic identity. Belief in the power of social solidarity and extrahousehold economic cooperation to fight economic privation and social injustice is expressed by many informants, among them Marina's grandfather, Antonio. Antonio is convinced that indigenous social organization enabled Chanchaleños to survive hacienda indenture: "We" are the people who survived owing to a distinct way of organizing ourselves. Antonio's descendants and many others have incorporated this idea into a strong community-solidarity ethic, pervasive in statements that differentiate Chanchaló from many other communities: "We" are people who "collaborate" to help one another and ourselves, unlike communities that have adopted "town" ways, where people either want to be more independent or expect the state to take care of them.[5]

The perception is strong that everyone will benefit more from participation in cooperative endeavors than from going it alone. Roughly half of the families in Chanchaló belong to production associations. Most people also engage in economic reciprocity with relatives or friends. When an individual objects to the requirement to contribute labor or material resources to communal or other cooperative activities, she or he is likely to be reminded that cooperative effort will ultimately yield greater individual economic returns and social security than private labor alone, and that it is the right thing to do. Neither pure altruism nor pure self-interest motivates this form of economic cooperation. Traditional ideals of mutual obligation coexist with the belief in greater individual benefit through collaboration. It is possible that the concept of strength through collaboration has contributed to a strong preference for collaboration *within* the household, as well.

Men and women contrast respectful local treatment of women with the physical intimidation that women must endure in Ecuadorean cities and coastal provinces, where mestizo gender ideology is dominant. Beatriz's practice of segregating her daughters from "town" boys while allowing them to mix with local boys is based in the widespread perception that women are valued more highly in Chanchaló and other indigenous communities than in urban (and coastal) mestizo society. My own country also receives unfavorable marks from Chanchaleños concerned for the welfare of women. Marina says that the United States is a nice place to visit but she wouldn't want to live there because women "have to be afraid in the street." As she attests, in Chanchaló women can walk alone at night without fear, because "no one wants to hurt us." When Eduardo quizzed me about my husband's treatment of me while expressing sympathy for my having to work so far away from my family, he explained delicately that local people are aware that women in my country may not be treated as well as women in Chanchaló. Highly valuing women's persons emerged from many conversations as a we/they distinguishing factor. Whether or not this ideal is always practiced, its existence is important to many people of both genders in Chanchaló.

Strong socialization against physical abuse of women appears to be mirrored in a low incidence of domestic violence. I did not hear women discuss physical fights between husbands and wives in the gossip networks to which I had access (where nonphysical domestic fights are among the preferred topics); nor did I observe any physical intimidation of women. The one incident I did observe involving physical violence against a woman occurred when a father avenged an earlier attack on his daughter by another young woman. He slapped the attacker and was immediately condemned by all who witnessed the incident, which took place amid a crowd. The consensus was that provocation did not excuse his hitting a female.

When Clemencia told me about her parents' boxing her ears in an attempt to force her to abandon her plan to marry Alejandro, she added that they had never hurt her before. She did not appear to be accustomed to familial violence. Clemencia was ultimately free to leave her parents' household and marry the man of her choosing.

I did not conduct a study of domestic violence, and I am well aware that the absence of physical, public behavioral, or gossip evidence is not evidence of absence. However, I do believe that both the public enforcement of nonviolence ideology and the fact that women do not discuss violence as a recurring problem in their communities, as coastal women do, suggest a relatively low level of violence against women.

## Women's Control of Fertility

Women's personal physical autonomy is more reliably evidenced in family-planning practices. Several women in my ethnographic sample have sought family-planning services with the cooperation of their husbands. This behavior is in direct contrast to reports of sierran mestizo communities where men control women's fertility to a greater extent (Phillips 1987; Stolen 1985), and the report of the local mestiza nurse's aide who runs the rural social security dispensary in Chanchalito. In her opinion, the reason women do not come to the dispensary for help with family planning is that their husbands will not allow it. In the opinion of both women and men in my ethnographic sample, the reason women do not seek family-planning aid at the dispensary is that the nurse's aide is not knowledgeable and does not offer effective methods.

During my first visit to her home, Clemencia asked me to help her find a doctor who would prescribe a method of contraception. She said that Alejandro was concerned for her health because each of her seven successive pregnancies had been more difficult than the one before. She had visited a public clinic but the physician had told her not to speak to him of such things. She had also heard about an herbal tea that would prevent conception but did not know where to obtain it. I located a female physician in Salcedo who would discuss the full array of contraceptive options and accompanied Clemencia and Alejandro to her office. I did not stay for the consultation, but Clemencia told me that the doctor explained options to both of them, and that Alejandro accepted her choice of contraceptive.

Beatriz practiced chemical contraception successfully for thirteen years.

When she came to ask about other options, she brought fifteen-year-old Nancy along. Beatriz and Lucho want Nancy to succeed in her ambition to become a physician. They do not appear to be concerned about virginity per se, Beatriz's remarks about "town boys" notwithstanding. She is much more concerned with equipping her daughter to avoid an unwanted pregnancy.

Rubén mentioned the lack of access to family-planning services among poor families who cannot afford private physicians as one of the most serious development problems in the region. This conversation came about the first time I talked with him. I simply asked him how many children he had and their ages, as one does when getting to know someone. He replied that he has two children and that the youngest is nine. "Family planning!" he added emphatically and proudly. "Nine years and no babies."

Rubén further stated that men are as concerned about having too many children as women, and that he has talked to many men who want to learn about effective contraception. He says there is not enough land in most families to bequeath each child enough for the survival of a new family; just making ends meet is difficult for poor people with many children. Rubén accompanies his wife to an expensive private physician in a provincial capital once every three months for her gynecological examination. He also has helped his neighbors find less expensive physicians, but he says many people still do not know that effective contraception exists.

None of the several women who asked me about family planning expected their husbands to object to contraception. One woman did say her husband was reluctant to follow the Peace Corps volunteer's recommendation of male sterilization, made during an informal meeting in Chanchaló, when several women asked her how they could obtain contraceptives. The recommendation was put forward by the same volunteer who castrated Valentina's pig with such an unhappy result. It is not surprising that the local woman was seeking other alternatives. I have no doubt that Chanchaleñas have the freedom, if not the technology, to control their fertility. Gender-egalitarian participation in family planning appears to be a feature of less integrated indigenous Andean communities, according to Harris, who reports that Laymi women also control their own fertility (1978).

## Women's Social and Political Activism

Chanchaleños are proud of their distinguishing social traditions, which include respect for women's physical persons, equal valuation of women's work, and the perception of survival through social solidarity and economic collaboration. Who "we" are is defined, at least partly, by how we treat one another. Women's apparent relative freedom from violence and sexual coercion suggests that these norms do influence practice.

Other indicators of women's physical independence include high levels of participation in communal and regional public organizations. There are no public organizations in which women may not participate. Women are active in public works, in local governance of the rural social security service, in the Women's Production Association, and in public ritual. In 1993, a most prestigious and demanding ritual position—*prioste* of the annual fiesta celebrating the community's founding—was held by a woman.

Informants give several reasons for the fact that only two women belong to the quesería (cheese factory) production association, and only one to the cattle production cooperative. No one says that male members or women's husbands try to prevent women from joining. According to Marina, the members of the quesería and its parent production association were recruited by FUNDAGRO and other agencies from a preexisting male-oriented political group. This pattern has been observed elsewhere in the Andes (Fernández 1988). In contrast, a mestizo development practitioner told me that women were not recruited because "women are not interested in production. They don't do it and they don't know anything about it." This agricultural professional has visited the community many times and observed women in the fields. Without having investigated the subject, he concluded that women must be merely unpaid family labor without decision input.

A number of women and men agreed with Marina's assessment of the reason wife and husband do not join the same economic organization: it would be inconvenient for both partners to participate in organizational meetings and *minga*s, because there would be no one left to work on the farm. Although wives and husbands compensate for the absence of one partner by increasing their individual workload and performing tasks regularly performed by the absent partner, they prefer to avoid obligating both partners for extrahousehold service in the same projects. One member of the Women's Production Association summarized this preference for independent participation in parallel organizations:

We don't want to work in the same association. If my husband is working on the farm or in the house, I can go to the *minga*. If I am working, he can go. Well, sometimes we both have to work in the fields because of the harvest or something else and no one can go to a *minga*. And sometimes we both have to leave our work and go to a *minga* when it is time to clean the canals. But there is no need for us to join the same association. We have one for women and two for men and women.

It should be noted here that women are not marginalized from control of economic resources accessed through the quesería and cattle production cooperatives. All informants agreed that women manage the income derived from their husbands' participation. This appears to be an important reason

why women are not more interested in independent membership in these organizations, but approve of what they consider to be household membership
accessed through their husbands' labor.

Women are independent voting members of the comuna. They participate
equally with men both in public debate, which often concerns community
development, and in the labor of community maintenance. This pattern is in
striking contrast to that described for communities in Peru (C. Allen 1988)
and Bolivia (Harris 1985), where women do not have voting membership in
the community's jural body but make their views known in informal town
meetings or by influencing their husbands' votes.

In Laymi (Aymara) communities, egalitarian relations between husbands
and wives are distinguished from more asymmetrical relations between
groups of men and women (Harris 1985). Although a man's vote will represent a household consensus, women cannot participate directly in formal political affairs. Women are perceived to be vulnerable to spirit attacks and thus
are not permitted to participate in collective activities taking place at night,
when most political activities occur (see Larme 1993). Such perceptions can
result in exclusion from work on irrigation networks and ultimate denial of
access to formal decision-making concerning irrigation or communal land
management (Fernández 1988).

In Quechua, the community studied by Allen (1988), women appear to be
satisfied with their public and organized forms of political expression, which
lie outside the communal assembly. Both women and elder men participate in
public political debate, although they do not vote in the assembly. Allen reports that no formal political action can be taken without a consensus including the voices of women.

The formal political organizations of many Andean communities have
been mandated by national law and may not represent a great deal of the actual political power within a community (Belote and Belote 1988). Thus the
fact that women do not hold office or even vote in these organizations may
not always indicate that they are being excluded from political power, or even
that they must participate through their husbands.

In Chanchaló, women make their views known by speaking at formal and
informal meetings of the comuna. At the meetings I attended in Chanchaló
and Sacha, women held the floor as often as men and were attended with
equal respect. Many women, however, express a reluctance to become involved in the electoral politics of the comuna. Several state that women do
not go to all of the comuna meetings because they do not want to spare the
time, and their husbands will represent the family. However, they say,
women will *always* go to the meetings in which officers are elected, because

they do not want to be "volunteered" by their husbands for time-consuming positions. If they attend the meeting, they can refuse to serve. The practice of husbands' volunteering their absent wives for prestigious but time-consuming posts has been observed elsewhere in the Andes (Fernández 1988). No women in Chanchaló hold office in the comuna.

A number of women also say that the comuna has no real political power except the vote of its president to elect the president of the regional campesino organization, the Casa Campesina of Cantón Salcedo. Officers of the women's organizations belonging to the Casa Campesina are members of its directorate, which holds elections for the regional presidency. They and the male officers of institutions other than the comunas observe and debate election procedure, but only the comuna presidents can vote. During the 1993 presidential elections, politically motivated women of Chanchaló, Sacha, and other indigenous communities in Cantón Salcedo (Clemencia and Valentina among them) successfully lobbied the directorate to award voting status in the next election to the presidents of women's associations.

Women speak for themselves politically and appear to be satisfied with the level of political participation they have in the community. They are taking positive steps to redress inequality at the regional level. Chanchaleñas also prefer to have parallel structures available to them at the local level. Women are not merely members of households represented politically by men.

## Dualistic Structures in Kinship and Inheritance

The households profiled in chapter 3 exemplify an important feature of traditional Andean kinship in both concept and practice: marriage is the equal joining of two kin groups. Kinship is reckoned bilaterally in Chanchaló. Most nuclear-family households engage in economic reciprocity with the extended families of both household heads. Both women and men supply land, labor, and loans accessed through their natal families. Flexible marital residence patterns and the proximity of most women to their families of origin, either in Chanchaló or in neighboring communities, facilitate observed gender equality in accessing resources through families of origin.

The NSF/FUNDAGRO Household Surveys do not include measures of access to labor or loans through kinship networks. The survey does include measures of women's landownership, and whether their land was inherited or purchased together with their husbands. I will describe local women's access to land, contextualize this information with informants' statements regarding inheritance patterns, and place Chanchaló in its regional context using patterns reported throughout the Andes.

*Women's Ownership of Land*

More than three-fourths of surveyed women own land, a slightly higher proportion of the sample than men reporting ownership. Women were asked to quantify landholding during the third phase of the household survey, when, because of sample attrition, seventy female household heads remained in the survey. Table 10 analyzes landholding according to the percentage of surveyed women whose only landholdings are independently owned; the percentage of women whose only landholdings are jointly owned with their husbands; and the percentage who own both independently held and jointly held land. Another way to analyze forms of landholding is to note that, among women who own land, half own land independently from their husbands, generally the result of inheritance, while over three-fourths have bought land jointly with their husbands.

Women and men own land in equal quantities. Among surveyed women, the average amount of land owned is 1.8 hectares (SD 2.5). Surveyed men reported owning 2.3 hectares (SD 4.6). Mean differences in the amounts of land owned by women and men are not statistically significant (two-tailed probability of t = .430).

The high percentage of women owning land may seem surprising, as Chanchaló, Sacha, and Cumbijín are located on lands of former haciendas and, to some degree, participated in the Ecuadorean land-reform program of the 1960s and 1970s.[6] This program by law permitted only "household heads" (nearly always male) to receive hacienda subsistence plots formerly worked by their households, or to access communal lands expropriated from a hacienda (see Phillips 1987). However, most land in the study communities was acquired originally through negotiated purchase from absentee hacendados

*Table 10. Women's Ownership of Land, Cantón Salcedo, 1993*

| Type of Ownership | Percentage of Women Reporting Ownership |
|---|---|
| Independent | 13% |
| Purchased with husband | 39% |
| Both independent and jointly purchased with husband | 26% |
| TOTAL owning land | 78% |

*Source:* NSF/FUNDAGRO Household Surveys, round 3, June–July 1993.
   *Note:* N = 70 female household heads remaining in survey sample during round 3, June–July 1993.

rather than through legal expropriation. Owners who acquired land from the haciendas proudly display their deeds, registered in the names of both husband and wife, as do owners who later bought land from other community members. Thus the effects of land reform for the generation of women whose households dealt with the haciendas have been much less negative than in many other Andean regions (Deere 1986).

Less than half of the women in the survey have inherited land. I do not have an equivalent measure for males, as men were not asked if they own land independently from their wives. This pattern may reflect the fact that the survey sample is relatively young and many younger women have not yet received their inheritances. However, women over the age of fifty or so are also unlikely to have inherited land, as their parents may have had none to bequeath. Thus both women such as Rosa (aged fifty-eight) and very young women are more likely to own land jointly than to have inherited independently. Women's independent ownership does not depend on the location of their families of origin. Women whose parents and inherited land are located in other communities usually do not have to travel far to access these lands and are likely to farm them with their husbands.

Among the women in my ethnographic sample whose parents owned land and had already parceled it out among their children, the women have inherited land equally with their male siblings. This pattern is consistent with Stark's (1984) report that women in the northern Ecuadorean sierra have begun to inherit lands that came into their families' possession as a result of land reform. Within my ethnographic sample, ideals of gender-blind inheritance appear to be strictly enacted. Parents attempt to award land of comparable size and quality to all of their children. Marina and her brother Alejandro have each inherited one hectare from their parents, as has each of their siblings. These plots are considered by all of the children to be of similar quality.

Chanchaleños say that the youngest child, regardless of gender, is expected to remain in the parents' house following marriage. This child thus inherits the house and surrounding land of an approximately equal value with that of other siblings. In Marina's family, the youngest child is a girl; she has inherited the house, garden, and surrounding plot. Valentina has inherited land of equal quantity and quality with her brothers. Susana's parents have ceded to her and her brother equal amounts of land. Although her brother is younger and could be expected to inherit the house, she currently lives in it and says that her parents gave it to her. Susana's inheritance has not yet been legally formalized, although both she and her brother regard the house as hers. He expects to inherit the family's home in Salcedo.

Clemencia has not yet inherited land. Her parents have said that she will come into the land on which her house now stands and its surrounding hectare, plus an additional two hectares in the *páramo*. She is well satisfied with this distribution of fertile lands and hopes that it will not be contested by any of her siblings. If siblings do not feel that their inheritances are strictly equal, they may exert pressure on their parents or siblings to alter the distribution.

Measures of ownership actually underrepresent the amount of land women bring into their households for productive use. Surveyed women were not asked if they sharecrop land with their parents or siblings. In my ethnographic sample, most women who have not yet inherited land do sharecrop with their parents. Clemencia and Beatriz exemplify this pattern.

In sum, it can be said that women are as likely to bring land into their households as are men. Although all lands are jointly worked and the proceeds from all lands are pooled within households, women's independently held lands cannot be appropriated by their husbands. Relationships among bilateral kinship reckoning, individual ownership of resources, and pooling of resources within the household, observed in several indigenous Andean communities, will place patterns observed in Chanchaló within a pan-Andean and historical context.

## Kinship and Land in Andean Communities

Ethnographic studies of indigenous highland populations in Ecuador conclude that women are likely to own, or control the usufruct of, land and animals independently from their husbands.[7] These sources agree that male and female siblings inherit land equally, and that husbands and wives cannot inherit or otherwise appropriate one another's land. Ideally, land is to be held for their children's inheritance.

Upon marriage, both spouses are likely to receive at least a part of their inherited land. Moreover, husbands and wives will work on and enjoy the income from one another's landholdings in a joint enterprise, but neither can unilaterally control the other's holdings. This is also true of livestock holdings; animals may be individually owned but provide products for the entire household.

Both land and animals acquired during marriage may also be owned jointly by wife and husband. It is likely that land bought during marriage will be jointly owned (Alberti 1986; Belote and Belote 1988). In one community it was found that when one spouse dies, the survivor will receive half-ownership of joint property while the other half will be divided equally among the children. When the remaining spouse dies, all of the land will be passed on to the children (Alberti 1986).

Within these ideal patterns, which are widely observed, there is plenty of room for disputes, as children may expect more of their inheritance upon marriage than their parents choose to give them, or they may be dissatisfied with their "equal" share. Not all holdings of the same size are equal, depending on altitude, soil, climate, improvements, and numerous other factors that can vary within a single community. Furthermore, individually held land ultimately is disposed of as the individual wishes (Alberti 1986). Nonetheless, there is no pattern of males receiving more or better land than females, or vice versa. Although Belote and Belote report that there is a tendency for the youngest son to inherit the parents' house, this pattern is not reported for other Ecuadorean communities.

As a general principle, individual ownership of productive resources applies to persons of both genders and all ages. Children begin to care for and own animals at an early age. As children mature, it is likely that they will contribute to the household fund, but they also retain individual ownership of animals and may have savings accounts in their own names.

In Ecuadorean communities studied by ethnographers, principles of bilateral kinship govern inheritance. Daughters and sons are perceived to be related equally to, and inherit equally from, both mothers and fathers. There are, however, traces of parallel descent that may be vestiges of pre-Conquest forms. According to Belote and Belote, although kinship is reckoned bilaterally, Saraguro boy babies are believed to be implanted in the womb by their fathers, whereas girls are believed to be formed by their mothers alone following stimulation by their fathers (1977). Parallel hierarchical ritual offices also are held by both Saraguro women and men at every fiesta; important ritual objects are handed down from mother to daughter. Alberti reports an informant's statement that females took their mothers' surnames and males, their fathers', until it became necessary for women to add their fathers' names if they wished to inherit from them legally (1986).

These forms resemble patterns of parallel descent and inheritance documented in pre-Conquest Peru (Silverblatt 1980) and contemporary Quechua (Isbell 1978) and Aymara (Collins 1986) communities in Peru. According to Collins: "A woman's access to land resources upon marriage is not dependent on membership in her natal household but on her position in a line of women extending back over several generations. The same is true for a man" (1986, 658). Isbell states that Chuschinos continue this practice, although it is against Peruvian law (1978, 79). Lambert's characterization of these apparent survivals or vestiges of parallel descent is particularly useful: "an idiom of parallel descent has persisted in some present-day Andean societies as a way of thinking about kinship" (1977, 17). This idiom is yet another expression of the separateness and independence of female and male: separate names, ancestors, and ritual identities for women and men.

Bilateral and parallel forms of gender-egalitarian inheritance will ensure that both women and men have access to inherited land so long as neither state intervention in land-tenure and inheritance patterns nor marital residence patterns favor males. In the Ecuadorean cases, equal inheritance is observed in communities where land reform favoring males did not affect freeholders (Belote and Belote 1988); where indigenous forms have been reinstated in the generation that is now inheriting parcels granted during the land-reform initiatives of the 1960s and 1970s (Stark 1984); and where indigenous patterns were maintained despite laws favoring males (Alberti 1986).

In some Andean communities, however, inheritance is biased in favor of males. Harris reports gender-biased inheritance in a Laymi Aymara population where land is controlled not by nuclear families but by a few persons who distribute it to their agnatic kin (1978). Residence tends to be virilocal. Thus, women are often without individual access to land, as children of either sex who marry out of their localities may have to relinquish rights to land (Lambert 1977). However, Harris also reports that women may inherit land in the absence of male heirs and "frequently retain right in their agnatic land" (1978, 39). Lambert summarizes a number of studies from southern Peru and Bolivia that reported this pattern during the 1960s and 1970s; he notes, also, that these rules are flexible, allowing room for new couples to cooperate with those relatives who have more resources. Collins, working in the same region, finds parallel inheritance patterns (1986).

It is possible that state intervention at least partly accounts for male bias in some Andean inheritance patterns. Parallel kinship reckoning and inheritance and flexible marital residence were legally altered by colonial governments as early as the first century of Spanish rule. When ruling on conflicting land claims put by members of intercommunity marriages, Viceroy Toledo decreed that a couple must reside in the husband's community and that their children should belong to the paternal kin group (Spalding 1967, 122, cited in Silverblatt 1980, 167). Although some groups attempted to settle disputes by reinstating or upholding the traditional pattern of women inheriting from their mothers and men inheriting from their fathers, others did not (Silverblatt 1980, 167). In areas where land was expropriated by the conquerors or otherwise controlled by the state, women's lands were more vulnerable than those of men (Silverblatt 1980). Most contemporary land-reform laws stipulate that claims be put by heads of households; Andean states recognize men as heads of the households in which they reside (Deere 1986; Collins 1986; Harris 1983a).

Nearly all contemporary ethnographic studies report that husbands and wives cannot unilaterally control one another's holdings; even though land is worked jointly and animals exploited by all household members, individual owners retain the ultimate decision authority concerning the disposition of their own property. Neither joint decisions concerning the use of land and animals nor the pooling of products derived from these sources indicate that household members have assumed the control of one another's individual property. A singular exception to this generalization is the finding by Bourque and Warren that husbands can exert control over their wives' inherited land. For this reason, daughters lose out to sons, who are expected to retain control of their inheritance and thus "are generally given the choicest lands in central locations for irrigation and transportation to town" (1981, 140).

The predominant traditional patterns of inheritance observed throughout the Andes thus result in women's independent ownership of land, animals, and other resources. In most of the areas studied, males are not favored by traditional inheritance norms. State interventions in the form of adjudicated preference for male heirs and patrilocal or virilocal residence patterns may have influenced practice in some areas; in others, indigenous people resisted state attempts to prevent women from inheriting greater wealth than their brothers or from inheriting at all.

The structural context for the two-headed household in Chanchaló is thus embedded within traditional Andean forms of gender-egalitarian inheritance and reciprocal access to productive resources through kin groups. Women's equal control of household economic resources and decision processes takes place in a context of equal ownership of productive resources, including land. Bilateral kinship reckoning and ambilocal marital residence patterns mean that women are as likely to access resources through kin groups as are men. These structural features have not been modified by legislation favoring male "household heads." In Chanchaló, *head* is a generational term rather than an engendered one.

## Conclusion

Indigenous forms of gender ideology and kinship structure that contribute to gender egalitarianism have proved robustly resilient in Chanchaló, having survived both subservience to paternalistic hacienda overlords and unequal integration into modern Ecuadorean society. A fundamental belief in the power of balance within two-headed households appears to be a distinctly Andean ideological construct. Among the clues to its durability in a setting where so many national institutions are both hierarchical and patriarchal is a local concept of resistance, in which native social forms are viewed as a vital defensive strategy enabling subjugated people to survive domination. The legacy of hacienda repression borne by Chanchaleños appears to be one of commitment to collaboration, rather than a desire to emulate patterns of dominance and subordination. Both men and women view the power of balance as worth defending.

Other components of gender ideology appear to be nontraditional. Andean gender fundamentalism idealizes the achievement of a dynamic balance of power within female-male dyadic units including the household. The ability to perpetuate the unit is believed to require tapping the strengths of both its female and its male parts. Although Chanchaleños embrace this dualistic concept of power and dynamism, they do not for the most part attribute differing, "separate but equal" strengths to women and men. Chanchaleños are quick to defend their nondifferentiated egalitarian ideals, such as the one underlying the claim that women plow with draft animals. The absence of perceived gender boundaries in the distribution of abilities, aptitudes, and character traits indicates that neither traditional Andean gender parallelism nor mestizo marianismo ideals underlie cultural constructions of gender in Chanchaló. I have speculated that labor patterns on the hacienda may have contributed to the absence of even perceived complementarity in the current division of household productive and reproductive labor. Perhaps women's work on the hacienda, where they reportedly demonstrated an ability to plow as well as men, contributed to current valuations of women's and men's equal capabilities.

Structures of kinship and inheritance that endow women and men equally with land and access to other economic and social resources provide a material foundation for the two-headed household. Local commitment to the preservation of these forms is undoubtedly linked with gender-egalitarian ideology. The structural basis for women to enter marriage as equal partners has been perpetuated together with the belief that women and men are equally worthy trustees of family material and social wealth.

Women's apparent relative freedom from violence and sexual coercion and their observed independent roles in community organizations and regional politics reflect ideological constructions of gender, household, and society, as well as their status as property owners and economic actors. Women are co-operating members of household units; they also have considerable personal autonomy both inside and outside their households. Speaking of the effects of tradition and change on women's household and public roles, Harris concludes that, in less integrated Andean communities, "women enjoy a freedom and self respect unusual in peasant societies" (Harris 1983a, 13). Although

Chanchaló is a highly integrated indigenous community, Harris's characterization rings true. As survivors of hacienda repression, Chanchaleños value both freedom and self-respect. They have retained traditional institutions— and shaped nontraditional ones—that support equal measures of these goods for women and men.

The two-headed household is a product of both tradition and change. Lessons learned on the mestizo-controlled hacienda are expressed in fundamentally indigenous Andean ideological and social forms. Dualistic power-sharing within the household persists in a political-economic environment characterized by processes of change that have elsewhere disadvantaged women. If Chanchaleños do not respond to economic change in the widely expected way, it may be because they have compelling reasons to view egalitarianism and collaboration as irreplaceable lines of defense in an unequal world.

SEVEN  Gender and Economic Change
in Cantón Salcedo
*The Myth of the Masculine Market*

---

IN CHAPTERS 3 AND 5, we observed gender-egalitarian control of productive resources and incomes in households practicing high-technology commercialized agriculture. We saw that women manage pooled household incomes, having both an equal voice in establishing household accumulation goals and veto power concerning expenditures. Women's financial authority was observed in households that depend on wages earned by migrating husbands, as well as in households where women's own production contributes a larger share to total household income. These patterns appear to contradict trends identified in research and practice concerning gender and development in Ecuador and elsewhere in the Andes. In this chapter I shall explore the bases for the widespread expectation that processes of planned and unplanned development will inevitably marginalize Andean women from resource control. I shall present additional evidence from Cantón Salcedo that this influential gender-and-development paradigm is flawed.

Deconstruction of gender-and-development literature suggests that patterns reliably observed in mestizo populations have been generalized to Andean rural populations without regard to ethnicity. Allowing that methods of ethnic categorization are not uniform in the literature, and that ethnic identification can be attributed in a dynamic and fluid manner both by those who bear it and by observers, I am proposing that it is inappropriate to generalize to the Andean cultural area on the basis of studies of populations characterized as mestizo. A majority of rural highland people are indigenous. Although this population is not homogeneous with respect to gender relations, a number of contrasts between indigenous and mestizo research populations in the region demonstrate that patterns observed in one ethnic context are unlikely to apply to the other. Further, comparison of studies of indigenous populations at varying stages of integration into capitalist commodities and labor markets does not support the argument that economic change inevitably has a negative effect for Andean women. Analysis of empirical evidence, especially the work concerning market-oriented agriculture, suggests that the case of Cantón Salcedo is not as surprising as a review of research conclusions and trend predictions would indicate.

In my view, the study of gender and development must incorporate a search for patterned inequalities associated with economic and social change. The quantitative component of this research was designed to produce information allowing me to test a model of household resource control that would statistically differentiate the independent effects of commodities and wage markets on women's control of economic resources. In Chanchaló I encountered a gender-egalitarian division of material wealth, perceived human capital, personal freedoms, and participation in intrahousehold and community power structures that could be called "patterned equalities." Because these patterns at times seemed impossibly neat, and because there is a small degree of variation in the extensiveness of women's control of household economic resources, I performed a statistical test that would help determine whether I had missed interactions with other potential determinants of women's resource control that could account for the apparently negligible effects of generally male-dominated markets.

Review of the case materials presented in chapters 3–5 indicates that women's equal participation in the management of commercial agriculture and incomes derived from market-oriented production occurs on farms of all sizes, whether husbands are absent or present, and regardless of the age of the woman. It does not appear that commercialization or male presence on the farm constrains women's control of economic resources. It would appear that women need not be elders who have accumulated decision authority to be exempt from the theoretically negative effects of the market. Women with more extensive control of productive resources have either contributed inherited land or bought land with their husbands. They are also full-time farmers who work in all phases of commercial production. In a nonpatriarchal setting such as Chanchaló, women could be expected to have control over the use and products of their lands; women's labor also could be expected to entitle them to decision authority over productive processes and incomes. I wanted to apply a quantitative test that would help sort out such interactions.

Results of multivariate regression analysis proved consistent with case-by-case analysis presented earlier but are not conclusive. I have appended results to the text (appendix C, table 3) and will discuss the model I tested in this chapter. I am offering this discussion for two reasons. First, it is important to explore sources of variation that can be masked by concentrating on norms, even norms as representative as the 80-plus-percent frequencies reported for women's control of land and incomes in the research communities. Although inconclusively tested, the regression model is based both on gender-and-development theory and on local knowledge; thus it provides a structure for this exploration that I hope will prove useful. Second, the model does not include measures that in retrospect I believe would contribute to an understanding of variation in gendered resource-control patterns. I hope that discussion of some of the model's flaws will prove helpful, as well.

## Gender and Planned and Unplanned Development in the Andes

In my first chapter, I summarized a pattern emerging from review of social science literature concerning women's roles in economic production and household resource control in highland Ecuador and elsewhere in the Andes. The thread running through these studies is that traditional indigenous patterns of gender-egalitarian landownership, participation in agricultural labor and decision-making, and access to household incomes are being threatened by both planned and unplanned development processes. In those regions where planned development in the forms of gender-biased legal structures limiting women's access to land or agricultural cooperative membership (Phillips 1987) or the targeting of production-oriented projects to men exclusively (Garrett and Espinosa 1988) have been operative, women have suffered decreasing access to the means of production. Unplanned development in the form of male participation in capitalistic labor markets has been ubiquitous, as the tiny land bases of many indigenous families will not support them. Those households increasingly rely on cash earned by men, while subsistence agriculture, managed by women, stagnates. Capitalistic commodity production on larger farms is an additional form of unplanned development that can marginalize women, as men tend to control the processes and/or the fruits of cash cropping (Bourque and Warren 1981). All of these processes are generally considered either to have weakened women's economic status within the household or to pose an observed threat to that status, even if women currently cling to their traditional equal share of economic resources.

Poised against the material and ideological influences of state restructuring and capitalism are traditional Andean forms of social organization and resource control, in which women's roles and status are generally viewed as equal with men's (Belote and Belote 1988; Poeschel 1988; Stark 1984; Allen 1988; Harris 1978, 1980, 1983a, 1985). There is general agreement that the survival of traditional forms may soon give way under the continued influence of capitalism and national government and culture. Egalitarianism in inheritance patterns, subsistence production systems, gender ideology, and social practice will be no match for economic change favoring male earning power in patriarchally oriented national institutions (see Belote and Belote 1988).

A comparison of the methodologies, theoretical perspectives, and results of these and other researchers indicates that the exogenous cultural-evolutionary pull felt by most analysts is not confirmed by their cumulative findings (Hamilton 1995, 323–36). Women in indigenous communities such as Chanchaló, where men have been migrating to wage labor for many years and many households have become heavily dependent on commercial agriculture, are observed to have maintained equal control of economic resources, including the cash earned by migrant men. However, as reported norms can mask considerable household-level variation within a research community, and the effects of integration into commodities and wage markets are not analyzed across households in these studies attesting to gender-egalitarian control of economic resources, the evolutionary paradigm cannot be dismissed.

## Modeling the Household Economy:
## The Making of Market Myths

### Effects of Male Outmigration and Labor Market

Although most researchers conclude that male bias in labor markets has, or ultimately will, reduce the proportion of household income controlled by women, studies report diverse findings concerning the observed effects of male outmigration and labor markets. Outmigration and the gender-bias of labor markets are linked issues, as rural labor markets generally do not offer women or men much in the way of well-paying employment. Desirable income-earning opportunities are concentrated in urban areas, and in occupations more accessible to men such as construction (see Belote and Belote 1988). Thus, we are looking at both effects due to men's physical absence from the farm, and results of increasing household dependence on wages earned by men.

Concerning women's participation in agricultural decision-making, results are contradictory. Two studies conclude that migrant men return to make decisions concerning what to plant and other issues of land use (Barsky et al. 1984; Balarezo 1984); male control is viewed as the status quo. In contrast, Poeschel (1988) finds that women make these agricultural decisions unilaterally in the absence of men, a continuation of their traditional full partnership in subsistence-based production.

A number of researchers conclude that intrahousehold gender reciprocity becomes more asymmetrical as a household comes to depend more on men's cash earnings, while women's agricultural production provides less and less of the household's sustenance (Weismantel 1988; see Collins 1986 and Gisbert, Painter, and Quitón 1994). The breakdown of traditional kinship and fictive kin reciprocity in labor and other forms of mutual aid—which is likely to accompany male outmigration and cultural integration—further erodes women's economic base. In their husbands' absence, women have less labor to exchange and may not have sufficient cash to hire labor. In addition, male outmigration provides a conduit for ideas prevalent in national mestizo culture encouraging machismo and patriarchal control of women's personal freedom and household economic resources. In indigenous households where migrant men have come to accept these ideas and women cannot resist them, patriarchal control increases and women's decision input decreases (see Balarezo 1984). Income pooling and women's management of pooled income give way to individual control, often to the detriment of women and children.

Other studies report, however, that in similar production systems where households depend on men for all or nearly all of their cash, women control the incomes of migrant men (Poeschel 1988; Barsky 1984; see Belote and Belote 1988). For methodological reasons, it is difficult to account for reported differences in the effects of male absence and wage labor on women's economic decision input. Although all of the studies deal with indigenous women from the smallholding sector of the Ecuadorean sierra, most are based on a very small number of cases, and methods of selecting socioeconomically representative cases differ among studies.

Barsky et al. present data derived from interviews and participant observation of four households representing a range of socioeconomic levels characterized by farm size in Cantón Cayambe in the northern sierra. This area contains over four thousand farming households. The rural economy is dominated by large dairy haciendas; most male smallholders work for wages locally or migrate to nearby Quito, returning to the farm on weekends.

Balarezo presents information collected during a period of two months
from interviews of fourteen families and an unspecified number of focus
groups from a rural population of over fifty thousand. Her research population includes two *cantones* of Cañar Province in the south-central sierra. Most
of these families derive part of their income from craft production, as well as
from wages earned by men during seasonal migration to the coast. The
sources of household income, rather than socioeconomic level, determined
Balarezo's sample.

Both Weismantel and Poeschel spent lengthy periods in the field, each living with a local family. Weismantel does not detail the number of households
studied nor the range of either household socioeconomic levels or economic
bases encompassed in her study of Parroquia (parish) Zumbagua, Cantón Pu-
jilí, located in the Western Cordillera of Cotopaxi Province not far to the north
and west of Cantón Salcedo. Her discussion of women's access to household
income concentrates on families who may go hungry without access to the
weekly wages earned in Quito by migrant husbands.

Poeschel (1988, 32) surveyed 42 households from a population variously
estimated by reported sources to be between 2,570 and 8,000 in Parroquia
Salasaca in Cantón Pelileo, Tungurahua Province, in the central sierra. Although this survey included questions concerning women's and men's economic activities, quantitative results are not reported other than the length of
time the 90 percent of men who work away from home have been absent
during the year. Rather, Poeschel used the survey to identify five socioeconomically representative families who would provide open interviews and life
histories concerning belief systems and developmental cycles as well as economic matters. She selected representative households according to a combination of socioeconomic level and income-earning strategies, including craft
production. Poeschel's discussion does not differentiate among households of
varying socioeconomic levels or income-earning strategies.

Methodological differences—including small sample sizes based on varying
criteria for representativeness—render it difficult to make comparative statements concerning differences in migratory patterns, microregional ecological
and economic bases, and households' income-earning strategies. For example, one cannot say that long-term male migration contrasts with short-term
male absence in terms of increased decision authority for wives of long-term
migrants, or that women practicing home-based craft production are more involved with agricultural production than those who work on dairy haciendas.
Patterns do not emerge that would explain women's greater or lesser involvement in agricultural labor and decision-making or in financial management,
in households from which men migrate to wage labor.

Differences in theoretical perspective, which can lead to differences in focus (and hence in observation) as well as in interpretation, do not account for contradictions in findings. Most of these studies were conducted within theoretical frameworks consistent with a global-economy perspective. While this perspective may underlie the generalized expectation that observed egalitarian patterns cannot endure, it does not contribute to contrasts in observation.

Although studies of *indigenous* women have found that male outmigration tends to have a negative or neutral effect on women's control of economic resources, studies of Andean *mestizo* women and farming systems find that men's absence can have a positive effect on women's control of productive resources. In a patriarchal setting, removal of the household patriarch can allow women to increase their management roles (Deere and León 1982). Since many policy analysts are unaware of ethnic contrasts (and/or are mestizo males), these findings have been highly influential in Ecuadorean development institutions, where the "feminization" of agriculture is generally attributed to unequal land distribution and male outmigration on the poorest farms. National-level studies also generalize this effect to sierran smallholders (see Preston 1980; Chiriboga 1984; Faulkner and Lawson 1991).

## Male Control of Commodities Markets and Household Capital Accumulation

As the discussion of male outmigration has implied, many analysts expect that women will be more heavily involved in agricultural production and resource control in subsistence (non-market-oriented) production, the dominant mode of agricultural production on the poorest, most marginal farms. The effects of agricultural commercialization and capital accumulation on women's participation in economic decision-making have been analyzed in several studies of women's roles in Andean production systems. One study will be analyzed in detail: Susan Bourque and Kay B. Warren's *Women of the Andes: Patriarchy and Social Change in Two Peruvian Towns* (1981). This work has widely influenced the study of gender and development, as it provides an analytically compelling and theoretically innovative analysis of patriarchy in a traditional setting. Methodological factors, however, make this work difficult to place in a comparative framework. A central thesis of Bourque and Warren's study is that traditional indigenous labor complementarity and gender ideology—coupled with increasing household agricultural commoditization and capital accumulation—marginalize women economically. The authors find that, in traditional households with greater capital accumulation (that is, larger private landholdings), women's field labor and economic decision input decrease. Households with more private land expand agricultural production to include cash cropping. Women's agricultural labor decreases owing to decreased labor demand in households with the resources to secure extrahousehold labor. Decreased involvement in field labor is considered detrimental to women's ability to control resources because they are thus further removed from cash-producing work than poorer women. In addition, men control the marketing of the household's products. Cash income may be administered by women, but men ultimately control the use of money. Women control the disposition of the family's harvests, deciding how much must be kept for household consumption. Thus, the more cash earned, the smaller the proportional share of total production under the control of the woman.

Bourque and Warren do not address the issue of women's greater or lesser degree of agricultural decision-making in market-oriented versus subsistence production; they generalize that men control agricultural decision-making. With reference to the decreased percentage of household production under the direct control of women in cash-cropping households, they conclude: "as a family increases the cultivation of cash crops and gears consumption to commercial products, women tend to lose their control over the management of family resources" (1981, 125). Since they also report that women decide what percentage of crops must be kept for home consumption (an important economic decision), the loss in authority to which they refer seems limited to that caused by households' increasing reliance on cash, over which women have less control than they have over agricultural products kept for home use.

Among the agricultural households described to demonstrate variation in traditional women's lives across levels of wealth, two focus on relations between their female and male heads. In the case of the poorer, less market-oriented household, the wife holds the view that men "should (as they actually do) direct these [agricultural] activities"; in her experience, men control household income (27). In a middle-income, more market-oriented household, wife and husband have bettered their economic circumstances through joint enterprises and purchase of land for commercial production and livestock (28–30). Although the husband markets products, purchased lands and herds are referred to as "theirs"; both take pride in their production and enjoy its economic fruits. In the absence of additional information regarding resource control in this family and case examples from wealthier market-oriented households, it is difficult to resolve the apparent contradictions between these cases and findings regarding women's loss of resource control in more market-oriented households.

Bourque and Warren's study has been used as the basis for the undocumented proposition that observed unequal participation by Andean women in household agricultural production is "undoubtedly" an artifact of commoditization (Sage 1993, 245). Alberti posits the following characterization of Andean farming systems, based on studies of mestizo populations and on Bourque and Warren's work: "If the household also raises a cash crop, it is likely to be under the control of the male head of household, even when women contribute labor to its cultivation" (1988, 66).[1] The generalization that indigenous women will have less responsibility for and control of commercial production is widely accepted in part because, to my knowledge, indigenous Andean women's management of market-oriented versus subsistence-oriented agriculture has been little investigated (Hamilton 1992; Hamilton 1995, 328, 335–36).[2]

A number of ethnographic accounts generalize that indigenous Andean women and men control the means and fruits of agricultural production jointly and in a gender-egalitarian manner (Belote and Belote 1988; Harris 1978; Fernández 1988; Poeschel 1988). When these studies are compared in terms of the relative market integration of the communities in question, women do not appear to have become more marginalized from economic resource control in more market-oriented settings (Hamilton 1995, 323–37). However, none of these studies analyzes variation in women's control of economic resources in households that derive more or less of their livelihoods from commercial production.

The most influential study of the negative effects of household capital accumulation on women's agricultural participation in the Andes is Deere and León's *Women in Agriculture: Peasant Production and Proletarianization in Three Andean Regions* (1982). This study is based on quantitative and qualitative analysis of large samples from mestizo populations in three microregions characterized by differing degrees of integration into capitalist relations of production (see also Deere and León 1981; Deere 1977, 1983). The authors find that intrahousehold relations of production tend to be more egalitarian in the poorest households, and more patriarchal in the wealthiest (Deere and León 1982, 94–104). In the "predominantly capitalistic" Peruvian region most like the study communities in Cantón Salcedo (where smallholders own their own land, but many families are semiproletarianized), decisions regarding land use, agricultural inputs, disposition of production, and household finance are likely to be controlled by men in the wealthier peasant households with larger landholdings and more market-oriented production.

Although wealthier women are less likely than poor women to perform field labor, they may work just as much as poorer women but have less control over production. Moreover, as the economic value of their work increases, wealthier women's control of relevant productive processes and incomes decreases. In land-poor households, "As men become increasingly proletari-anized, women take up the household's secondary activity, subsistence agri-cultural production, almost as an extension of domestic work" (Deere and León 1981, 360). The dialectical basis for more egalitarian relations in poor households is summarized by Deere: "Women's increased participation in agricultural production, decision-making, and community affairs have raised women's relative status within the family, and probably as well, within the community" (Deere 1977, 66).

Although Deere and León do not analyze the effects of gender ideology in the construction of intrahousehold resource-control patterns, they conclude that capitalist development in agriculture is produced by a "complex inter-ac-tion of economic, political and ideological factors" (1982, 140) and that the sexual division of labor and economic decision-making in peasant households are subject to similar influences. As the predominantly capitalistic population they study is characterized as mestizo/white, rather than ethnically indige-nous, it is probable that observed patterns reflect class differentials regarding the intrahousehold effects of patriarchal mestizo gender ideology. Thus struc-tural and cultural interactions would produce a system in which economic necessity overrules cultural strictures regarding women's labor, and poorer women take on more decision input with their individual responsibility for agricultural production and/or with the decreasing value of agricultural pro-duction to total household income.

Garrett and Espinosa, writing about both mestizo and indigenous farmers in highland Ecuador, report similar findings (1988). A sharp contrast is evi-dent between the conclusions of these studies and those of Alberti, who stud-ied both mestizo and indigenous women's participation in agricultural labor and household decision-making in Chimborazo Province, Ecuador (1986). Alberti finds that indigenous women of all socioeconomic levels participate equally with men in decisions concerning subsistence-based agricultural pro-duction. Contrasting indigenous patterns of resource control with the more patriarchal control observed in wealthier smallholding mestizo households, Alberti concludes: "Gender relations are relatively egalitarian regardless of household wealth. This suggests that where women are culturally accorded a productive role and economic independence is the cultural ideal, differences in wealth do not affect gender relations in the same way" (1986, 160).

Although Alberti's findings are suggestive, she regrets that her sample is too small (seventeen indigenous women) to allow for statistical cross-section-al analysis. She also does not compare households of differing wealth levels using qualitative information. Three-fourths of the women and men in her sample state in interviews that women participate equally in decisions concerning land use, purchase of inputs, and when to plant potato and maize. Both men and women also say that women have equal or greater control over all household cash income, although most of this is earned by men working off the farm. It is entirely possible that this proportion of her sample includes households of all socioeconomic levels.

The more widely accepted generalization concerning all Andean farming systems is that it is women on the most marginal farms who participate in agricultural field labor. These women may or may not have economic decision authority. In households capitalizing on larger land bases, men will make decisions even if their wives contribute considerable labor to the agricultural enterprise.

These studies treat an interaction between increasing household wealth and agricultural commoditization as related phenomena that tend to marginalize women from household economic decision-making. The research communities in Cantón Salcedo provide a good test case for these theoretical associations because there is a wide range of variation both in household wealth in landholdings and in the amount of total household income derived from commercial agriculture in the sample.

## Women's Land and Labor

Most researchers are confident that women's ownership of land in indigenous Andean communities contributes positively to their control of household economic resources (see Belote and Belote 1988; Alberti 1986; but see also a contrasting pattern in Deere and León 1982, where mestizo women's ownership does not entitle them to egalitarian control of production). These studies also emphasize, however, that women's ownership operates in conjunction with a work ethic that includes women's recognized equal contribution of labor, and also with gender ideology according women equal responsibility for economic survival. In the presence of these cultural conditions, ownership can be expected to yield decision authority.

More at issue in the literature is the very likelihood that women will have equal ownership of land, in communities that have been affected by land-reform and other planned development initiatives aimed at restructuring smallholder access to the means of production and integrating smallholders into national and international economies. As we have seen, women in Chanchaló, Sacha, and Cumbijín are as likely as men to own land. Women also own as much land as men.

This gender-egalitarian landholding pattern takes place in an area where the national government mandated land reform but was relatively powerless to oust politically influential hacendados. Most land came into the possession of Chanchaleños through purchase from the hacendado's heirs following labor strikes. In the other research communities, a variety of transfers were negotiated, some based on hacienda service. Thus legislation requiring land to be registered in the name of male household heads had less of an effect than one might expect. In the study region, attempts to increase the patriorientation of households and ownership of land through other forms of legislation by colonial and republican governments, such as those described by Silverblatt (1987), Collins (1986), and Isbell (1978), would have been subsumed within hacienda control of all local lands. Thus macrolevel political-economic determinants that have had varying, but often negative, effects on women's ownership of land have not marginalized women relative to men in Chanchaló.

Both social scientists and local informants expect that women's labor in commercial agriculture will help to entitle them to decision-making authority in agricultural production. To the degree that agriculture provides total household income, women's farm labor is expected to entitle them to agricultural and, perhaps, to other cash incomes (see Barsky et al. 1984). These associations can be expected in nonpatriarchal settings only (Deere and León 1982). Chanchaló is such a setting. In this chapter we shall evaluate evidence that women's labor entitles them to decision authority in cash-cropping households at all socioeconomic levels.

*Life Stage*

In many societies, a woman may accumulate authority with age, as she becomes the senior woman in an extended-family household or as she accumulates land or other forms of independently held wealth. A woman's place in her household's journey through a lifetime of production and reproduction has been shown to have an independent effect on women's economic authority in many settings (Buvinić 1990; Wolf 1992). Thus, analysis of market effects should control for age.

In the research area, most households are composed of nuclear families; older female heads are unlikely to control more resources than younger heads on the basis of intergenerational social status. However, the survey sample is relatively young and comprised of marital partners. As the sample does not include elderly female dependents, a woman's age could be expected to influence positively her decision authority. Older women, such as the land-rich matriarch Valentina (forty-seven), may be more likely to have inherited or accumulated land jointly with their husbands and may have built up more enduring and far-reaching reciprocity networks through which productive resources are channeled into their households.

Older women also may have had more opportunity to demonstrate the expertise that informants and some analysts expect will contribute to economic decision authority. Most women over thirty have been married for at least fifteen years, a generous amount of time in which to have accumulated social, economic, and human resources. In addition, we have observed that neither a woman's age nor her being the mother of a very young child constrains her equal participation with men in agricultural labor. To the degree that labor positively affects resource control, age would not be expected to marginalize women from economic decision-making.

## Testing the Markets

The multivariate statistical procedure I used tests the independent effects of male outmigration to wage labor, commercialization of household agriculture, women's independent and joint ownership of land, women's agricultural labor, and their ages, on the extent of women's control of their households' most valued economic resources. The model's dependent variable is a scale in which women receive points for control of land, incomes, agricultural technology, and the use of agricultural products, if they reported equal or greater control of these resources than their husbands during the NSF/FUNDAGRO Household Surveys. Measures of women's control over the four resource domains were reported in chapter 5 and shown to correspond with observed behavior. Variation on the cumulative scale is described in appendix C, together with operationalization of independent variables, sampling, and results.

Results are not conclusive; the sample available for testing is small (N = 48), owing both to sample attrition over time and to the fact that not all households provided complete information on all variables theorized to influence women's decision input. Although comparison of means tests indicate that the regression sample does not differ from the rest of the research population on relevant measures (appendix C, tables 1, 2), I shall emphasize qualitative evidence that the sample represents households in Chanchaló, Sacha, and Cumbijín, together with additional quantitative measures from the full sample of 108 households.

### *Integration into Capitalistic Labor and Commodities Markets Does Not Marginalize Women from Control of Economic Resources*

The model suggests that women's participation in control of household economic resources is not affected by their households' greater participation in capitalist agriculture, nor by their husbands' migration to wage labor.[3] Case descriptions and comparison of means tests confirm that women control important economic resources regardless of whether their husbands migrate to wage labor and regardless of the level of their households' dependence on commercialized agriculture.

*Male Outmigration to Wage Labor.* As more than 80 percent of women in Chanchaló, Sacha, and Cumbijín have an equal voice in the control of most household economic resources while fewer than one-fourth of the men have recently migrated, it is unlikely that male migration would account for the observed high level of women's control of productive resources in this predominantly nonpatriarchal setting. However, it is possible that the small minority of women who do *not* control economic resources equally with their husbands are concentrated among households in which men migrate to wage labor.

Both comparison of means tests, bivariate correlations, and behavioral observation demonstrate that women whose husbands migrate to work for wages do not become marginalized from control of economic resources. Because male outmigration could influence women's control of household income in ways that differ from the effect on other resources, I shall present comparison of means tests for the effect of male outmigration on women's control of particular resource domains (table 11).[4] The table demonstrates that there are only small and nonsignificant differences in women's control of both household finance and of resource domains relating more exclusively to control of agricultural resources within households where husbands migrate or do not migrate.

These findings are not surprising in light of intrahousehold relations described in the preceding chapters. In order for men to become dominant in matters of finance, women's roles as financial managers would have to be revised in light of both men's greater contribution to total household income and a cultural shift reconstructing gender roles along more patriarchal lines. Within the households of current migrants, women's roles do not appear to have been redefined. This may be partly owing to the continued importance of agriculture as a current income source within many of these households (see appendix C, table 4; Hamilton 1995, appendix 3).

As the case of Mariana and Enrique illustrates, women continue to manage financial resources in homes where the husband's wages account for most current cash income (see chapter 5). This case also suggests that generalizations concerning the reluctance to invest in agriculture attributed to land-poor sending households may not reflect microlevel diversity. In contrast to the scenario described elsewhere (see chapter 1), Mariana does not face a disastrous loss of extrahousehold labor owing to an inability to hire or exchange

Table 11. Women Report Gender-Egalitarian Control of Household Resources:
Comparison of Means on Households in Which Husband Migrates Versus Households
in Which Husband Does Not Migrate, Cantón Salcedo, 1992

| | Male Outmigration[a] (N = 21) | | No Outmigration (N = 79) | | |
| --- | --- | --- | --- | --- | --- |
| | Mean | SD | Mean | SD | Sig. t 2-tail |
| Percent of resource domains[b] equally controlled by woman | 82% | 25 | 83% | 28 | .946 |

Percentage of Women Reporting Equal or Greater Control than Husband in Four Resource Domains

| | Mean | SD | Mean | SD | Sig. t 2-tail |
| --- | --- | --- | --- | --- | --- |
| Land use | 86% | 36 | 81% | 40 | .622 |
| Finance | 81% | 40 | 89% | 32 | .427 |
| Input selection | 81% | 40 | 71% | 46 | .329 |
| Product use | 81% | 40 | 90% | 30 | .352 |

Source: NSF/FUNDAGRO Household Surveys, round 1, August–October 1992.

Notes: a. Husband reported leaving community to work during 1992; average amount of time spent away from the community: thirteen weeks (SD 14).

b. Cumulative scale reflecting women's self-reported equal or greater control than husband in four economic resource domains: (1) land use; (2) household finances, including production finance; (3) selection of agricultural inputs; and (4) disposition of products. Scale values: 0 = no participation; 25% = equal control of one resource domain; 50% = equal control of two domains; 75% = equal control of three domains; 100% = equal control of all resources.

labor. Enrique turns over most of his wage to Mariana, who applies this cash to their jointly determined production goals. These include the continuation of commercial agricultural production involving hired labor; capital outlay for membership in the cooperative, particularly advantageous to farmers with little land; and saving to buy additional land. In contrast to the scenario described in the Ecuadorean development literature, both household heads remain committed to investment in small-scale agriculture. The fact that the husband is in a better position to earn off-farm cash income to facilitate achievement of these goals does not alter gender-egalitarian reciprocities within the household.

Both structural and cultural factors contribute to this phenomenon. Although the households in Chanchaló that send male householders to urban areas are relatively poor, many have sufficient resources to continue commercial agricultural production. They simply are not as poor as many sending households throughout the Ecuadorean sierra (Chiriboga 1985). It is equally important that male and female householders continue to pool resources and that these may be invested in agriculture. Thus women's labor and management in agriculture continue to provide their households with relatively important material resources. Women's labor and management also continue to be perceived by their husbands as valuable resources per se.

Neither current nor former migrants have imposed more patriarchal control of economic resources. It is possible that returned migrants did not change originally positive attitudes concerning their wives' managerial abilities and the economic benefits to be derived from these abilities. It is also possible that men may have changed their attitudes but were nonetheless unable to exert patriarchal control over their wives. I observed several households including former migrants, some of whom had lived outside their indigenous communities for years serving in the Ecuadorean military (Alejandro) or working in cities (Nicolás) or working in coastal plantation agriculture (Esteban). I find the first explanation more likely: returned male migrants are as respectful and proud of their wives' economic performance as men who have stayed in the communities. If these men ever did attempt to duplicate the male dominance of economic processes idealized in mestizo society, they have since abandoned ideals of male physical superiority and exclusive providership or management responsibility relating to household economic activities.

*Agricultural Commercialization.* Observation of gender relations confirms, also, that there is no independent relationship between integration into commodities markets and resource control patterns. Within the households I observed, increased reliance on commercial agriculture has no effect on women's control of economic resources. Mariana and Enrique derive around 40 percent of their total annual income, including the subsistence value of agricultural production, from the sale of crops and animals. Susana and Nicolás derive two-thirds of their total income from commercial agricultural production, even though Nicolás contributes a locally earned daily wage. Clemencia and Alejandro derive 89 percent of total household income from the sale of their crops, animals, and animal products; during most of the year, 100 percent of their cash income is produced agriculturally. Alegría's household derives 100 percent of their considerable income from agriculture. All of these women participate equally in decisions regarding land use, product use, and agricultural technology; only Susana has somewhat less than equal participation in all decisions regarding household finance. The households of these women represent the full range of socioeconomic variation in the study communities.

Both macro- and microlevel structural factors contribute to women's control of economic resources in market-oriented households. Victoria Lockwood suggests that, among small-scale commercial producers in developing countries, both women's labor in cash cropping and bilateral principles of land inheritance tend to weaken men's otherwise dominant control of capital (1989, 200). In Chanchaló, women work with all crops and own land equally with men.

National agricultural policy and planned development interventions in the study area have not afforded men greater access to the means of commercialized production (see Deere and León 1987). Macroeconomic policies favoring the production of commodities for export have not been directed to smallholders in Cantón Salcedo. Commercial production is devoted primarily to potato and other traditional Andean crops, and to vegetable crops; all are marketed locally by both women and men. Thus new crop technology and marketing infrastructure, which are often offered only to men through development programs, have not affected this population.

Little of the commercial agricultural infrastructure created by governmental and quasi-governmental agencies has reached the smallholding sector in Salcedo. For example, women cannot be disadvantaged relative to men concerning subsidized cheap credit for commercial production, because cheap credit is not available to smallholders. Programs offering veterinary medical and other livestock technologies to small-scale producers *have* been targeted to men's groups only, but dairy and livestock production provides a relatively small proportion of production income to most households.

Progressive farmers like Clemencia worry about household productivity and sustainability losses resulting from *both* low levels of institutional outreach and differential institutional exclusion of women. Her concern regarding the exclusion of women is that household productive decision-making may not reflect optimal choices. Clemencia says that she and her husband teach one another what they have learned from their individual experience. However, she feels that women's greater responsibility for financial management and labor organization in many households may mean that women have more stringent criteria than men for evaluating potentially wasteful or nonsustainable practices. She is convinced that direct evaluation of all options by both household heads would provide the strongest informational base for decision-making. Clemencia is especially concerned that integrated pest-management technologies have not been promoted in Chanchaló, where representatives of chemical companies argue persuasively for nonsustainable application levels of hazardous materials.

Although the Women's Production Association produces potato and other crops, the agents of development who work with this group concentrate on family health and nutrition. Technical assistance offered to other associations is concentrated on livestock and dairy production. In a farming community whose primary source of income is potato, relatively little crop-oriented technical assistance is offered to either male or female producers.

## Woman's Age and Life Stage of the Household Do Not Influence Economic Decision Authority

Authority over household economic resources does not appear to accrue with age. One finding that may shed light on this factor is that older women are not more likely to have acquired land (see appendix C; Hamilton 1995, appendix 3, tables 6, 7). Ethnographic evidence also indicates that there is no relationship between a woman's age and control of resources. Susana, Marina, and other young women have already inherited land; many older women report that they and their husbands bought land together early in their marriages. Very young women like Nancy are encouraged to develop resource management skills and to begin accumulating capital. Young women and girls also work in their families' agricultural enterprises.

Thus it is not surprising that a young wife like Susana should be an equal partner in the management of agricultural resources. Although she is only twenty-three Susana has developed considerable agricultural expertise, which her husband cites as the reason she has more say in decisions relating to agricultural production. We have also seen that Nancy is being trained by her mother to guard the family's purse and to become a discriminating judge of potential bargains in the marketplace. Young women come to marriage well endowed with management experience. In a nonpatriarchal setting like Chanchaló, they do not face an enduring, uphill battle to overcome ideological barriers to equal participation in resource control.

## Women's Economic Decision Authority and Ownership of Land, Labor, and Household Wealth

In the model I tested, women's joint or independent ownership of land is the strongest predictor of women's overall economic-decision authority.[5] These results are consistent with observations of behavior. In this population, husbands cannot appropriate their wives' inherited land. Land purchased by husband and wife has been paid for by the wife's labor and financial management as well as by the husband's. Women who have invested an inheritance or the fruits of their labor in household production have a greater stake in that production than women who have not. It is reasonable to conclude that, in this nonpatriarchal setting, a woman's stake entitles her to a larger managerial role in household production. It is also possible that a woman's larger investment stake makes a larger managerial role more *attractive* to her.

Household capital accumulation also independently and positively predicts women's greater participation in economic decision-making in this model, suggesting an independent relationship that is not a shared outcome of agricultural commercialization (see bivariate correlations also, in appendix C, table 4). The association is small, however. We have seen that women from poor households (Susana and Mariana) and from middle-income households (Clemencia) control economic resources in much the same way as the more affluent Alegría and Rosa. Given the limitations within which we must interpret these results, the model does not support a conclusion that women are more likely to control resources in wealthier households.

What we can say is that formation of an extremely unequal distribution of wealth has *not* been accompanied by the development of more patriarchal control of economic resources within wealthier households. Unlike the situation described in Andean mestizo settings, wealthier women in Chanchaló work in the fields, participate in all phases of agricultural production, and are full decision-making partners in their households' economic enterprises. In the wealthiest household in Chanchaló, where sufficient capital has been accumulated to create a unique wealth-ranking by informants, there are *dos cabezas*.

Widespread female ownership of land is related to bilateral kinship structure, as is the failure of capital accumulation to bring with it patriarchal conditions in economically elite households. Influential studies of the positive association between greater capital accumulation and more patriarchal control of economic resources and women's activities have been carried out among patrilineal, patrilocal populations (Sacks 1979; see discussion in Mukhopadhyay and Higgins 1988) as well as among bilateral populations exhibiting patriorientation (Deere and León 1982). In the study population, neither male nor female household head enjoys exclusive membership in a descent group through which the household must access land and social benefits.

*"Mutual Interest" in Economic Resource Control.* In the study population, both spouses have a stake in increasing household accumulation, as both will own the fruits of production. Perhaps we should be asking not only how household accumulation affects women's control of resources, but also whether women's more extensive resource control contributes positively to greater household accumulation and, if so, what effect this would have on resource control configurations. Richard Wilk's model of the relationship between household wealth and economic resource control in Kekchi Maya household economies (Wilk 1990) may shed light on patterns observed in Chanchaló.

Wilk finds that households exemplifying a "mutual interest" pattern of shared economic decision-making, responsibility, and resources are able to accumulate more capital than households exemplifying a patriarchal pattern of authoritarian control with intrahousehold bargaining over individually controlled resources. When economic decision-making is "conceived as a group decision over group resources rather than as a process of bargaining between individuals" (Wilk 1990, 340), each householder has a stake in household productivity and becomes more willing to share tasks flexibly, to work hard, and to manage resources carefully. As with the forms of extrahousehold cooperation described earlier for Chanchaló, neither pure altruism nor pure self-interest accounts for observed patterns; hence the term *mutual interest*. The result is tangibly greater accumulation.

In Chanchaló, the perception is strong that "two heads are better than one" in terms of applied managerial expertise. Husbands at all socioeconomic levels are likely to attribute household accumulation successes to cooperative management of productive resources and to their wives' administration of household incomes. Perhaps regression results reflect a material basis for this attribution.

*The Cultural Context.* Egalitarian gender ideology contributes to all observed positive associations. In this population men explicitly recognize the value of their wives' labor and managerial contributions to household accumulation. Both gender and kinship ideology are important components of women's ability to retain control of inherited lands and to have their ownership recognized as a legitimate basis for economic-decision authority.

## Factors the Model Does Not Address

The model I tested explains relatively little of the variation in women's control of economic resources. Although I am not relying on the regression as a definitive test, owing to the limitations discussed, I think it is important to address additional reasons the model contains so little explanatory power. The model includes theoretically important material determinants of women's marginalization that can be interpreted in light of normative, egalitarian gender ideology and the consistency between norms and behavior. However, it does not include measures of individual women's and men's ideological constructions of gender. I also do not have measures for other influences on women's control of resources that I now expect would add considerably to a model's explanatory power for this research population, and perhaps for others.

Among the important missing factors is individual preference. I have as-

sumed that women prefer greater economic-decision input, and I think this is
largely true. The women I came to know best value their position as equal
managers of the resources upon which their livelihoods depend. However, I
believe it is possible that, among the minority of women who have less extensive control of economic resources, some may prefer that their husbands assume a greater share of resource management. The model would have been
improved by the construction of a control factor indicating the direction of
that preference.

During my fieldwork, informants repeatedly reminded me that, even
among poor people, individual preference plays a part in decisions concerning
the optimal investment of labor, land, and money toward the achievement of
a variety of individual and household goals.[6] And, as Valentina and others
emphatically state, not all people are alike. Idiosyncratic variation is a matter
of pride in a community where, until twenty-five years ago, the will of one
man ultimately determined how human labor and other agricultural resources would be used. Idiosyncrasy in management styles also should be addressed. Although the ideological norm dictates that joint management is the
best management, women may prefer a less inclusive role for a variety of reasons.

The personalities, goals, and individual experience of women and their
husbands, as well as women's perceptions of their own and their husbands'
strengths, influence women's desire for greater or lesser participation in resource control. A woman might conclude that it is in her own best interest to
exploit the comparative advantage of her mate's greater possession of particular skills, motivation, or temperamental qualities. Husbands have been observed to defer to their wives' greater experience, affinity, or desire; it is reasonable to expect that women may do the same.

Personality may influence women's preferred management style independently of perceived benefits. Both extremely assertive individuals and
women who fear loss of control may seek a more inclusive role in resource
management. On the other hand, a woman's claim to extensive control of resources could result in conflict within the household if her mate is assertive
and disinclined to share authority. A woman who is temperamentally disinclined to conflict may prefer the avoidance of emotional distress to a pitched
battle with a determined mate.

Individual goals may also play a role in women's preferences. An ambitious or future-oriented woman may consider that she has a larger stake in
more decision outcomes. A less ambitious or future-oriented woman may
choose not to bother with all aspects of resource control. Individual experience or family traditions may also influence women's desire to control re-

sources. A woman whose mother was less involved in resource control may choose, for purely personal reasons, either to emulate or to reject this pattern.

The myriad influences of the personalities and desires of women and their husbands that could result in a woman's preference for a more or less inclusive role in economic resource control could be elaborated in great depth. My purpose here is simply to acknowledge that the model I have tested does not allow for these influences. By the same token, the model does not allow for the influence of personality traits and other factors that might disable or otherwise result in nonvoluntary exclusion from resource control. The failure of this model to incorporate measures of preference and other idiosyncratic factors may account for some of the unexplained variation in women's greater control of economic resources in this population where "patterned equalities" are the norm.

## Summary: The Myth of the Masculine Market in Cantón Salcedo

I base the following conclusions on the consistency of patterns observed ethnographically, in descriptive and bivariate statistical procedures, and in multivariate analysis. Women are more inclusively involved in household economic resource control if they have contributed inherited land or if their contributions have helped to purchase land for household production. Chanchaleños' perception that labor is one form of entitlement to resource control, albeit not the only form, appears to be borne out. Women are inclusively involved in wealthier households, as well as in poorer ones. The perception that women's involvement in resource management contributes positively to the accumulation of capital appears to have a basis in material fact, helping to account for gender-egalitarian control of the population's largest concentrations of household capital. In this population, women's contributions of material resources, management expertise, and labor to the economic enterprise result in greater economic managerial authority. None of these effects is a shared outcome of a woman's age.

Women's economic-decision authority is not decreased by their husbands' migration to wage labor. Neither men's exposure to patriarchal gender ideology outside their communities nor increasing household dependence on migrants' cash earnings has decreased women's economic authority. Similarly, households' dependence on commercial, as opposed to subsistence, agriculture has no effect on women's productive decision-making in this population where no agricultural domains are closed to women. In Chanchaló, Sacha, and Cumbijín, there is no evidence of patterned inequality caused by male-dominated commodities and wage markets.

## Conclusion

Women's economic contributions translate into economic authority in indigenous Cantón Salcedo; in many other populations, labor, expertise, and even earned income do not always entitle women to equal participation in intrahousehold decision-making. The high valuation of women as economic actors observed in the study population is an important component of women's economic equality. Both cultural tradition and the perceived household material benefits derived from women's economic authority contribute to this high valuation. Just as egalitarian gender ideology provides a basis for the recognition of women's contributions to household accumulation, material evidence of women's managerial success helps to preserve this ideology. Bilateral kinship structure and egalitarian inheritance patterns, which provide a structural basis for women to enter marriage as equal partners, have been perpetuated together with the belief that women and men are equally worthy trustees of family social and material wealth.

Macro and micro linkages are relevant to the structural-cultural dialectic. Interactions of exogenous and indigenous or endogenous factors did not produce the widely expected forms of female subordination. This finding may be partly attributed to the place of indigenous communities in national class structures. Had the state been more committed to widespread transformation of highly unequal ownership structures during the land-reform initiatives of the 1960s and 1970s, gender-biased development processes might have had a more pervasive effect in communities like those in Cantón Salcedo. Were the state and other development institutions more committed to integrating small-scale producers into commodities markets as competitive producers, more infrastructural benefits might be targeted exclusively to men. Had the planned restructuring of agricultural production not bypassed indigenous communities in Salcedo, we might have found more male-dominated resource domains.

Other forms of gender-biased capitalistic development did not bypass Chanchaló. Yet the cultural hegemony theorized to accompany increased integration into capitalistic labor and commodities markets has not materialized. Migrant men working within patriarchally oriented institutions in urban areas have not become household patriarchs. Migrants may admire the economic power of their mestizo bosses, but they have not attempted to gain economic power at the expense of their wives. Some indigenous Ecuadorean communities that have been more directly affected by planned agricultural development have retained gender-egalitarian access to the means of production (Stark 1984; Alberti 1986). Dialectical analysis suggests that ethnicity can mediate the potentially negative effects for women of macrolevel political economic change.

## Development Implications

It is tempting to conclude that women in Chanchaló, Sacha, and Cumbijín have benefited from the relative exclusion of their communities from planned-development interventions that elsewhere target resources to male household heads. However, in two-headed households where resources are pooled, relations of production are less likely to become more asymmetrical owing to planned development per se. Such a statement, of course, can be tendered regarding *only* forms of planned development that do not imperil the well-being of smallholding women and their families through change processes *other* than increased intrahousehold gender hierarchy. In Clemencia's view, families suffer from the lack of certain forms of planned development in Chanchaló, some of which should be offered directly to women. In the following chapter, I shall review lessons learned from the women and men of Chanchaló regarding their development needs and agendas.

## Market Myths in Gender-and-Development Research and Practice

This chapter has demonstrated some of the ways that myths of universal male dominance come into being. In the case of the mythical pan-Andean male-controlled commodities market, a fairly limited statement from one influential study of indigenous gender relations became an article of faith with broader implications than the work would justify. In gender-and-development research and practice, failure to distinguish ethnically or locally differentiated patterns in household resource control contributed to a broadly diffused application of patterns observed in mestizo populations to the indigenous majority of rural Andean households.

I do not doubt that studies attesting to male control of market-oriented agriculture in mestizo Andean populations—and elsewhere in Latin America and the developing world—reflect a widely occurring source of gender inequality (Katz 1995; IDB 1995, 63–70). However, it is not simply the mode of household production but, rather, the macroeconomic policy environment in which smallholder production takes place that is likely to influence the proportion of household labor and other resources invested in production for the market, and women's roles in both labor and resource control (see Deere and León 1987, 2–12). Furthermore, the intrahousehold effects of increasing market-orientation within smallholder production systems, and of changing market structures, can be expected to vary with local structural and cultural configurations.

Variation in intrahousehold processes related to increasing market orientation in smallholder production has been demonstrated in a number of recent case studies. Research demonstrating that women control market-oriented productive resources and incomes in several African settings—where the pattern of increasing subordination of women owing to male control of cash cropping was first widely observed—"warrant a more nuanced approach to the subject" (Little 1994, 166) of the gendered effects of increased market integration (Conelly and Chaiken 1993; Stone 1988; Stone, Davis, and Netting 1995; Webb 1989; see Sørensen 1996). The observation that bilateral principles of resource access can weaken male dominance of market-oriented production (Lockwood 1989, 199–201) applies to a number of Southeast Asian and Latin American populations. Several studies of women's roles in commercial rice and vegetable production in the Philippines have found that women control the household production budget, allocating funds for purchase of inputs and arranging for hired labor, as well as working in the fields; women also market farm products and control incomes (Paris 1989; Hoque and Adalla 1993; Timsina et al. 1993). A similar intrahousehold division of resource domains is evidenced for Central and East Java, although the degree to which women control, rather than administer, incomes is contested among researchers (see discussion in Wolf 1992, 63–67). In fieldwork conducted among smallholding mestizo populations in Mexico in 1996, I found widely varying local forms of gendered labor and resource control in commercial agriculture within four communities where both farming systems and cultural configurations are quite similar. In two of the four communities, women are decision-making partners in market-oriented production (Hamilton 1996).[7]

Within these and other recent works, women are seen to resist male-biased market structures, carving niches for themselves in commercial production. Patterns of cooperation among women and men, and of their overlapping economic interests within commercializing households, also have been analyzed. It is time to reevaluate global concepts of gender inequality arising from male control of commodities markets.

EIGHT  Development and the
Two-Headed Household

*Lessons Learned in Chanchaló*

---

THIS STUDY BEGAN as a search for patterned inequalities related to development processes. I attempted to incorporate into this search lessons learned by researchers and practitioners during nearly three decades of analysis of gender and development from a variety of perspectives. My hope was to delineate forms of gender inequality and to identify political-economic and social structures that contribute to patterned inequality, together with their supporting ideologies. I expected that structural and cultural bases for gender inequality would operate at all levels of analysis, including household, kin group, community, economic sector, nation, and beyond. I planned to explore interactions between structure and culture—and among macrolevel and microlevel institutions—that would elucidate the linkages within processes that marginalize women. I hoped that revealed linkages would contribute to policy analysis and development practice in ways that would interdict processes of marginalization. These were the lessons of homework.

The lessons of fieldwork confirmed the necessity to examine linkages between structure and culture, macro and micro. The lessons taught by women and men in Chanchaló, however, redefined the nature of the inquiry. The task became the elucidation of patterned gender *equalities* in a community in-

235

tegrated into market economies on an unequal basis, but largely hidden from planned agricultural development initiatives.

## Patterned Equalities

Having become sensitized to the pitfalls of presuming that households possess unitary production and utility functions, and to the need to delineate nuanced asymmetrical gender reciprocities within households, I encountered in Chanchaló household units of production, consumption, distribution, and accumulation in which all of these processes involve the pooling and gender-egalitarian control of resources. Among the lessons repeatedly emphasized by my Chanchaló teachers, and observed in their practice, were two that are central to this inquiry. The first is that local households have *dos cabezas:* the concept of unitary headship is both exogenous to Chanchaló and unacceptable to Chanchaleños. The second is that dualistic authority applies to the joint management of all household economic resources.

The frequency and emphasis with which these lessons were verbalized indicate the salience of values concerning dualistic control of communal resources within households. An examination of structural and cultural patterns relating to kinship, inheritance, and community revealed a structural/cultural dialectic in which ideological constructions of gender roles and of survival through community solidarity, together with principles of social and political organization, contribute to resource-sharing and dualistic control within the household.

Bilateral kinship reckoning and gender-egalitarian inheritance patterns contribute to the equal ownership of the means of production brought into marriage by women and men. Constructions of gender placing high value on the physical labor and management expertise of women contribute to both joint ownership of property acquired during marriage and equal control of other household resources. Social ideology prescribing individual benefit through communal labor and resource-sharing at the extrahousehold level may have contributed to these same patterns within households. Recognition of women's leadership within the campesino regional-level political organization is among the fruits of women's social and political autonomy in their communities.

Patterned intrahousehold equalities are embedded in social, cultural, political, and economic institutions at the household, kin-group, and community levels, which, in my interpretation, have contributed positively to these patterns. As many of these institutions have been similarly described for other Andean communities where gender-egalitarian intrahousehold processes have also been observed, ethnicity appears to be an important factor among the sources of patterned equality.

However, within a small minority of households in Chanchaló and the other research communities in Salcedo, women do not share control of economic resources on an egalitarian basis. Gender hierarchies have been observed in other Andean settings as well, and repeating sources of inequality have been delineated. Integration into labor and commodities markets more accessible to men, state restructuring of the means of production in favor of men, and ideological shifts accompanying these processes have been shown to cross the ethnic divide with negative results for Andean women.

Both statistical tests and case-by-case analysis demonstrated that variation in women's control of resources does not stem from household participation in labor and commodities markets. Nor have the wealthiest households—whose capital accumulation has increased while others have become increasingly proletarianized—become more patriarchal. Rather, the source of variation in women's control of economic resources lies in their contributions of land and labor to their households. Women own land equally with men in Chanchaló; women work equally in all agricultural domains and their labor continues to be valued equally with men's. Thus, variation in ownership and labor, and in intrahousehold processes influenced by them, is not a consequence of patterned gender inequality. Moreover, the interaction of macro- and microlevel phenomena is dialectically dynamic rather than hegemonic; local-level structural and cultural institutions contributing to gender egalitarianism appear to have retained saliency despite at least twenty-five years of integration into gender-biased market structures. In indigenous Cantón Salcedo, capitalism and patriarchy are not a package deal.

Chanchaleños taught me that an equal valuation of women and men as economic, social, and political agents is possible at the household and community levels, and that gender equality in their community is related to indigenous Andean ethnicity. I do not wish to romanticize women's status in Andean tradition, however, or to imply that it is a static or undifferentiated phenomenon. Studies of the interaction of Andean tradition and political-economic change have revealed aspects of tradition that make women vulnerable to increasingly patriarchal intrahousehold relations expected to accompany planned and unplanned development. Most of these have to do with traditional gender complementarities in ideology and behavior that appear to be absent in Chanchaló.

I am unable to sort out all of the attributes of egalitarian gender relations in Chanchaló that derive from Andean tradition or from historical integration with national institutions. I am confident that I observed in Chanchaló ways of thinking about gender and patterns of resource control that contrast sharply with those reported for Andean mestizo populations. Thus I was able to delineate, with very broad strokes, the ethnic divide posited in chapter 6. I agree with Chanchaleños that women's status in their community appears to contrast positively with women's status in mestizo Ecuador, where the national press records daily the widespread abuses of a *machista* patriarchy.

However, I am unable to trace the historical interactions of pre-Hispanic and Hispanic institutions that have resulted in the current divide. I did not conduct the kind of historical research that would tell us, for example, whether gender complementarity in the division of labor was at one time a feature of indigenous Chanchaló that has been altered owing at least partly to the assignment of all labor domains to women as well as to men during hacienda indenture. If such a process did occur, it may have contributed to current egalitarian valuations of women's and men's labor.

I also do not wish to romanticize current observations of gender relations. I have stated my admiration and affection for friends and teachers of both genders in Chanchaló. I am sure these feelings have colored my interpretation of processes within their households and community. It is also fair to say that their behavior *caused* me to admire them.

I have described gender-egalitarian access to the means and fruits of economic production, to social welfare and political expression. I have reported that women have the authority to control their own biological fertility, if not the technical means to enact their wishes, and I have suggested that ideals of nonviolent behavior influence a relatively low incidence of violence against women. Some of these goods are in shorter supply for women of my own society than for women in Chanchaló. I admire the ways I believe women are valued in Chanchaló.

It has been my intention to allow patterns in gendered processes to emerge within this study as they did during my own impressionistic experience of life in Chanchaló, and then to test my observation against quantitative evidence collected by other researchers. Qualitative and quantitative evidence proved highly congruent. Patterned equality in the intrahousehold division of labor and local wage rates, and in ownership and control of economic resources, has been documented both quantitatively and qualitatively. In turning to some of the uses I hope will be made of this information by development analysts and planners, I shall apply indigenous knowledge regarding gender and development. I shall not attempt to improve on Chanchaleños' development prescriptions.

## Planned Development and the Future of
## Women in Chanchaló

Aside from gender-biased urban labor markets that draw men away from Chanchaló without offering comparable opportunities for women, social and economic problems faced by women in Chanchaló are those relating to class inequalities, rather than gender inequalities. Planned development efforts have not marginalized women from the means of production. Land reform favoring male household heads has had little effect, as legal land reform per se did not result in significant redistribution of land in the study area. Legal constitution of agricultural production cooperatives that has prohibited membership by wife and husband in a single cooperative has not prevented women from joining male-oriented production associations in Chanchaló. Moreover, women emphasize a preference for maintaining parallel production organizations, as it is detrimental to both household and production-association output if wife and husband have to abandon farmwork to attend the same meetings or labor rotations. If both attend, home production suffers. If one spouse must stay home to manage a critical agricultural activity, the association produces less and member benefits decline. Whereas male-oriented organizations produce more income for members than does the female-oriented association, all incomes are pooled within households and managed by women. Thus, increased male earning power and the application of male labor to association activities have not disadvantaged women.[1]

Losses suffered through planned development interventions that do not take into account women's roles in agricultural decision-making have primarily affected households, rather than women. One concern voiced by local women with respect to production associations is that FUNDAGRO, the Roman Catholic Church, and other institutions supporting their efforts do not channel production-oriented technical assistance to the Women's Production Association. Although information and other forms of technical assistance are likely to be pooled within households, so that women will have access to assistance offered to male-oriented groups through member husbands (see Alberti 1986, 166), Chanchaleñas want to evaluate the usefulness of new technologies on the basis of direct observation rather than their husbands' reports. It was suggested that women and men may have differing standards by which to judge the costs and benefits of new technologies, and that joint decisions based on knowledge disseminated to only one household head are not founded on the optimal informational base. Half of all male household heads do not belong to the production associations; information offered to male-oriented groups will bypass most wives of nonmembers.

More important to women in Chanchaló than gender-biased access to production-oriented technical assistance is the fact that relatively little agricultural development assistance has reached the community. In an area inundated with promotional campaigns by agrochemical companies, none of the development agencies working in Salcedo has offered assistance in the implementation of integrated pest-management technologies. In an area where incomes and household subsistence are heavily dependent on potato production managed by both women and men, agencies have offered men technical assistance in dairy production and women assistance in income earning through craft and guinea-pig production, together with raising vegetable gardens and other contributions to family nutrition.

Aside from issues of technical assistance, modernized agricultural infrastructure is largely unavailable to farmers of either gender in Chanchaló. Development needs cited most often in the community are centered on irrigation, marketing, and credit. Chanchaleños must compete in commodities markets with larger producers whose influence within the Ministry of Agriculture and other national institutions has yielded them access to large-scale irrigation works and subsidized credit. Local farmers have little hope that the state water ministry will support their efforts to access the water to which they are currently legally entitled through small-scale canal works, but which is sometimes diverted by large landholders. Although not constrained by monopsonistic control of marketing, farmers face collusion among buyers in regional markets accessible to the community.

Chanchaleños have taken collective steps to improve their ability to compete in capitalistic commodities markets. The primary function of the cheese factory and the Women's Production Association is to produce commodities for sale. Profits provide credit funds available to members at low interest. The quesería has joined an independent national association of thirty-four queserías and has accessed more competitive markets in Quito and Guayaquil. Members have been able to expand production to fourteen products and expect to further expand national marketing. Local people have defended their water rights, although their ability to press claims against powerful landholders is severely constrained. They have periodically removed the means of illegal diversion of their water, but access continues to be precarious.

Although many Chanchaleños have also taken steps independently to ameliorate the effects of the community's lack of social infrastructure, these individuals as well as others state that lack of clean water, education, and health care is as damaging to the community as their limited access to economic infrastructure. Undernutrition is cited as a serious problem by many men and women who are well aware of the synergistic relationship between childhood disease (exacerbated by contaminated water supplies) and poor diet in contributing to high local rates of undernutrition (Maxwell and Fernando 1989; von Braun 1988; Schiff and Valdéz 1990).

Prominent among needed services listed by women and men are reproductive health care and family planning. Access to modern birth-control technology will not solve the problem of large families with small landholdings having too little land to bequeath sustainable holdings, cited by several informants as the reason families want to limit the number of children they have. Ecuador has one of the most unequal distributions of land in the developing world (Seligson 1984); Salcedo typifies this unequal distribution (Chiriboga 1985). Simply limiting family sizes will not eliminate poverty for smallholders. However, access to birth control will reduce serious health risks currently associated with childbirth, reduce child-care costs for both mothers and fathers, and improve the economic circumstances of children growing up in smaller families.

In sum, agricultural development interventions have played a relatively small role in the business of making a living in Chanchaló. Women have not been disadvantaged by projects offering production benefits to men only, partly because only limited production-oriented assistance has been offered to farmers. The lack of social infrastructure also disadvantages entire households. Lack of reproductive health care and family-planning services is more debilitating for women but also negatively impacts family welfare. A planned development prescription for Chanchaló that would improve the lives of women would concentrate on community access to social and economic infrastructure rather than redressing gender inequalities caused by poorly planned agricultural development efforts. As Chanchaleñas evaluate their situation, the sins of development institutions impacting their lives are those of omission, rather than commission.

The women of Chanchaló have little to fear, should their community become more visible to national and international development institutions. Formative intrahousehold processes reflecting the influence of local institutions have mediated the impact of market integration along lines consistent with gender-egalitarian power-sharing. Income earned by men in agricultural development projects is managed by, and contributes to the accumulation of, their wives. Neither clerical pieties nor the activities of "mothers' groups" sponsored by the Roman Catholic Church have remade the women of Chanchaló in the image of marianismo. Chanchaleños take advantage of lending and social services offered through the church, for which they are grateful, without altering their constructions of gender. Local women and men have managed to serve many of their own interests through individual or household participation in all of these institutions. One of these interests is sustaining an intrahousehold balance of power that both women and men believe has served them well.

## The Power of Balance: Lessons for
## Gender-and-Development Studies

The women and men of Chanchaló want their individual and collective stories to be told. They do not want their community to remain "well hidden" from national and international institutions. They are proud of their egalitarian and collaborative traditions, of their strong women and strong families. They believe patterned equalities have helped them survive against long odds, over many generations, and they want to impart the social value of these traditions. I hope that my study will serve these purposes.

For students of gender and development, the exemplum of the two-headed household entails other forms of instructive value. The presence of patterned equalities where many of us would not expect to find them calls us to reexamine an ideologically driven expectation that women in developing countries will be victimized by an evolutionary and unified trend encompassing economic development and patriarchal social institutions. We are encouraged to look for women's successes in resisting or adapting the institutions of market economies and directed economic change to serve their own ends. We are encouraged, also, to reconstitute both analysis and activism in partnership with local women.

Moreover, we are reminded that interactions of gender and development work both ways: women are economic agents whose priorities can profoundly affect the playing out of development policy. Macroeconomic policy that is blind to gender bias in instrumental agricultural development, employment, and social structures will result in multiple losses rather than in efficient and equitable investment in rural development. Where women are unable to resist or transform gender-biased processes, their labor will be allocated inefficiently. Where women are able to overcome gender bias, their labor may be allocated more efficiently, but misdirected development investment will have been wasted. In either case, investing in unequal structures cannot produce the sectoral growth that is often a primary goal of development policy.

Results of this case study suggest that a dialectical approach examining interactions among structural and cultural factors and macro- and microlevel institutions contributes to an understanding of intrahousehold economic processes and engendered human agency. In the case of three Ecuadorean indigenous communities, this approach produced evidence of remarkably egalitarian gender relations; elsewhere, recent research has revealed productive niches women have carved for themselves within more patriarchal systems. I do not suggest, however, that a focus on local institutions, cultural factors, or the nuances of gender reciprocity can be expected to result in similar findings across populations. The primary task facing scholars and practitioners in the field of gender and development must be the continued search for—and transformation of—patterned inequalities attributable to development processes.

# Appendix A

*Research Methods*

## Institutional Affiliations

This study was carried out in conjunction with National Science Foundation (NSF) Project "Farming Systems and Socio-cultural Determinants of Child Growth in Two Ecological Zones of Ecuador" (SBR 9106378), with Dr. Kathleen M. DeWalt the principal investigator. (The project will be referred to as NSF Child Growth Project.) The central research objective of this project was to examine the influence of socio-economic, cultural, and biological factors on child growth in highland and coastal smallholder populations. Among the determinants expected to influence child growth were the gendered division of labor in agriculture, women's control over subsistence production of food and income, and women's time allocation and child-care patterns. I was invited to join the project to provide survey instrument design assistance and qualitative information regarding these determinants.

The NSF Child Growth Project was instituted in collaboration with the Fundación para el Desarrollo Agropecuario, Quito (FUNDAGRO), a foundation that plans and coordinates agricultural research and extension efforts in Ecuador. Project research design was based, in part, on the results from a series of baseline surveys of small-holder populations in areas served by FUNDAGRO commodity programs. These surveys were conducted during 1988–1990 by FUNDAGRO staff and (through the Cooperative Agreement for Nutrition and Agriculture) by consultants from the University of Kentucky (see B. DeWalt et al. 1990). Results of these surveys suggested that women have larger roles in commercial agriculture than other studies had found (Hamilton 1992) and contributed to the research design of the current study.

## Site Selection

Baseline data indicated that the highland communities surveyed in Cantón Salcedo in 1988 were, on average, both poor and undernourished. Most landholders had far less than the five–eight hectares estimated by the Ministry of Agriculture to be necessary for household economic survival (B. DeWalt et al. 1990; Seligson 1984). These communities thus formed an appropriate research population for the NSF Child Growth project. Each of these communities was shown to exhibit variation on household and individual measures important for my own study: male out-migration; degree of agricultural commercialization; socioeconomic status; and integration into national society and culture. The NSF project population includes three communities served by the FUNDAGRO Dairy Commodity Program in Cantón Salcedo: Sacha, Chanchaló, and Cumbijín.

## Quantitative Methods

### Sampling

A stratified probabilistic sample of 117 households was drawn by NSF Child Growth Project staff from a July 1992 project census of 332 households representing a population of approximately 470 households. Population figures are based on co-muna records. The project census includes 87 percent of the 135 households in Chanchaló; 56 percent of the 243 households in the largest and most dispersed community, Cumbijín; and 88 percent of the 93 households in Sacha. Censused households were stratified according to the presence of children under the age of sixty months; a random sample was then drawn from among households with young children. This method of stratification was employed because the project's ultimate outcome measure is the nutritional health of young children.

This method of stratification produced a sample that is younger than the communities' total populations (see chapter 2, "Demography and Social Organization"). Women's intrahousehold social status and household socioeconomic levels could be expected to co-vary with the age of the female household head. However, interviews with key informants and reports of land-tenure patterns for the research area (SEDRI 1981; Chiriboga 1988b) indicate that the sample does reflect the range and distribution of household wealth encompassed within the research population. Obtaining information for the full population age range was addressed by including older women in an ethnographic sample.

The survey was conducted in three rounds, in order to capture seasonal variation in agricultural production, income, and consumption over a period of one year, and to track child growth during this period: August–October 1992, March–April 1993, and June–July 1993. Both male and female householders were surveyed. Eighty-two households participated in the second round; seventy-two participated in the third round.

Comparison of means tests indicate that samples are comparable across rounds in terms of socioeconomic status, demographic measures, and income sources (Hamilton 1995, 286–88). Some variables used in analysis of women's labor and control of economic resources were included only in individual waves, reducing sample size for some procedures. The smallest subsample used in statistical testing—which includes households who participated in all rounds and gave complete information on several economic variables—is comparable to surveyed households not included in the analysis (Hamilton 1995, 287–88). Nonetheless, qualitative information is relied upon to confirm patterns reported for all samples. The effects of attrition and nonresponse regarding samples available for individual statistical procedures will be addressed together with the analyses.

Univariate analysis (chapters 4, 5) include the 108 cases (94 percent) from the first-round sample and the 80 cases (98 percent) from the second-round sample in which the surveyed woman is a female household head, rather than an unmarried young woman still living with her parents. I have excluded surveyed women without male partners because I want to examine women's intrahousehold economic roles relative to those of their male counterparts, rather than relative to their parents' authority.

## Measures

*Household Agricultural Production and Socioeconomic Status.* Measures of agricultural production and socioeconomic status include the amount of land and livestock held or accessed by male and female householders. They also include land quality; the amount produced, consumed, and marketed of all household agricultural products, animal products, and livestock; income from all products and from off-farm sources; types, amounts, and costs of agricultural inputs; amount and cost of labor of household members and others. Male informants were asked to identify household members who administer all types of income.

*Women's Labor and Control of Economic Resources.* Measures of women's agricultural labor include women's recall of time allocation for the preceding twenty-four hours and average amount of time spent in agricultural production weekly during each season. Recent anthropological studies of agriculturalists in Peru (Thomas et al. 1988) have demonstrated significant comparability between recall data and direct observation of daily activity. As women can be expected to perform more than one task simultaneously, they were asked to list both primary and secondary activities for each half-hour period during the twenty-four hours.

Measures of the range of women's agricultural activities include ranking by women of their involvement relative to that of their husbands in a variety of tasks: planting, weeding, harvesting, processing, marketing, applying agrochemicals, and animal care. Women were also asked to rank involvement in decisions concerning use of the land, selection of agrochemicals and other inputs, and the disposition of products for sale or home consumption. Women's institutional and informal sources of technology, information, and credit were elicited. Women were asked to rank their participation relative to that of their husbands in the management of total household income and income derived from the sale of animals and animal products.

*Household Census; Proximity of Extended Kinship Networks.* The age, gender, occupation, educational level, and relationship to the female householder of all persons residing in the household were given by the female householder. Both men and women were asked for migration histories. Women were asked to locate their parents, grandparents, and siblings geographically.

*Consumption.* Measures of food consumption include one-week and twenty-four-hour recalls of all foods consumed in the household, whether each food is produced or purchased, and the amount spent for each food during the week; twenty-four-hour recall of all food consumed by the mother and the target child whose nutritional status is being measured; whether the mother is nursing and the number of times a day she nurses. Nonfood consumption measures include quality of housing and the material goods owned by the family. This information was collected from female householders.

*Nutritional Status.* Anthropometric measures of nutritional health were taken from one "target" child under the age of sixty months in each household. These include stature or recumbent length, body weight, mid-arm and mid-calf circumferences;

and skinfold measurements at six selected sites. Weights were collected using portable dial-face spring scales suspended from any suitable anchor in the house. Heights and lengths were collected using a board with a metal meter tape embedded in it on a sliding headboard. Heights and weights of children were standardized relative to the National Center for Health Statistics (NCHS) norms (Hamill et al. 1979) adapted for international application by the World Health Organization (WHO 1983; see Latham 1984; Stephenson, Latham, and Jansen 1983; Gopalan 1983; Habicht et al. 1974). Data on nutritional status are presented in terms of (1) height for age, (2) weight for age, (3) weight for height. Generally speaking, children who are below –2 standard deviations (that is, Z < –2.0) from NCHS/WHO norms are considered to be at nutritional risk (Frisancho 1986).

## Data Collection Personnel and Procedures

Both NSF Child Growth Project and FUNDAGRO staff participated in survey instrument design and administration, and in preliminary analysis of data. The interdisciplinary team was headed by Dr. Kathleen DeWalt, Dr. Billie DeWalt, and Dr. William Leonard, anthropologists, principal investigator and coprincipal investigators of the NSF project; Dr. Jorge Uquillas, sociologist, Director of Evaluation, FUNDAGRO; and Dr. Hector Ballesteros, veterinarian, Director of the Dairy Commodity Program, FUNDAGRO. Interviewers included James Stansbury, anthropologist, NSF project ethnographer and coordinator of survey administration; FUNDAGRO evaluation and commodity program field staff Dr. Oscar Silva, veterinarian, Alex Portillo, agronomist, Favian Tapia, student agricultural extensionist, and Gloria Cordoba, extensionist in nutrition; two graduate nutritionists from the Escuela Politecnica de Chimborazo, Susana Chávez and Lilián Leyedra; and Patricia Gutiérrez, biologist.

In general, specialists in veterinary and agricultural science and extension interviewed male householders concerning agricultural production, access to agricultural infrastructure, and household socioeconomic indicators. Nutritionists interviewed female householders concerning household demography, consumption, health, livestock and animal-product production, women's participation in household agricultural production and control of economic resources, and women's income.

It was the original intention of NSF Child Growth Project principal investigators to administer the agricultural production instrument to the householder primarily responsible for production, whether male or female (K. DeWalt, personal communication; see B. DeWalt 1990 et al.). However, this methodology proved impracticable in the field. In the judgment of the survey coordinator, administering both production and consumption questionnaires to female householders would place an onerous burden on interviewees' time (James Stansbury, personal communication). Therefore, the agricultural production questionnaire was administered to male householders.

The result of this procedure is that only one production function can be analyzed per household, as measures of inputs, outputs, and income per crop and field were taken from male producers only with reference to the entire household. Whereas women's *participation* in household agricultural production can be analyzed, women's *productivity* cannot be analyzed. Research findings indicate that households in the study population pool productive resources, agricultural products, and incomes; thus, using a single production function per household does not obscure gendered differences in productivity.

## Qualitative Methods

Qualitative methods included participant observation in the research community, regular observational visits to an ethnographic sample of ten families, and interviewing of these families and other community members. During the first two months of fieldwork, I observed family agricultural activity, women's group meetings and other community events, FUNDAGRO dairy program extension activities, marketing, and other activities in Chanchaló. I also interviewed several key informants, both women and men, in order to gain a basic understanding of agricultural production, men's and women's roles in production and resource management, and gender ideology. These early observations and interviews served to map the domain of agricultural work and decision-making, to chart the perceived likelihood of women's involvement in particular domains, and to reveal patterns in gender ideology concerning the ability and appropriateness of women's participation in each domain.

During this early experience, in December 1992–February 1993, I was invited into many homes and made a number of friends. Using survey information from the first wave, together with personal observations, I identified an ethnographic sample of ten families who represented the full community range on several key variables: household wealth; women's independent ownership of land; male outmigration; importance of commercial agriculture to family income; women's age and intrahousehold social status (unmarried daughter, young wife, elder wife); and women's and men's experience of life outside their community. During the remaining months of fieldwork, I visited these families at least once every two weeks for observational visits, which lasted an average of four hours, and spoke with them more frequently. Three of these families I visited informally several times a week.

I did not schedule visits more than one day in advance, nor did I have a fixed rotational schedule. I had intended to measure women's time allocation, using a statistically randomized schedule of spot-check visits. However, during my preliminary investigation, I quickly learned to expect that all women would be full-time farmers, even those with small children, those who were ill, or who hired help. I also learned that valuable opportunities presented themselves serendipitously, and that if I anticipated likely opportunities too rigorously, I would miss many events well worth observing. For these reasons, I did not adhere to a randomized rotation but made sure to visit each household regularly. On many days, I simply walked down the roads, stopping to visit with any informant who called out a greeting. After a socially acceptable interval, I would stay for an observational visit if the informant were doing something I wanted to learn more about and seemed willing. At times, I asked to be included in certain activities. At other times, informants invited me to participate in or observe an activity they thought I would be interested in. Using this methodology, I observed both male and female roles in all phases of agricultural production, processing, and marketing. Families also conducted financial and other intrahousehold allocative negotiations in my presence. In sum, I relied on the population representativeness of my ethnographic sample and the NSF project sample to reveal the distribution of observed phenomena.

Although I did interview and observe each woman and her husband or parents concerning key variables, I did not administer a formal interview schedule for my ethnographic sample. I interviewed both women and men, sometimes separately and sometimes together, along with several adolescents and children. Interviews focused on questions such as access to land through inheritance, purchase, and sharecropping; income streams; household consumption needs and budgeting; specific fields, crops, and animals with which each producer works; advantages and disad-

vantages of investment in various crops and animals; production problems and successes; the weighing of costs and benefits in decisions concerning land use, labor allocation, varietal choice, and selection of agrochemicals, together with the relative
participation of household members in these decisions. Informants were also asked
to discuss preferences concerning production tasks and domains and to delineate
patterns of substitution for unavailable family members' labor.

I wanted to gain some idea of the gender distribution of knowledge and preferences in each family as well as perceived participation. I also wanted to gain an understanding of family members' reproductive responsibilities, knowledge, and task
preferences. All family members were asked about dietary preferences and food
preparation. Both men and women were asked to describe their participation in
housework and child care, as well as cooking.

Interviews were open-ended. I always worked with a list of questions I had prepared for anticipated interviews, and usually managed to elicit relevant information.
However, I prefer a relaxed, conversational interview atmosphere, and my informants often told me that they liked talking to me for this reason. Informants objected
to the use of a tape recorder, so field notes provide the only record of these interviews. I have been a teacher and practitioner of rapid, accurate note-taking techniques for many years; I am confident these notes accurately reflect interview content.

## The Population: Congruence Between Quantitative and Qualitative Samples

In order to demonstrate intersample congruence for ethnographic observation
conducted in Chanchaló and quantitative data collected from a three-community
sample, Chanchaló will be compared to the other communities included in the probabilistic sample. The three communities resemble one another in terms of level and
distribution of wealth, services, education, and nutritional health; importance of
commercial agriculture to household economy; household demography; and political and social organization. Analysis-of-Variance tests demonstrate that the three
communities do not differ significantly (test of mean differences) on the following
measures (see Hamilton 1995, 314–22; all tables in ibid., appendix 1):

• Household landholdings (table 1)
• Total household income (table 2)
• Percentage of total household income derived from commercial agriculture
(table 3)
• Percentage of total household *cash* income derived from commercial agricul-
ture (table 4)
• Number of women owning land independently or jointly with their husbands
(table 6)
• Women's age (table 7)
• Women's education (table 8)
• Child weight for age (table 9)
• Child height for age (table 10)
• Child weight for height (table 11)

The following measures of women's participation in agricultural labor and economic resource control do not differ among communities:

• Decisions concerning land use (table 12)
• Selection of agricultural inputs (table 13)

• Management of pooled household income, including production finance (table 14)
  • Disposition of household agricultural products for use or sale (table 15)
  • Application of agrochemicals (table 17)

Table A.1 presents a summary of socioeconomic, health, and demographic indicators for the probabilistic sample.

This table demonstrates that characteristic features of Chanchaló (chapter 2) also describe the entire sample. Including all three communities, the population comprises poor smallholder households heavily dependent on commercial agriculture for their economic survival. Most women and men own land; virtually all households access land for agricultural production. The distributions of both land and income are sharply and positively skewed among households. During the year preceding the survey's first round, nearly one-fourth of male household heads worked outside their communities for an average of three months.

Nearly all households are headed by a conjugal pair; the overwhelming majority of these are also nuclear families. Most families have access only to poor local primary education and sporadic public health services. More than one-third of all families did not have enough calories to sustain them during the week they were surveyed. Over one-fourth of the children under five are undernourished. In sum, the probabilistic sample represents a population of poor, underserved people trying to make a living from commercial agriculture on small land bases.

Because the communities are similar in areas central to my analysis, I shall use qualitative information gathered in Chanchaló to interpret statistical results derived from the entire probabilistic sample. On one relevant variable, Chanchaló is different from one other sample community (Sacha): Chanchaló has significantly less temporary male outmigration (Hamilton 1995, 316, appendix 1, table 5). However, the farming systems do not differ in Chanchaló and Sacha. Moreover, the inclusion of a community with more male outmigration makes the probabilistic sample more directly comparable to several other Andean populations in which women's economic roles have been studied.

Both qualitative and quantitative samples represent the full range of variation within the study population in terms of household socioeconomic level and male outmigration to wage labor, key variables in the analysis of women's roles within small-farm household economies. The size and composition of these samples are appropriate for a cross-sectional analysis of variation in intrahousehold economic processes in which both multivariate statistical modeling and interpretive analysis based upon intensive interviewing and behavioral observation provide evidence of observed patterns.

*Table A.1. Socioeconomic, Health, and Demographic Indicators in Three Communities, Cantón Salcedo, 1992*

| *Income (N = 104 with complete information)* | |
|---|---|
| Average per capita/month: | $47 (SD 47) |
| Median per capita/month: | $35 |
| Distribution: | poorest 20% hold 4% of the wealth |
| | top 20% hold 50% of wealth |
| Household cash income: | 87% from commercial agriculture |
| | (on average, SD 25) |
| All household income: | 56% from commercial agriculture |
| | (on average, SD 27) |

| *Land* | |
|---|---|
| Landownership: | 78% of women and 72% of men own land |
| Access to land: | 98% of households access land through |
| | ownership, sharecropping, or rental (N = 97) |
| Total household average: | 2.6 hectares (SD 2.6) |
| Total household median: | 2.0 hectares |

| *Education* | |
|---|---|
| None: | 39% of women (N = 127) |
| | 19% of men (N = 124) |
| Completed primary school: | 57% of women |
| | 76% of men |

*Health*

37% below FAO norms for household food security
27% of children under 5 at nutritional risk
(over 2 SD below NCHS/WHO standard weight for age)

| *Demographics* | |
|---|---|
| Average age of adult females: | 29 (SD 7) |
| Average age of adult males: | 34 (SD 11) |
| Average family size: | 6 (SD 2) |
| Female-headed households: | 1% |
| Conjugal-pair households: | 94% |
| Nuclear-family households: | 80% |
| Women native to community: | 67% |
| Males worked outside community in 1992: | 22% |
| The average time away from community: | 13 weeks (SD 14) |

Source: NSF/FUNDAGRO Household Surveys, round 1, August–October 1992 (116 households).
    *Note:* Both male and female household heads were interviewed.

# Appendix B

The following tables provide correlational and multiple regression analyses examining women's agricultural labor and women's control of agricultural technology.

## Multiple Regression and Correlation Tables (B.1, B.2)

The relatively small sample size (a result of sample attrition and incomplete information on some measures for some cases) suggests caution in the interpretation of associations that appear nonsignificant. However, bivariate models that delete missing cases pairwise raise the number of cases to nearly 100 and demonstrate similar results. A multiple regression model with pairwise deletion of missing cases also produced similar results (Hamilton 1995, appendix 3, tables 1–3). The sample size indicates that a high significance level, such as .10, will be required to reject the null hypothesis. In all these models there is nothing close to statistical significance for relationships between the number of hours a woman works in agriculture and her age, child-care needs, household socioeconomic status, or husband's absence from the farm.

## Women's Participation in Selection of Agricultural Technology

In the multiple regression model reported below (table B.3), hypothesized determinants of women's self-reported equal participation in pesticide selection for household production include: whether the woman applies pesticides; household level of pesticide use; household wealth in land; whether the woman owns land independently of her husband; and whether her husband is absent from the farm. I wanted to see whether women were being marginalized from control of this input on larger or higher-technology farms where men are widely expected to control all expensive inputs (as is theorized in much of the Ecuadorean development literature). I also wanted to determine whether women's independent ownership of productive resources or the absence of their husbands would exert a positive effect on their participation in this decision domain (as the ethnographic literature would suggest). Finally, I wanted to test local informants' perceived positive association between labor and decision-making for a given productive domain. (Variation on the dependent variable is described in chapter 5.)

Small sample size (a result of sample attrition affecting the last round of the NSF/FUNDAGRO household surveys and nonresponse of some male householders) indicates the need for caution in interpreting results, especially nonsignificant results. However, qualitative information is consistent with the regression results.

*Table B.1. Regression of Women's Agricultural Labor Hours on Selected Individual and Household Characteristics, Cantón Salcedo, 1993*

*Multiple regression model $R^2$ = .044; significance of F = .639*

| Independent Variables | Beta | Significance |
|---|---|---|
| Woman's age | .115 | .412 |
| Child under two | −.131 | .336 |
| Household wealth[a] | .002 | .991 |
| Male outmigration[b] | .114 | .408 |

*Source:* NSF/FUNDAGRO Household Surveys, round 2, March–April 1993 (80 households).

   *Notes:* Variation on the dependent variable is discussed in chapter 4. N = 60 cases with information on all variables. Women's weekly agricultural labor hours were estimated by informants concerning general practice. One case was identified statistically as an outlier influential to the regression and therefore was not included in the regression. Cases are deleted listwise.

   a. Total household landholdings.

   b. Whether husband lived away from the farm during the year preceding the survey.

*Table B.2. Zero Order Correlations Among Women's Agricultural Labor Hours and Selected Individual and Household Characteristics, Cantón Salcedo, 1993*

| | Woman's Age | Child Under Two | Household Wealth[a] | Husband's Absence |
|---|---|---|---|---|
| Labor hours | r = .137 | r = -.134 | r = .018 | r = .097 |
| (weekly av.) | p = .149 | p = .154 | P = .447 | p = .231 |
| Woman's age | | r = -.157 | r = .269 | r = .007 |
| | | p = .115 | p = .019 | p = .480 |
| Child under two | | | r = -.070 | r = .133 |
| | | | p = .298 | p = .156 |
| Household wealth | | | | r = -.211 |
| | | | | p = .053 |

*Source:* NSF/FUNDAGRO Household Surveys, round 2, March–April 1993 (80 households).

   *Note:* N = 60 cases with information on all variables; one outlier removed. Cases are deleted listwise.

   a. Total household landholdings.

*Table B.3. Regression of Women's Participation in Choice of Agrochemicals on Selected Individual and Household Characteristics, Cantón Salcedo, 1993*

*Multiple regression model R² = .473; significance of F = .000*

| Independent Variables | Beta | Significance |
|---|---|---|
| Woman applies pesticides | .574 | .000 |
| Household level of pesticide use[a] | .330 | .002 |
| Woman's independent ownership of land[b] | −.130 | .203 |
| Total amount of land held by the household | −.006 | .951 |
| Male outmigration | .087 | .409 |

*Source:* NSF/FUNDAGRO Household Surveys, round 3, July 1993 (70 households with both male and female household heads [conjugal pairs]).

*Notes:* Dependent variable is women's self-reported participation (equal to or greater than husband's) in decisions concerning selection and quantity of pesticides used in household agricultural production. N = 61 households in which male householder provided information on pesticide use and female householder provided information on her participation in decision-making concerning types and quantities of pesticides used.

a. Number of applications per field reported by male householder.

b. Dummy variable.

# Appendix C

## Multiple Regression Model

### Independent and Dependent Variables: Operationalized Measures and Variation within the Regression Sample

In order to test statistically the independent influence of theoretically relevant conditions on women's control of economic resources, six independent variables are proposed in a least-squares multiple regression model in which variables are entered stepwise and missing cases are deleted listwise (table C.3). Complete information on all variables was obtained from only forty-nine households. The regression's sample size indicates not only that results should be interpreted with caution, as the probability of Type 2 errors is high for small samples, but also that it is important to examine the sample itself, in order to determine whether it is representative of the entire probabilistic sample. Following a description of operationalized measures and the number of cases lost to sample attrition and incomplete information on individual measures, I shall summarize a series of t-tests which demonstrate that the regression sample does represent the entire probabilistic sample.

In this model, the dependent variable is a cumulative scale reflecting women's self-reported equal or greater participation than their husbands in four domains of resource control important to household economies: (1) land-use decisions, (2) household financial management, (3) selection of agricultural inputs, and (4) the disposition of agricultural products for sale or use within the household. I did not weight the individual measures of resource control that comprise the scale, although an argument could be made that land and financial management are more indicative of overall economic authority than product disposition or input selection. This scale reflects the reach of a woman's intrahousehold economic authority. Of all women surveyed, 62 percent report equal participation on all four measures (100 percent) of resource control; 19 percent report equal participation on three measures (75 percent); 11 percent report equal participation on two measures (50 percent); 6 percent report equal participation on only one measure (25 percent); two women report zero participation in economic resource control.

Socioeconomic and demographic independent variables include (1) the household's total landholdings, a measure of capital accumulation or household wealth in this population dependent for survival upon agricultural production; (2) a dichotomous variable measuring whether the female householder owns land, including both independent and joint ownership; (3) the percentage of total household income derived from commercial agriculture during the cropping cycle preceding the survey's first round, a measure of the household's integration into the capitalist mode of production; (4) a dichotomous variable measuring whether the male household head lived outside his community during the year preceding the survey's first round; (5) the female household head's self-reported average weekly agricultural labor hours, a measure of women's involvement in agricultural labor in this sample where women's agricultural labor input does not vary seasonally. An additional demographic control variable is entered into the regression: the age of the female householder. (Variation on these measures is discussed in chapter 2 regarding Chanchaló and summarized regarding all three communities in the probabilistic sample in appendix A.)

Levels of measurement include both individual and household. In this population, one can speak of relatively undifferentiated "household" economies: the land, labor, and income of individuals are pooled within households. Although households have two heads, it is the household—rather than the individual—that functions as the unit of production. The regression model "navigates between these multiple units of analysis and attempts to capture their various interrelationships" (Wolf 1992, 23).

I am concerned with the *independent* effects of each of these variables. Bivariate correlation tables are presented in this appendix for the sample included in the regression (table C.4). Additional bivariate and multiple regression tables for a sample in which cases are deleted in pairwise fashion are reported in Hamilton 1995 (appendix 3, tables 6, 7); these tables demonstrate that relationships reported also hold when cases are deleted pairwise. Bivariate associations demonstrate that each variable can be expected to exert an independent effect. Although there is a tendency for larger farms to be more commercialized and for men to remain at home on these farms, correlations are not high. Each of these variables interacts independently with the dependent variable. Although households that include a landholding woman tend to have more land, this correlation is also not high. Women's ownership and household wealth in land are discrete phenomena.

One of these variables (women's landholding) was derived from the third round of the household survey; sample attrition thus reduced the potential regression sample to seventy cases. Six of the eighty female household heads surveyed during the second round did not provide information concerning number of hours usually worked in agriculture. Incomplete information on other variables taken from first-round interviews with male householders further reduced the regression sample. Of the original 116 households surveyed, 9 men did not provide information concerning total household landholdings; 15 did not report income from all sources including commercial agriculture; 8 did not respond to questions concerning outmigration. Measures of women's control of economic resources were collected during the first round of the survey; only one woman did not respond. My decision to include only households in which both female and male household heads responded to the survey (108 of the original 116) further reduced the size of the sample available for analysis.

Comparison of the 49 households included within the regression sample with the remaining households surveyed during the three rounds of quantitative data collection demonstrates that the regression sample is representative of the entire population (tables C.1 and C.2).

The regression includes as its dependent variable a cumulative measure of women's control of household economic resources. The regression sample does not differ from the population on the individual measures of which this scale is composed (table C.2).

Women's participation in control of household economic resources does not appear to be affected by their households' greater participation in capitalist agriculture, nor by their husbands' migration to wage labor. While the small size of the regression sample indicates considerable caution in interpreting the lack of statistical significance, probabilities of Type 2 error do not approach the .05 level. Additionally, bivariate associations in which nearly 100 cases are included also do not approach statistical significance (Hamilton 1995, 343).

*Table C.1. Comparison of Means on Measures Included in Multivariate Analysis of Women's Control of Economic Resources: Multiple Regression Sample Versus Households Omitted from Regression*

| | Multiple Regression Sample (N = 49)[a] | | Other Households (N varies per measure total = 59)[b] | | Sig. t 2-tail |
|---|---|---|---|---|---|
| | Mean | SD | Mean | SD | |
| Percentage of resource-control areas in which woman has equal control[c] | 84% | 24 | 81% (N = 59) | 26 | .560 |
| Percentage of total household income from commercial agriculture | 61% | 36 | 71% (N = 44) | 30 | .137 |
| Husband migrated out during 1992 | 19% | 39 | 24% (N = 51) | 43 | .566 |
| Woman owns land[d] | 78% | 41 | 79% (N = 20) | 41 | .939 |
| Total household landholdings/ha. | 2.7 | 2.3 | 2.2 (N = 48) | 1.6 | .205 |
| Women's weekly agricultural labor hours | 47 | 14 | 45 (N = 25) | 18 | .568 |
| Woman's age | 30 | 8 | 28 (N = 59) | 7 | .064 |

*Sources:* NSF/FUNDAGRO Household Surveys, rounds 1–3, August 1992–July 1993, Cantón Salcedo.

*Notes:* a. Multiple regression model includes the 49 cases with information on all variables hypothesized to affect women's economic resource control.

b. Number of cases excluded from the regression per measure (sample attrition over time and incomplete information on some measures reduced the number of cases available).

c. Scale reflecting self-reported equal or greater participation than husband in resource control concerning four areas: (1) land use; (2) selection of inputs; (3) household finances, including production finance; and (4) disposition of products. Scale values: 0 = no participation; 25% = participation in one resource-control area; 50% = participation in two areas; 75% = participation in three areas; 100% = equal participation in all areas of resource control.

d. Dummy variable measuring whether woman owns land (independently or jointly with husband) or does not own land.

Table C.2. Comparison of Means on Percentage of Women Reporting Equal or Greater Control than Husband in Four Resource Domains: Multiple Regression Sample Versus Households Omitted from Regression

| | Multiple Regression Sample (N = 49)[a] | | Other Households (N = 59) | | Sig. t 2-tail |
|---|---|---|---|---|---|
| | *Mean* | *SD* | *Mean* | *SD* | |
| Land use | 88% | 33 | 80% | 41 | .276 |
| Finance | 89% | 33 | 88% | 33 | .921 |
| Input selection | 75% | 44 | 69% | 47 | .419 |
| Product use | 88% | 33 | 89% | 31 | .707 |

*Source:* NSF/FUNDAGRO Household Surveys, round 1, August–October 1992.

*Note:* a. Multiple regression model includes the 49 cases with information on all variables hypothesized to affect women's economic resource control.

Table C.3. Regression of Women's Control of Economic Resources on Selected Individual and Household Characteristics

$R^2 = .287$; significance of F = .002; stepwise entry of variables

| Independent Variables in the Equation | Beta | Significance |
|---|---|---|
| Household wealth[a] | .307 | .024 |
| Woman's ownership of land[b] | .423 | .002 |
| Woman's agricultural labor hours (weekly average) | .221 | .090 |

| Independent Variables Not in the Equation | Beta Calculated to Enter Equation | Significance |
|---|---|---|
| Male outmigration | −.053 | .684 |
| Woman's age | .109 | .446 |
| Proportion of total household income[c] from commercial agriculture | −.126 | .325 |

*Sources:* NSF/FUNDAGRO Household Surveys, rounds 1–3, August 1992–July 1993 (N = 48).

*Notes:* Cumulative scale reflecting self-reported equal or greater participation than husband in control of (1) land use, (2) selection of agricultural inputs, (3) household finance, and (4) disposition of agricultural products. Cases are deleted listwise.

a. Total household landholdings.

b. Dummy variable measuring whether woman owns land (independently or jointly with husband) or does not own land.

c. Includes subsistence value of agricultural production.

Two variables positively predict women's greater resource control with very low probabilities of Type 1 error: women's ownership of land and household wealth. For a sample of this size, relationships with a probability of up to .10 could be considered marginally significant. Thus women's agricultural labor also appears to have a small positive effect on the extensiveness of their resource control.

A model in which cases are deleted pairwise is presented in Hamilton 1995 (appendix 3, table 3). A bivariate correlation table for the regression sample reported here is appended below (table C.4).

Table C.4. Zero Order Correlations Among Women's Control of Economic Resources and Selected Individual and Household Characteristics

|  | Household Wealth | Woman's Land | Ag. Labor Hours/wk. | Husband's Outmigration | Woman's Age | Commercial Ag.[a] |
|---|---|---|---|---|---|---|
| Greater resource control[b] | r = .229 | r = .473 | r = .230 | r = -.077 | r = .293 | r = -.068 |
|  | p = .118 | p = .001 | p = .115 | p = .601 | p = .044 | p = .645 |
| Household wealth[c] |  | r = .230 | r = .029 | r = -.215 | r = .331 | r = .253 |
|  |  | p = .116 | p = .846 | p = .143 | p = .022 | p = .083 |
| Woman's land[d] |  |  | r = -.031 | r = -.016 | r = .259 | r = -.029 |
|  |  |  | p = .833 | p = .912 | p = .075 | p = .847 |
| Woman's labor hours (weekly average)[e] |  |  |  | r = .103 | r = .202 | r = -.003 |
|  |  |  |  | p = .488 | p = .168 | p = .986 |
| Husband's outmigration |  |  |  |  | r = -.037 | r = -.103 |
|  |  |  |  |  | p = .803 | p = .485 |
| Woman's age |  |  |  |  |  | r = .040 |
|  |  |  |  |  |  | p = .787 |

Sources: NSF/FUNDAGRO Household Surveys, rounds 1–3, August 1992–July 1993.
  Notes: N = 49 cases with information on all variables entered into multiple regression analysis. Cases are deleted listwise.
  a. Proportion of total household income, including subsistence value of agricultural production, from commercial agriculture.
  b. Scale reflecting self-reported equal or greater participation than husband in control of land use, selection of inputs, production finance, and disposition of products.
  c. Total household landholdings.
  d. Independent ownership or joint ownership with husband.
  e. Self-reported average number of hours worked in agriculture per week.

# Notes

## 1. Gender and Rural Development

1. Chanchaleños are descended from pre-Columbian Andean peoples (see chapter 2). Until the late twentieth century, their primary language was Quichua, the lingua franca of the Inca empire. Following the anthropological convention of naming groups of indigenous persons after their primary language, Chanchaleños may be referred to as a Quichua group. Although most people in the community no longer speak Quichua, they proudly claim the language as part of their indigenous heritage.

2. Unless otherwise noted, translations from the original Spanish are my own.

3. The term *mestizo* refers to persons of mixed indigenous and Spanish ancestry.

4. A "natural experiment" in the social sciences is one in which the researcher tests a proposition regarding human behavior or thought without recourse to environmental or behavioral control. The researcher identifies potential determinants of observable, existing variation and evaluates the effects of those determinants (see Bernard 1988, 62–65).

5. A number of scholars have detailed the importance of understanding the ways intrahousehold or gendered divisions of labor, access to productive resources, and control of incomes affect the results of planned development projects aimed at improving the welfare of resource-poor families (see Feldstein, Flora, and Poats 1989; Moser 1989; Parpart 1993; Katz 1995). Jane Parpart encourages development planners to incorporate into their models for economic and social change women's "interpretation of the world they inhabit, their successes and failures and their desires for change. The goals and aspirations of Third World women would be discovered rather than assumed, and strategies for improving their lives could be constructed on the basis of actual experiences and needs" (1993, 454). The "gender variable" thus refers to the use of knowledge concerning the "lived realities of Third World women" (454) and men in policy-oriented analysis of development processes.

6. Perhaps upon longer acquaintance, we would find economic coercion underlying the elderly Rosa's killing workday in a wealthy family's enterprise. Rubén's words of praise for his wife's managerial skills may resemble those of an employer who congratulates himself on having found the ideal administrative assistant, a competent manager who makes one-tenth of his salary. Perhaps Beatriz's politically active, alcohol-consuming husband has abandoned a more generalized male prerogative to allocate economic resources; Beatriz may control only the portion of household finance based on income she has earned independently or income her hus-

261

band has elected to share—in effect, a "household allowance" she must stretch to cover daily and long-term needs. Mariana's apparent control of her husband's off-farm earnings may be an isolated case; perhaps most women whose husbands earn most of the family's income working away from home will have less success in negotiating access to this form of income. Similarly, Valentina's agricultural production may account for only a small portion of the household's total income; her apparent control of marketing may mask asymmetrical gender reciprocities related to male-biased wage structures.

7. See Boserup 1970, 1990; Rogers 1980; Benería and Sen 1986; Leacock 1986; Obbo 1990; Bossen 1984; Charlton 1984; Buvinić and Mehra 1990; IDB 1995.

8. See Kandiyoti 1985; ICPEDC 1986; Deere 1977, 1986; Palmer 1985; Bossen 1984; Charlton 1984; Phillips 1987; Rogers 1980; Jaquette 1985; Venema 1986.

9. For Africa and Asia see Boserup 1970, Rogers 1980, and Lockwood 1993; also Conelly and Chaiken 1993, Little 1994, Stone 1988, Webb 1989. For Latin America see Katz 1995 and Bourque and Warren 1981.

10. Concepts of household formation that influenced practice within many donor agencies were grounded in neoclassical economics. The New Household Economics, a neoclassical approach pioneered by Gary Becker (1965, 1981), assumes the existence of a single household utility function, which reflects all members' preferences (Senauer 1990; Pitt and Rosenweig 1985). Becker (1981) delineates the assumptions within this theoretical approach. Whether all members have the same preferences or one member—an "altruistic dictator"—imposes his or her preferences on other household members, the emerging single set of preferences aims to maximize the welfare of all household members. Altruism underlies decision-making within the household. This approach has been criticized by researchers who assume that preferences vary among household members, who enter into a bargaining process to reconcile their differences (Folbre 1984; McElroy and Horney 1981, drawing on the cooperative game theory developed by Nash [1953]). An individual's bargaining strength is determined by his or her potential ability to survive without the household; this ability is conceived of in economic terms by the individual's wage rate should he or she enter the labor market. Amartya Sen (1990) has pointed out that although the bargaining model is an improvement over the single-utility-function model, it assumes that household members are motivated exclusively by self-interest, a questionable assumption concerning families. Sen posits a model of negotiation within the household that is centered on "cooperative conflict," a dynamic reflecting the dual motivation of household members to forward their own self-interest while maintaining the unit and discharging their perceived obligations toward other family members.

A central issue in modeling household economics, then, is to allow for the importance of kinship relations within an economic unit devoted to both production and consumption. Although the terms *family* and *household* are often used interchangeably in development literature, they are conceptually separate. Utilizing Yanagisako's (1979) discussion, Jane Jaquette summarizes the distinction between the two:

People actually live in households as opposed to families. Thus "household" refers to geographic propinquity—notwithstanding the fact that absent members are sometimes considered to be part of a household. Moreover, the household (not the family) is the location of a set of activities that reproduce members daily (through the domestic work of cooking, washing, cleaning and so on) and intergenerationally (not only through biological reproduction but also through the socialization of children). "Family," on the other hand, refers to kinship, and it presents a normative system whereby people are recruited into households. That is, "families organize households" (Rapp 1992:51); through the rights and duties defined by kinship, the family regulates the activities of household members. People's entrance into household relations of production and consumption and their experience of household resource allocation depend on the normative system of the family (Curtis 1986; Jaquette 1993, 48)

Gillian Hart (1992) has proposed that these normative systems be analyzed in terms of how their rules become constituted, as well as how these constitutions influence behavior. Guyer and Peters (1987) emphasize the ideological basis of the household as both a social unit and as an analytical construct. Household ideologies influence not only the members of households under study, but also researchers' methodologies and conclusions (see also Collins 1986).

11. See Frank 1969, 1972; Emmanuel 1972; Deere and de Janvry 1979; de Janvry 1981; also Barkin 1990.

12. See Deere 1976, 1977; Saffioti 1977; Leacock 1977, 1986; Nash 1975; also Nash and Safa 1976, Nash and Fernández-Kelly 1983, and Chaney 1976.

13. In the phrase *ideologies of gender,* the term *ideology* refers to a body of ideas—beliefs, values, ways of thinking—that serves to legitimate a social, political, or economic structure. "Gender ideology," for example, serves to legitimate patterned forms of gender relations within a cultural entity and may be contrasted among cultural entities.

14. Martin (1994), Nash (1995), Safa (1995b), and others have also demonstrated ways Latin American women have used their status as mothers and housewives and their work in mothers' volunteer groups to create political platforms that address social problems and contribute to an expanded concept of citizenship and political participation for women.

15. For Africa see Carney and Watts 1991; Guyer 1988b, 1991; and Guyer and Peters 1987. For Asia see Wolf 1992, Hart 1992, and Lepowsky 1993.

16. See Parpart 1993, 1995; Hirschman 1995; Parpart and Marchand 1995; de Groot 1991; Chowdhry 1995; and Rathgeber 1995.

17. Two notable exceptions are the innovative projects by Fundación para el Desarrollo Agropecuario (FUNDAGRO), promoting organized women's production activities for quinoa and other crops and for cassava processing, and an integrated-pest-management pilot project by the Secretariat of Integrated Rural Development (SEDRI) with a limited inclusion of women. Both of these organizations have received funding from international agencies.

18. This pattern is repeated throughout Latin America (Deere and León 1987).

## 2. An Introduction to Chanchaló

1. Except where noted, the following discussion is based on Salomon (1986, 122–42).

2. Servile labor relations on traditional haciendas were similar throughout the Ecuadorean sierra. Patterns reported for Chanchaló are similar to those recorded for the northern sierra (Barsky et al. 1984; Rosero 1984). In addition to those indigenous families living on estates and laboring under servile relations or huasipungaje, many others were bound to the haciendas through seasonal labor contracts (and other forms of exchange) for access to hacienda resources such as water, forest resources, or grazing rights. Although free to apply their labor elsewhere, in effect these landless or smallholding families depended on hacienda wages and resources and were thus obliged to provide labor (see Seligson 1984). Not all indigenous communities or regional groups were bound to haciendas. Among contemporary groups who maintained independence are the Salasacas, Saraguros, and Otavaleños (Casagrande 1974; Chiriboga 1983).

3. Elsewhere in the sierra, wives of hacienda workers assigned to livestock management often assumed most of their husband's hacienda labor requirement, together with their children, in order to free the man to work on the family plot (Barsky et al. 1984; Rosero 1984). A contrasting pattern of women's agricultural labor as it relates to the articulation between hacienda agricultural production and that of the huasipunguero family is reported by Salamea and Likes (n.d.) and by Chiriboga (1983, 74). These authors find that women were likely to take primary responsibility for the family's agricultural and livestock production while their husbands performed their hacienda work obligations.

4. The fluidity of the gendered division of labor reported for Hacienda Chanchaló contrasts with employment patterns for women and men on more modernized and specialized haciendas in Cantón Salcedo and throughout sierran Ecuador. During the 1950s and 1960s, a number of local hacendados converted their holdings from diversified and labor-intensive crop and livestock production to high-technology dairy operations requiring much less nonspecialized field labor. These landowners opted to pay a small permanent workforce trained to manage mechanized dairy production, while converting the lands of their former huasipungueros to pasture. They terminated huasipungo relations and contracted with free laborers or with other hacendados to obtain the domestic and agricultural labor needed on their properties (Farrell 1983). Although women's permanent employment on these haciendas was largely limited to hand milk-

ing (Barsky et al. 1984), both women and men continued to be employed as seasonal field labor (local informants; see Martínez 1984, 1985). Gendered wage differentials on dairy haciendas reflect both the specialized training offered to men only, and the fact that hacendados, by a number of ruses, claimed nearly a full working day from women but paid them only for the part-time hours actually devoted to milking.

5. During the colonial era land appropriation, forced labor, and excessive tithes and tributes resulted in a number of indigenous uprisings in Cotopaxi Province and throughout the sierra. In some locations, these rebellions succeeded in removing *encomenderos,* together with the bureaucrats, overseers, and priests who also claimed their share of indigenous production. Eventually, however, the revolts failed to sustain claims for the reinstatement of indigenous lands and cultural patrimony (Hurtado 1980, 33). Similarly, although individual uprisings proved successful during the Republican era, the ouster of locally dominant elites did not result in widespread change. Nonetheless, indigenous rebels continued their struggle; eventually several units joined forces with the followers of Eloy Alfaro in the successful Liberal revolution of 1895 (Spindler 1987, 83). Indigenous support of the Alfarista regime resulted in important legal reforms, among them the legal abolition of concertaje informal slavery (Spindler 1987).

6. Elsewhere in the Andes, the hacienda system fostered forms of household and extended-family organization that differed markedly from those of independent smallholding communities (Deere 1990); this does not appear to have been the case in Ecuador (Martínez 1984; Chiriboga 1983). Both hacienda-tied and economically independent communities of smallholders maintained interhousehold exchange systems reminiscent of traditional reciprocity, perhaps in response to the asymmetrical nature of their interaction with either landholders or regional labor and product markets (Chiriboga 1983; Casagrande 1974). One researcher concludes that even though internal hacienda communities often did not emerge from servile relations with their indigenous character intact, "ethnic cohesion" is realized in basic structures of social organization, which do not differ from those maintained in independent communities such as Saraguro, Salasaca, or Otavalo (Chiriboga 1983, 85–86). Indigenous communities internal and external to the hacienda system "were not worlds apart" (77). Intrahousehold socioeconomic organization is also similar within formerly hacienda-dependent and independent groups such as the Salasacas and Saraguros, with whom patterns observed in Chanchaló will be compared in later chapters.

7. Estimated daily household caloric intake was figured as a percentage of estimated needs (from FAO/WHO 1973): intake ÷ requirements x 100. Households with less than 115 percent of requirement (allowing for waste) are considered to be at risk (ibid.). According to weekly food consumption recalls, it appears that 41 percent of surveyed households were at risk during August–October 1992.

8. Height for age and weight for age were standardized in relation to WHO/NCHS standards (appendix A). In a well-nourished population, only 2 percent of all children would fall below two standard deviations from the reference-population median on these measures. Percentages in the text refer to percentages of children who are below two standard deviations from the median. Measurements were taken August–October 1992.

9. Although many land transfers in Chanchaló have not been legally registered because of high legal costs, most of these are matters of inheritance; deeds registered to parents agree with statements by parents and children regarding the amount of land inherited by children.

10. Gamma correlations among the three informant rankings of household wealth are as follows (N = 38):

|  | *Informant 1* | *Informant 2* |
| --- | --- | --- |
| Informant 2 | .868 | |
| Informant 3 | .964 | .912 |

11. I cannot explain why so many Chanchaleños insist that their best chance for a better life is to work together on private and public projects of mutual benefit, whereas individuals from two neighboring communities express a preference for taking their chances with their own re-

sources. It has been suggested that poorer people are more likely to engage in traditional socio-economic reciprocity while those with more resources, because they can afford to do so, prefer to avoid the obligation of labor and resources (Belote and Belote 1977). It has also been suggested that people with alternate investment opportunities will not want to devote resources to re-ciprocal economic institutions (Walter 1981). Yet, according to informants from nearby commu-nities, Chanchaló is neither poorer nor more lacking in investment opportunities than they are.

One of the bordering communities was chartered on former hacienda lands; their legacy of repression and of a past need to cooperate for survival is the same, although fewer members of the contemporary community worked together on the former hacienda. Moreover, the same families live in all three bordering communities; they intermarry and many have lived in more than one of the communities. The economic base, historical tradition, and gene pool are the same. Two additional communities studied by the NSF Child Growth Project—Sacha and Cumbijín—also were formed of hacienda lands; these communities collaborate somewhat less than Chanchaló, but considerably more than Chanchaló's immediate neighbors.

12. There is very little crime in Chanchaló, including theft. Although everyone keeps houses locked up tight, their tools, machinery, and other goods often lie protected only by the barking of their many dogs. When asked if anything has ever been stolen or if they know anyone who has experienced theft, most people say no. There is little evidence of physical violence, including domestic violence. During the time I was in the community, I heard of only one incident; what impressed me was that the perpetrator was roundly criticized by everyone, even though the vi-olence was minimal. The victim was a young woman who had previously attacked the daughter of the man who publicly slapped her. Violence by men against women is considered shameful, including a doting father's revenge. Even very small children run loose; their parents are confident that neighbors will help if a child should be hurt. Essentially, people feel safe. No one is asking for a local police force, nor are they asking for policing from Salcedo.

13. Negative stereotypes of *indios* (Indians) perpetrated by mestizos seemed racist to me; however, Chanchaleños, who discussed *racismo* (racism) as a social problem for *morenos* (people of African ancestry), did not appear to associate racism with their own social and economic mar-ginalization within national society. Social and economic discrimination are perceived to be problems of class rather than of ethnicity or genetic endowment. Although I was told by urban Ecuadoreans that "hacienda Indians" still adopt a superficially subservient stance when dealing with whites, I did not observe such behavior.

## 3. Managers, Mothers, Maiden, and Matriarch

1. FUNDAGRO assisted Clemencia and Marina in their applications for this scholarship. Al-though there were many applicants, all three of the winning entries from Cotopaxi Province were sponsored by the FUNDAGRO field project in Cantón Salcedo.

2. In a typical sharecropping arrangement, the landowner provides prepared land; the ten-ant provides seed, labor, and varying proportions of fertilizer, pesticides, and other inputs. The owner and tenant split the profits evenly. Family sharecropping arrangements are similar to those between nonrelatives.

3. Although FUNDAGRO's office is stocked with pamphlets advising contour plowing and integrated pest management, the extensionists concentrate on veterinary medicine and milk production. The project's commodity focus does not preclude promotion of environmental pro-tection. Some information is provided, but these topics are not central to FUNDAGRO's mission as it is perceived by the field staff. Moreover, to justify continued funding, the project must demonstrate that milk production has been improved in the region, and that improvements have contributed to increased economic or nutritional well-being. The project's field director as-sures me that if clients express an interest in learning about soil conservation or the costs of agrochemical use, his staff will be happy to provide information to them. He does not plan to in-crease project work on environmental issues otherwise.

Two peace corps volunteers worked in Chanchaló during 1992–1993. Both volunteers were trained in and focus on livestock production. A USAID-funded environmental-protection proj-ect operating in Cantón Salcedo does not include the communities of the Eastern Andean

Cordillera, where Chanchaló is located. The slopes of the Western Cordillera are much more severely eroded, and limited funds are targeted to those areas in which nonsustainable practices are most destructive.

4. Among the chemical pesticides most frequently used in Chanchaló are (1) Dithane M-45, containing the active ingredient mancozeb, which has been removed from most products in the United States, and (2) Monitor, containing methamidophos, also restricted in the United States.

5. Bourque and Warren (1981) discerned a contrasting pattern in an indigenous Peruvian community, where a woman's economic decision authority implies weakness in her husband. Not only are women more subordinated in this community than in Chanchaló, but informants conceive of intrahousehold authority as a limited good.

6. The term *fuerza* implies the possession of power and strength. The term also connotes the ability to withstand disease.

## 4. Women's Work

1. See Benería 1979, 1982; Bossen 1989; Wainerman and Recchini 1981; Deere and Léon 1982, 1987; Aguiar 1986; Dixon 1985.

2. The percentage of men working away from home varies tremendously among indigenous communities in the Ecuadorean sierra, and among communities in Cantón Salcedo at any given time (Chiriboga 1984, 1985). Male outmigration also varies according to men's age and agricultural and labor market conditions (see Hamilton 1992). In the relatively moist and fertile Eastern Cordillera of Cantón Salcedo, where Chanchaló and the other current research communities are located, temporary male outmigration varies between 40 percent and 10 percent for relatively young men (those most likely to migrate) according to the 1988 baseline surveys (B. DeWalt et al. 1990) and current research. This is a relatively low percentage by sierran standards.

3. Maria Fernández states that, in the Andes, men are responsible for "purchase of supplementary inputs" (1988, 213). I assume these would include agrochemicals if used by the household.

4. The term *agricultural production* refers to any activity that adds value to a plant or animal product, whether the product is destined for exchange or for household consumption. Activities include soil preparation, seed selection and planting, cultivation, pest management, fertilization, harvesting, processing, animal care, pasturing, milking, marketing. Local women tended to exclude hours spent marketing from their evaluation of labor hours devoted to farm production.

5. Differences in the general valuation of women's labor are also marked between these Peruvian settings and the study communities: in the Peruvian communities women's labor earns less cash or reciprocal labor-exchange credit than does men's labor. In the study communities, as reported in the text, women and men earn an equal wage.

6. See Harris 1978, 1980, 1985; Allen 1988; Weismantel 1988; Poeschel 1988; Belote and Belote 1977, 1988; Bourque and Warren 1981; Silverblatt 1987; Hamilton 1995, 331–34.

7. Catherine Allen, Linda Belote, and Jim Belote report that both women and men routinely perform most of one another's duties, using one another's tools, although they continue to perceive the tasks as belonging to the opposite gender. Allen summarizes: "Male and female activities are conceptually distinct but flexible in practice" (1988, 78). In the Peruvian and Ecuadorean communities they studied, there is no shame involved in men's doing women's work, or vice versa. Allen finds that any person can perform any task, as long as the work is done in a manner befitting the gender of that person. Belote and Belote state that the only term they heard denoting inappropriate female gender-role performance translates as "like-a-man" but refers to a woman's ineptitude at performing women's work, rather than her performing men's work (1988). Allen also reports that although men and women frequently perform tasks associated with the opposite gender, within any given household a man and a woman should not do the same work at the same time. Roles thus remain properly distinct, though flexibly shifting, and complementarity is preserved.

8. Discussion of reproductive labor is based on observations of behavior and interviews in Chanchaló. The NSF/FUNDAGRO household surveys do not include questions concerning women's and men's participation in child care, housework, food preparation, and other reproductive labor domains. Although the survey does include twenty-four-hour activity recalls, both women and men report primarily productive activities, failing to include simultaneous child care. Work performed in and around the house—versus in the field—also appears to be underreported by both women and men.

## 5. Women's Control of Household Economic Resources

1. Most pesticides are applied to the potato crop, which is highly vulnerable to the fungus late blight *(Phytophtera infestans)* and to the Andean weevil *(Prenotrypes vorax)* (SEDRI 1981, 76–80; Crissman and Espinosa 1993, 16). In a three-month period, the average household sprays each field five times; some households apply once a week. These levels are fairly consistent throughout the year, and in the upper ranges are as high as any in Ecuador (Zuloaga et al. 1990, 165). The major limitation to the number of applications is the availability of household funds (see Uquillas et al. 1990, 21).

## 6. The Power of Balance

1. Belief in the power of balance may have contributed to dualistic power-sharing in pre-Conquest Andean political entities ranging in size from community or chiefdom to empire, as well as within traditional Andean households (Dillehay 1979; Murra 1968).

2. Bourque and Warren (1981) also find that it is considered improper for women to attempt to make it alone. These authors, however, consider this to be detrimental to women.

3. Weismantel extends the engendered control of differing productive zones to include the urban sites of male wage labor, where cash is earned (1988); she finds, however, that separate is far from equal, as women's products no longer contribute an equal share to household reproduction nor entitle them to share in their husband's earnings.

4. Concepts of women's strengths in Chanchaló also differ sharply from negative valuations of women's physical or emotional weakness *(debilidad)* in indigenous Peruvian communities studied by Susan Bourque and Kay B. Warren (1981) and by Anne Larme (1993). These studies find that traditional Andean constructions of gender serve to marginalize women from key productive domains or tasks, and from most cash-earning activities, owing to women's perceived weaknesses. Larme places the locus of patriarchal sanctions in the ethnomedical concept of women's *debilidad*. Women's reproductive apparatus, childbirth experience, and propensity to suffer negative emotions such as fear and sadness are believed to render them vulnerable to airborne illness and thus unsuited to "heavy" work or travel to coastal areas. Their "light" work does not earn cash and becomes devalued vis-á-vis the cash-earning activities of men. Bourque and Warren report not only that women are proscribed from participation in activities during which most value is added to agricultural production, including traveling to market, but also that men from households where women do control economic resources are perceived by neighbors to be weak. Authority within the household is conceived of as a limited good: "In this cultural system, authority in the family appears to be conceived of as limited in quantity. Thus, a woman's extension of competence in decision-making is seen as inevitably challenging and undermining her husband's position" (1981, 105).

Larme, Bourque, and Warren describe gender constructions as unlike those in Chanchaló as the *marianismo* of mestizo Ecuador. Beliefs concerning airborne illnesses are present in Chanchaló, but are less differentiated and supernaturally associated than those reported to threaten women in Cuyo Cuyo (Larme 1993). In Chanchaló women are not believed to be more susceptible to airborne disease than men. Beliefs concerning women's vulnerability during and following childbirth appear to be differently associated with weakness in Chanchaló and Cuyo Cuyo, as well. No one in Chanchaló attributes women's vulnerability during childbirth to their unique biology (believed in Cuyo Cuyo to "open" them to airborne natural and supernatural illness during childbirth). Although Chanchaleños who speak about childbirth are impressed by the danger to women, no one describes that danger as being associated with either women's biological weakness or airborne illness. In fact, I was assured that women's postpartum confinement is not necessitated by any weakness on their part.

Women in Chanchaló not only travel and participate in heavy labor and value-adding agricultural activities, they are described as *fuerte*, the logical opposite of the term *débil*. Intrahousehold authority is not conceived of as a limited good; men are proud of their strong wives, whose accomplishments appear to enhance household prestige. I do not find it surprising that such striking differences exist among Andean indigenous populations with respect to gender constructions, as these differences may be accounted for by (among other factors) differing degrees of integration into national mestizo society, or differences among traditional medical beliefs throughout the large Andean region.

I offer a differing interpretation from that of Bourque, Warren, and Larme, for the direction of change that might account for these differences. They find that traditional Andean institutions are more patriarchal than most other ethnographers have reported, such ţhat the absence of these negative and exclusionary constructions of gender in Chanchaló would be attributable to social and cultural integration. I find this interpretation plausible with respect to exclusion through traditional labor complementarity (which does not exist in Chanchaló) and medical beliefs (which appear to be much less pervasive in Chanchaló). However, my own experience of indigenous and mestizo societies in Ecuador suggests that machismo and its attendant conception of intrahousehold authority as a limited good are more characteristic of mestizo than indigenous society. In Ecuadorean indigenous communities more characterized by gender complementarity than Chanchaló, researchers do not find that women are marginalized from resource control owing to exclusion from productive tasks or domains (Belote and Belote 1988; Stark 1979); it does not seem to me that these researchers have "romanticized" the effects of perceived male-female differences (see Jaquette 1986, 251). Thus, I would not attribute the absence of beliefs in women's *debilidad* to loss of tradition in Chanchaló.

5. The association of urban lifeways with social-welfare infrastructure reflects the greater access to social programs afforded both poor and middle-class families in urban areas than is available to poor rural people. In the view of Chanchaleños it would be futile—as well as maladaptive—to rely on the extension of social-welfare programs to indigenous communities.

6. See discussion of real effects of land-reform legislation in Cantón Salcedo in chapter 2; also Chiriboga 1988a, 1988b; and Waters 1985.

7. Belote and Belote 1977, 1988; Walter 1981; Stark 1979, 1984; Weismantel 1988; Alberti 1986.

## 7. Gender and Economic Change in Cantón Salcedo

1. Alberti cites Deere and León's 1982 study, which does present comparisons across households and quantitative information concerning economic strata, and her own 1986 study. In both of these studies (discussed later in this chapter), women's marginalization in commercial production and wealthier households is described for mestizo populations. Although Alberti's generalization is to Latin American farming systems, her only three citations refer to Andean populations.

2. It should be noted that some researchers may have characterized production of food crops as being subsistence-based, without examining the proportion of crops destined for household use or sale (see Preston 1980 and related discussion in Cancian 1989). One rapid rural reconnaissance survey concluded that cash cropping is practiced by small farmers throughout the sierra (Blumberg and Colyer 1990).

3. Although the small size of the regression sample indicates considerable caution in interpreting the lack of statistical significance, probabilities of Type 2 error do not approach the .05 level. Additionally, bivariate associations in which nearly one hundred cases are included also do not approach statistical significance (Hamilton 1995, appendix 3).

The husband's absence from the farm serves as a measure of the effects of household dependence on wages earned in a gender-biased labor market. Migrants working in construction earn between four and five times the standard local gender-egalitarian wage for a day's work. Migrants earned a much larger proportion of their households' total income than did men who earned local wages. On average, migrants' wages accounted for 59 percent of their households' cash income; local wages or salaries accounted for 35 percent. At the median, migrants' wages accounted for 58 percent of household income, while local wages or salaries accounted for only 20 percent.

4. Use of the t-test for analysis of ordinal dependent variables is discussed in Bernard 1988, 411, and in Pagano 1990, 26. Also see Gaito 1980.

5. In the regression model, two variables positively predict women's greater resource control with very low probabilities of Type 1 error: household wealth and women's ownership of land. For a sample of this size, relationships with a probability of up to .10 could be considered marginally significant. Thus women's agricultural labor also appears to have a small positive effect on the extensiveness of their resource control.

6. See Diane Wolf's excellent discussion of the role of individual preference in the decision by young women from land-poor Javanese households to seek factory work (Wolf 1992).

7. Preliminary analysis suggests that migration histories partially account for this variation, in a scenario similar to that described by Deere and León (1982). However, wives retain considerable influence over commercial production as much as twenty years after their husbands' return, even in households that have become relatively wealthy. Patriarchal control of market-oriented agriculture may not be a universal norm even among Latin American mestizo populations.

## 8. Development and the Two-Headed Household

1. These associations access severely limited resources through FUNDAGRO and other NGOs, which are funded at least partly by international agencies, as well as through Ecuadorean state agencies.

# Bibliography

Acevedo, Luz del Alba. 1995. Feminist Inroads in the Study of Women's Work and Development. *In* Women in the Latin American Development Process, ed. Christine E. Bose and Edna Acosta-Belén, 65–98. Philadelphia, Pa.: Temple University Press.

Acosta-Belén, Edna, and Christine E. Bose. 1995. Colonialism, Structural Subordination, and Empowerment: Women in the Development Process in Latin America and the Caribbean. *In* Women in the Latin American Development Process, ed. Christine E. Bose and Edna Acosta-Belén, 15–36. Philadelphia, Pa.: Temple University Press.

Afonja, Simi. 1986. Changing Modes of Production and the Sexual Division of Labor Among the Yoruba. *In* Women's Work, ed. Eleanor Leacock and Helen Safa, 122–35. South Hadley, Mass.: Bergin and Garvey.

———. 1990. Changing Patterns of Gender Stratification in West Africa. *In* Persistent Inequalities: Women and World Development, ed. Irene Tinker, 198–209. New York: Oxford University Press.

Afshar, Haleh. 1991. Women and Development: Myths and Realities, Some Introductory Notes. *In* Women, Development and Survival in the Third World, ed. Haleh Afshar, 1–10. London: Longman.

Agarwal, Bina. 1992. The Gender and Environment Debate: Lessons from India. *Feminist Studies* 18 (1): 119–58.

———. 1994. Gender, Resistance and Land: Interlinked Struggles over Resources and Meanings in South Asia. *Journal of Peasant Studies* 22 (1): 81–125.

Aguiar, Neuma. 1986. Research Guidelines: How to Study Women's Work in Latin America. *In* Women and Change in Latin America, ed. June Nash and Helen Safa, 22–33. South Hadley, Mass.: Bergin and Garvey.

Alberti, Amalia M. 1986. Gender, Ethnicity, and Resource Control in the Andean Highlands of Ecuador. Ph.D. dissertation, Stanford University.

———. 1988. From Recommendation Domains to Intra-Household Dynamics and Back: Attempts at Bridging the Gender Gap. *In* Gender Issues in Farming Systems Research and Extension, ed. Susan V. Poats, Marianne Schmink, and Anita Spring, 61–72. Boulder, Colo.: Westview Press.

Alchon, Suzanne Austin. 1992. Native Society and Disease in Colonial Ecuador. Cambridge, England: Cambridge University Press.

Allen, Andrea M. 1993. Dos Gatazos: Politics and Production in Two Andean Communities. Ph.D. dissertation, University of Kentucky.

Allen, Catherine J. 1988. The Hold Life Has: Coca and Cultural Identity in an Andean Community. Washington, D.C.: Smithsonian Institution Press.

Andrade, Xavier, and Fredy Rivera. 1988. El movimiento campesino e indígena en el último período: Fases, actores y contenidos politicos. *In* Nueva historia del Ecuador, vol. 11, Epoca republicana V: El Ecuador en el último período, ed. Fernando Tinajero and José Moncada, 267–77. Quito: Corporación Editora Nacional.

Arias, Patricia. 1994. Three Microhistories of Women's Work in Rural Mexico. *In* Women of the Mexican Countryside, 1850–1990, ed. Heather Fowler-Salamini and Mary Kay Vaughan, 159–74. Tucson: University of Arizona Press.

Arizpe, Lourdes, and Carlota Botey. 1987. Mexican Agricultural Development Policy and Its Impact on Rural Women. *In* Rural Women and State Policy, ed. Carmen Diana Deere and Magdalena León, 67–83. Boulder, Colo.: Westview Press.

Arizpe, Lourdes, and Josefina Aranda. 1986. Women Workers in the Strawberry Agribusiness in Mexico. *In* Women's Work, ed. Eleanor Leacock and Helen Safa, 174–93. South Hadley, Mass.: Bergin and Garvey.

Ayala Mora, Enrique. 1993. Resumen de historia del Ecuador. Quito: Corporación Editora Nacional.

Babb, Florence. 1986. Producers and Reproducers: Andean Marketwomen in the Economy. *In* Women and Change in Latin America, ed. June Nash and Helen Safa, 53–64. South Hadley, Mass.: Bergin and Garvey.

———. 1989. Between Field and Cooking Pot: The Political Economy of Marketwomen in Peru. Sourcebooks in Anthropology, no. 15. Austin: University of Texas Press.

———. 1996. After the Revolution: Neoliberal Policy and Gender in Nicaragua. *Latin American Perspectives* 23 (1): 27–48.

Balarezo, Susana P. 1984. Tejedoras de paja toquilla y reproducción campesina en Cañar. *In* Mujer y transformaciones agrarias en la sierra ecuatoriana, ed. Susana Balarezo et al., 147–244. Quito: Centro de Planificación y Estudios Sociales (CEPLAES)/Corporación Editora Nacional.

Barkin, David. 1990. Distorted Development: Mexico in the World Economy. Boulder, Colo.: Westview Press.

Barsky, Osvaldo. 1978. Iniciative terrateniente en la reestructuración de las relaciones sociales en la sierra ecuatoriana, 1959–1964. *Revista de ciencias sociales* 2 (5).

———. 1984. La reforma agraria ecuatoriana. Quito: Facultad Latinoamericana de Ciencias Sociales.

Barsky, Osvaldo, and Gustavo Cosse. 1981. Tecnologia y cambio social: Las haciendas lecheras del Ecuador. Quito: Facultad Latinoamericana de Ciencias Sociales.

Barsky, Osvaldo, Lucía Carrión, Patricia de la Torre, and Lucía Salamea. 1984. Modernización hacendal y nuevos roles de la mujer campesina. *In* Mujer y transformaciones agrarias en la sierra ecuatoriana, ed. Susana Balarezo et al., 47–146. Quito: Centro de Planificación y Estudios Sociales (CEPLAES)/Corporación Editora Nacional.

Barsky, Osvaldo, et al., eds. 1980. Ecuador: Cambios en el agro serrano. Quito: FLACSO/CEPLAES.

Basile, David G. 1974. Tillers of the Andes: Farmers and Farming in the Quito Basin. Chapel Hill: University of North Carolina Department of Geography.

Becker, Gary. 1965. A Theory of the Allocation of Time. *Economic Journal* 75:493–517.

———. 1973. A Theory of Marriage. *Journal of Political Economy* 1 (81): 813–46.

———. 1974. A Theory of Marriage. *Journal of Political Economy* 2 (82): 511–26.

———. 1981. A Treatise on the Family. Cambridge, Mass.: Harvard University Press.

Bell, Diane. 1986. Central Australian Aboriginal Women's Love Rituals. *In* Women's Work, ed. Eleanor Leacock and Helen Safa, 75–95. South Hadley, Mass.: Bergin and Garvey.

Belote, Jim, and Linda Belote. 1977. The Limitation of Obligation in Saraguro Kinship. *In* Andean Kinship and Marriage, ed. Ralph Bolton and Enrique Mayer, 106–16. Washington, D.C.: American Anthropological Association.

Belote, Linda, and Jim Belote. 1981. Development in Spite of Itself: The Saraguro Case. *In* Cultural Transformations and Ethnicity in Modern Ecuador, ed. Norman Whitten, 450–76. Urbana: University of Illinois.

———. 1988. Gender, Ethnicity, and Modernization: Saraguro Women in a Changing World. Michigan Discussions in Anthropology. Ann Arbor: Department of Anthropology, University of Michigan.

Benería, Lourdes. 1979. Reproduction, Production, and the Sexual Division of Labor. *Cambridge Journal of Economics* 3:203–25.

———. 1982a. Accounting for Women's Work. *In* Women and Development, ed. Lourdes Benería, 121–47. New York: Praeger.

———, ed. 1982b. Women and Development: The Sexual Division of Labor. New York: Praeger.

———. 1995. Toward a Greater Integration of Gender in Economics. *World Development* 23 (11): 1839–50.

Benería, Lourdes, and Gita Sen. 1986. Accumulation, Reproduction, and Women's Role in Economic Development: Boserup Revisited. *In* Women's Work, ed. Eleanor Leacock and Helen Safa, 141–57. South Hadley, Mass.: Bergin and Garvey.

Benería, Lourdes, and Martha Roldán. 1987. The Crossroads of Class and Gender: Industrial Homework, Subcontracting, and Household Dynamics in Mexico City. Chicago: University of Chicago Press.

Bernard, H. Russell. 1988. Research Methods in Cultural Anthropology. Newbury Park, Calif.: Sage Publications.

Berti, Peter R. 1996. Dietary Adequacy and Its Relationship to Anthropometric Status in a Highland Ecuadorian Community. Ph.D. thesis, University of Guelph.

Berti, Peter R., William R. Leonard, and Wilma J. Berti. 1995. *Somos iguales:* The consequences of the equal sharing of food between spouses in rural highland Ecuador. *American Journal of Physical Anthropology.* Supplement 20:65 (abstract).

Bidegaray, Pedro. 1992. Social Networks and the Reproduction of the Peasant Domestic Unit. Paper presented at the Annual Meeting of the Society for Applied Anthropology. Memphis, March 24–28.

Birdsall, Nancy, and William P. McGreevey. 1983. Women, Poverty, and Development. *In* Women and Poverty in the Third World, ed. Mayra Buvinić, Margaret Lycette, and William P. McGreevey, 3–13. Baltimore: Johns Hopkins University Press.

Blankstein, Charles S., and Clarence Auvekas Jr. 1974. Agrarian Reform in Ecuador. Madison, Wis.: Land Tenure Center.

Blumberg, Rae Lesser. 1978. Stratification: Socioeconomic and Sexual Inequality. Dubuque: William C. Brown.

———. 1979. Rural Women in Development: Veil of Invisibility, World of Work. *International Journal of Intercultural Relations* 3:447–72.

———. 1988. Income Under Female Versus Male Control. *Journal of Family Issues* 9 (1): 51–84.

———. 1989. Making the Case for the Gender Variable: Women and the Wealth and Well-Being of Nations, ed. Mari H. Clark. Washington, D.C.: Office of Women in Development, USAID.

———. 1990. Gender and Development in Ecuador. Informe borrador para AID-Quito.

———. 1991. Introduction: The "Triple Overlap" of Gender Stratification, Economy, and the Family. *In* Gender, Family, and Economy: The Triple Overlap, ed. Rae Lesser Blumberg, 7–32. Newbury Park, Calif.: Sage Publications.

———. 1995a. Gender, Microenterprise, Performance, and Power: Case Studies from the Dominican Republic, Ecuador, Guatemala, and Swaziland. *In* Women in the Latin American Development Process, ed. Christine E. Bose and Edna Acosta-Belén, 194–226. Philadelphia, Pa.: Temple University Press.

———. 1995b. Introduction: Engendering Wealth and Well-Being in an Era of Economic Transformation. *In* EnGENDERing Wealth and Well-Being: Empowerment for Global Change, ed. Rae Lesser Blumberg, Cathy Rakowski, Irene Tinker, and Michael Monteón, 1–16. Boulder, Colo.: Westview Press.

Blumberg, Rae L., and Dale Colyer. 1990. Social Institutions, Gender, and Rural Living Conditions. *In* The Role of Agriculture in Ecuador's Agricultural Development: An Assessment of Ecuador's Agricultural Sector, ed. Morris D. Whitaker, Dale Colyer, and Jaime Alzamora, 247–66. Quito: USAID.

Bolton, Ralph, and Enrique Mayer, eds. 1977. Andean Kinship and Marriage. Washington, D.C.: American Anthropological Association.

Borlagden, Salve B., Edna M. Alegado, Isabel M. Carillo, and Joselito Frances A. Alcaria. 1989. The Cebu Integrated Social Forestry Project. *In* Women's Role in Resource Management: A Reader, ed. B. van der Borg, 123–38. Bangkok: Food and Agriculture Office of the United Nations.

Boserup, Ester. 1970. Women's Role in Economic Development. New York: St. Martin's Press. 2d edition, Aldershot, England: Gower Publishing, 1986.

———. 1990. Economic Change and the Roles of Women. *In* Persistent Inequalities: Women and World Development, ed. Irene Tinker, 14–24. New York: Oxford University Press.

Bossen, Laurel. 1981. The Household as Economic Agent. *Urban Anthropology* 10:287–303.

———. 1984. The Redivision of Labor: Women and Economic Choice in Four Guatemalan Communities. Albany: State University of New York Press.

———. 1989. Women and Economic Institutions. *In* Economic Anthropology, ed. Stuart Plattner, 318–50. Stanford, Calif.: Stanford University Press.

Bourque, Susan, and Kay Barbara Warren. 1981. Women of the Andes: Patriarchy and Social Change in Two Peruvian Towns. Ann Arbor: University of Michigan Press.

Braidotti, Rosi, et al. 1994. Women, the Environment, and Sustainable Development: Towards a Theoretical Synthesis. London: Zed Books, in association with INSTRAW.

Brush, Stephen. 1987. Who Are Traditional Farmers? *In* Household Economies and Their Transformations, ed. Morgan D. Maclachlan, 143–54. Lanham, Md.: University Press of America, Society for Economic Anthropology.

Burton, Michael L., and Douglas R. White. 1987. Sexual Division of Labor in Agriculture. *In* Household Economies and Their Transformations, ed. Morgan D. Maclachlan, 107–30. Lanham, Md.: University Press of America, Society for Economic Anthropology.

Buvinić, Mayra. 1980. Una estrategia para la mujer en el Ecuador. Centro Internacional de Investigaciones sobre la Mujer. Manuscript.

———. 1983. Women's Issues in Third World Poverty: A Policy Analysis. *In* Women and Poverty in the Third World, ed. Mayra Buvinic, Margaret Lycette, and William P. McGreevey, 14–31. Baltimore: Johns Hopkins University Press.

———. 1984. Projects for Women in the Third World: Explaining Their Misbehavior. Washington, D.C.: International Center for Research on Women. April.

Buvinić, Mayra, and Rekha Mehra. 1990. Women and Agricultural Development. *In* Agricultural Development in the Third World, ed. Carl K. Eicher and John M. Staatz, 290–308. 2d ed. Baltimore: Johns Hopkins University Press.

———. 1993. The Intergenerational Transmission of Poverty in Santiago, Chile. *In* Understanding How Resources Are Allocated Within Households, 13–14. Washington, D.C.: International Food Policy Research Institute and the World Bank.

Buvinić, Mayra, Margaret Lycette, and William P. McGreevey, eds. 1983. Women and Poverty in the Third World. Baltimore: Johns Hopkins University Press.

Çağatay, Nilüfer, Diane Elson, and Caren Grown. 1995. Introduction. *World Development* 23 (11): 1827–36.

Cancian, Frank. 1989. Economic Behavior in Peasant Communities. *In* Economic Anthropology, ed. Stuart Plattner, 127–70. Stanford, Calif.: Stanford University Press.

Carney, Judith, and Michael Watts. 1991. Disciplining Women? Rice, Mechanization, and the Evolution of Mandinka Gender Relations in Senegambia. *Signs* 16:651–81.

Casagrande, Joseph B. 1974. Strategies for Survival: The Indians of Highland Ecuador. *In* Contemporary Cultures and Societies of Latin America, ed. Dwight B. Heath, 93–107. 2d ed. New York: Random House.

CEIS. *See* Centro Ecuatoriano de Investigaciones Sociales (CEIS).

Central Ecuatoriana de Servicios Agrícolas (CESA). 1987. Formas de participación de la mujer en cinco zonas rurales del Ecuador. Quito: CESA.

Centro de Planificación y Estudios Sociales (CEPLAES) y Instituto Latinoamericano de Investi-gaciones Sociales (ILDIS). 1993. Ecuador: Análisis de Coyuntura 6. Perspectivas 1993. Quito: CEPLAES-ILDIS.

Centro Ecuatoriano de Investigaciones Sociales (CEIS). 1988. Problems That Concern Women and Their Incorporation in Development: The Case of Ecuador. *In* Women and Economic Development: Local, Regional, and National Planning Strategies, ed. Kate Young, 31–73. New York and Paris: Berg/Unesco.

CEPLAES. *See* Centro de Planificación y Estudios Sociales (CEPLAES).

CESA. *See* Central Ecuatoriana de Servicios Agrícolas (CESA).

Chafetz, Janet Saltzman. 1991. The Gender Division of Labor and the Reproduction of Female Disadvantage: Toward an Integrated Theory. *In* Gender, Family, and Economy: The Triple Overlap, ed. Rae Lesser Blumberg, 74–94. Newbury Park, Calif.: Sage Publications.

Chaney, Elsa M. 1976. Women and Modernization: Access to Tools. *In* Sex and Class in Latin America, ed. June Nash and Helen Safa, 160–80. South Hadley, Mass.: J. F. Bergin.

———. 1987. Women's Components in Integrated Rural Development Projects. *In* Rural Women and State Policy, ed. Carmen Diana Deere and Magdalena León, 191–211. Boulder, Colo.: Westview Press.

Charlton, Sue Ellen. 1984. Women in Third World Development. Boulder, Colo.: Westview Press.

Chayanov, A. V. 1966. The Theory of Peasant Economy, ed. D. Thorner, B. Kerblay, and R. E. F. Smith. Homewood, Ill.: Irwin.

Chibnik, Michael. 1978. The Value of Subsistence Production. *Journal of Anthropological Research* 34 (4): 551–76.

———. 1987. The Economic Effects of Household Demography: A Cross-Cultural Assessment of Chayanov's Theory. *In* Household Economies and Their Transformations, ed. Morgan D. Maclachlan, 74–106. Lanham, Md.: University Press of America, Society for Economic Anthropology.

Chiriboga, Manuel. 1983. El analysis de las formas tradicionales: El case de Ecuador. *Anuario Indigenista* 43 (December): 37–99.

———. 1984. Campesinado andino y estrategias de empleo: El caso Salcedo. *In* Estrategias de supervivencia en la comunidad andina, ed. M. Chiriboga et al. Quito: CAAP.

———. 1985. La crisis agraria en el Ecuador: Tendencias y contradicciones del reciente proceso. *In* Economía política del Ecuador: Campo, región, nación, ed. Louis Lefeber, 91–132. Quito: Corporación Editora Nacional.

———. 1988a. Estructura de la producción agropecuaria. *In* El problema agrario en el Ecuador, ed. Manuel Chiriboga, 421–38. Quito: ILDIS.

———. 1988b. La reforma agraria ecuatoriana y los cambios en la distribución de la propiedad rural agrícola, 1974–1985. *In* Transformaciones agrarias en el Ecuador, ed. Pierre Gonard et al., 39–58. Quito: CEDIG.

———. 1989. Movimiento campesino e indígena y participación politica en Ecuador: La construcción de identidades en una sociedad heterogenea. *Ecuador Debate* 13:87–122.

Chiriboga, M., G. Ramon, J. Sanchez-Parga, A. Guerrero, J. Durston, and A. Crivelli, eds. 1984. Estragias de supervivencia en la comunidad andina. Quito: CAAP [Center of Artists for Popular Action].

Chowdhry, Geeta. 1995. Engendering Development? Women in Development (WID) in International Development Regimes. *In* Feminism/Postmodernism/Development, ed. Marianne H. Marchand and Jane L. Parpart, 26–41. London: Routledge.

Chrissman, Charles C., and Patricio Espinosa. 1993. Implementing a Program of Research on Agricultural Sustainability: An Example of Pesticide Use in Potato Production in Ecuador. Paper presented at the Latin American Farming Systems Meetings, Quito, March 3–6.

Cloud, Kathleen. 1985. Women's Productivity in Agricultural Households: How Can We Think About It: What Do We Know? *In* Women as Food Producers in Developing Countries, ed. Jamie Monson and Marion Kalb, 11–18. Los Angeles: UCLA African Studies Center.

Collier, Donald. 1946. The Archaeology of Ecuador. *In* Handbook of South American Indians, 2:767–84. Bureau of American Ethnology Bulletin, no. 143.

Collier, Paul. 1990. Women and Structural Adjustment. Washington, D.C.: The World Bank.

Collins, Jane. 1986. The Household and Relations of Production in Southern Peru. *Journal of the Society for Comparative Study of Society and History*, pp. 651–71.

———. 1988. Unseasonal Migrations: The Effects of Rural Labor Scarcity in Peru. Princeton, N.J.: Princeton University Press.

Commander, S., and P. Peek. 1986. Oil Exports, Agrarian Change, and the Rural Labor Process: The Ecuadorian Sierra in the 1970s. *World Development* 14:79–86.

Conelly, W. Thomas, and Miriam S. Chaiken. 1993. Inequality and Gender in the Control of Resources in Agropastoral Systems: The Luo and Luhya of Western Kenya. Paper presented at the Association for Women in Development International Forum, Washington, D.C.

Cornick, Tully R., et al. 1985. Institutionalizing Farming Systems Research and Extension: Cornell University's Experience in Ecuador and the Philippines. Ithaca: Cornell International Agricultural Mimeograph, no. 115.

Cosse, Gustavo. 1984. Estado y agro en el Ecuador. Quito: Facultad Latinoamericana de Ciencias Sociales.

Crain, Mary. 1991. Poetics and Politics in the Ecuadorean Andes: Women's Narratives of Death and Devil Possession. *American Ethnologist* 18 (1): 67–89.

Crandon, Libbet. 1984. Why Susto? *Ethnology*, pp. 153–67.

———. 1985. Women, Enterprise, and Development: The Pathfinder Fund's Women in Development: Projects, Evaluation, and Documentation. Washington, D.C.: Pathfinder Fund.

———. 1986. Medical Dialogue and the Political Economy of Medical Pluralism: A Case from Rural Highland Bolivia. *American Ethnologist* 13:463–76.

Curtis, Richard F. 1986. Household and Family in Theory on Inequality. *American Sociological Review* 51:168–83. (Cited in Jaquette 1993, 48.)

DAWN. *See* Development Alternatives with Women for a New Era (DAWN)

Deere, Carmen Diana. 1976. Rural Women's Subsistence Production in the Capitalist Periphery. *Review of Radical Political Economics* 8:9–17.

———. 1977. Changing Social Relations of Production and Peruvian Peasant Women's Work. *Latin American Perspectives* 4:48–69.

———. 1983. The Allocation of Familial Labor and the Formation of Peasant Household Income in the Peruvian Sierra. *In* Women and Poverty in the Third World, ed. Mayra Buvinic, Margaret Lycette, and William P. McGreevey, 104–29. Baltimore: Johns Hopkins University Press.

———. 1986. Rural Women and Agrarian Reform in Peru, Chile, and Cuba. *In* Women and Change in Latin America, ed. June Nash and Helen Safa, 189–207. South Hadley, Mass.: Bergin and Garvey.

———. 1990. Household and Class Relations: Peasants and Landlords in Northern Peru. Berkeley and Los Angeles: University of California Press.

Deere, Carmen Diana, and Alain de Janvry. 1979. A Conceptual Framework for the Empirical Analysis of Peasants. *American Journal of Agricultural Economics* 61 (4): 601–11.

Deere, Carmen Diana, and Magdalena León (León de Leal). 1981. Peasant Production, Proletarianization, and the Sexual Division of Labor in the Andes. *Signs* 7:338–60.

———. 1982. Women in Agriculture: Peasant Production and Proletarianization in Three Andean Regions. Geneva: International Labor Organization.

———. 1987. Introduction. *In* Rural Women and State Policy, ed. Carmen Diana Deere and Magdalena León, 1–20. Boulder, Colo.: Westview Press.

de Groot, Joanna. 1991. Conceptions and Misconceptions: The Historical and Cultural Context of Discussion on Women and Development. *In* Women, Development and Survival in the Third World, ed. Haleh Afshar, 107–35. London: Longman.

de Janvry, Alain. 1981. The Agrarian Question. Baltimore: Johns Hopkins University Press.

de Janvry, Alain, and Elizabeth Sadoulet. 1990. Investment Strategies to Combat Rural Poverty in Latin America. *In* Agricultural Development in the Third World, 2nd ed., ed. Carl K. Eicher and John M. Staatz, 442–58. Baltimore: Johns Hopking University Press.

de Velasco, Juan. 1981. Historia del reino de Quito en la America Meridional. Caracas: Biblioteca Ayacucho.

Development Alternatives with Women for a New Era (DAWN). 1987. Development, Crises, and Alternative Visions (1985). *Reissued in* Development, Crises, and Alternative Visions, ed. Gita Sen and Caren Grown. New York: Monthly Review Press.

DeWalt, Billie R. 1979. Modernization in a Mexican *Ejido:* A Study in Economic Adaptation. Cambridge and New York: Cambridge University Press.

DeWalt, Billie R., et al. 1990. Dairy-Based Production and Food Systems in Mejia and Salcedo. The Research Extension and Education Project Baseline Surveys Report, no. 1. Quito: Fundación para el Desarrollo Agropecuario.

DeWalt, Kathleen M. 1981. Diet as Adaptation: The Search for Nutritional Strategies. Federation Proceedings 40:2606–10. Anaheim, Calif.: Federation of American Societies for Experimental Biology.

———. 1983a. Income and Dietary Adequacy in an Agricultural Community. *Social Science and Medicine* 17:1877–87.

———. 1983b. Nutritional Strategies and Agricultural Change. Ann Arbor: UMI Research Press.

DeWalt, Kathleen M., and Jorge Uquillas. 1989. Potato Production and Consumption in the Sierra of Ecuador: A Diagnostic Survey Conducted by the Nutrition and Agriculture Cooperative Agreement. Culture and Agriculture 39:6–11.

DeWalt, Kathleen, Billie R. DeWalt, José Carlos Escudero, and David Barkin. 1990. The Nutrition Effects of Shifts from Maize to Sorghum Production in Four Mexican Communities. Unpublished manuscript.

Dillehay, Tom D. 1979. Prehistoric Resource Sharing in the Central Andes. *Science* 204:24–31.

Dinham, Barbara, comp. 1993. The Pesticide Hazard: A Global Health and Environmental Audit. London: Zed Books in Association with the Pesticide Trust.

Dixon, Ruth. 1985. Seeing the Invisible Women Farmers in Africa: Improving Research and Data Collection Methods. *In* Women as Food Producers in Developing Countries, ed. Jamie Monson and Marion Kalb, 19–36. Los Angeles: UCLA African Studies Center.

Edirisinghe, Neville. 1991. Income and Employment Sources of the Malnourished Rural Poor in Kandy District, Sri Lanka. *In* Income Sources of Malnourished People in Rural Areas: Microlevel Information and Policy Implications. Working Papers on Commercialization of Agriculture and Nutrition, no. 5, ed. Joachim von Braun and Rajul Pandya-Lorch, 139–44. Washington, D.C.: International Food Policy Research Institute.

Elson, Diane. 1995. Gender Awareness in Modeling Structural Adjustment. *World Development* 23 (11): 1851–69.

Elson, Diane, and Rosemary McGee. 1995. Gender Equality, Bilateral Program Assistance and Structural Adjustment: Policy and Procedures. *World Development* 23 (11): 1987–1994.

Emmanuel, Arghiri. 1972. Unequal Exchange. New York: Modern Reader.

FAO/WHO. 1973. Energy and Protein Requirements. WHO Technical Report Series, no. 522. Geneva: WHO.

Farrell, Gilda. 1983. Participación de la mujer en el sector moderno de la economía. Revista Economía y Desarrollo. Quito: IIE-PUCE.

Farrell, Gilda, and Sara da Ros. 1983. El acceso a la tierra del campesino ecuatoriano. Quito. Mundo Andino/FEPP.

Faulkner, Anne H., and Victoria A. Lawson. 1991. Employment Versus Empowerment: A Case Study of the Nature of Women's Work in Ecuador. *Journal of Development Studies* 27:16–47.

Feldman, Robert, and Michael E. Moseley. 1983. The Northern Andes. *In* Ancient South Americans, ed. Jesse Jennings, 139–78. W. H. Freeman.

Feldstein, Hilary Sims, Cornelia Butler Flora, and Susan V. Poats. 1989. The Gender Variable in Agricultural Research. Ottawa: International Development Research Centre.

Fernández, Maria E. 1988. Technological Domains of Women in Mixed Farming Systems of Andean Peasant Communities. *In* Gender Issues in Farming Systems Research and Extension, ed. Susan V. Poats, Marianne Schmink, and Anita Spring, 213–21. Boulder, Colo.: Westview Press.

Fernández-Kelly, M. Patricia, and Saskia Sassen. 1995. Recasting Women in the Global Economy: Internationalization and Changing Definitions of Gender. *In* Women in the Latin Amer-

ican Development Process, ed. Christina E. Bose and Edna Acosta-Belén, 99–124. Philadelphia, Pa.: Temple University Press.

Ferrin, R. 1982. De la forma huasipungo de trabajo a la economía comunitaria: Un caso de
transformación de las relaciones sociales de producción. *In* Estructuras Agrarias y Reproducción Campesina, ed. C. Sepulveda et al. Quito: IIE-PUCE.

Finerman, Ruthbeth D. 1983. Experience and Expectation: Conflict and Change in Traditional
Family Health Care Among the Quichua of Saraguro. *Social Science and Medicine* 17:1291–99.

———. 1989a. The Forgotten Healers: Women as Family Healers in an Andean Indian Community. *In* Women as Healers: Cross-Cultural Perspectives, ed. Carol McClain, 24–267. New
Brunswick, N.J.: Rutgers University Press.

———. 1989b. Tracing Home-Based Health Care Change in an Andean Indian Community.
*Medical Anthropology Quarterly* 3:162–74.

Finn, M., and C. Jusenius. 1976. La posición de la mujer en la fuera laboral de Ecuador. *Estudios
Andinos* 5:99–116.

Flora, Cornelia Butler. 1987. Income Generation Projects for Rural Women. *In* Rural Women
and State Policy, ed. Carmen Diana Deere and Magdalena Leon dé Leal, 212–38. Boulder,
Colo.: Westview Press.

Flora, Cornelia Butler, and Blas Santos. 1986. Women in Farming Systems in Latin America. *In*
Women and Change in Latin America, ed. June Nash and Helen Safa, 189–207. South
Hadley, Mass.: Bergin and Garvey.

Folbre, Nancy. 1984. Household Production in the Philippines: A Non-Neoclassical Approach.
*Economic Development and Cultural Change* 32 (2): 303–30.

———. 1986. Hearts and Spaces: Paradigms of Household Economics. *World Development* 14 (2).

———. 1988. The Black Four of Hearts: Toward a New Paradigm of Household Economics. *In* A
Home Divided: Women and Income in the Third World, ed. Daisy Dwyer and Judith Bruce.
Stanford, Calif.: Stanford University Press.

Fordham, Miriam, Billie R. DeWalt, and Kathleen M. DeWalt. 1985. The Economic Role of
Women in a Honduran Peasant Community: Socioeconomic Constraints to the Production,
Distribution, and Consumption of Sorghum in Southern Honduras. The International
Sorghum and Millet Project, Report no. 3. Lincoln: Institute of Agriculture and Natural Re-
sources, University of Nebraska.

Frank, André Gunder. 1969. Capitalism and Underdevelopment in Latin America. New York:
Modern Reader.

———. 1972. The Development of Underdevelopment. *In* Dependence and Underdevelopment,
ed. James Crockroft, 19–46. New York: Anchor.

Frank, Robert H. 1991. Microeconomics and Behavior. New York: McGraw-Hill.

Frisancho, A. R. 1974. Triceps Skinfold and Upper Arm Muscle Size Norms for Assessment of
Nutritional Status. *American Journal of Clinical Nutrition* 27:1052–57.

———. 1986. Anthropometric Standards for Evaluating Growth and Nutritional Status Using
the Frameter. Ann Arbor, Mich.: Health Products.

Gaito, J. 1980. Measurement Scales and Statistics: Resurgence of an Old Misconception. *Psycho-
logical Bulletin* 87:564–67.

Garrett, Patricia, and Patricio Espinosa. 1988. Phases of Farming Systems Research: The Relevance of Gender in Ecuadorian Sites. *In* Gender Issues in Farming Systems Research and Extension, ed. Susan V. Poats, Marianne Schmink, and Anita Spring, 198–212. Boulder, Colo.:
Westview Press.

Ghimire, D. P. 1991. Gender Analysis in a Migrant Community. Paper presented at the Eleventh
Annual Symposium of the Association for Farming Systems Research-Extension. East Lansing, Michigan.

Gisbert, María Elena, Michael Painter, and Mery Quitón. 1994. Gender Issues Associated with
Labor Migration and Dependence on Off-Farm Income in Rural Bolivia. *Human Organization*
53:110–22.

Gladwin, Christina H., and Carrie M. Thompson. 1995. Impacts of Mexico's Trade Openness on
Mexican Rural Women. *American Journal of Agricultural Economics* 77 (August 1995):712–18.

Goetz, Anne Marie. 1991. Feminism and the Claim to Know: Contradiction in Feminist Approaches to Women in Development. *In* Gender and International Relations, ed. Rebecca Grant and Kathleen Newland. Bloomington: Indiana University Press.

Gonzáles Montes, Soledad. 1994. Intergenerational and Gender Relations in the Transition from a Peasant Economy to a Diversified Economy. *In* Women of the Mexican Countryside, 1850–1990, ed. Heather Fowler-Salamini and Mary Kay Vaughan, 175–91. Tucson: University of Arizona Press.

Gopalan, C. 1983. Small Is Healthy? *New Delhi: Nutrition Foundation of India Bulletin* 5:33–37.

Gose, Peter. 1991. House Rethatching in an Andean Annual Cycle: Practice, Meaning, and Contradiction. *American Ethnologist* 18 (1): 39–66.

Gregory, C. A., and J. C. Altman. 1989. Observing the Economy. London: Routledge.

Gross, Daniel R. 1984. Time Allocation: A Tool for the Study of Cultural Behavior. *Annual Review of Anthropology* 13:519–58.

Guerrero, Andrés. 1984. Haciendas, capital y lucha de clases andina. Quito: Editorial El Conejo.

Guyer, Jane I. 1988a. Dynamic Approaches to Domestic Budgeting: Cases and Methods from Africa. *In* A Home Divided: Women and Income in the Third World, ed. Daisy Dwyer and Judith Bruce, 157–72. Stanford, Calif.: Stanford University Press.

———. 1988b. The Multiplication of Labor: Historical Methods in the Study of Gender and Agricultural Change in Modern Africa. *Current Anthropology* 29:247–59.

———. 1991. Female Farming in Anthropology and African History. *In* Gender at the Crossroads: Feminist Anthropology and the Postmodern Era, ed. Micela di Leonardo, 257–77. Berkeley and Los Angeles: University of California Press.

Guyer, Jane I., and Pauline E. Peters. 1987. Introduction. *Development and Change* 18:197–214. Special issue, Conceptualising the Household.

Habicht, J. P., et al. 1974. Height and Weight Standards for Pre-School Children: How Relevant Are Ethnic Differences in Growth Potential? Lancet, i: 611–14.

Hamill, P. V. V., T. A. Drizd, C. L. Johnson, R. R. Reed, and A. R. Roche. 1977. NCHS Growth Curves for Children from Birth to Eighteen Years: United States. Publication no. PHS 78-1650: Vital and Health Statistics Series 11, no. 165. U.S. Department of Health, Education, and Welfare, Hyattsville, Md.

Hamilton, Sarah. 1992. Visible Partners: Women's Labor and Management of Agricultural Capital on Small Farms in the Highlands of Central Ecuador. *Urban Anthropology* 21:353–83.

———. 1994. Gender and Agrochemicals: Linking Productivity, Environment, and Health in an Andean Ecosystem. Paper presented at the Ninety-third Annual Meeting of the American Anthropological Association. Atlanta, Nov. 30–Dec. 4.

———. 1995. The Two-Headed Household: Gender and Agricultural Development in an Andean Setting (Cotopaxi Province, Ecuador). Ph.D. dissertation, University of Kentucky.

———. 1996. Unpublished fieldnotes. Field sites included communities in the following Mexican *municipios*: Axochiapan, Morelos; Abasolo, Tamaulipas; Cerritos, San Luis Potosí; and Apatzingán, Michoacan.

Hamilton, Sarah, Thelma Paris, and Irene Tanzo. 1997. Women's Roles in Rice-Vegetable IPM in Central Luzon, Philippines. IPM CRSP Working Paper Series. Blacksburg, Va.: Office of International Research and Development, Virginia Tech.

Hamilton, Sarah, William R. Leonard, and Peter Berti. 1996. Somos Iguales: A Bio-Socio-Cultural Model of Intrahousehold Gender Parity and Economic Change in the Ecuadorean Andes. Paper presented at the Ninety-fourth Annual Meeting of the American Anthropological Association. San Francisco, November 20–24.

Handelman, Howard. 1981. Ecuadorian Agrarian Reform: The Politics of Limited Change. *In* The Politics of Agrarian Change in Asia and Latin America, ed. Howard Handelman, 63–81. Bloomington: Indiana University Press.

Handwerker, W. Penn. 1992. West Indian Gender Relations, Family Planning Programs and Fertility Decline. *Social Science and Medicine* 35 (10): 1245–57.

Harris, Olivia. 1978. Complementarity and Conflict: An Andean View of Women and Men. *In* Sex and Age as Principles of Social Differentiation, ed. J. S. La Fontaine, 21–40. London: Academic Press.

————. 1980. The Power of Signs: Gender, Culture and the Wild in the Bolivian Andes. *In* Nature, Culture and Gender, ed. Carol P. MacCormack, 70–94. London: St. Martin's Press.

————. 1981. Households as Natural Units. *In* Of Marriage and the Market: Women's Subordination in International Perspective, ed. Kate Young, Carol Wolkowitz, and Roslyn McCullogh. London: Committee of Socialist Economists Books.

————. 1983a. Women's Organizations in Bolivia: Peasants and Miners. *In* Latin American Women, ed. Olivia Harris, 12–13. London: Minority Rights Group.

————, ed. 1983b. Latin American Women. London: Minority Rights Group.

————. 1985. From Asymmetry to Triangle: Symbolic Transformations in Northern Potosí. *In* Anthropological History of Andean Politics, ed. John Murra, Nathan Watchel, and Jaques Revel, 260–79. Cambridge, England: Cambridge University Press.

Hart, Gillian. 1992. Imagined Unities: Constructions of "The Household" in Economic Theory. *In* Understanding Economic Process, ed. S. Ortiz and S. Lees, 111–29. Lanham, Md.: University Press of America.

Hill, Polly. 1986. Development Economics on Trial: The Anthropological Case for a Prosecution. Cambridge, England: Cambridge University Press.

Hirschman, Mitu. 1995. Women and Development: A Critique. *In* Feminism/Postmodernism/Development, ed. Marianne H. Marchand and Jane L. Parpart, 42–55. London: Routledge.

Holdridge, Leslie R. 1967. Life Zone Ecology. San José, Costa Rica: Tropical Science Center.

Holmboe-Ottesen, Gerd, Ophelia Mascarenhas, and Margareta Wandel. 1989. Women's Role in Food Chain Activities and the Implications for Nutrition. ACC/SCN Nutrition Policy Discussion Paper, no. 4. Geneva: UN ACC/SCN.

Hoque, M. M., and C. B. Adalla. 1993. Integrating Gender Issues into Farmer-Participatory Research: The Case of Vegetable IPM Technology Generation in Calamba, Laguna, Philippines. *Journal for Farming Systems Research-Extension* 3 (2): 1–12.

Hurtado, Osvaldo. 1980. Political Power in Ecuador. Translated by Nick D. Mills Jr. Albuquerque: University of New Mexico Press.

ICPEDC. *See* International Center for Public Enterprises in Developing Countries (ICPEDC)

IDB. *See* Inter-American Development Bank (IDB)

IECAIM. *See* Instituto Ecuatoriano de Investigaciones y Capacitación de la Mujer (IECAIM)

Ifeka-Muller, Caroline. 1975. Female Militancy and Colonial Revolt: The Women's War of 1929, Eastern Nigeria. *In* Perceiving Women, ed. S. Ardener. New York: John Wiley and Sons.

ILDIS. *See* Instituto Latinoamericano de Investigaciones Sociales (ILDIS)

INEC. *See* Instituto Nacional de Estadística y Censos (INEC)

Instituto Ecuatoriano de Investigaciones y Capacitación de la Mujer (IECAIM). 1992. Investigación de datos estadísticos sobre la mujer ecuatoriana: Demografía, salud, educación y empleo. Quito: IECAIM.

Instituto Latinoamericano de Investigaciones Sociales (ILDIS). 1993. Informe social no. 1, Ecuador: Ajuste y situación social. Quito: ILDIS.

Instituto Nacional de Estadística y Censos (INEC). 1990a. IV, V: Censo de población y IV de Vivienda. Quito: INEC.

————. 1990b. Anuario de astadísticas vitales: Nacimientos y defunciones. Quito: INEC.

————. 1991. Censo de población, San José de Chanchaló. Latacunga: INEC.

————. 1992. Sistema estadístico agropecuario nacional. Quito: INEC.

Inter-American Development Bank (IDB). 1992. Self-Help for Indigenous People. *IDB* 19 (9–10): 9.

————. 1995. Women in the Americas: Bridging the Gender Gap. Washington, D.C.: IDB/Johns Hopkins University Press.

International Center for Public Enterprises in Developing Countries (ICPEDC). 1986. The Role of Women in Developing Countries. Ljubljana, Yugoslavia.

International Center for Research on Women. 1988. What to Do About WID? A Report for AID/Ecuador. By Mayra Buvinic and Michael Paolisso. Unpublished report.

————. 1989a. Institutionalizing Women in Development (WID) at USAID/Ecuador. By Michael Paolisso and Rae Lesser Blumberg. Unpublished report.

———. 1989b. Non-Traditional Agricultural Exports: Labor, Gender and Socio-Economic Considerations. By Michael Paolisso and Rae Lesser Blumberg. Unpublished report.

Isbell, Billie Jean. 1978. To Defend Ourselves: Ecology and Ritual in an Andean Village. Prospect Heights, Ill.: Waveland Press.

Jacobs, Susie. 1991. Changing Gender Relations in Zimbabwe: The Case of Individual Family Resettlement Areas. *In* Male Bias in the Development Process, ed. Diane Elson. Manchester: Manchester University Press.

Jacobson, Margaret. 1991. Conservation and a Himba Community in Western Kaokoland, Namibia. Manuscript.

Jaquette, Jane. 1985. Women, Population and Food: An Overview of the Issues. *In* Women as Food Producers in Developing Countries, ed. Jamie Monson and Marion Kalb, 1–10. Los Angeles: UCLA African Studies Center.

———. 1986. Female Political Participation in Latin America: Raising Feminist Issues. *In* Women in the World, 1975–1985: The Women's Decade, ed. Lynne B. Iglitzin and Ruth Ross, 243–69. 2d rev. ed. Santa Barbara, Calif.: ABC-Clio.

———. 1990. Gender and Justice in Economic Development. *In* Persistent Inequalities: Women and World Development, ed. Irene Tinker, 54–69. New York: Oxford University Press.

———. 1993. The Family as a Development Issue. *In* Women at the Center: Development Issues and Practices for the 1990s, ed. Gay Young, Vidyamali Samarashinghe, and Ken Kusterer, 45–62. West Hartford, Conn.: Kumarian Press.

Jiménez Rodríguez, Leonidas. 1990. Evaluación de la adopción de prácticas mejoradas en bovinos (ganadería de leche) Salcedo-Cotopaxi. Tesis de Grado, Facultad de Ciencias Agrícolas, Universidad Central del Ecuador.

Joekes, Susan, with Noeleen Heyser, Ruth Oniang'o, and Vania Salles. 1994. Gender, Environment and Population. *Development and Change* 25:137–65.

Jordán, Fausto, et al., eds. 1984. Mujer y transformaciones agrarias en la sierra ecuatoriana. Quito: CEPLAES/Corporación Editora Nacional.

Kabeer, Naila. 1994. Reversed Realities: Gender Hierarchies in Development Thought. London: Verso.

Kandiyoti, Deniz. 1985. Women in Rural Production Systems: Problems and Policies. Paris: UNESCO.

Katz, Elizabeth G. 1995. Gender and Trade Within the Household: Observations from Rural Guatemala. *World Development* 23:327–42.

Kennedy, Eileen. 1989. Income Resources of the Rural Poor: The Case of Southwestern Kenya. Washington, D.C.: International Food Policy Institute.

Knapp, Gregory. 1991. Andean Ecology: Adaptive Dynamics in Ecuador. Boulder, Colo.: Westview Press.

Kumar, Shubh K. 1991. Income Sources of the Malnourished Poor in Rural Bangladesh. *In* Income Sources of Malnourished People in Rural Areas: Microlevel Information and Policy Implications. Working Papers on Commercialization of Agriculture and Nutrition, no. 5, ed. Joachim von Braun and Rajul Pandya-Lorch, 155–61. Washington, D.C.: International Food Policy Research Institute.

Lambert, Bernd. 1977. Bilaterality in the Andes. *In* Andean Kinship and Marriage, ed. Ralph Bolton and Enrique Mayer, 1–27. Washington, D.C.: American Anthropological Association.

Larme, Anne C. 1993. Environment, Vulnerability, and Gender in Andean Ethnomedicine. Paper presented at the American Anthropological Association Meetings, Washington, D.C., November 18, 1993.

Laslett, Peter. 1984. The Family as a Knot of Individual Interests. *In* Households: Comparative and Historical Studies of the Domestic Group, ed. R. Netting, R. Wilk, and E. Arnould, 353–82. Berkeley and Los Angeles: University of California Press.

Latham, Michael C. 1984. Strategies for the Control of Malnutrition and the Influence of the Nutritional Sciences. *Food and Nutrition* 10:5–31.

Lawson, Victoria. 1990. Work Force Fragmentation in Latin America and Its Empirical Manifestations in Ecuador. *World Development* 18:641–58.

Leacock, Eleanor. 1977. Women, Development, and Anthropological Facts and Fictions. *Latin American Perspectives* 4 (1 and 2): 8–17.

———. 1986. Postscript: Implications for Organization. *In* Women's Work, ed. Eleanor Leacock and Helen Safa, 253–66. South Hadley, Mass.: Bergin and Garvey.

León, Magdalena. 1984. Measuring Women's Work: Methodological and Conceptual Issues in Latin America. *Institute of Development Studies (IDS), Sussex, Bulletin*, no. 15.

Leonard, William R. 1995. Comparison of Heart Rate–Monitoring and Factorial Methods: Assessment of Energy Expenditure in Highland and Coastal Ecuadoreans. *American Journal of Clinical Nutrition* 61:1146–52.

Leonard, William R., Kathleen M. DeWalt, and Jorge E. Uquillas. 1993. Ecology of Childhood Growth and Nutritional Status in Highland Ecuador. Paper presented in the symposium "Landscapes of Health in the Andes," American Anthropological Association Annual Meeting. Washington.

Leones, Julie. 1991. Rural Household Data Collection in Developing Countries: Designing Instruments and Methods for Collecting Time Allocation Data. Working Papers in Agricultural Economics, no. 91-16. Ithaca, N.Y.: Cornell University Department of Agricultural Economics and Cornell Food and Nutrition Policy Program.

Lepowsky, Maria. 1993. Fruit of the Motherland. New York: Columbia University Press.

Leslie, Joanne. 1989. Women's Work and Childhood Nutrition in the Third World. *In* Women, Work and Child Welfare in the Third World, ed. Joanne Leslie and Michael Paolisso. Boulder, Colo.: Westview Press.

LeVine, Terry Yarov. 1987. Inka Labor Service at the Regional Level: The Functional Reality. *Ethnohistory* 34:14–62.

Little, Peter. 1994. Maidens and Milk Markets: The Sociology of Dairy Marketing in Southern Somalia. *In* African Pastoralist Systems: An Integrated Approach, ed. Elliot Fratkin, Kathleen A. Galvin, and Eric Abella Roth. Boulder, Colo.: Lynne Rienner.

Llanos Albornóz, Martha. 1985. Observations on the Role of Women in the San Julian Colonization Project. Development Anthropology Network. Binghamton, N.Y.: Institute for Development Anthropology.

Llovet, Ignacio D. 1986. Capitalism and Social Differentiation: The Case of Ecuador's Rural Population. *Latin American Perspectives* 13:60–75.

Lockwood, Victoria. 1989. Tubuai Women Potato Planters and the Political Economy of Intra-Household Gender Relations. *In* The Household Economy: Reconsidering the Domestic Mode of Production, ed. Richard R. Wilk, 197–220. Boulder, Colo.: Westview Press.

———. 1993. Tahitian Transformation: Gender and Development in a Rural Society. Boulder, Colo.: Lynne Rienner.

Luzuriaga, C. 1980. Situación de la mujer en el Ecuador. Quito: Gráficas San Pablo.

Luzuriaga, C., and C. Zuvekas. 1983. Income Distribution and Poverty in Rural Ecuador, 1950–1979. Tempe: Arizona State University.

Maclachlan, Morgan D., ed. 1987. Household Economies and Their Transformations. Monographs in Economic Anthropology, no. 3. Lanham, Md.: University Press of America, Society for Economic Anthropology.

Mallon, Florencia. 1986. Gender and Class in the Transition to Capitalism: Household and Mode of Production in Central Peru. *Latin American Perspectives* 48:147–74.

———. 1987. Studying Women's Work in Latin America: Reflections on the Direction of Feminist Scholarship. *Latin American Perspectives* 14:255–61.

Marchand, Marianne H. 1995. Latin American Women Speak on Development: Are We Listening Yet? *In* Feminism/Postmodernism/Development, ed. Marianne H. Marchand and Jane L. Parpart, 56–72. London: Routledge.

Marcus, George E., and Michael M. J. Fischer. 1986. Anthropology as Cultural Critique: An Experimental Moment in the Human Sciences. Chicago: University of Chicago Press.

Mardešic, Vjekoslav Darlić. 1992. Estadísticas de la mujer: Ecuador 1992. Quito: Fondo de Desarrollo de las Naciones Unidas para la Mujer (UNIFEM) y el Instituto Latinoamericano de Investigaciones Sociales (ILDIS).

Marroni de Velázquez, Maria da Glória. 1994. Changes in Rural Society and Domestic Labor in Atlixco, Puebla, 1940–1990. *In* Women of the Mexican Countryside, 1850–1990, ed. Heather Fowler-Salamini and Mary Kay Vaughan, 210–24. Tucson: University of Arizona Press.

Martin, JoAnn. 1994. Antagonisms of Gender and Class in Morelos. *In* Women of the Mexican Countryside, 1850–1990, ed. Heather Fowler-Salamini and Mary Kay Vaughan, 225–42. Tucson: University of Arizona Press.

Martínez V., Luciano. 1984. De campesinos a proletarios: Cambios en la mano de obra rural en la sierra central del Ecuador. Quito: Editorial El Conejo.

———. 1985. Articulación mercantil de las comunidades indígenas en la sierra ecuatoriana. *In* Economía politica del Ecuador: Campo, región, nación, ed. Louis Lefeber, 133–78. Quito: Corporación Editora Nacional.

Maxwell, Simon, and Adrian Fernando. 1989. Cash Crops in Developing Countries: The Issues, the Facts, the Policies. *World Development* 17:1677–708.

Mayer, Enrique. 1977. Beyond the Nuclear Family. *In* Andean Kinship and Marriage, ed. Ralph Bolton and Enrique Mayer, 60–80. Washington, D.C.: American Anthropological Association.

Mayoux, Linda. 1995. Beyond Naivety: Women, Gender Inequality, and Participatory Development. *Development and Change* 26:235–58.

McElroy, Marjorie B., and Mary Jean Horney. 1981. Nash-Bargained Household Decisions: Toward a Generalization of the Theory of Demand. *International Economics Review* 22 (2): 333–50.

McGuire, Judith S., and Barry M. Popkin. 1988. The Zero Sum Game: A Framework for Examining Women and Nutrition. *Ecology of Food and Nutrition* 10:27–32.

McKee, L. 1980. Ideals and Actualities: The Socialization of Gender-Appropriate Behaviour in an Ecuadorian Village. Ph.D. thesis, Cornell University.

Meggers, Betty J. 1966. Ecuador. New York: Frederick A. Praeger.

Mehra, Rekha. 1993. Gender in Community Development and Resource Management. *In* Women at the Center: Development Issues and Practices for the 1990s, ed. Gay Young, Vidymali Samarashinghe, and Ken Kusterer, 145–61. West Hartford, Conn.: Kumarian Press.

Mencher, Joan P. 1988. Women's Work and Poverty: Women's Contribution to Household Maintenance in South India. *In* A Home Divided: Women and Income in the Third World, ed. Daisy Dwyer and Judith Bruce, 99–119. Stanford, Calif.: Stanford University Press.

Middleton, Dwight. 1979. Migration and Urbanization in Ecuador: A View from the Coast. *Urban Anthropology* 8:313–32.

Mohanty, Chandra. 1988. Under Western Eyes: Feminist Scholarship and Colonial Discourses. Feminist Review 30: 61–88.

Molnar, Augusta. 1989. Forest Conservation in Nepal: Encouraging Women's Participation. *In* Seeds: Supporting Women's Work in the Third World, ed. Ann Leonard. New York: Feminist Press.

Moreno Yánez, Segundo E. 1988. Formaciones políticas tribales y señoríos étnicos. *In* Nueva historia del Ecuador, vol. 2, Epoca aborigen II, ed. Segundo Moreno Yánez, 9–134. Quito: Corporación Editora Nacional.

Moser, Caroline O. N. 1989. Gender Planning in the Third World: Meeting Practical and Strategic Gender Needs. *World Development* 17:1799–825.

Mosse, Julia Cleves. 1993. Half the World, Half a Chance. Oxford: Oxfam.

Mukhopadhyay, Carol C., and Patricia J. Higgins. 1988. Anthropological Studies of Women's Status Revisited: 1977–1987. *Annual Review of Anthropology* 17:461–95.

Mummert, Gail. 1994. From *Metate* to *Despate:* Rural Mexican Women's Salaried Labor and the Redefinition of Gendered Spaces and Roles. *In* Women of the Mexican Countryside, 1850–1990, ed. Heather Fowler-Salamini and Mary Kay Vaughan, 192–209. Tucson: University of Arizona Press.

Murra, John. 1946. The Historic Tribes of Ecuador. *In* Handbook of South American Indians, vol. 2, pp. 785–821. Bureau of American Ethnology Bulletin, no. 143.

————. 1968. An Aymara Kingdom in 1567. *Ethnohistory* 15 (2): 115–51.

————. 1980 [1956]. The Economic Organization of the Inca State. Greenwich, Conn.: JAI Press.

Nash, John. 1953. Two-Person Cooperative Games. *Econometrica* 21 (1): 128–40.

Nash, June. 1975. Certain Aspects of the Integration of Women in the Development Process: A Point of View. United Nations World Conference of the International Women's Year.

————. 1979. We Eat the Mines and the Mines Eat Us: Dependency and Exploitation in Bolivian Tin Mines. New York: Columbia University Press.

————. 1986. A Decade of Research on Women in Latin America. *In* Women and Change in Latin America, ed. June Nash and Helen Safa, 3–21. South Hadley, Mass: Bergin and Garvey.

————. 1995. Latin American Women in the World Capitalist Crisis. *In* Women in the Latin American Development Process, ed. Christina E. Bose and Edna Acosta-Belén, 151–66. Philadelphia, Pa.: Temple University Press.

Nash, June, and Helen Safa, eds. 1976. Sex and Class in Latin America. South Hadley, Mass: J. F. Bergin.

————. 1986. Women and Change in Latin America. South Hadley, Mass.: Bergin and Garvey.

Nash, June, and Maria Patricia Fernández-Kelly, eds. 1983. Women, Men, and the International Division of Labor. Albany: SUNY Press.

Navarro, Marysa. 1988. Women in Pre-Columbian and Colonial Latin America. *In* Restoring Women to History: Latin America and the Caribbean, 3–40. Bloomington, Ind.: Organization of American Historians.

Navas A., Oswaldo. 1986. El Cantón Salcedo; Sintesis de sus valores espirituales y fisicos. No publication information included on frontispiece.

Obbo, Christine. 1990. East African Women, Work, and the Articulation of Dominance. *In* Persistent Inequalities: Women and World Development, ed. Irene Tinker, 210–22. New York: Oxford University Press.

Oberem, Udo. 1988. El período incaico en el Ecuador. *In* Nueva historia del Ecuador, vol. 2, Epoca aborigen II, ed. Segundo Moreno Yánez, 135–66. Quito: Corporación Editora Nacional.

Office of Women in Development, USAID. 1990. Women in Development: A Report to Congress by the U.S. Agency for International Development, FY89–FY90. Washington, D.C.: US-AID.

Oficina Nacional de la Mujer, eds. 1984. Seminario sobre la Participación de la Mujer en la Vida Nacional. Quito: Productora de Publicaciones.

Orrego de Figueroa, Teresa. 1976. A Critical Analysis of Latin American Programs to Integrate Women in Development. *In* Women and World Development, ed. Irene Tinker, Michele Bo Bramsen, and Mayra Buvinic. New York: Praeger.

Padilla, Martha Luz, Clara Murguialday, and Ana Criquillon. 1987. Impact of the Sandinista Agrarian Reform on Rural Women's Subordination. *In* Rural Women and State Policy, ed. Carmen Diana Deere and Magdalena León, 124–41. Boulder, Colo.: Westview Press.

Pagano, Robert R. 1990. Understanding Statistics in the Behavioral Sciences. 3rd ed. New York: West Publishing Company.

Palmer, Ingrid. 1985. The Impact of Agrarian Reform on Women, and the Impact of Male Out-Migration on Women in Farming. West Hartford, Conn.: Kumarin Press.

————. 1992. Gender Equity and Economic Efficiency in Adjustment Programmes. *In* Women and Adjustment Policies in the Third World, ed. Haleh Afshar and Carolyne Dennis, 69–86. New York: St. Martin's Press.

Papanek, Hanna. 1990. To Each Less Than She Needs, From Each More Than She Can Do: Allocations, Entitlements, and Value. *In* Persistent Inequalities: Women and World Development, ed. Irene Tinker, 162–81. New York: Oxford University Press.

Paris, Thelma. 1989. Women in Rice Farming Systems, Crop-Livestock Project, Sta. Barbara, Pangasinan. *In* Working Together: Gender Analysis in Agriculture, ed. Hilary Sims Feldstein and Susan V. Poats, 209–39. West Hartford, Conn.: Kumarian Press.

Parpart, Jane L. 1993. Who Is the "Other"?: A Postmodern Feminist Critique of Women and Development Theory and Practice. *Development and Change* 24:439–64.

———. 1995. Deconstructing the Development "Expert": Gender, Development, and the "Vulnerable Groups." *In* Feminism/Postmodernism/Development, ed. Marianne H. Marchand and Jane L. Parpart, 221–43. London: Routledge.

Parpart, Jane L., and Marianne H. Marchand. 1995. Exploding the Canon: An Introduction/ Conclusion. *In* Feminism/Postmodernism/Development, ed. Marianne H. Marchand and Jane L. Parpart, 1–22. London: Routledge.

Pearsall, Deborah M. and Dolores R. Piperno. 1990. Antiquity of Maize Cultivation in Ecuador. *American Antiquity* 55 (2): 324–37.

Pedersen, Duncan, and Carlos Coloma. 1983. Traditional Medicine in Ecuador: The Structure of the Non-Formal Health Systems. *Social Science and Medicine* 17:1249–55.

Peek, Peter. 1980. Agrarian Change and Labor Migration in the Sierra of Ecuador. *International Migration Review* 119:609–21.

Pelto, Gretel, Lindsay Allen, and Adolfo Chavez. 1989. Maternal Care-Giving and Child Growth in a Highland Mexican Area. Abstracts of the Thirteenth International Conference of Nutrition, Seoul, Korea, August 1989.

Phillips, Lynne. 1987. Women, Development, and the State in Rural Ecuador. *In* Rural Women and State Policy, ed. Carmen Diana Deere and Magdalena León, 105–23. Boulder, Colo.: Westview Press.

———. 1990. Rural Women in Latin America. *Latin American Research Review* 25 (3): 87–107.

Pitt, Mark, and Mark Rosenweig. 1985. Health and Nutrient Consumption Across and Within Farm Households. *Review of Economics and Statistics* 67 (2): 212–23.

Placencia, M. M. 1984. Integración de la mujer a los procesos de desarrollo. *In* Seminario sobre la Participación de la Mujer en la Vida Nacional, ed. Oficina Nacional de la Mujer. Quito: Productora de Publicaciones.

Poats, Susan V., Hilary S. Feldstein, and Dianne E. Rocheleau. 1989. Gender and Intra/Inter-Household Analysis in On-Farm Research and Experimentation. *In* The Household Economy: Reconsidering the Domestic Mode of Production, ed. Richard R. Wilk, 245–66. Boulder, Colo.: Westview Press.

Poeschel R., Ursula. 1988. La mujer salasaca: Su situación en una época de reestructuración económico-cultural. 2d ed. Quito: Ediciones Abya-Yala.

Popkin, Barry. 1980. Time Allocation of the Mother and Child Nutrition. *Ecology of Food and Nutrition* 9:1–14.

Portes, Alejandro. 1985. Latin American Class Structures: Their Composition and Change During the Last Decades. *Latin American Research Review* 20:7–39.

Preston, David A. 1980. Rural Emigration and the Future of Agriculture in Ecuador. *In* Environment, Society, and Rural Change in Latin America, ed. David Preston, 195–208. New York: John Wiley.

Proyecto de Desarrollo Rural Integral Salcedo (SEDRI). 1981. Diagnóstico, vol. 1, ed. Gonzalo Muñoz, Roberto Susman, et al. Quito: Instituto Interamericano de Cooperación para la Agricultura (IICA).

Pumasunta Chacha, Elsa. 1992. Historia general de Chanchaló. Unpublished manuscript.

Radcliffe, Anne. 1986. Gender Relations, Peasant Livelihood Strategies and Migration: A Case Study from Cuzco, Peru. *Bulletin of Latin American Research* 5:29–47.

Rakowski, Cathy A. 1995a. Planned Development and Women's Relative Power: Steel and Forestry in Venezuela. *Latin American Perspectives* 22 (2): 51–75.

———. 1995b. Conclusion: Engendering Wealth and Well-Being: Lessons Learned. *In* EnGENDERing Wealth and Well-Being: Empowerment for Global Change, ed. Rae Lesser Blumberg, Cathy Rakowski, Irene Tinker, and Michael Monteón, 285–94. Boulder, Colo.: Westview Press.

Rapp, Rayna. 1992 (1978). Family and Class in Contemporary America: Notes Toward an Understanding of Ideology. *In* Rethinking the Family: Some Feminist Questions, ed. B. Thorne and M. Yalom. Boston: Northeastern University Press. (Cited in Jaquette 1993, 48.)

Rasnake, Roger Neil. 1988. Domination and Cultural Resistance: Authority and Power Among an Andean People. Durham, N.C.: Duke University Press.

Rathgeber, Eva M. 1995. Gender and Development in Action. *In* Feminism/Postmodernism/Development, ed. Marianne H. Marchand and Jane L. Parpart, 204–20. London: Routledge.

Redclift, Michael. 1978. Agrarian Reform and Peasant Organization on the Ecuadorian Coast. London: Athlone Press.

Redclift, Michael R., and David A. Preston. 1980. Agrarian Reform and Rural Change in Ecuador. *In* Environment, Society, and Rural Change in Latin America, ed. David Preston, 53–63. New York: John Wiley.

Rogers, Barbara. 1980. The Domestication of Women. New York: Tavistock.

Roldán, Marta. 1988. Renegotiating the Marital Contract: Intra-Household Patterns of Money Allocation and Women's Subordination Among Domestic Outworkers in Mexico City. *In* A Home Divided: Women and Income in the Third World, ed. Daisy Dwyer and Judith Bruce, 229–47. Stanford, Calif.: Stanford University Press.

Roseberry, William. 1989. Anthropologies and Histories: Essays in Culture, History, and Political Economy. New Brunswick, N.J.: Rutgers University Press.

Rosenweig, Mark R., and T. Paul Schultz. 1982. Market Opportunities, Genetic Endowments, and Intrafamily Resource Distribution: Child Survival in Rural India. *American Economic Review* 72:803–15.

Rosero, Rocío. 1984. Las mujeres campesinas de la sierra Ecuatoriana. Notas para una metodología de investigación. *In* Mujer y transormaciones agrarias, ed. Susana Balarezo et al., 13–45. Quito: Centro de Planificación y Estudios Sociales (CEPLAES)/Corporación Editora Nacional.

Rothstein, Frances Abrahamer. 1995. Gender and Multiple Income Strategies in Rural Mexico: A Twenty-Year Perspective. *In* Women in the Latin American Development Process, ed. Christina E. Bose and Edna Acosta–Belén, 167–93. Philadelphia, Pa.: Temple University Press.

Rozelle, Scott. 1991. Rural Household Data Collection in Developing Countries: Designing Instruments and Methods for Collecting Farm Production Data. Working Papers in Agricultural Economics, no. 91-17. Ithaca, N.Y.: Cornell University Department of Agricultural Economics and Cornell Food and Nutrition Policy Program.

Russo, Sandra, Jennifer Bremer-Fox, Susan Poats, and Laurene Graig. 1989. Gender Issues in Agriculture and Natural Resource Management. In cooperation with Anita Spring. Edited by Bruce Horwith. Washington, D.C.: Robert R. Nathan Associates.

Sacks, Karen. 1975. Engels Revisited: Women, the Organization of Production, and Private Property. *In* Toward an Anthropology of Women, ed. Rayna R. Reiter, 211–34. New York: Monthly Review Press.

———. 1979. Sisters and Wives: The Past and Future of Sexual Equality. Westport, Conn.: Greenwood.

Safa, Helen Icken. 1986. Runaway Shops and Female Employment: The Search for Cheap Labor. *In* Women's Work, ed. Eleanor Leacock and Helen Safa, 58–71. South Hadley, Mass.: Bergin and Garvey.

———. 1995a. Economic Restructuring and Gender Subordination. *Latin American Perspectives* 22 (2): 32–50.

———. 1995b. Women's Social Movements in Latin America. *In* Women in the Latin American Development Process, ed. Christina E. Bose and Edna Acosta-Belén, 227–41. Philadelphia, Pa.: Temple University Press.

Saffioti, Heleieth I. B. 1977. Women, Mode of Production, and Social Formations. *Latin American Perspectives* 4 (1 and 2): 27–37.

Safilios-Rothschild, Constantina. 1990. Socio-Economic Determinants of the Outcomes of Women's Income Generation in Developing Countries. *In* Women, Employment, and the Family in the International Division of Labor, ed. S. Stichter and J. Parpart. Philadelphia, Pa.: Temple University Press.

Sage, Colin. 1993. Deconstructing the Household: Women's Roles Under Commodity Relations in Highland Bolivia. *In* Different Places, Different Voices: Gender and Development in Africa, Asia, and Latin America, ed. Janet H. Momsen and Vivian Kinnaird, 243–55. New York: Routledge.

Salamea, Lucia, and Mary Frances Likes. N.d. The Changing Role of Rural Women in Ecuador. Quito: Manuscript.

Salomon, Frank. 1986. Native Lords of Quito in the Age of the Incas: The Political Economy of North Andean Chiefdoms. Cambridge, England: Cambridge University Press.

Sarmiento Rogrígues, Fausto. 1988. Antología·ecologica del Ecuador. Quito: Casa de la Cultura Ecuatoriana, Museo Ecuatoriano de Ciencias Naturales.

Schiff, Maurice, and Alberto Valdéz. 1990. Nutrition: Alternative Definitions and Policy Implications. *Economic Development and Cultural Change* 38:281–92.

Scrimshaw, Susan. 1981. Adaptation and Family Size from Rural Ecuador to Guayaquil. *In* Cultural Transformations and Ethnicity in Modern Ecuador, ed. N. Whitten. Urbana: University of Illinois.

———. 1985. Bringing the Period Down: Government and Squatter Settlement Confront Induced Abortion in Ecuador. *In* Micro and Macro Levels of Analysis in Anthropology, ed. Billie R. DeWalt and Pertti J. Pelto, 121–46. Boulder, Colo.: Westview Press.

SEDRI. *See* Proyecto de Desarrollo Rural Integral Salcedo (SEDRI).

Seligson, Mitchell A. 1984. Land Tenure Security, Minifundization and Agrarian Development in Ecuador: A Preliminary Assessment. Report submitted to USAID, Quito.

Sen, Amartya K. 1990. Gender and Cooperative Conflicts. *In* Persistent Inequalities: Women and World Development, ed. Irene Tinker, 123–49. New York: Oxford University Press.

Sen, Gita. 1996. Gender, Markets, and States: A Selective Review and Research Agenda. *World Development* 24 (5): 821–29.

Sen, Gita, and Caren Grown. 1987. Development, Crises, and Alternative Visions. New York: Monthly Review Press.

Senauer, Benjamin. 1990. The Impact of the Value of Women's Time on Food and Nutrition. *In* Persistent Inequalities: Women and World Development, ed. Irene Tinker, 150–61. New York: Oxford University Press.

Senauer, Benjamin, and Marito García. 1988. The Determinants of Food Consumption and Nutritional Status Among Preschool Children: Evidence from the Rural Philippines. University of Minnesota, St. Paul. Mimeograph.

Senauer, Benjamin, Marito García, and Elizabeth Jacinto. 1988. Determinants of the Intrahousehold Allocation of Food in the Rural Philippines. *American Journal of Agricultural Economics* 70:170–80.

Sepulveda, C., et al., eds. 1982. Structuras agrarias y reproducción campesina. Quito: IIE-PUCE.

Silverblatt, Irene. 1980. Andean Women Under Spanish Rule. *In* Women and Colonization, ed. Mona Etienne and Eleanor Leacock, 149–85. New York: Praeger.

———. 1987. Moon, Sun, and Witches: Gender Ideologies and Class in Inca and Colonial Peru. Princeton, N.J.: Princeton University Press.

Smith, Carol A. 1985. Local History in Global Context: Social and Economic Transitions in Western Guatemala. *In* Macro and Micro Levels of Analysis in Anthropology: Issues in Theory and Research, ed. Billie R. DeWalt and Pertti J. Pelto, 83–120. Boulder, Colo.: Westview Press.

Smith, M. L., and G. V. Glass. 1987. Research and Evaluation in Education and the Social Sciences. Englewood Cliffs, N.J.: Prentice-Hall.

Sørensen, Pernille. 1996. Commercialization of Food Crops in Busoga, Uganda, and the Renegotiation of Gender. *Gender and Society* 10 (5): 608–28.

Spindler, Frank M. 1987. Nineteenth-Century Ecuador: An Historical Introduction. Fairfax, Va.: George Mason University Press.

Spradley, James P. 1979. The Ethnographic Interview. New York: Holt, Rinehart and Winston.

Stark, Louisa. 1979. Division of Labor and the Control of Economic Resources Among Indian Women in the Ecuadorian Highlands. *Andean Perspectives* 3:1–5.

———. 1984. The Role of Women in Peasant Uprisings in the Ecuadorian Highlands. *In* Political Anthropology of Ecuador: Perspectives from Indigenous Cultures, ed. Jeffrey Ehrenreich, 3–23. Albany: Society for Latin American Anthropology and Center for the Caribbean and Latin America, State University of New York at Albany.

Stephenson, L. S., M. C. Latham, and A. Jansen. 1983. A Comparison of Growth Standards: Similarities between NCHS, Harvard, Denver and Privileged African Children and Differences with Kenyan Rural Children. Ithaca, N.Y.: Cornell International Nutrition Monographs Series, no. 12.

Stevens, Evelyn P. 1973. *Marianismo:* The Other Face of Machismo in Latin America. *In* Female and Male in Latin America, ed. Ann Pescatello, 89–101. Pittsburgh, Pa.: University of Pittsburgh Press.

Steward, Julian H. 1963. Native Population of South America. *In* Handbook of South American Indians, vol. 5. New York: Cooper Square Publishers.

Stohlke, Verena. 1983. Position Paper for the Social Science Research Council Workshop on "Social Inequality and Gender Hierarchy in Latin America." Mexico City, 1983.

Stolen, Kristi Anne. 1985. Mujer doméstica y domesticada: Realidad económica y machismo en la sierra ecuatoriana. Quito: CEPLAES.

———. 1989. En media voz. Quito: CEPLAES.

Stoler, Ann. 1976. Class Structure and Female Autonomy in Rural Java. *In* Women and National Development, ed. Wellesley Editorial Committee, 74–88. Chicago: University of Chicago Press.

Stone, M. Priscilla. 1988. Women, Work, and Marriage: A Restudy of the Nigerian Kofyar. Ph.D. thesis, University of Arizona.

Stone, M. Priscilla, Glenn Davis, and Robert McC. Netting. 1995. The Sexual Division of Labor in Kofyar Agriculture. *American Ethnologist* 22 (1): 165–86.

Stubbs, Jean, and Mavis Alvarez. 1987. Women on the Agenda: The Cooperative Movement in Rural Cuba. *In* Rural Women and State Policy, ed. Carmen Diana Deere and Magdalena León, 142–61. Boulder, Colo.: Westview Press.

Subedi, Anil. 1991. Involving Women Farmers in Technology Generation and Transfer: An Experience of Lumle Regional Agriculture Research Centre's FSRE Approach in the Western Hills of Nepal. Paper presented at the Eleventh Annual Symposium of the Association for Farming Systems Research-Extension. East Lansing, Michigan.

Taussig, Michael. 1980. The Devil and Commodity Fetishism in South America. Chapel Hill: University of North Carolina Press.

Terán, Francisco. 1990. Geografía del Ecuador. Quito: Libresa.

Thomas, R. B., T. L. Leatherman, J. W. Carey, and J. D. Haas. 1988. Biosocial Consequences of Illness Among Small-Scale Farmers: A Research Design. *In* Capacity for Work in the Tropics, ed. K. J. Collins and D. F. Roberts, 249–76. Cambridge, England: Cambridge University Press.

Thompson, Karen, Kathleen DeWalt, and Billie DeWalt. 1985. Food Consumption and Nutrition in Three Highland Honduran Communities. INTSORMIL Report, no. 3. Lexington: University of Kentucky.

Thurner, Mark. 1993. Peasant Politics and Andean Haciendas in the Transition to Capitalism: An Ethnographic History. *Latin American Research Review* 28 (3): 41–82.

Timsina, D., A. L. Ferrer, T. Paris, and B. Duff. 1993. Rural Women in Irrigated and Rain-Fed Rice Farming in the Philippines: Decision-Making Involvement and Access to Productive Resources. *Journal of Farming Systems Research-Extension* 3 (2): 147–61.

Tinker, Irene. 1990a. A Context for the Field and for the Book. *In* Persistent Inequalities: Women and World Development, ed. Irene Tinker, 3–13. New York: Oxford University Press.

———. 1990b. The Making of a Field: Advocates, Practitioners, and Scholars. *In* Persistent Inequalities: Women and World Development, ed. Irene Tinker, 27–53. New York: Oxford University Press.

USAID/Ecuador. 1990. The Role of Agriculture in Ecuador's Economic Development: An Assessment of Ecuador's Agricultural Sector, ed. Morris Whitaker, Dale Colyer, and Jaime Alzamora. Quito: USAID Office of Agriculture and Natural Resources.

Uquillas, Jorge, et al. 1990. La papa en los sistemas de producción agropecuaria de la sierra ecuatoriana. Quito: Kellogg Foundation.

Van Willigen, John, and Billie R. DeWalt. 1985. Training Manual in Policy Ethnography. Special

Publication of the American Anthropological Association, no. 19. Washington, D.C.: American Anthropological Association.

Vargas, José María. 1977. Historia del Ecuador, siglo XVI. Quito: Ediciones de la Universidad Catolica.

Velasco, F. 1979. Reforma agraria y movimiento campesino indígena de la sierra. Quito: El Consejo.

Venema, Barnhard. 1986. The Changing Role of Women in Sahelian Agriculture. *In* Women Farmers in Africa, ed. Lucy Creevey. Syracuse, N.Y.: Syracuse University Press.

von Braun, Joachim. 1988. Effects of Technological Change in Agriculture on Food Consumption and Nutrition: Rice in a West African Setting. *World Development* 16:1083–98.

von Braun, Joachim, and Graciela Wiegand-Jahn. 1991. Income Sources and Income Uses of the Malnourished Poor in Northwest Rwanda. *In* Income Sources of Malnourished People in Rural Areas: Microlevel Information and Policy Implications. Working Papers on Commercialization of Agriculture and Nutrition, no. 5, ed. Joachim von Braun and Rajul Pandya-Lorch, 117–30. Washington, D.C.: International Food Policy Research Institute.

Vosti, Stephen A., and Julie Witcover. 1991. Income Sources of the Rural Poor: The Case of the Zona da Mata, Minas Gerais, Brazil. *In* Income Sources of Malnourished People in Rural Areas: Microlevel Information and Policy Implications. Working Papers on Commercialization of Agriculture and Nutrition, no. 5, ed. Joachim von Braun and Rajul Pandya-Lorch, 47–68. Washington, D.C.: International Food Policy Research Institute.

Wainerman, Catalina, and Zulma Recchini de Lattes. 1981. El trabajo domestico femenino en el Banquillo de los Acusados: Medición censal en America Latina. Mexico City: Terra Nova.

Walter, Lynn. 1981. Social Strategies and the Fiesta Complex in an Otavaleño Community. *American Ethnologist* 8:172–95.

Wandel, Margareta, and Gerd Holmboe-Ottesen. 1988. Women as Nutrition Mediators: A Case Study from Sri Lanka. *Ecology of Food and Nutrition* 21:117–30.

Warren, Kay B., and Susan C. Bourque. 1991. Women, Technology, and International Development Ideologies: Analyzing Feminist Voices. *In* Gender at the Crossroads: Feminist Anthropology and the Postmodern Era, ed. Micela di Leonardo, 278–311. Berkeley and Los Angeles: University of California Press.

Waters, William F. 1985. Access to Land and the Form of Production in the Central Ecuadorian Highlands. Ph.D. thesis, Cornell University.

Webb, Patrick. 1989. Intrahousehold Decisionmaking and Resource Control: The Effects of Rice Commercialization in West Africa. Working Papers on Commercialization of Agriculture and Nutrition, no. 3. Washington, D.C.: International Food Policy Research Institute.

Weiner, Annette. 1986. Forgotten Wealth: Cloth and Women's Production in the Pacific. *In* Women's Work, ed. Eleanor Leacock and Helen Safa, 96–110. South Hadley, Mass.: Bergin and Garvey.

Weismantel, Mary. 1988. Food, Gender, and Poverty in the Ecuadorian Andes. Philadelphia, Pa.: University of Pennsylvania Press.

Weiss, Wendy A. 1985. Es el que manda: Sexual Inequality and Its Relationship to Economic Development in the Ecuadorian Sierra. Ph.D. thesis, Bryn Mawr College.

WHO. *See* World Health Organization (WHO)

Wilk, Richard. 1990. Household Ecology: Decision Making and Resource Flows. *In* The Ecosystem Approach in Anthropology: From Concept to Practice, ed. Emilio F. Moran, 323–56. Ann Arbor, Mich.: University of Michigan Press.

Wilson, Fiona. 1988. Women and Agricultural Change in Latin America: Some Concepts Guiding Research. *World Development* 13:1017–35.

Wolf, Diane. 1992. Factory Daughters: Gender, Household Dynamics, and Rural Industrialization in Java. Berkeley and Los Angeles: University of California Press.

World Bank. 1984. Ecuador: An Agenda for Recovery and Sustained Growth. Washington, D.C.: World Bank.

World Health Organization (WHO). 1979. Measurement of Nutritional Impact. Geneva: WHO.

———. 1983. Measuring Change in Nutritional Status. Geneva: WHO.

Yanagisako, Sylvia. 1979. Family and Household: The Analysis of Domestic Groups. *Annual Review of Anthropology* 8:161–205. (Cited in Jaquette 1993, 48.)

Young, Kate. 1978. Modes of Appropriation and the Sexual Division of Labour: A Case Study from Oaxaca, Mexico. *In* Feminism and Materialism: Women and Modes of Production, ed. Annette Kuhn and Ann Marie Wolpe. London: Routledge and Kegan Paul.

Zambonino J., Agosto. 1984. Sintesis monográfica del Cantón Salcedo. No publication information included on frontispiece.

Zevallos, José Vicente. 1989. Agrarian Reform and Structural Change: Ecuador Since 1964. *In* Searching for Agrarian Reform in Latin America, ed. William C. Thiesenhusen, 42–69. Boulder, Colo.: Westview Press.

Zuloaga, Alberto et al. 1990. El sistema technologico de la papa en el Ecuador. Quito: FUNDAGRO (Fundación para el Desarrollo Agropecuario).

Zuñiga, Neptali. 1936. Monografía de la Provincia de León. Quito: Imp. de la Escuela de Artes e Industrias.

———. 1968. Historia de Latacunga Independencia. 2 vols. Quito: Talleres Gráficos Nacionales.

# Index

245–47, 249, 254, 263*n17*, 265*nn1, 3,* 269*n1*

general assembly, 64
gender: boundaries, 162; complementarity, 26–28, 195, 162–64, 239–43; and cultural construction of ideologies, 16, 182–88, 189–201; and cross-cultural role differences, 16; and division of labor, 2, 72–73, 160–64; and domestic bias, 2, 8–10, 165, 232, 242; and egalitarianism, 17, 168, 236; and empowerment, 15; and equity, 14, 15, 64; hierarchies of, 13; ideology, 16, 21, 27, 160, 163, 189–92, 219; identity, 31; inheritance patterns and, 17, 204–07; and land ownership, 168, 204–07; and patterned equalities, 236–41; and patterned inequalities, 12–13, 18, 21, 31, 235–37, 243; perceptions of, 162; reciprocities, 261*n6;* roles, 163; among Sarajuro, 28, 163, 166, 182, 188; specialization, 163; variable, 3, 11, 264*n11;* and violence, 7, 8, 195–97, 265*n12;* and violence compared to U.S., 8, 113, 196. *See also* spouse abuse
gender-and-development: analysts, 11; discourse and deconstruction, 13, 189, 210; diversity, 21; division of labor, 21, 72–73, 160–64; equity goals and global economy, 19; feminists, 19–21; and the future, 239–42; and policy implementation, 22; research and practice, 32; sociocultural linkage, 21; studies on, 18
Gender-and-Development Model, Dependent Variable Components: and access to agricultural technology, 178–81, 214–21; and agricultural production, 211–21; and household economic resources, 210–22; and income, 174–78, 210–26; and land, 170–76, 204–07, 220–26
Gender-and-Development Model, Independent Variables: and commercialization of household agriculture, 3, 5, 25–26, 30–31, 90–99, 136–39, 210–19, 225–26; and male out-migration, 213, 222; and women's agricultural labor, 219–21; and women's age or life stage, 221–23; and women's independent and joint ownership of land, 202–04, 210–22
Gender-and-Development Model, Testing: multivariant statistical procedures for, 222; dependent variable components of, 222–28; and independent variables, 222–28, 256–57;
Gender-and-Development Model, Test Results: dependent variable components and independent variables, 231–33
gender ideologies: and bilateral and parallel inheritance, 206–07; change in, 188, 213–15; cultural, 16, 182–201; and emotional and moral strength, 190; and fundamentalism, 186–87; historical, 8–19, 185–86; and intellectual strength, 192–93; and land, kinship, and inheritance, 201–09, 213–15; and *marianismo,* 193–95; mythic, 187–88; parallelism and complementarity, 195; and physical strength, 142–43, 189–90; social and political, 195–201, 214, 219–20; and spiritual strength, 193–94; traditional, 30, 184–85, 207–08; and women's ownership of land, 202–04

Guayas (province), 156
Guayaquil, 240

hacienda system: 102, 104, 117, 134, 163, 164, 195, 207, 208, 221, 264*nn6, 11;* colonial and modern history of, 2–3; in Chanchaló, 44, 47–49, 103; and land for women, 23; and lands, 58, 64
Harris, Olivia, 187, 200, 206, 208, 213
Hart, Gillian, 32, 262*n10*
health: and Clemencia, 80; and illness, 150; levels of, 55–60, 137; and Marina, 117; reproductive, 138–39; services, 61–63; and Susana, 119
Hirschman, Mito, 20
Holdridge, Leslie, 39
household: budgets of, 2, 92–95; decision-making and, 183; economic resource control in, 18, 27, 30, 92–95, 167–69, 174–78; gender complementarity and, 26–28, 174–78, 195; and gender egalitarianism, 27; head as concept, 11, 207–09; ideology, 182–209; income composition and control of, 13, 167–82, 216–20; production, 210–22, 247; productive labor of, 201–22; reproductive labor of, 11, 166; structure of, 13, 182–209; women's subordination in, 19, 182–209
*huasipungaje,* 45–48, 50
Humid Mountain Forest, 40

Inca, empire: 23, 41, 43, 261*n1;* invasion of, 43
income: from crafts and gardens, 24; household, 57; women's control of, 13, 167–82, 216–20
independent variables, 256–60. *See also* Gender-and-Development Model
indigenous *(indigena):* in Chanchaló 65–67; community, 33, 44, 120; farmers, 1, 8, 22–23, 33–34, 240–81; and inheritance, 183–85; land, 204–07; and mestizos, 118; politics, 43; resistance, 45–48; society, 42; women, 216–18
inheritance patterns, 17, 23, 188, 201–09, 232
integrated pest management, 96–99
investment patterns, 10

Jacquette, Jane, 9–10, 12, 22, 262*n10*